BOOKS BY MAJOR DESMOND CHAPMAN-HUSTON

A CREEL OF PEAT AND OTHER ESSAYS.

HILLS OF HELL AND OTHER VERSES.

THE MELODY OF GOD: Essays and Biographical Studies.

SIR JAMES RECKITT: A Memoir.

THE LIFE OF GENERAL SIR JOHN COWANS, G.C.B., QUARTERMASTER-GENERAL OF THE GRAT WAR. (In collaboration with Major Owen Rutter.)

Editor of:

BY THE CLOCK OF ST. JAMES': By Percy Armytage, C.V.O.

DAISY PRINCESS OF PLESS: By Herself.

SUBJECTS OF THE DAY: By the Marquess Curzon of Kedleston, K.G.

MYSELF.

From a drawing by Sargent, 1913.

Frontis.

DAISY
PRINCESS OF PLESS

By HERSELF

Edited with an Introduction by
MAJOR DESMOND CHAPMAN-HUSTON

WITH TWENTY-EIGHT ILLUSTRATIONS

NEW YORK
E. P. DUTTON & CO. INC.

DEDICATED
TO
MY THREE SONS
HANSEL, LEXEL, AND BOLKO

ACKNOWLEDGMENTS

Thanks
And thanks: and ever oft good turns
Are shuffled off with such uncurrent pay.

WITH my humble duty, I have to offer to His Majesty King George V. my sincere thanks for his kindness in graciously allowing me to publish a letter addressed to me by King Edward VII. in 1901.

To Lord Rosebery I am specially indebted for his permission—which is very rarely given—to quote several interesting letters which he at various times wrote to me. I also offer my sincere thanks to Lady Mary Erroll, Lord Albemarle, Sir Arthur Crosfield, Colonel W. E. Gordon, V.C., Lord Grey of Fallodon, Captain Robin Grey, the Honourable Ivan Hay, and Lord Winterton, for permission to make use of some of their letters.

If there are any others whom I should have asked for leave to use their letters, and through inadvertence have not done so, I beg for forgiveness.

It is not possible to name individually all those who have helped me with this book; many of them had to suffer tedious hours having it read aloud to them over and over again. I must not, however, fail to record my great indebtedness and warm gratitude to Major Chapman-Huston, Colonel Guy Wyndham, Miss Frances Alexina Todd, Miss Dorothy Crowther, Mrs. Ralph Beck, and Mr. Edward Ellul, for invaluable help in preparing the manuscript and seeing the volume published: nor would I forget little Joe Craven, who last winter at Munich spent hours making a Chronology when he might have been skating; if any of the dates are wrong the fault is mine, not his.

D. OF P.

LA NAPOULE, ALPES MARITIMES,
May, 1928.

INTRODUCTION

WHEN Daisy Princess of Pless did me the honour of consulting me about her intention to write her Reminiscences, I ventured to advise her to be perfectly frank about herself and others. Fortunately this advice accorded with her own open temperament and outspoken manner of expression and, except when to be candid would have hurt living persons, she has followed it: autobiography that is neither revealing nor self-revealing is merely futile.

The Princess's book, which ends dramatically in November, 1918, covers the twenty-five years immediately preceding the Great War and has the supreme merit of being founded on her own diaries and on letters she has written and received. Consequently, in her volume we get what she felt, thought and knew at the time, a genuineness of feeling, of thought and knowledge uninfluenced by subsequent reaction or recantation. While this fixed quality is always a great merit in a volume of recollections, it seems to me to be specially precious when crystallized in the mind of a writer who has watched from behind the scenes during great historic events.

Very widely known in Europe and America for many years as Princess Henry of Pless, the authoress was formerly Mary Theresa Olivia Cornwallis-West, elder daughter of Colonel Cornwallis-West, of Ruthin Castle, Denbighshire, and Newlands Manor, Hampshire. Colonel Cornwallis-West's grandfather was a younger son of the third Earl de la Warr. The Barony of de la Warr dates from 1209, the Barony of West from 1342, and although the Earldom dates only from 1761, the Sackville branch of the family held the Dukedom of Dorset from 1720 until 1843, when the sixth Duke and fourteenth Earl dying unmarried, it became extinct.

Through her maternal grandmother, Lady Olivia, daughter of Thomas, second Marquess of Headfort, who married the Reverend Frederick FitzPatrick, the Princess is connected with the distinguished Irish families of Taylour and FitzPatrick, and amongst her kinsfolk are the Maxwells, Stanhopes, Churchills, Wynyards, Grosvenors, Lumleys, Wyndhams, Russells, and many other great families.

In 1891 Daisy Cornwallis-West married Prince Henry of Pless, eldest son of Hans Heinrich XI., the then reigning Prince. For the marriage the Cornwallis-West family had to produce the long pedigree and the innumerable quarterings considered indispensable on the Continent; this was quite easily done, incidentally proving the bride's royal descent from Henry III.; Prince Henry in return was able to show a descent equally illustrious, his family, even then an ancient one, being first ennobled in 1650: the Principality of Pless became an appanage of the Hochberg family in 1847, when Count Hans Heinrich X. of Hochberg succeeded the last Duke of Anhalt-Cöthen-Pless.

The Princess was married almost direct from the schoolroom, having had only one short season in London. A very young and totally inexperienced girl, she suddenly found herself the wife of the heir to one of the richest Princes in Europe, and plunged into all the difficulties of Court and social life in Germany. Her English training, her love of freedom, her love of nature, the open-air life she had led with animals and flowers in Wales and Hampshire, and her total lack of social experience, ill-fitted the Princess for the complexities of existence at a Court enslaved by a narrow and rigid etiquette, and presided over by the dictatorial mind of the Emperor William II. However, with an ardent, courageous, and perhaps unduly impulsive nature she made a personal success that has become almost legendary; and while her beauty, which was world-famous, inevitably aroused some jealousies, her extraordinary charm, sincerity and simplicity made her innumerable friends.

In 1907, upon the death of his father, Prince Henry became reigning Prince of Pless, the possessor of vast wealth and the owner of Fürstenstein, a country palace in Silesia containing over six hundred rooms; the castle of Pless, also in Silesia, with an estate larger than an English county; the castle of Albrechtsburg in Saxony; a palace in Berlin, a château on the Riviera, and several smaller castles and houses.

On becoming a Serene Highness and consort of the Head of the Princely House of Pless, the Princess found herself compelled by her position to live a life that she considered to be impossible. In England, where Court life itself is comparatively simple, and where state and ceremony are customary only on the greatest occasions, we have no conception of the stiffness of the etiquette and the extraordinary amount of ceremony observed before the War at the Courts of even the less important German Princes. Brought up as a simple English country girl and with her ancestral inheritance of Welsh and Irish blood, the Princess found herself stifled and bored by the magnificence of Fürstenstein and Pless. Ceremonial life for a few weeks in Berlin during the season she would, and could, have cheerfully borne; but the state maintained by her husband in his homes she found ridiculous and, let it be confessed, even a little vulgar!

The stables, with their two hundred-odd thoroughbred horses, many of them race-horses and hunters, were a source of endless delight, because, although never the incomparable horsewoman that her sister Constance Duchess of Westminster is admitted to be, the Princess was a keen rider and an admirable whip. What she disliked most were the postilions and outriders, the Jägers who followed her when she went for a scamper in the endless forests surrounding her homes, and the three powdered footmen who were on duty outside her door day and night. She was never permitted to be a moment alone, and when on a journey, she travelled with a lady-in-waiting, two secretaries, a courier, three maids and mountains of luggage. She records how even her father-in-law, who was kindness and indulgence itself to her, told her it was not etiquette to allow a young Royal Prince to sit beside her on a sofa in the drawing-room! Custom reserved that privilege for elderly Royalties and for ladies who were her equal, or whom she particularly wished to honour! A German lady-in-waiting and the three German lady's-maids she might have endured, but found it ridiculous that, no matter how late she happened to be, two bed-chamber maids should have to be on duty in her bedroom for the sole purpose of turning down the sheets. This, for Daisy Cornwallis-West the tom-boy who hated dressing up, loved stables and kennels better than Courts and drawing-rooms, and who could climb trees quite as well as her brother George! The Jägers, the Bodyguard, the Master of the Horse, the Comptroller of the Household, the numberless Grooms of the Chambers, Footmen and so on, were bad enough, but to have even her bedroom continually encumbered by servants seemed to the Princess unendurable. Moreover, to a girl who loved best a punt on a pond at Newlands, or her own little private garden at Ruthin, the twenty or thirty square miles of private park at Fürstenstein in the centre of a vast forest, and the finest gardens in Silesia, were a weariness. The castle of Pless, it is true, dates in part from the thirteenth century, but most of it was rebuilt about 1870 and, like Fürstenstein it was, in those days, magnificence and gilded discomfort from end to end. Homeliness, privacy, simplicity—none of all this she found. Is it any wonder that the young Princess hated it all? The expenditure was on a ridiculous scale, the kitchens and cellars alone costing thirty thousand pounds sterling a year. Everything else was equally lavish. Even that was not enough.

When his father died the Prince of Pless started remodelling, enlarging and rebuilding Fürstenstein. It is now decorated and furnished in perfect taste. The work took twenty years and cost a King's ransom. The result, however, is that the house is not only one of the largest, but one of the most interesting in Europe: one of the most extraordinary items of information in this unusual book is that the building operations went on right through the War! Another is that in the highest German circles everyone seems to have spoken or written English without let or hindrance. Nearly all the correspondents of the Princess, including her husband and family, used English only. A German married in England or France dare not have acted thus!

II

Richly endowed by nature with brains, charm, wit, understanding, and, one might say, from her cradle intimate with prominent and influential personages, the Princess could never have been satisfied with mere social triumphs or content with her place and fame as the most lovely Princess in Europe. She aspired to a position, not indeed of prominence, but of usefulness in the organization of practical affairs, which is the inevitable and therefore not the least important mission of those who would be worthy of their high station; as we shall learn, she was never at her ease in being merely ornamental. Throughout her married life the Princess has taken the keenest interest in international politics, in which she frequently interposed with advantage. For years she persisted in warning the German Emperor against neglecting Russia and throwing her into the arms of France—which is exactly what he did do. The Princess knew and liked Russia, was acquainted with the Czar and Czarina and numbered many members of the Imperial family amongst her intimate friends. Her main preoccupations, however, were the relationships between England and Germany; again and again she acted as an unofficial peacemaker between the two countries. Knowing well and having a high regard and affection for both King Edward VII. and the Emperor William II., she always poured oil on the oft-troubled waters of their intercourse. The Emperor was ever her kind, indulgent and helpful friend, and she saw perhaps an amiable side of his nature, now too often forgotten by both his foes and his former friends. She quotes in her pages some of the frank letters of advice she frequently sent him and which, it is only fair to emphasize, he accepted in the sincere, loyal and truthful spirit in which they were written.

From the early 'nineties until 1914 the Princess was one of the most notable ladies of fashionable and social life in Germany and England. Indeed it is hardly too much to say that she has known every man of famous accomplishments and every woman of famous beauty in England, Germany, France and Austria during the past twenty-five years; and every one who reads these pages will admit that she has exercised an important, and always pacific and benevolent, influence on Anglo-German relations. Through whosoever fault it might be that the European war broke out, it was certainly not through hers; for years she foresaw and dreaded it, and did all that one woman could possibly do to avert it.

III

The outbreak of War in 1914 put the Princess in a terribly difficult—almost an impossible—position. Finding that in Silesia in the neighbourhood of her home she was looked upon as a foreigner and a spy and her presence resented, she became a Sister in a Berlin War Hospital, served successively on the French, Austrian and Serbian fronts, was watched all the time as a possible traitor, and, towards the end of the War, had the bitterness of seeing her eldest son go out to fight against the country of her birth. She had, however, at least two real consolations. One was her personal work for British Prisoners-of-War in Germany; the other was the sympathetic understanding and moral support of practically all her intimate English, Austrian, Spanish, American, and German friends.

All her life, and perhaps more particularly during the period of the War, the Princess kept up a close correspondence with members of nearly all the German Royal Houses and, through her great friend the Crown Princess (Princess Margaret of Connaught) with the Swedish Court. From these letters she quotes in her Reminiscences as far as it is at present wise and discreet to do so. She gives us intimate views of the German Emperor, the Crown Prince, the Crown Princess, the Emperor's youngest sister, Princess Margaret (Princess Frederick Charles of Hesse)—another of Princess Daisy's greatest friends—his second sister, Victoria Princess Adolphe of Schaumburg-Lippe (Frau Alexander von Zoubkoff), the Emperor Karl of Austria, the Grand Duke of Mecklenburg-Strelitz, and many others of similar authority: Princess Frederick Charles of Hesse, the Crown Princess of Sweden and the Princess of Pless had all the same "little name" and were known to their intimates as "the three Daisies." The letters to the Princess from Prince Eitel Fritz of Prussia, the second son of the Emperor, were they available, would in themselves make a complete picture of the War as seen from the German High Quarters in the field. From the end of 1914 to the downfall of Russia, Pless was the Headquarters of the German Armies in the East, and to it came the Emperor, the young Austrian Emperor Karl, the Kings of Saxony and Württemberg—indeed all the German federated Princes—Prince Henry of Prussia, the German Crown Prince, the King of Bulgaria, the Turkish Crown Prince, prominent Generals like Hindenburg, and statesmen like Bethmann-Hollweg. We catch glimpses of them at the council table, walking and talking in the gardens, or making themselves agreeable to their hostess in her private sitting-room. The Princess reveals fully for the first time the authentic history of the tragic suicide of the young Duke of Mecklenburg-Strelitz in 1918.

IV

The Princess, who now lives a good deal in Munich, is on intimate terms with many members of the Bavarian Royal Family; the late King, Ludwig III., was her friend, as are the Crown Prince Rupprecht, the Duke Luitpold, Prince Ludwig Ferdinand, his wife, Marie de la Paz, an Infanta of Spain, and their daughter, Princess Pilar, who has for Princess Daisy an enduring affection. All through the War King Ludwig went out of his way to be charming to Englishwomen married to Germans, and to the Princess, as to many others, Bavaria was an oasis of peace in a desert of hate.

Through her three sons, her daughter-in-law, her cousin Countess Larisch and her innumerable relations and connections, the Princess is in touch with the post-war generations in England, Germany, France, Poland, Spain, Austria and Czecho-Slovakia. Statesmen and diplomats have whispered guarded secrets to her; artists have clamoured to portray her perfect English beauty. Utterly frank about herself, her family, her beautiful mother Mrs. Cornwallis-West, and her friends, she is never merely scandalous; yet her gentle malice opens windows to truth: her Irish wit stings but never wounds.

No such intimate picture of the brilliance, wealth, gaiety and fascination of social life in pre-war England and Germany as this has ever been painted, because no other woman of our time was so completely at home in the two countries. To the world the Princess became known as the typical English beauty with golden hair, perfect complexion, graceful stature, and ineffaceable charm. She could walk, ride, hunt, shoot, sail, sing, play and dance to perfection. She looked the fairy Princess. She could talk. She could do her utmost to obey King Edward's parting behest at her wedding, " to learn German and become a faithful subject of her adopted country " ; she could do most things—but she could never quite forget she was an Englishwoman, and in pre-war Prussia that helped no one. Possibly it does not to-day! That may be why the Princess now lives mostly in Bavaria and in France.

V

Perhaps it may be permissible to interject here a word of explanation about my own modest share in this volume. The business of an Editor is, in my view, to interfere as little as possible with the author whom he is introducing. It is a natural, and on the whole an engaging, weakness for a new writer to desire to enter the arena of authorship hand in hand with a friend, however humble ; we are all inclined to be apprehensive of the freemasonry of a craft, or of a section of society, of which we are ignorant. Therefore —although assuredly she needs no introduction—I obeyed the Princess's commands and accepted the privilege of putting my name on her title-page. In the matter of footnotes I found difficulties ; in a book of this kind they are at best a tiresome necessity ; yet, a new generation of readers is growing up, people's memories are short ; therefore a number of reminders could not be avoided. As far as possible I have confined myself to making clearer such points as might be obscure and to making such transpositions or corrections in the text as were obviously needed. Except where they bear the initials of the authoress, all footnotes may be accepted as mine.

A few words seem desirable about the extracts which the Princess has chosen from her diaries. Omission marks signify either redundancies or passages at present unsuitable for publication. The industry of the Princess was extraordinary and one keeps wondering how she found time to do half of what she accomplished. She kept her diary regularly and with considerable fullness practically all her life.

It is in several fat volumes and I have calculated that it contains more than half a million words—that is to say, nearly half as many words as Stevenson used in writing twelve novels!

If the Princess's book is an intimate picture of her own time, it is also a record of the deepest human interest: showing frankly and faithfully a woman's heart; her triumphs, passions, mistakes and failures. It tells how she surmounted great and seemingly unending difficulties and disappointments, and how, in the end, she won great content.

She has had everything the world can give. On her wedding day, she became entitled to wear, amongst many jewels, the world-famous rope of Pless pearls, seven yards long, the mere thought of which might perhaps be sufficient to test the composure of any very young girl. She enjoyed all the advantages of princely rank without its more tiresome isolations and restrictions: She had command of wealth beyond belief.

These things are now of the past, and in her record the Princess shows plainly that the gifts with which you are endowed at birth, such as health, a sense of humour, the capacity to win and keep love and friendship, a deep and quenchless love for nature, flowers, animals, travel, books, and the possession of congenial friends, surroundings and occupations, are in truth the only enduring sources of human peace and happiness: to these the Princess would assuredly add the doing of some regular work for the public weal.

And if, in addition, you give to the world three stalwart sons, as the Princess has done, you are, I venture to think, amply entitled to look back on the past without any cankering regrets, and to face the future with a smile.

D. C.-H.

CRICKET HILL,
YATELEY, HAMPSHIRE.
21*st April*, 1928.

CONTENTS

CHAPTER EIGHT

PAGE

CHAPTER NINE

CHAPTER TEN

LIST OF ILLUSTRATIONS

CHAPTER ONE

1873–1891

The bolt's from the door: let us rise and go.
What shall we take? A violin,
Poems in plenty, a coin or so,
And a leather purse to hold them in.

Down the highway and up the street,
And the whole will make a beautiful song:
Oh! the merry heart, and the heart's wild beat,
And the mirth in the eyes that have wept too long!

And now all tunes that ever you play,
And the wild things said by your fiddle-strings,
Are perfectly sure to come true some day;
And you and I will be Queens and Kings.

LADY MARGARET SACKVILLE.

I THINK these lines by my cousin Margaret Sackville express better than any others I have ever read a child's ideas about life. "Growing up" is to be just the opening of magic doors; the beginnings of many wonderful and endless journeys; the music of laughter, dance and song. We are to meet none but chivalrous knights and peerless ladies and all whom we love are to become queens and kings: perhaps in a way all these things do happen to us; but not quite as we imagined in childhood.

My mother, Mrs. Cornwallis-West, was one of the loveliest women of her time and thought both her daughters plain: compared with her I dare say we were. My governesses and nurses were always telling me how ugly I was; that my ears were too small, my mouth too big and my nose turned up. To remedy this they were continually pulling my ears to make them bigger and tweaking my nose to make it aquiline. This made me suspect that beauty was probably a curse, and I do not find that time has greatly modified that babyish impression. These remarks about my looks are the only shadows I can remember during a radiant childhood. No one could have had a happier, freer, more joyous youth than my brother George, my sister Shelagh and I had at romantic Ruthin Castle in North Wales, and exquisite, beloved Newlands in Hampshire—but, mine at least, contained some horrible moments. I did not like being told that I was ugly; no one does, not boys—or even men, as I found out later.

But perhaps I had better say just a word or two to explain who we were. I will not go much into the tiresome ancestry business, which anyway I could never properly understand. This was a bad handicap later when I became a German Princess and had to remember exactly how every member of the twenty odd German Reigning Houses was related, and how they all went in to dinner. Besides, Major Chapman-Huston, in his introduction, has explained as much as is necessary. We thought it best to put it there because no one ever reads introductions, although I feel quite sure this one is beautifully written. The only ancestor in whom as a child I took much personal interest was Thomas the second Baron West, who at Crécy is said to have picked up the French King's crown and handed it to the Black Prince with the courtly remark, *Jour de ma Vie*, which remains the family motto to this day.

I am told all authors are vain; it may be so, but I am not a trained writer; I received no education in the proper sense of the word, and have not the art to choose words that read nicely together. The critics, therefore, may not like my style, though I do most eagerly hope that they and every one who reads this book will like me and be indulgent to my literary—and all my other—shortcomings, and remember that so far as the extracts from my diaries are concerned, they were nearly always hurriedly written, and frequently in railway trains or under similar uncomfortable conditions, especially during the War.

George, my only brother, is Major George Frederick Myddelton Cornwallis-West, and is known to the family as Buzzie. I was baptized Mary Theresa Olivia, but every one calls me Daisy or, in the intimacy of the family circle, Dany: it was my own name for myself before I could speak properly, and my dearest loved ones always use it. My sister's name is Constance Edwina, and her pet name is Shelagh or Biddy. My father we called Poppets or anything else that came into our heads; my mother we treated like a sister, and shocked all our Victorian relations—of which we had an extraordinary number—by calling her Patsy. Poppets had his own private "little name," for her, which was Mussie. I understand that in these days most children call their parents by their Christian names. I see nothing wrong in this, although I must confess to having been mystified by two mites, both of whom were less than five years old, always talking of "Jane and James." These I imagined to be dolls, ponies or dogs, until one day to my astonishment I learned they were their parents!

As we are making "personal remarks" in a manner that would also have upset the Victorians, I may as well add that my brother George was endowed with his full share of the family good looks, and that women have never been shy of showing that they thought so. Shelagh I have always considered to be much handsomer than I am. She has the loveliest large, deep, dark, mysterious eyes, my mother's chestnut hair—now turning a most becoming grey—a marvellous figure, and the West complexion, which is undeniably lovely. Blue eyes and quantities of golden hair gained for me the name of being a "typical English beauty," an early label which I have never succeeded in living down! I am as tall as Shelagh and, although I was a better dancer, I could not ride or skate nearly so well. I love horses and riding, but Shelagh is a magnificent horsewoman. She is cleverer than I am, an excellent organizer and an able business woman. We could both run a large establishment, or indeed any number of them; although I think Shelagh enjoyed doing so more than I did. It fell to both our lots to entertain on a vast scale, she at Grosvenor House, and at Eaton, where her house-parties for polo and racing were famous, and I at Pless and Fürstenstein.

Perhaps Shelagh does not get on with people at first quite so easily as I do, as her stronger will and deeper nature are not for the shallow. I am impressionable, shy and apt to become unduly excited; Shelagh has great poise and self-control. Yet we both inherited a generous share of Irish-Welsh temperament and, while we may outwardly appear quite cool, often seethe within: we are both, I should say, mettlesome and difficult to handle. I am at times too fond of my own way and do not always foresee that to gain it one must sometimes have to pay a foolish price.

I need say no more here about Patsy, Poppets, Shelagh, George or myself, because the reader will get to know all about us as we go along. This will, I hope, prove interesting, because, although much could be said for and against us as a family, at least no one could say we were dull or ordinary. Indeed the chief accusation against us was that we were too lively. King Edward, who loved us all, christened us the "Wild West Show" and once sent a telegram addressed to "the Wild West Show, New Forest," which safely reached us. On another occasion he addressed one to "the Queen of Ireland, Hampshire," which was duly handed to my mother. We were always jolly and happy and, looking back now, I thank God for every blessed moment of that glad joyousness and laughter. The sundering years of tragedy and sorrow only make those far-off days the more precious; and I always cherish the memory of my mother and father as bubbling over with laughter and pray that, wherever they are, they are laughing now. Because of our own feelings of loss and desolation we always associate the next life with pain and gloom. But, whatever it is, it is not that: either we are just asleep, or we are full of a serene and quiet joy.

It would be merely silly to pretend that, as I grew up, I did not realize that I had inherited good looks from my parents. It could not well be otherwise; my father was a splendid-looking man and, as I got older, people took good care not to leave me in doubt as to what they thought about my appearance. Shelagh being dark and I fair, there could never be any question of jealousy or rivalry between us.

Ruthin, which is in the very north of Wales in the beautiful Vale of Clwyd, is a real castle or fortress, not as in Germany, where every building with a roof that is not obviously a farm-house is called a *Schloss*. It dates from 1400, and was a place of defence against the Scots when they descended upon Wales. All my childish ideas of early English history were associated with the Scots, who always seemed to be "descending" upon somebody or something. In those days they occasionally returned home with their spoils; now they always remain and consume them in sight of their defenceless victims. Of course Ruthin had to have a moat round it to protect it against the Scottish invaders. How we loved playing hide-and-seek in the dungeons and the old ruins, which seemed as if designed by a fairy king for our playground; indeed, to a child, the very word moat is filled with glamour and magic.

My father had a shooting-box called Llanarmon on his Llanarmon Dyffryn Estate up in the mountains, and when he went there I felt he was as far away as if he were at the North Pole. I copy an early undated letter I sent to him while he was there. I think it must have been written in 1880 when he was contesting West Cheshire. It is evident that I was learning French at the time, because the letter reads like a translation and I use the English equivalents for phrases such as *mon vieux* and *ta petite*:

RUTHIN CASTLE, NORTH WALES.

MY DEAR OLD POPPETS,—

I am thinking how dreadful it must be in the wild mountains among the Welsh people and I think I must write you a little note to comfort you. I am taught that there are no roses without thorns, but I am sure the thorns for getting into Parliament are very prickly. . . . It is very hot to-day at Ruthin. . . . Take care of your little self, dear old Dads, and come home soon to your little chickens who send you a lot of big kisses and hugs. Your loving little daughter,

DAISY.

My father did not get into Parliament then, but in 1885 he was elected member for the Western Division of Denbighshire, which he represented until 1892, first as a Liberal Unionist and later as a Conservative; he and Mr. Gladstone having parted company on the Home Rule question.

My mother, as I have said, was a most beautiful woman, twenty years younger than my father and with a vitality that death itself could scarcely draw into its arms. She could not be bothered with young children and nurseries, but wanted to live her own free, vital existence. Consequently we were left a great deal to ourselves and to governesses.

If I worshipped from a distance my lovely mother, I adored my father, who was not only the finest specimen of the older type of English gentleman, but a real friend and comrade to his children.

In due time we got a "finishing" governess called Miss Clark or some such name. I think the name "finishing governess" is most sad, as it means finishing off the dreams of girlhood. Miss Clark used to put cherry tooth-paste on her face and black cork on her eyebrows and wear gold buttons all down the bodice of her frock. I remember she tried to teach me good English, but never succeeded.

Yet, as I have said, we had great compensations. Games and sports delighted us. One favourite game was circuses. We had an old horse called Jimmy Jones, which we tried to ride standing on its back.

We found this did not answer, because as soon as Jimmy Jones moved on we moved off! We liked George to be the clown, but this always displeased him as he wanted to be the circus master and crack a whip. Then Shelagh thought of another idea. She somehow fastened Jimmy Jones to a wooden box in which I was to sit like a lady reading *The Bride of Lammermoor*. All my life long people have always insisted on my being a lady, and I have never really wanted to be anything but a tomboy. Sometimes the cord broke as we galloped (if any action of Jimmy Jones's deserves that name) up and down the avenue. Shelagh said I must not be frightened or hurt, keep my skirt over my legs and pay no attention to the sand and pebbles which used to get into the box. I remember to this day how difficult I found it to combine being romantic like the Bride of Lammermoor and dignified and ladylike (with my legs covered), while my knees were dirty and bleeding from being repeatedly thrown on the gravel.

II

My great-grandfather West was the third son of John eighth Baron West and second Earl de la Warr. I never saw him, as he died many years before I was born. Known in the family as "the Honourable Frederick" he had great interest for us because of his two very prudent and, I hope, happy marriages. He specialized in heiresses and married first, in 1792, Charlotte, daughter of Richard Mitchell, of Culham Court, in Berkshire. This lady obligingly died three years later, leaving him all her belongings and one small daughter. Losing no time, he, as the newspapers say, "led to the altar" three years later Maria, only daughter of Richard Myddleton, of Chirk Castle, in Denbighshire, by whom he had an only surviving son, who became my grandfather.

The story goes that when "the Honourable Frederick" died in 1852 his daughter and her stepbrother drew lots as to which should have Chirk and which Ruthin, and grandfather drew Ruthin. Be that as it may, father duly inherited the Castle and estate, and I am glad he did.

My grandfather also inherited from "the Honourable Frederick" the agreeable knack of falling in love with heiresses, a habit which in our family seems, in the old phrase of the Heralds, to have fallen into abeyance. His first wife was Lady Georgiana, daughter of the fifth Earl of Chesterfield. She lived only a few years and they had no children, but the marriage connected our family with the Stanhopes, many of whom were famous and nearly all of whom are delightful. Grandfather's second wife was Theresa, only daughter of Captain John Whitby, R.N., who was the friend of Nelson and Cornwallis.

About 1805 Admiral Sir William Cornwallis, that very gallant sailor brother of the Marquess Cornwallis who was Viceroy of Ireland in 1801 at the time of the Union, having by his fearless seamanship compelled Napoleon I to abandon his idea of invading England, decided to retire. Of course he wanted to live within sight of the English Channel which he had long defended with such courage and sagacity. He found an old house on the spot on which Newlands now stands. Hardly a mile from the seashore and exactly opposite the Needles, it commands lovely views of the Channel and the Isle of Wight, standing high over the intervening waters of the Solent. The old farm-house was burned down one Sunday morning and the Admiral built the Newlands we know and love. It is in the rather bad "Strawberry Hill" Gothic style then so fashionable, with turrets, battlements and semi-pointed windows, the glass of which is cut into fascinating little panes. Time, however, and the velvety sea-drenched air of South Hampshire, have combined to make the place lovely. The house is covered with all sorts of coloured creeping things, and Patsy, who adored gardens, and was no mean gardener, had made it a blaze of azaleas, rare rhododendrons, hydrangeas and other gay, singing shrubs which thrive there quite as well as they do on the Riviera: cosy nooks, herbaceous borders, brick (lovely warm old red brick) pergolas, water gardens, heather, and many wild and careless patches here and there, delighted her. Under her care it became a perfect *English* garden. Patsy, like me, loved adventure, travel and change and yet, like me, always remained absurdly and unchangeably English. Wherever I have lived I have always tried to make an English garden. I have one now at La Napoule, and I am making one at Munich.

Captain John Whitby was Admiral Cornwallis's Flag Captain and dearest friend. After they had both retired from the Navy, Whitby married Theresa Symonds, a remarkable member of a remarkable family. They had one little girl, who was baptized Theresa Cornwallis. When she was about a year old her father died.

From that moment Admiral Cornwallis constituted himself the guardian of the widow and only child of his dead friend. In due course he made his will, leaving almost everything he had in trust for Theresa Cornwallis Whitby and her descendants. Later she married grandfather and had two sons, one of whom became my father. I love to think of the romantic friendship of the old Admiral for the widow and child of his dearest friend and the happy result it had on all our lives.

All my own recollections of Newlands are associated with the enchanting music of woods and the sea.

With Newlands my grandmother brought into our family the pompous name of Theresa, which I have never liked and which is the only legacy I personally received from the Whitby family. I need say no more here of how we came to inherit the family name of Cornwallis; my brother has given a very full and interesting account of it all in his new book[1] where anyone who cares to do so can read more about it.

[1] *Life and Letters of Admiral Cornwallis*, by Major G. Cornwallis-West. Holden. 1928.

My father adored every old stone in Ruthin, and knew and loved every tree in the woods and parks at Ruthin and Newlands. He did not share my mother's love of society and was more than contented with his painting, music and the life and duties of an English country gentleman. For forty-five years he was Lord-Lieutenant of Denbighshire and for many years a Member of Parliament, and always devoted himself faithfully to discharging his public and private responsibilities.

I loved Ruthin and Newlands as much as my father did, and would have made any sacrifice to keep them in the family. To me all other places have been but houses; Ruthin and Newlands were homes. I would not have exchanged them for those two great possessions of other branches of the family, splendid Buckhurst and incomparable Knole.

And now I must say something about the relatives I most associate with my girlhood. Patsy's mother, Lady Olivia FitzPatrick, was born a Taylour, being Olivia, a daughter of the second Marquess of Headfort, who was for many years Lord Chamberlain to Queen Victoria. I do not think I ever saw him, although I remember his eldest son, Uncle Headfort, the third Marquess, quite well because he had a crooked foot which was a great source of interest and curiosity to us children. He was an old dear, or seemed to us very old, and used to bring us sweets, pat our heads and pet us—a thing dogs, horses and children love.

Granny Olivia, I have been told, was most lovely as a young woman; indeed, she remained handsome and distinguished-looking to the end of her days. Her husband, the Reverend Frederick FitzPatrick, was a Church of Ireland clergyman and was for some years Rector of Cloone in County Leitrim; but, as they say abroad, "that did not go," and eventually he gave it up and bought Warren Hall, in Cheshire, where he could hunt to his heart's content. The Irish are not, or perhaps I should say were not in those days, squeamish about the social proclivities of their clergy, but I have been told it did offend some of the more

English-minded of his parishioners to see grandfather FitzPatrick take the early Communion Service with a surplice over his hunting boots and rush through it because the Meet was a distant one. Nor can I imagine Granny Olivia ever contenting herself with life in an Irish country house. Grandfather bought and lived in Cloone Grange, a place of some pretensions, where he kept up much greater state than was considered fitting for a clergyman. His curates, who I am afraid did all the work, lived in Cloone Rectory.

Prominent amongst other visitors whom I remember at Ruthin or Newlands was dear Alice Bective. A daughter of the fourth Marquess of Downshire, she married my cousin Lord Bective, eldest son of the third Marquess of Headfort, who, however, died in 1893 without succeeding. She was my mother's friend. Alas! even as I correct these lines I see that this sweet, gracious, lovable woman has passed away at the age of eighty-six. She had only one child, a girl called Olivia, who has inherited all her mother's goodness and fragrant charm, and who married Lord Henry Bentinck in 1892.

Another visitor was Lily Pocklington, who was beautiful, unlucky in marriage and finance, and who was, I think, the first woman in Society to start a bonnet shop. I fear it was not a great success, although patronized by Princess Christian and other Royalties. Rumour had it that many of Mrs. Pocklington's friends were readier at buying than at paying.

Colonel Austin Mackenzie and his wife used to come frequently, and he would thrill me by telling me shivery ghost stories. The lovely Mrs. Wheeler was another radiant figure that flitted across the scenes of my girlhood. In her day she was a famous beauty and, with Mrs. Langtry, existed in the blaze of publicity, then so novel, but to-day so commonplace in the experience of all those who by chance, guile, notoriety, or sometimes even merit, succeed for a few brief hours in catching public interest.

As I grew older I was taken periodically to London

where we had a town house, 49 Eaton Place. Even there I can have seen but little of the great world of London, because the house is chiefly associated in my memory with father's studio where he carried on the painting he so much loved and to which he devoted a great deal of time; those who ought to know said his work had considerable merit: some of it hangs on my walls now.

Of course all kinds of people used to come to see us, and the two who stand out most vividly are King Edward VII. and Lord Charles Beresford. King Edward was, of course, still Prince of Wales; he was very kind, but sometimes his visits were an awful bore, because it meant being hurried into our best clothes and having our hair re-done, and all at express speed as the Prince hated to be kept waiting. I remember one such occasion when we were lying down resting after lunch—I was about ten, and my sister seven—he called on my mother and asked to see the children. We had to be got up and have our hair done all over again, and came downstairs feeling rather cross. The Prince asked us all kinds of questions, laughing all the time: why, we did not know. But anyhow, we did not laugh. Then he put his hand in his pocket and produced two little brooches like ladybirds—those little red insects with black spots which are supposed to bring you so much luck. We accepted them with some awe but were secretly very pleased, and felt it was really a compensation for having hurriedly to get up and listen to the nurse's grumbles.

Lord Charles Beresford we used to meet at Portsmouth. We were very proud of knowing him, but we had to pay for it as his visit always meant that our hair was put into curl papers the night before, and these were twisted so tightly that they hurt. But our hair looked beautiful the next day! Then, too, we were usually dressed in clean sailor frocks which came back from the wash with all the hooks bent in, to the great annoyance of our nurse, and which sometimes had shrunk so much that though I was a slender child the waistband used to cut into my flesh, and I could scarcely eat anything. *Il faut souffrir pour être belle*, of course, but it was an early beginning, and I remember one luncheon which was a torment to me because I wanted more mutton cutlet than my waist allowed, and was agonized by this disappointment and the fear of forgetting to say grace after lunch.

The seventh Lord and Lady de la Warr used to come often. He was cheery, good-looking and very nice. His widow, Constance, is a writer of distinction and her daughter, Margaret Sackville, whose little fairy verses I quote at the beginning of this chapter, a poet of great and acknowledged merit. Nor would I forget the visits to Newlands and Ruthin of cousin Adelaide Taylour. A daughter of the third Lord Headfort, she is a gracious, charming and faithful figure, still visiting me every year at La Napoule.

Mr. Gladstone was a great friend and admirer of my mother, whom he loved hearing sing *The Wearin' o' the Green* as only she could sing it. We went quite often to Hawarden Castle, and I can quite truthfully say that Mr. Gladstone was my first love. Somehow he never struck me as old and both he and Mrs. Gladstone were perfectly delightful to children. One day after shamelessly flirting with the old gentleman I boldly asked for their photograph, which was at once given to me. They both signed it; I have it to this day, and love to look at the two kindly venerable figures seated side by side. Though only a photograph, it has something of the pathos of that most tender and appealing of all masterpieces—Whistler's portrait of his Mother.

When I was about sixteen or so, Patsy, Poppets, Shelagh and I went to Florence. Shelagh and I were to learn Italian and singing. Pawskie, our governess, was there to chaperon us, while Patsy and Poppets visited galleries and churches and Poppets amused himself by making excellent copies of the masterpieces he particularly liked in the Uffizi and elsewhere. Dear old Bolton (who was then quite young and my father's valet) carried the easels and paint brushes to and fro: I cannot honestly say that the experience aroused in him any marked devotion to Italian art. Like Sir Frederick Ponsonby, Poppets could copy an Old Master so faithfully and well that only an expert could tell it was not an original.

My voice was tried by Vanuchini, Director of the Opera and then famous in Florence. He taught me himself and laid the foundations of all I ever knew about singing. He was enthusiastic about the possibilities of my voice and told my father he would train me for nothing if I would promise to learn Italian and French thoroughly and adopt singing as a career. Of course I was enchanted; I was born with a love of singing and acting, and my quaint and enthusiastic teacher was quite certain, after the fashion of those days, that he could make my mezzo-soprano into a pure, fine soprano. I saw nothing but rapture ahead, and was intoxicated with visions of myself as *Elsa*, *Elizabeth*, *Marguerita*, or one of a score of other lovely and unlucky heroines. I was not quite sure whether I wanted most to be fair, frail and consumptive (but enduring), or dark, passionate and mysterious like *Delilah*, and, in my more confident moments, I felt quite sure that I could interpret either type of rôle to the acclamations of an astonished and ravished world.

Women are often accused of foolish economies, and I dare say they indulge in them almost as frequently as men. We spent the winter at an hotel, the name of which I have quite forgotten. I realized that our stay in Italy was a considerable expense to my father, and that it was really made for my sake, because Shelagh was too young to derive much benefit from it. In a spirit of unselfishness I secretly decided to help to "keep down the bills" by drinking plain instead of bottled water. Sanitation in Italy in those days was even worse than it is now, and the result was a severe attack of typhoid fever. As soon as it could possibly be managed I was taken home to England

MYSELF.

Aged about Fourteen.

for my convalescence—all my hopes of a career on the operatic stage drowned in a glass of water!

From that time onward my life was spent mostly at Ruthin or Newlands. Between lessons were alluring excitements such as visits from people famous in the great outside world. The War seems to have set one's childhood back to a hundred years ago. Could there ever have been a time when every one seemed gay, happy, contented and reasonably well off! People loved coming to Ruthin and Newlands. A warm welcome and an appreciative audience awaited all who had personality or distinction; wit, gaiety, light-heartedness and good comradeship counted with us far more than long purses or long pedigrees.

III

I remember so well a man who used to come to Ruthin to see my mother. Her beauty, lively and audacious wit, and unquenchable charm gained her innumerable devoted admirers, many of whom were indeed almost her slaves. This particular man was gallant and kind and sang beautifully. I think it was he who first aroused in my heart—not love—but the thought of love. The sort of secret ecstasy a young girl so often experiences just before she falls in love with love. During this period she will do many foolish and impulsive things, but seldom, indeed almost never, wrong ones, because she has no desire for or understanding of reality: she is unawakened. Happy the girl and happy her husband if he is the first to open her eyes to the real meaning of life and love and to do it with gentle understanding and tenderness.

I remember thinking how nice it would be to be loved by such a big, strong, *gentle* man. One day I was sitting out in the sun beside him when my mother called. He picked me up, chair and all, and carried me to her. Another day while he was there she and I started playing hide-and-seek. We hid in an angle of the old castle walls and made bogy noises. He found us and caught my hand and drew me to him. Later I often recalled what was probably to him nothing more than a childish romp, and wondered why he had ever let me go.

On one of my birthdays he gave me a moonstone heart with little diamonds round it and suspended from a slender gold chain. One of the bitterest memories of my youth was, before my engagement, obeying my mother's order to give it back to him. I could not bear the thought of doing so myself, but took it in tears to the dear old family butler, who gave it to him for me.

In those early days I do not think he loved me; perhaps he never really did so in the full sense of the word. Yet, during my first and only season in London, I met him often. I knew he had no money and that I should never be allowed to see him, much less to marry him, and told him so. He replied that he did not care a hang: "You are out now, and free to make your own choice, and I shall see you whenever I can."

Brave, futile words: defiant, foolish words of youth that make the heart beat high, even now long years after.

Once again, after my marriage, I met him in a restaurant. He asked: "When may I come and see you, Princess?" I turned to him a haughty little face: "I am sorry, but I am staying at an hotel and never know when I shall be at home." Poor trite little social excuse under which to bury my first romance. I never saw him again; he died in South Africa not very long after.

IV

When my mother married she was only sixteen and a half: her three children were born before she was twenty-one. It therefore seemed to her very natural that her daughters should marry young; she was too much accustomed to homage and admiration to want them clinging to her skirts. Her beauty was of the brilliant, brunette type, and she had the loveliest teeth and smile and a perfect figure. My father simply worshipped her and let her do exactly what she liked —perhaps too much so: he was intensely proud of her and in his eyes she could do no wrong. As for her beauty and the interest it aroused, one can hardly realize it nowadays. The 'eighties and 'nineties originated the rather vulgar term, Professional Beauties, amongst whom my mother was numbered. There was a photograph taken of her wearing an ermine coat and muff sitting on an artificial rock during an artificial snowstorm, which sold by the million. That her loveliness was of the first order is proved by the fact that amongst her peers were such universally acknowledged beauties as the Duchess of Leinster and her sister Lady Helen Vincent (Viscountess d'Abernon), Thérèse Lady Londonderry, Georgiana Lady Dudley, Lady de Bathe (Mrs. Langtry), Mrs. Wheeler and several others. My mother talked well, had a brilliant rather than a profound mind, a great sense of humour, overflowing vitality, and she had a fine voice and her passionate singing of *The Wearin' o' the Green* would have aroused a revolutionary outburst in Ireland any day. Both she and Granny Olivia had an enchanting little Irish brogue.

It is no exaggeration to say that Patsy had the reputation of being the fairest woman in the three kingdoms. Abraham Hayward, a writer famous in his day and now almost forgotten, wrote a long poem in her honour, the last verse of which ran:

> For though envy itself should disarm,
> And in praise of thy beauty agree,
> On none will thy fulness of charm
> Ever flash as it flashed upon me.

Hayward, who was himself a brilliant talker, could appreciate my mother's wit, her resilient personality, her mind like flashing quicksilver, and his approval was powerful enough to place any woman of fashion far above her contemporaries. The unusual thing about Patsy's fascination was that it never faded. To the end of her life men, and women also, would do anything for her.

All this being so, it was decided that I should come out early. I was never told that I must marry rank and money, but I think it must always have been an understood thing that I should do so because, for our position and the scale on which we lived, we were poor. When I was duly Presented to Queen Victoria I wore, for the first time, a long dress, an enormously long train and three white plumes in my hair. I tried to look nice, but simply felt what a little donkey I was.

Of course I at once began going to dances, and one in particular I remember. I wore on my head, in the rather silly fashion of those days, a wreath of corn with poppies and cornflowers in it. I must confess I thought it rather fine and my chagrin can be imagined when a nice man came up to me and said: "What on earth made you put that silly wreath on? You look like a harvest festival." I could not take it off there and only felt embarrassed, shy and afraid to dance. My evening was quite spoiled. People, even very kind people, seldom realize how easily girls, and boys too, are hurt.

V

I first met my future husband, Prince Henry of Pless, at a ball. Although in the German Diplomatic Corps and recently appointed a Secretary of the German Embassy in London, he did not at that time speak perfect English. I was shy and hardly understood a word he said, and a stupid little Peer who was there and who wanted to marry me, began to giggle. He is alive still and I hope he reads this and will realize how cross he made me. Although only a girl, I felt he was being very rude to a foreigner, and I did not like it. Far from furthering his cause it only made me sorry for Prince Henry and inclined to be kinder to him than I might otherwise have been.

We had a neighbour, a very charming Peer, owner of a fine property, whom it was thought I might marry, and whom I think I could easily have loved. Unfortunately he was at the time blatantly in love with a married woman. I remember the very morning after my husband proposed to me we were riding in the Row when this very dear man galloped up on a big chestnut horse and asked a question which gave no happiness. Some years later he married and had children, but after a time he and his wife separated and he is now dead. What a queer mixed-up affair is life! However, I am happy to say that I kept his chivalrous friendship to the very end: like so many of us, he just missed his way.

My husband proposed to me at a masked ball at Holland House. I did not know what on earth to say or do. I realized that my mother was ambitious and desired the match. In those absurd days it was a big feather in a mother's cap if she could marry a daughter off during her first season. "Marry her off"—an odious phrase. I told Hans I did not love him. He said that did not matter; love came after marriage. Perhaps it does sometimes, but I fear not often.

In Germany every bride, whatever her rank, provides furniture, linen, trousseau—everything. Often she provides the house as well. In France the custom is similar although perhaps not quite so general. I could provide nothing; and my family could not even give me my trousseau on a fitting scale. Prince Henry, knowing all this, dazzled me with descriptions of life in Silesia. I was to have hunters, jewels, castles, two ladies-in-waiting, visit England every year, and goodness knows what. It all sounded splendid and romantic. I did not realize it clearly at the time, but I was just being bought. Yet, after all these years, I must be perfectly fair to my husband. He did not, and never could, see it from my point of view. Instead of a wife who would add to the riches of his family, he was marrying someone without a penny. Braving the age-old customs of his own country, he was prepared to do all himself, even to paying for the trousseau! Nothing could have exceeded the generosity with which he treated my family right up to the end of the War and even after it. Again and again he came to the help of one member or another. These things must not be forgotten. Even now when his revenues are much diminished by the cruel post-war taxation in Germany and by the confiscatory policy of the present Polish Government, he lets me want for nothing in reason. But I am wandering and anticipating—as I fear a woman will.

For breakfast on my wedding morning I had sausages and bacon and wondered if they had anything so nice in Germany, or only porridge. The wedding reception was given by Princess Alexis Dolgorouky at her house in Portman Square. Born a Fleetwood Wilson, she was a great friend of my mother's. The house was of course upside down, so I went out early and walked in the garden in the centre of the Square. I put on my oldest shoes, a funny little old turban hat and soiled gloves. I had only an allowance of twelve pounds a year for shoes and gloves and had learned to be careful. I remember rather wishing that Hans could see me looking such a fright, not want to marry me and go back to Germany without me.

The marriage took place at St. Margaret's, Westminster, but I was far too excited to remember much about the ceremony, except that I had to wear a diamond coronet which my father-in-law had given me as a wedding present. Amongst my new titles I was a Countess of the Holy Roman Empire, and the crown was a copy of the one worn in the old days by ladies of that rank: I have it still. Of course the Prince and Princess of Wales were there and signed the register. My father, who looked so proud and handsome, gave me away. I remember wondering how little Shelagh was getting on in her first half-long frock

—and they really were long in those days—because, after all, she was only a child, being three years younger than me. I do not remember much else about the service except that, as I left the church, the dear English crowd with its unique mixture of Cockney wit and sentiment—bless it—called out, "God Pless you." At the reception I was rather pleased when the servants addressed me as "Your Highness."

What I do remember, and with real regret, is that I never properly carried out dear King Edward's friendly parting advice to learn German and become a good subject of my adopted country; I became, I hope, a good and loyal subject, but I never succeeded in thoroughly learning the language.

Gossip had it that my husband, who did not want to marry a German, got sent to London with the daring hope of trying to marry the fair young English Princess who is now Queen of England. It was said that the Duke and Duchess of Teck were not unfavourably disposed to the idea, which may have been true, as the Duke, who was the son of a Prince of Württemberg, was far from well off. The Hochbergs have frequently married Royalties; indeed Pless came to them through the marriage of the then head of the family with the last princess of one of the old Polish reigning houses[1]—a fact which, oddly enough, became for a time of considerable political importance during the Great War: moreover, in olden times the family has given kings to Hungary and Bohemia.

However, Hans met me, and never hesitated a moment. Admittedly he loved me. I suppose I should have felt flattered at being chosen, because my husband's position and great wealth were considered as entitling him to aspire to a bride in the highest quarters. But in those days I attached little importance to such considerations, and I do still less in these.

When we married, my husband gave up diplomacy, telling me that the German Foreign Minister of that

[1] See pages 10 and 111.

day refused to allow junior diplomatists to marry. Even then I thought this such nonsense, because the one thing they want is a charming and agreeable wife who is sufficiently intelligent to keep her ears open and her mouth closed when serious matters are being discussed. The decision was unfortunate in another way. It deprived my husband of a regular occupation during my father-in-law's lifetime, and me of a life the variety and interest of which would perhaps have done something to make up for the absence of that deep and lasting love and respect without which no marriage (however suitable otherwise) can be a real success.

We went to Paris for our honeymoon as my husband had served there and in Brussels before being transferred to the German Embassy in London and therefore knew the Continent well.

I began my married life totally unprepared for any of its experiences, duties or responsibilities. Literally I knew nothing. A short time before I had overheard my mother telling a woman friend that " So-and-so was in love with Daisy." I kept pondering what " being in love " meant.

My experience was by no means an unusual one. Many girls of my period went through as bad or worse. But the convention ordaining such things was horrible and cruel. My parents, with hearts full of tender love, did nothing whatever to prepare me for life and its ordeals. I suppose I knew something, but only in a vague furtive way. I had no fixed principle ; no clear guiding thought. Without a rudder or chart, I was at the mercy of any wind that blew close enough to reach me. Either of my parents would have done anything in the world for me—except tell me the truth.

I ascribe many of the errors and misfortunes of my life to the fact that I not only married a man who was a stranger to me, but that I had no idea of how even to begin to get to know, much less to guide and influence, him.

Women, at any rate, will understand how utterly

without knowledge of any kind I was ; how scamped and short had been my social training, when I say that I did not even know how my smart French going-away frock should be worn. I put it on back to front. My husband, who has the keenest eye for women's clothes, was half-amused and half-cross when he saw it. He scolded me.

It had to be hurriedly changed, and I drove away for my honeymoon consumed with grief, humiliation and dread of the unknown.

CHAPTER TWO

1892–1900

WHEN I arrived in Pless I found a great white palace built on the site of an older one by my father-in-law about 1870. It is very French, as are most large German houses of that period, and was full of rather bad, heavy, over-gilded furniture, which was also supposed to be French and which was nothing but ugly German. There were acres of terraces and gardens and much indifferent statuary. A great deal of state and heavy luxury, no comfort or convenience, and not a single bathroom! My husband had made for me an ornate one of gold mosaic, now in Fürstenstein, rather horrid, but much better than none.

For my reception all the retainers and servants were assembled in their best uniforms and liveries. Both at Pless and Fürstenstein the organization of the household was on strictly military lines, and every servant had to do daily drill. The women servants were all dressed alike in native Silesian costume carried out in the livery colours of dark crimson and silver. The magnificent staircase was lined with masses of men wearing blue coats with white gaiters and gloves, a uniform which I thought horrid. Their numbers puzzled and frightened me: the only thing I liked was the maid-servants in their short crimson dresses, white aprons, fichus and stockings, and caps of white cambric, and their hair in plaits down their backs—they looked too amusing.

I soon found the etiquette was unbelievably boring. I knew no German and could not make my wishes known. When I wanted to leave one room for another a bell was rung, a servant opened the door and a footman walked in front of me to wherever I wished to go. And all I wanted to do was to steal quietly away with a tight throat, or perhaps wait for the English post. One of the first things I did was to learn enough German to tell them that this ceremony was no longer necessary and that I *could* open doors, and liked to go to bed by myself. This my husband disapproved of and, all our lives together, we had constant misunderstandings about what he called interfering with the servants. Even during the War, when all the younger men-servants were in the Army, he was cross because I told his valet to turn on the heating instead of summoning the particular persons without whose immediate help one had to go on being either asphyxiated or frozen! Hans comes of a nation which attaches absurd importance to trifles.

However, my unfailing consolation was my father-in-law, Hans Heinrich XI. The family all called him Vater and I did the same. Like my own father, he was a very great gentleman. He gave me the warmest of welcomes and was ever my dear and faithful friend and protector. He understood me, I think. Above all, he believed in me. When any of my new, frightening German relations were severe with me, he would say: "Leave the child alone; she will come in front of you all in time." This gave me courage and I did my utmost to please him by being tactful and learning to do things as I should. But there was something wild and untamable in my English spirit—or is it Irish or Welsh?—that at times outraged his old-fashioned ideas of what was ladylike, and then even he and I would be at cross-purposes for a little moment. I had often to swallow unshed tears. A stubborn streak of English pride has always made me want to hide pain or disappointment.

I never cared for Pless, but my father-in-law loved it. In his eyes one of its most interesting features was his famous stud of magnificently bred horses. A roan chestnut was his favourite colour and I can see now in my mind's eyes a perfect stallion called *Rapid Roan*. The Master of the Horse was a dear old gentleman with an Italian wife. When he conducted us round the stables or the breeding establishment he always wore a grey top-hat and gave the impression that we were being shown a holy sanctuary where hardly a word might be spoken. As in England, this performance usually took place on Sunday mornings after church and before luncheon, and it was certainly felt to be the most important and impressive ceremony of the day. I seem to remember that Vater once ran a horse for the Derby and very nearly won it.

To please my father-in-law I did my best to memorize the pedigrees of the more famous stallions and mares. I would say: "What a lovely foal; I am sure *Rapid Roan* is the father and *Pless Beauty* the mother." Sometimes, by a lucky hit, I was correct and every one would smile and say, "Yes, Your Highness." I love horses, just as I love people, but I never could understand pedigrees. To me, trying to memorize the ancestry and relationships of either race-horses or families is as hard as trying to grasp the Athanasian Creed. So far, the most difficult part of writing this book has been to get into my head who exactly my great-grandparents were. Fortunately I need only keep such points in my head long enough to write them down. Like the reader, I can then speedily forget them.

We had nearly always to be at Pless for Christmas, which was not a bit like Christmas at home. We had pretty German Christmas songs, but no crackers, mince pies or plum puddings. Later on I used to procure these from England and have a private little celebration in my own room, in which my English maid and my husband's English valet joined. Had I done this in public every one would have thought that I was seriously trying to undermine the constitution of the Kingdom of Prussia.

At Pless we had a great number of men called *Oberförster* or head foresters, who wore a beautiful green uniform. At stated times they were invited to luncheon and then we would use the big dining-room, which is enormous. I shall never forget the first time this happened. I was much impressed by their picturesque appearance, until my husband warned me by saying: "Do not look surprised, my dear girl, if you see them spitting into their finger-bowls!" I thought he was what my sons call "pulling my leg" until, to my horror, I saw them put a peppermint and water mixture, served for the purpose, into their finger-bowls, gargle, and then pass it back: it almost made me sick! All over Germany the disgusting spitting habit used to be general. It is now much better, but even in spotless Munich you see notices forbidding it everywhere; and in all shops are displayed the orders of the City authorities, *Nicht auf den Boden spucken*. This may be a good thing, but the sight of the notice in a café, dairy, or food shop arouses unpleasant suggestions.

My second son, Lexel, now aged twenty-two, reminds me that when he was fifteen he was made almost ill every evening at his Uncle Bolko's country house, Rohnstock, in Silesia, by this revolting gargling practice. The establishment was maintained on very old-fashioned lines. Ugly blue glass finger-bowls, with a blue glass tumbler inside them containing the necessary mixture, were placed in front of each guest and, at the end of the meal, conscientiously and noisily used. The party then entered the drawing-room and, before coffee was served, all the relations gave each other an emphatic and resounding kiss, at the same time saying *Mahlzeit*, meaning good digestion.

The nasty kissing habit has fortunately quite died out, but in many middle-class families it is still the custom for anyone entering a room while a meal is in progress or leaving the table before it is ended to say *Mahlzeit*. The Danes have a similar custom, and in that country to omit to say *Vel bekomme* in such circumstances would be considered very rude indeed.

Lexel adds that, horrid as the gargling in the dining-room was, it at least served to mitigate the beastliness of being kissed by a lot of people whose mouths and beards smelled and tasted of dinner! But then Lexel never did like promiscuous embraces, and, as a very small boy, once flatly refused to kiss even the Emperor's hand.

II

I much preferred our occasional Christmases at Fürstenstein. They were very happy, almost sacred, because all our Guards, servants and dependants and their families came and celebrated Christmas with us. There were presents for every one and it was great fun choosing suitable ones. Some of my English friends used to come over and stay and help us and, for the time, every one was free and happy. This is one of the very nicest sides of German life that on such occasions perfect equality obtains between prince and peasant.

The Castle of Fürstenstein occupies a magnificent position: it crowns a great pointed pine-clad rock over two hundred feet high on the south-west and north, and dominates an enormous stretch of country filled with forests, lakes and wide stretches of open plain which fade away to the distant Silesian mountains. Many of the old rooms in one part of the house are actually in the rock and, to reach the Castle, one must approach it from the east and cross the great stone bridge which spans a river flowing far down below at the bottom of a deep ravine. The roads to the Castle all gradually ascend and the approach from any direction is an ever-changing vista of enchanting loveliness.

It is situated close to the western border of Silesia, where it touches what was the old Bohemian frontier in the picturesque mountain country known in Germany as *Sudeten Gebirge*. It was originally a moated fortress and *Burgwarte*, or watch-tower, and was erected for the purposes of defending the frontier by Duke Bolko I. of Löwenberg-Schweidnitz about 1292. But fortresses in those days were always changing hands and some time after the Castle came into the possession of Ritter Conrad I. of Hochberg of Giersdorf, the founder of the Fürstenstein line, and has been held by his descendants to this day.

From the main Park gates a splendid avenue of linden trees leads gradually to the entrance towers guarding the bridge and passes through the outer and inner court-yards gay with flowers, to the principal entrance on the east front.

Fürstenstein is not really a peaceful place; one cannot get on the green grass away from servants. One is always passing a Musketeer, and the terraces are stiff, and there are always old men and women working on them, keeping them far too tidy and formal-looking. There are no corners massed with roses of no particular kind, where butterflies dance and bees hum. Except in the forests, every tree in Germany is grown as a standard; maples, may trees, lilacs, everything. Just at the end of the winter when the poor little things think no one cares, they start to burst, but all the little quivering green twigs are cut off. They have to grow and live and flower by rule. So many German gardens are like a prim little *Gretchen* in a stiff cotton frock with eyes cast down, white cotton stockings and black boots and lots and lots of thin little plaits round her head. Such gardens resemble ferns and a fern always seems to me such a proper plant—no colour or scent or mystery: it is the Mrs. Grundy of the plant world. To me, Fürstenstein has always brought a sense of loneliness, but that of course is largely because it is in a foreign country. If only there had been some nice simple countrified neighbours instead of the gossipy, jealous, narrow-minded Counts and Countesses, it would have made all the difference. On moon-lit nights I used to wander on the terraces alone, and then come up the steps to hear German, and smell cigars—and the sound of the river in the valley made me think of the sea at Newlands, one wave following another for ever and ever!

The state, too, as I have said, irked me. For years

I was not allowed to use a motor but was always met at the station by a semi-state carriage with postilions. At Pless and Fürstenstein a gorgeously dressed man with a cocked hat and a tall silver staff was always on duty outside the front door. He signalled one's approach to the servants, flourished his great stick and saluted like a regimental drum-major of the English Guards. Privately I christened him *Guy Fawkes*.

I have always been, in a way, a Socialist; and hated our liveries all smothered in silver lace, and the unnecessary servants for nothing but show. On gala occasions at least thirty men waited at dinner. I am quite sure it is wrong to flaunt one's riches and power. To do things well in a quiet and dignified way is quite another matter. One expects to see a lady well-dressed and with good shoes and *lingerie*—but she need not lift up her skirts and say, "Look at my Valenciennes." All the display made me feel like a *nouveau riche*, and eventually I persuaded my husband to reduce some of it.

One day I did a perfectly mad thing; it was to try to learn how to ride postilion. Of course I had to have a lady's saddle, no other was possible in Germany in those days. Well, try to ride postilion with a lady's saddle. See how uncomfortable it is. I did not dare to go through the villages or meet anybody, or I should have got into a terrible family row when I got home; such an incomprehensible game would not have been tolerated. Why is it a man can do anything and a woman nothing? At any rate, they are doing more now; to my mind, perhaps too much. I would rather they stayed more at home, had more babies and personally looked after them.

I remember so well the Emperor being at Pless one Sunday soon after my marriage; he and my father-in-law, mother-in-law and sister-in-law had walked on. I said I would follow in a minute. I wanted to change my clothes, and, hurriedly doing so, joined them in a short red-brown walking frock and cap with a walking stick. My "in-laws" had put on long skirts for church and had not changed. The Emperor looked at me and said: "Now that is what I call properly dressed; a short skirt and stout shoes." I felt very shy and said nothing.

In the evenings in those days we all sat round a table with a lamp in the middle, the women of the family with their embroidery. I used to get up in the morning very simple-minded and good-tempered, and we all sat under the lime trees and wrote letters or sewed. Nothing else was permitted.

At Promnitz, the principal shooting-box in Pless, we were not allowed to wear evening dresses or jewels. This, thank goodness, made it more homely. So one evening, to tease dear old Vater, I came down in a sack-cloth skirt and bodice made of two new sacks I had got from the stables. In one I made holes for my two arms to come through and I cut the bottom of it off to make sleeves. With the other sack I made a skirt and put on a red tie, waistband and bows at my wrists. I said nothing but sat down next to Vater at dinner. In the middle of the meal the dear old gentleman said: "I cannot understand this extraordinary smell of horse and hay near me," and turned round as if to ask a servant. Of course they knew the joke. At last he put his head close to me, whispering in German: "Excuse me, my child, but I am afraid that it comes from you!" On which I could not keep back my laughter and said, also in German: "Vater, you are quite right, these are two brand-new sacks out of your stables—don't you think I look very smart? I have no jewels on, as you see. I shall be quite sorry to throw this nice useful dress away."

When I first married I was told that it was not considered *fürstlich*, that is princely, for me to go about among our people at Fürstenstein and Pless, but after a few years I took the law into my own hands, ordered my carriage and went where I chose. I remember in those early days going to see a new hospital in Schweidnitz. I thought the doctor who conducted me round was most brutal. I did not want to see all the horrors he showed me, or to disturb the poor sick people. Some of the sights almost made me ill. Afterwards my husband told me that most probably the doctor did it on purpose to disgust me so that I should never wish to go there again. Those middle-class men in authority preferred to rule their own roosts and have no critical eye from outside to mark their shortcomings. This man was one of those who, later on, most bitterly opposed our efforts to cleanse the filthy river into which many towns drained. At one time the death-rate of those towns was enormous. My English ideas of sanitation were outraged and for many years I fought to have this disgraceful state of affairs put right, as I will tell later.

Breslau is the nearest town of any size to Fürstenstein. It is fifty miles away and we of course used it a great deal. I remember that when I first stayed in the town—it is really a city and being the old capital of Silesia it contains many interesting and historic buildings and corners—in 1892—the little old inn was unbelievably primitive, no carpets or comfort of any sort. In the principal public room there was just a long narrow table with felt mats to put beer glasses on, and there one sat among other people's coachmen and footmen! I was only nineteen, and when I went to bed I was so terribly hungry that Hans went out to the Club and got me some bread and butter and ham.

But all Germany was primitive then. I remember leaving England with its beauty and perfection of life (which has since been to some extent copied in Germany) and thinking to myself, "Have I really got to live here? Is this uncivilized and ungentlemanly country to be my home?" But I learnt to treat it all as a huge joke. At first I wanted to cry, and you know how it is when you can't cry you must laugh, and when you mustn't laugh you squeeze the inside of your mouth with your teeth. You need not bite, but it keeps your lips from trembling.

Life in Germany was so utterly different from what it is in England that it is hard to explain. I remember

MY GREAT-GRANDPARENTS, THE 2ND MARQUESS OF HEADFORT AND HIS WIFE.

I and some of our guests rode to the *Alte Burg*, a rock, or rather baby mountain, near Fürstenstein one afternoon. It being a weekday, I did not think there would be anyone about. But to my horror the *Gesangverein* from one of the towns was there and a lot of tourists. They came to meet us on the bridge and lined up and sang. I spoke to them and thanked them and asked if they would not come and sing under the windows of the garden-house where I and the boys and our guests were having tea. This pleased them enormously and they sang slow good wholesome heavy steadfast German choir songs. I tried to look dignified with a hot face and a safety riding skirt. There is, as is well known, a great deal of singing in Germany, and much of it is very good. But some of the men sound as if they were singing into empty metal pots—there is a sort of dull echo and uncertainty about every note.

I really did try to obey King Edward's parting advice, but unsuccessfully. No one can blame me more than I do myself for not having learnt German properly, but in my house everybody talked English. All my friends came from Austria and Hungary, many had American or English wives. It was not because I did not try—but the idea of my talking German made them all laugh. I started once to have lessons and a dear old lady came up from the village to teach me at half-past ten. The door of my sitting-room would open and in would come one of the guests and throw a cushion at my head and then three or four others would come in and say: "For goodness' sake come out, we don't know what to do with ourselves, there is no one to tell us about anything or show us round. Come out, life is short, and we are going away next week." Then a last cushion would come at my head, perhaps fall on the table, on an ink-pot, or on the head of the old governess.

The only German I can speak really well is medical German, which I used during the War when working in the Red Cross with the doctors and nurses.

I must now try to recollect some further impressions of the first years of my married life as a very young and shy *Prinzessin*.[1]

Soon after I first arrived in Berlin, very, very terrified, I was taken to stay at Friedrichshof, near Cronberg, with the Empress Frederick, mother of the Emperor, and the elder sister of King Edward. The Empress was the most great-hearted, great-souled lady I ever met. She had a rare tenderness, and I felt there was a loneliness in her thoughts. The first day after luncheon I did not remember the way upstairs or know quite where to go. Seeing the Empress sitting outside alone on her balcony I went to the piano, opened it and sang *Home, Sweet Home* by heart. I felt the Empress might have been thinking of England. I did not go out to speak to her—but just shyly shut up the piano and went away: from that hour the Empress was my unfailing friend. I walked often with the Empress in her garden of roses which was beautiful. I told her so—and all she answered was: "Pick one, dear, for you are the most beautiful rose in my garden."

My husband was always, and always will be, what dear General Oliphant used to call "pompous Hans." In the Empress's personal Book, which she gave me to sign, I wrote "Daisy of Pless"—using the Christian name by which I had always been known and called; but when I had to do it again in the visitors' book before leaving, my husband turned and told me severely to write "Mary Theresa of Pless"—which I had never done in my life: I felt perfectly idiotic and as if it were the name of someone else, or a very old grand lady.

My visits to the Empress must have been kept in her dear remembrance or she would not, just before dying, have thought of me so lovingly. I suppose she recalled her own life when she first came to Germany as a lovely, young, high-spirited girl of only seventeen and a half. Even before the marriage she

[1] I was not, of course, a *Fürstin* or reigning Princess until after the death of my father-in-law in 1907.—D. of P.

had unpleasant experiences to meet. There was some question of the wedding taking place in Prussia. Queen Victoria was aghast at the very idea and wrote quite tartly to Lord Clarendon, then our Ambassador in Berlin: "Whatever may be the usual practice of Prussian Princes, it is not *every* day that one marries the eldest daughter of the Queen of England. The question therefore must be considered as settled and closed."[1] This, to some extent, was my own feeling. Hans's family is certainly very distinguished, but it was my view then, and it is now, that the daughter of a well-born English gentleman is a good enough consort for any foreign prince.

Remembering her own early difficulties, the Empress Frederick had fears for my future. As long as she lived she never failed me, and one of her last acts was to charge the Emperor her son to protect and help me.

My father-in-law looked so well in Berlin in his silk hat and black coat, very tall, with a beautiful figure, and he used to like to walk with me in the mornings down the Wilhelmstrasse, the Whitehall of Berlin, where every one would see us. One day I came down with a very pretty quiet grey frock on—one of Jay's best. He looked at me very kindly and sadly and said: "Child, have you no black frock?" I said: "But, Vater, we are not in mourning, I never had a black frock yet." So he replied: "Never mind then, come out as you are," and we went. No lady was supposed in those days to walk in the street in Berlin in anything but black!

I should never have been allowed to have been "at home" alone to a man in my father-in-law's house in Berlin; indeed one might not even speak to a man alone. Of course this was a terrible bore sometimes, but it is better to talk too little than too much, particularly if one is pretty, young and married. One day in our own house in the country—my father-in-law and others were there—I sat on a sofa after dinner and

[1] *Letters of Queen Victoria*, Vol. III. John Murray.

Prince Eitel Fritz, then, like myself, young and shy, sat beside me and drank his coffee. I thought nothing of it—why should I, it seemed so natural. But the next day Vater explained to me, saying, " Child, don't do that in Germany ; we never let a man sit on the same sofa as a lady. He can get a chair for himself." This made me smile, but he was too dear for me to argue with him.

I was not even allowed to drive alone in an open carriage in Berlin, and as the house was very often overheated I longed for air. A darling old aunt of my husband (now dead) took pity on me and we went out driving together in an open carriage, as alone I never could have gone.

Berlin society was, and still is, very boring. Occasionally I used to feel I could not stand another minute of it. The Germans have never acquired the art of mixing their guests. Everything is done according to rank and precedence, and the inevitable result is devastating dullness. No one really wants always to sit next to the same people. One dare not ask a husband to dine without his wife or they would both have fits (even if they hated each other) ! Worse still, people are segregated according to ages ! Could anything more invidious or soul-destroying be imagined ? Even now at a tea-party in Munich the " young people " are herded into one room and the " old people " into another, there to sit round a tea-table and never budge. The procedure is disastrous. I really do not want to sit next to a man because he is a Prince. I know all the Princes in Germany, Imperial and otherwise ; I know everything they are going to say and would be grateful for a change. I have often amused myself by speculating as to who are the hostesses who have the temerity to decide when an unmarried girl is no longer " young " and show her into the room sacred to the " old." And does " the girl " relish this particular moment in what, I suppose, one might call her " social descent " ? Is she welcomed by her new circle with effusion, or do they pretend not to notice her advent and act as if the poor dear had been always an " old "? I have never been present on one of these dramatic occasions, and hope I never shall be.

It is not easy to describe how we were placed at Court. To the right of the thrones of the Emperor and Empress was the Diplomatic Circle; to the left, in order, were reserved places for the Princesses and Duchesses and, further down, the Countesses and Baronesses. Often there were not many of us Princesses or Duchesses present. For instance, dear old Aunt Anna Reuss never came, or could have come, for the Reuss Princesses claimed the right to have pages to carry their trains at Court, but the Emperor would not agree to this. One of the Empress's nieces married a Reuss some years ago; indeed they are quite as well-born as the Hohenzollerns. Times, however, have changed. The Emperor's second wife was born Princess Hermine of Reuss; her first husband, a Prince of Schönaich-Carolath, was connected with the Hochberg family.

There were rules, of course, at Court about the ladies' dresses, one being that at a Schleppencour (so-called from the Schleppen, or train, about fifteen feet long, worn by the ladies), one's train must not hang from the shoulders, but from the waist. I thought this perfectly hideous, so I had two broad strips made of the same stuff as my train and put them over my shoulders so as to look as if they were necessary to hold it on, but from the side one could see no waist. I do not know if they guessed or if anybody noticed. I always wore a piece of tulle or chiffon over my shoulders, either pale blue or white. Once the Mistress of the Robes came to me and said: "Why hide your shoulders with that piece of stuff, it is much nicer showing them." And she pulled a bit down. I at once pulled it up and said: "You see, Countess, the least little draught gives me a chill." I would not go about with shoulders like Queen Victoria's early pictures, with a *décolletage* coming straight across the front to the top of the arms, which I think makes the most hideous line, and is only possible when the hair is worn in ringlets.

The only dances permitted at Court Balls were the gavotte and minuet, and only those who had practised them together beforehand were allowed to take part! I thought it so ridiculous to dance them with a man in a modern German uniform that I gave up doing so. If, instead, they had been dressed in satin coat and breeches or if we had all been in fancy dress, I would have liked it, but otherwise it did not interest me. There was one very well-known, extremely tall, middle-aged man, and all his friends were sorry for him. He held the office of Grand Huntsman and had to stand all the time in front of the Thrones wearing a large white wig with thick white curls and a three-cornered black hat: his suit was of green velvet most beautifully embroidered.

At Court Balls we did not wear the regulation long trains, but ordinary ball dresses; and supper was served early, at 10.30, at small tables. On one occasion I sat between two distinguished old gentlemen, one of whom asked me why we were staying at an hotel instead of in our own big ugly palace in the Wilhelmstrasse. I said because my husband preferred it as in our house there were no bath-rooms. "Mein Gott!" said one of the old gentlemen, "must he absolutely have a bath every day?"

Many people were of course very anxious to become *hoffähig*, that is, eligible to go to Court and as a result to get into Berlin society. I said to my husband years ago: "But, Hans, the time will come when Frau X and Frau Y, and other persons will come to Court—one wants them, the entrance to the Palace is not a holy door." In a few years many of them were made "von" and had lovely dresses at Court. One is a dear Englishwoman called Frau von Weinberg. She has a splendid house near Frankfurt containing many beautiful things. In the old days lots of English and Hungarians used to go there to play polo. Her husband and brother-in-law, who made fortunes in dye-stuffs, had one of the finest racing stables in Germany.

The Emperor, in later years, welcomed the opportunity of meeting prominent business men and even Jews in ordinary society. And why not? In every country in the world they are the people from whom the aristocracy has, and is being recruited. England is the only country I know where a Jew is thought of not primarily as a Jew but as an Englishman: if he is a good citizen his religion is solely his own affair and concerns no one but himself. Even so, in Berlin Jews were not admitted to Court. It is true some were ennobled and granted the coveted prefix "von," but, before this happened, they were required to submit to the indignity of going through some form of baptism in a Christian church!

III

However, the greatest happiness in my married life was derived from our visits to England. These did not take place every year, as my husband had promised before marriage, but they were fairly frequent, and I had really no cause to complain.

We used to hunt in Leicestershire. I had great times there learning to ride, which I had not done thoroughly as a child, never having jumped big fences; I got to love them and timber was what I liked best. Dear Gordon Wood, one of the best riders in Leicestershire, used often to pilot me: I can see it all now. I was once trying a small bay horse and came to a big drop fence. I went hard at it, the horse stopped dead, and I gracefully shot over its head—unhurt. This sounds difficult, but with safety riding skirts it is quite easy and comfortable. One day I was going through a gate in the Pytchley country. I did not then know that many people had the reputation of being very rough going through gates. Consequently lots of riders put red ribbons on their horses' tails whether they kicked or not. I got so tied up once near a man's leg that off came my stirrup. I had to beg someone to find it for me, as without a stirrup it would have been impossible with safety to myself or the horse to clear a big fence.

A favourite horse I had was a chestnut stallion; he never kicked and was a great broad friend. We have many of his descendants in Silesia even now. Another horse I loved was called *Pilewell*. When the time came for me to get on my second horse and we saw the second horseman approaching, *Pilewell* used to turn round his head and calmly bite me gently on my toe. He hated going home. One day we had not had much of a run, so the darling old boy was not tired; when he turned round as usual to kiss my toe in farewell I could not bear to let him go and took him on. As it turned out, the last run of the day was by far the best, and both *Pilewell* and I had a perfect time. I do not go so far as to say that a horse or a dog knows what every one thinks. But, if they are loved by, and in constant touch with their master or mistress, they do know and share any strong feelings such as joy, grief, anger or fear. In fact, their minds are a sounding-board to those whom they really love, and that is why their companionship is often so close and comforting. That also is the fundamental reason why it is quite impossible to become a good horseman if you are afraid of horses. They always know.

From the very first moment I set foot in Germany I determined to do all in my power to foster everything that made for friendship and understanding between the country of my birth and that of my adoption. One obvious way was to keep reminding people of the fact that the Empress Frederick was born a British Princess and that the Emperor was Queen Victoria's eldest grandson.

During the autumn of 1896 and the early part of 1897 I therefore busied myself raising money amongst English women married to Germans for the purpose of making a present to beloved Queen Victoria on the occasion of her Diamond Jubilee. I wrote innumerable personal letters, although the chief secretary at Fürstenstein, Herr Freytag, relieved me of all the more tedious details. The scheme was a great success. The Queen desired the money to be given to a charity, but we rather insisted on a personal gift. Eventually everything was satisfactorily arranged and the Queen agreed to accept a diamond and emerald bracelet and an album containing all the signatures. I have often wondered where the bracelet is now. I hope nice, kind, music-loving Princess Beatrice has it.

In August, 1897, we paid a visit to Ireland and stayed at Vice-Regal Lodge with the dear Cadogans. There was a large party, including Frederick Lord Dufferin, surely one of the most courtly and delightful men who ever lived. I asked him for a copy of his Mother's *Poems and Verses*. He sent it with his own *Letters from High Latitudes*, and the following characteristic letter. The *Poems* are amongst my treasured autographed volumes in my own upstairs sitting-room to this day:

CLANDEBOYE, CO DOWN, *August* 31, 1897.

MY DEAR PRINCESS,—

In accordance with your gracious commands, I send you the two books you are good enough to wish to have.

I was so glad to have found myself next to you at dinner on the last night of our stay at the Vice-Regal Lodge, for there is nothing so agreeable as to terminate a visit under the pleasantest auspices that the situation can provide.

Believe me, yours sincerely, DUFFERIN AND AVA.

No one could pay a compliment or turn a phrase like Lord Dufferin. To the end of his days he enjoyed the society of pretty ladies; I was only one of many young women who would far rather talk to him than to the younger men. Here is another of his letters, written the same year and well worth preserving, because he wrote and spoke with the utmost distinction:

CLANDEBOYE, IRELAND, *December* 12, 1897.

DEAREST PRINCESS,—

I cannot say how pleased I was to get your letter, especially as it heralded the photograph you graciously promised me. The letter I got when I was staying with my daughter Helen[1] at Raith, and yesterday morning, on arriving at Clandeboye, the first thing which greeted me was your lovely face. The portrait is a real work of art, and I intend having it framed for the delight of all who come to this place. I do not think, however, you need fear being ever forgotten by any of your friends, for, apart from your sweet face, which it is a delight to look upon, you are so kind and cheery that the sunshine falls upon any place that you inhabit, and still lingers there after your departure.

And now I obey your request, and send you my wife's and my own photographs.

Besides a nice shooting party at my daughter's, I have been spending a few days with my old friend the Duke of Argyle at Inverary, but to tell the truth I hate leaving home, for being so deaf, I am unfit for Society, though I hope still to enjoy paying you a little *tête-à-tête* visit when you come to London, for when talking alone with anyone I forget my affliction, and hear as well as ever.

And so God bless you, dear Lady; with my respects to your husband,

Yours sincerely, DUFFERIN AND AVA.

I do not think I ever saw the writer of this charming letter again. The South African War came. His good-looking eldest son, Lord Ava, was killed during the siege of Ladysmith, and his second son, Lord Frederick Blackwood, his successor in the Marquisate, severely wounded. Lord Dufferin died in 1902, leaving his name and achievements to history, and a memory which is to this day green and fragrant in the minds of all who knew him.

IV

During the summer and autumn of 1899 we had a very quiet time. We were at Newlands for a bit

[1] Viscountess Novar.

and then again went to Ireland, where we took a house at Bray in lovely County Wicklow. I rather think that we shared it with uncle Pat FitzPatrick. If not, he, at any rate, came and stayed with us. I loved the sea and the scenery of the Wicklow mountains, amongst which we had many interesting excursions. I had written to the Emperor to thank him for some things which he had sent me for a Bazaar and his reply, written in English, will explain why I was "keeping quiet":

KIEL, *June* 2, 1899.

MY DEAR PRINCESS DAISY,—

Best thanks for your very kind letter. I am so glad that the few things I sent you brought you so much money. I am sure the fair Stallholder was however the real attraction. How very glad I am that you are really expecting! May God give you a nice baby. If a boy, may he be like his grandfather, and if a daughter, may she be as like as possible to her beautiful and winning mama. I hope that all will go right and well. I am very sorry to miss Cowes! But my wife's accident prevented it! I won Queen's Cup. Believe me, Ever yours truly,

WILLIAM, I.R.

The Second Boer War and the attitude of the Emperor, Press and public towards it and towards England did not make things too agreeable for an Englishwoman married to a prominent German and living in Germany between 1899 and 1902. The effect of the Emperor's wild and foolish telegram to Kruger at the time of the Jameson Raid in December, 1895, and of all the subsequent vulgar abuse of England in the German Press, had remained, and made things extremely difficult.

I think it must have been about that time that I first became alive to the suspicion and jealousy of England fermenting in official Germany, and the danger of this developing into an active hatred, leading eventually to war. If I was aware of this risk long before others, it is entirely owing to my experiences during the wretched years when all our anxieties were centred in South Africa. I have been blessed (or cursed) with an acute intuition of the thoughts and feelings of others. The fact that a thought, friendly or unfriendly, is carefully concealed, only makes me the more aware of its existence. Throughout my married life in Germany people for politeness or some other reason often tried to deceive me as to their real feelings about England, and never once succeeded. Only too often this reacted on my domestic relations, as indeed it was bound to do, and was the root cause of much that otherwise need not have happened.

The year 1900 was a very full one. My eldest boy, Hans Heinrich XVII, or, as we call him, Hansel, was born at Berlin on February 2nd. The Emperor and King Edward were his sponsors and he therefore bears the additional names of William Albert Edward. His birth after nine years of married life was a source of great happiness to me. A darling little baby girl had been born earlier, but she died.

Naturally the birth of an eldest son and heir overshadowed all else in importance for Hans and myself. I arranged my life so that when at Fürstenstein or Pless I should have at least an hour every evening to spend with my baby, and always insisted on bathing him myself and hearing him say his little prayers when he grew old enough to learn them. This rule I never afterwards broke. My father-in-law was delighted with little Hansel, and not the least part of my delight was watching his.

My brother George, who was in the Scots Guards, had, like every one else, been serving in South Africa. Being invalided home with enteric fever, he travelled on Lady Randolph Churchill's famous Hospital Ship *Maine*, and he and his hostess became engaged. George is exactly the same age as Lady Randolph's eldest son Winston. I always liked Jennie, who was gay, courageous and kind. Her sister, Lady Leslie, is my friend to this day. George and Jennie were married at St. Paul's, Knightsbridge; the reception was at the home of Jennie's other sister, Mrs. Moreton Frewen, in Chesham Place, and the honeymoon was spent at Lord Saye and Sele's wonderful old home, Broughton Castle. It was lent by Lord and Lady Algernon Gordon-Lennox, who were then the tenants. Jennie let it be known that she did not wish to keep her title, and one of the daily papers put it thus:

> The papers give this information,
> At Lady Randolph's own request
> That now her proper designation
> Is Mrs. George Cornwallis-West.

So much has been written about Jennie and she was so well-known that I need say little about her here. In spite of the disparity of their ages we were all pleased with the marriage and hoped it would bring lasting happiness to them both. It made Winston Churchill a connection of ours, a prospect we viewed with somewhat mixed feelings. I cannot honestly say I ever cared for him much, but at any rate, like his friend Lord Birkenhead, he is intensely alive and individual, and in this age of stereotyped personalities that is much. Moreover, he has brains, and a keen sense of personal opportunity, two characteristics that have kept reappearing in the Churchill family since the days when John, the great Duke, bartered his favours to such ladies of the Court as commanded power and influence. The present Duke of Marlborough has inherited the brains, but is entirely without the self-seeking spirit and thick skin, in the absence of which very few can hope to play a successful part in the political turmoil of a modern democracy.

In January, 1901, Queen Victoria died and King Edward succeeded. Of course the Queen's death made a world-wide impression, and threw the German Court into deep mourning. I cannot say it personally affected me greatly, as I saw the august figure only a few times, and my memories of her were shadowy. Moreover, an exciting family event was then engaging all our interest.

In February Shelagh was married to the Duke of Westminster at St. Paul's, Knightsbridge. Owing to the Court mourning, the wedding was as quiet as we could make it. The pages were Guy Wyndham's handsome boy Dick, once a soldier and now a painter of great distinction and originality, and Lord Arthur Grosvenor's small boy Robert. They wore suits copied from the *Blue Boy*, then one of the glories of Grosvenor House and now alas! in America. Bend Or's sister Lettice Grosvenor and Lady Lettice Cholmondeley were the bridesmaids. Dr. Edwards, then Bishop of St. Asaph and now Archbishop of Wales, and Dr. Jayne, the Bishop of Chester, performed the ceremony. I can only remember Mr. Balfour in the church looking far more vague and ethereal than any bishop and, apparently, wondering how on earth he got there; Bend Or's mother, dear Sibell Grosvenor, who had married brilliant and handsome George Wyndham; and Dolly of Teck and his wife Meg,[1] who is Bend Or's aunt, although almost as young as he is! Prince Dolly was, of course, Queen Mary's eldest brother. Sibell and George had the reception in their house in Park Lane and the honeymoon was spent at Eaton. Bend Or gave Shelagh presents not unworthy of an Empress. Here I must say a word about the origin of his nickname, which, by the way, I have often heard used by people who do not even know him by sight! He was born at Eaton in March, 1879, and that year his grandfather, the first Duke, won the Derby with his famous horse *Bend Or*. Personally I nearly always called him Benny, a "little name" used only by the family.

The marriage was no surprise to his family or to ours. He and his sisters, now Constance Shaftesbury and Lettice Beauchamp, used often to come over to Ruthin, which is quite near Eaton, and play with us when we were all children. When I was a lanky, ugly girl of about twelve I one day dressed myself up in the schoolroom tablecloth, arranged the

[1] Afterwards Marquess and Marchioness of Cambridge.

From a picture by Ellis Roberts.

From a miniature.

MY FATHER AND MOTHER, COLONEL AND MRS. CORNWALLIS-WEST.

table as an altar, got a prayer book and solemnly read the marriage service to the very end over Shelagh and Benny, they giving the responses with equal solemnity. His two sisters were bridesmaids dressed in some old finery of my mother's, with feathers in their hair. I found the butler and a stray housemaid in the passage and brought them in as witnesses, and secretly " borrowed " a ring from our governess's room. For years after that they always called each other " my darling wife " and " dearest husband " and tenderly preserved every childish letter they ever wrote to each other. Then came the age of shyness—Shelagh worked in the schoolroom, Benny went to Eton and Oxford. When he was eighteen he came to stay with us and they wanted to be engaged. Of course this was not allowed as both my father and Benny's grandfather thought they were too young, and for two years he was sent abroad to learn French. Suddenly he arrived one day at Fürstenstein with a guide-book and practically no luggage. Of course Shelagh was there. He was supposed to be making a riding tour for a fortnight round the old castles in the North of France. " My man and the horses," he said, " are waiting for me in some village, and when I get this dam guide-book by heart I shall have to go home pretending I have been all the time in France."

After that he went to the War in South Africa, but just as he came of age his grandfather died, and Bend Or came home, again spoke to my father, and the engagement was announced. Of course every one said they were still far too young ; and, if I had been older, I should probably have said the same. As it was I helped them as much as ever I could.

Shelagh was with me in Silesia a great deal before she married, and when she did so I felt absolutely lost without her, and thought what a lucky man my new brother-in-law was.

CHAPTER THREE

1901–1904

THE German Emperor's famous telegram to President Kruger in 1896 at the time of the Jameson Raid had not annoyed me so much as it did most English people. I am very impulsive myself and can therefore understand and sympathize with impulsive acts. The way the incident was regarded in official Germany did, however, open my eyes to the fact that the Emperor had around him few, if any, devoted, wise, tactful and absolutely disinterested advisers. When I really got to know something of Germany I began to feel, and I still feel, that had the Emperor's action not aroused the storm of protest that it did, had it in fact as well as in intention put England out of court, there were those close to the Emperor, notably his Foreign Secretary, Baron Marschall von Bieberstein, who would have been quite ready to claim credit for having inspired its dispatch. It was a failure and *therefore* all the blame was thrown on the Emperor: few realized it at the time (I doubt if even the Emperor himself did), but it was a significant shadow of sinister events to come.

The Baron was never friendly towards England. In May, 1912, he succeeded my old friend Count Wolff-Metternich as German Ambassador to the Court of St. James's, but only occupied the post for a very short time, as he died suddenly a few months later; making way for Prince Lichnowsky, a much more sympathetic figure.

My own small part in the events of the time was to do what I could to make harmony out of discord and to smooth over as far as one individual could the jealousies and suspicions aroused in Germany by the South African War. If the Boers were German-Dutch and their conquerors English, at least they were equal in honour and heroism in their soldier graves.

With some such thoughts as these I proceeded at the beginning of 1901 to organize a Guild of Women to raise funds to mark and care alike for the graves of Boer and Briton in South Africa. The long guerrilla campaign had dragged its weary course without anything being done. I could not bear the thought of the thousands of sorrowing ones in both countries made unhappy by the knowledge of those neglected resting-places; and I also hoped the efforts would not only comfort individuals, but perhaps do something to heal the wounds of war. Nor could I forget that Gordon Wood and many other dear friends who had died gallantly were in lonely graves in that far-off Southern land. I had put on Gordon's grave the words, *Blessed are the Pure in Heart, for they shall see God*, because he was the cleanest-minded man I had ever known.

In July, 1901, we all went to Russia. The Anthony Drexels invited us to join their magnificent steam yacht *Margareta*. First we cruised in Scandinavian and Baltic waters. I love the sea and find no holiday equal to one on a well-appointed yacht or ship surrounded by congenial people. What can be more perfect (if you are a good sailor)! To go ashore, motor to some famous or lovely spot, return on board and find your own food, bed, servants and maid waiting for you. Like the snail, you carry on your back a house designed in every way for your comfort and convenience and—unlike the snail's—it can in turn carry you. In addition to our host and hostess the party included Arthur Crichton (Lord Erne's son), Brinsley FitzGerald, and Reginald Lister, then Secretary of the British Legation at Copenhagen. I do not think the Drexels' beautiful daughter, now Lady Winchilsea, was on board.

I enjoyed St. Petersburg and Moscow; and of course we met a great number of Grand Dukes and Russian Royalties. I visited Tsarskoe Selo, which is the Russian Windsor, and was much interested, as it was then also, as far as I could make out, a sort of Aldershot of the Russian Army. The Grand Duke Vladimir, who was in command, was the brother of Czar Alexander III. and uncle of Nicholas II., and had married a Princess of Mecklenburg. I remember best their three sons, the Grand Duke Kyrill (now rightful Emperor of Russia), the Grand Dukes Boris and André, and their daughter the Grand Duchess Hélène, who afterwards married Prince Nicholas of Greece.

I was fascinated by Russia and like to feel that some of the warm friendships I made there endure to this day.

In August I went to Scotland to stay at Loch More, in Sutherland, with Shelagh and Bend Or, and we were joined there by Patsy and Poppets, while Hans went to Cowes. The holiday was spoiled for me by hearing of the death of the Empress Frederick. It was as if I had lost a second mother, and made me feel very lonely and defenceless in Germany.

Following so closely upon the death of her great mother Queen Victoria, which brought to the British Throne an uncle whom he did not like, this event, to my mind, did much to make it possible for the Emperor William II. to start on the downward slope leading eventually to his downfall. The dismissal of Bismarck and the passing of the Empress opened the way to the path which in the end led to the destruction of the German Empire.

If ever any man in a position of great responsibility needed always close to him advisers who were sagacious, disinterested and courageous, that man was William II. He succeeded twenty years too soon.

Great as was my sense of personal loss, however, the death of the Empress did much to give me, personally, the key to her son's true character. As in duty bound, I wrote to him, using the following words:

May I be permitted to write one little line to Your Majesty to express my deepest sympathy on the occasion of the death of the Empress Frederick. Perhaps, Sire, it is a happy relief, as one hated so to think of her great suffering. She was always so dear and gentle and kind to every one—and her lovely home and rose garden will know her no more . . .

In reply I received the following letter. No fair-minded person can deny its obvious feeling and sincerity. It shows how truly devoted the Emperor was to his mother, and contradicts much that has been foolishly written to the contrary. I know that, like myself, the Empress Frederick was too impulsive in her youth. Recognizing this failing in me, her tender motherly instinct desired to shield me even after she had left this earth: such is the enduring power of unselfish love that it does so even now:

WILHELMSHOHE, *August* 17, 1901.

DEAR PRINCESS DAISY OF PLESS,—

I am very much touched by your kind letter of condolence to me, on the death of my beloved mother. It was an event foreseen since long and yet dreaded when it came! What awful times of suffering and agonies my poor dear mother went through in the last two years no human being can conceive. Words are unable to describe it! It leaves a blank in our home, for she was the spiritual centre for all of us, in her activity and liveliness, in the interest she took in everything. Poor dear Mama! Thank God the last days she was without pain and went to sleep quite quietly and peacefully. One of my last conversations on the 15th of June this year was about you. She had a great liking to you, and when I told her that I know no woman whom I admired and loved more than you, she said I was perfectly right, that she thought you the most sweet, lovely and lovable being she had ever seen; that your arms, neck and hands were perfection and happy the man whom you possessed and who was beloved by you, and that she hoped I would always prove a friend to you and not let you be maliced or anything said against you as long as I could put a stop to it. I thought you would like to know how dear Mama spoke of you, and it is unnecessary for me to say that I fully endorse and approve of *all* that Mama said: What a blessing indeed for a man who is worthy to be possessed and loved by you!

Once more thanking you for your kind sympathy, I remain,
Ever yours most sincerely, WILHELM, I.R.

The Emperor's English is quaint, but his meaning is clear. In the letter he inferentially promised to continue towards me the care and protection his mother had always shown, and to be honest and truthful, I must say that in all the difficult after years he never once failed.

The Emperor's idea of his mother as the spiritual centre of her family and of all its interests is fine and true. He was a young man—we were all then very young—and it must sadly be admitted that as time goes on every one of us loses some of the ardent ideals of youth.

Of course I also wrote at once to King Edward, who replied as follows. His letter also illustrates the great gift the Empress Frederick had of arousing and retaining affection:

NEUES PALAIS, POTSDAM, *August* 10, 1901.

MY DEAR PRINCESS DAISY OF PLESS,—

Your kind letter of sympathy has touched me very much, but I was well aware what a warm heart you had.

The loss of my beloved Sister is an irreparable one to me as not a week elapsed without our writing to one another.[1] I loved her dearly and shall miss her terribly, but she suffered so intensely and for so long a time that one would not have wished her life prolonged. We have just laid her to rest next to her beloved and excellent husband in the lovely mausoleum which she herself built.

To-night I leave for Homburg, having decided to take a three weeks "cure" there.

It is indeed a long time since we last met and so many sad events have occurred since then, but trusting to see you again at no very distant date, Believe me,

Yours very sincerely, EDWARD R.

Early in October we went to Wolfsgarten, near Darmstadt, to stay with the Grand Duke and the

[1] This extremely interesting correspondence, numbering between two and three thousand letters and throwing much first-hand light upon contemporary history, was at his special request handed back to King Edward VII. on the death of his sister.

Grand Duchess of Hesse. She was formerly Princess Victoria Melita of Edinburgh and is the younger sister of Queen Marie of Rumania. The castle, a long, low building built round three sides of a square, is really only a *Jagdschloss* or hunting-box. The party consisted of Lady Georgiana Buchanan, whose husband had just been appointed Secretary of the British Embassy in Berlin; Ruth Mercier, an artist of merit who used to paint in the studio of the Grand Duchess and encourage her hostess in an art she loves, and in which, for an amateur, she is unusually proficient. Prince Nicholas of Greece (whom I had last seen in Russia in July) was also there. One night we played *Consequences*—I think it is called. Some of the questions and answers were quite amusing. The Grand Duchess asked: "Why does virtue take so many different forms?" To which someone replied: "Because, being a woman, she likes to change dresses." Another of our hostess's questions was: "Why should tears prove joy as well as sorrow?" To this there was no satisfactory answer. I asked: "Do you believe in eternal joy after death?" To which Prince Nicholas replied: "I believe that joy is a sensation entirely moral and that, as such, it is inseparable from the soul." I also wanted to know: "Would you rather have a great love that might die, or an everlasting affection?" Prince Nicholas said: "Before having experienced either I am inclined to believe the second preferable; but usually a man's egotism is more flattered by the passion he inspires, however brief, than by winning a sincere and lasting affection." I then asked: "What is the greatest help to us in life?" and Prince Nicholas wrote: "The belief that we might be worse." I hope this thought has been found a real consolation to him in the difficult years through which he and his family have passed since the War. Fortunately he is very happily married and one may dare to guess that in his home he has found both the great love and the everlasting affection perfectly combined.

The Grand Duchess inquired: "Why does one so

often hurt the person one loves best?" the Prince thought it was "because we know them best and, being their friends, we have the courage to tell them the truth; truth being the most painful thing we can tell."

That same year the Grand Duchess divorced her husband and, five years later, married the Grand Duke Kyrill. They now reside at Coburg, or in their delightful little villa at St. Briac which, it is hardly an exaggeration to say, the Grand Duchess made with her own hands.

Exactly a year later (August, 1902) Prince Nicholas returned to Russia and married at Tsarskoe Selo the handsome and delightful Grand Duchess Hélène or, as she signed it in my book, "Ellen"; they have now three charming daughters and reside a great deal at Cannes, where I have the pleasure of seeing them frequently. Their eldest girl, Princess Olga, recently married Prince Paul of Serbia and has a small boy called Alexander; Princess Elizabeth and Princess Marianne are not yet married.

From Wolfsgarten we went to Eaton for the Chester Races, and the end of the month found us at Keele Hall with the Grand Duke Michael Michaelovitch and Sophy Torby. The Prince of Lynar was there and a large party, and I particularly remember that visit because I went down a coal-mine. Rosamund de Ramsey, born a Churchill, was also there and her girl Alexandra Fellowes. Little did we then foresee the drama of August, 1914.

Our next port of call was Newlands, where we found Patsy, Poppets, George, Shelagh and Bend Or, and Count Jare Moltke, a Danish diplomat who was also to come dramatically into my life in 1914. From there we went to lovely Rufford to Lord Savile. There was a large and amusing house-party, including Mar and Kellie and Violet, Juliet Lowther, Jack Brinton who afterwards married Mrs. Willie James, the late Lord Lansdowne's second son Lord Charles Fitzmaurice,[1]

[1] Major Lord Charles Fitzmaurice (afterwards Mercer Nairne), 1st Dragoons, Equerry to the King, killed in action in the early autumn of 1914.

Pat de Bathe, Muriel Wilson, Lord Scarbrough and Cecilia, and Terence Clandeboye (afterwards Lord Dufferin). Haddon Chambers was there and was uncommonly good company, and Nellie Melba not only sang for us, but was most amusing and wrote in my album *l'art est un ami qui ne trompe jamais*, which is not only terse but true. We rushed home to Fürstenstein to a small party we had for Prince Albert of Schleswig-Holstein, Princess Christian's only surviving son and brother of Princess Helena Victoria and Princess Marie Louise.

In December we had a party at Pless. The Emperor was the chief guest and was extremely pleased because he shot two wild aurochs, one with a single bullet. These huge fierce animals, a species of buffalo resembling those which used to roam the western prairies of America, are very rare in Eastern Germany. Ours were, I think, the first, having been imported from the Caucasus by my father-in-law when he was a young man. The Emperor had his stuffed and personally placed one in the hall of the beautiful Royal Castle which he built in Posen to please the Poles. The only other thing I remember about that particular party is that the Emperor proved himself an adept at the then fashionable game of ping-pong, revived in these days under the grand name of table tennis.

The middle of December found us at Trachenberg, in Silesia, with Prince and Princess Hatzfeldt (Hermann and Natalie). They were both delightful and Natalie was very like her brother Count Benckendorff, who was Russian Ambassador in England when war broke out. Poor man, he died in London in 1917 and, as his body could not be taken home, he remains unburied to this day beneath the altar of Westminster Cathedral.

II

In January, 1902, I was at Chatsworth, and it was perhaps the one visit to that hospitable and kindly home I did not thoroughly enjoy. I was worried and unhappy about politics. Lord Rosebery, whom I have always greatly admired, was there. I wanted to talk over various things with him, but found no suitable opportunity. He had not, I think, approved of the South African War, and was commonly supposed to be in favour of a sympathetic understanding with Germany. At any rate, I knew that during his Foreign Secretaryship and Premiership relations between Germany and England had seemed to improve. When the Chatsworth visit was over I wrote to him and received the following letter. I should say that I had covered my approach by a request for his autograph. His political reference is to the large Conservative majority which, during the South African War,[1] had brought Lord Salisbury in as Prime Minister with Mr. Chamberlain as his Colonial Secretary. I think that I had besought Lord Rosebery (as many others have done) to take a more active part in political life :

38 BERKELEY SQUARE, W., *January* 21, 1902.

DEAR PRINCESS HENRY OF PLESS,—

I send my signature for your album at the end of this note. I am grateful for your kind and interesting letter, though I do not quite understand it, for some of the phrases require development to a person who does not see much good to be done in the present state of Parliament. But you do me great injustice in saying that I should not have enjoyed a talk at Chatsworth. Unfortunately in a great Vanity Fair of that kind one only sees those or converses with those whom one shoots with or golfs with or Bridges with or sits next at dinner !

Yours sincerely, ROSEBERY.

That I was not preoccupied with politics all the time I was at Chatsworth is clear, because we acted *A New Year's Dream*, specially composed for the occasion by Leo Trevor ; and the present Lord Clarendon, then Lord Hyde, and I sang the duet from *Samson and Delilah.*

[1] On September 18, 1900, the London *Gazette* contained the formal announcement of the Dissolution.

In February we were at Warter Priory. Charlie and Lady Marjorie Wilson were there; also Patsy, who was, as usual, the life and soul of the party. There were, of course, theatricals, and I remember Gwendoline Maitland,[1] Lord Ingestre,[2] Lord Hyde and Reggie Fellowes taking part. The three daughters of the house, Millie Hartopp, Enid Chesterfield and Gwladys Wilson (now Viscountess Chaplin), helped nobly to keep up the fun: I was always very fond of Millie. Soon after she and Charlie Hartopp were divorced and she married the late Lord Cowley.

After a few days in London we went to Blenheim to enchanting Consuelo Marlborough and the Duke. Albert Mensdorff was there, as were Arthur Stanley and John Spencer Churchill. Mensdorff-Pouilly, whom I liked very much, was Austrian Ambassador in England for many years and was *persona grata* everywhere. He made no secret of the fact that he was connected with the British Royal Family, a connection of which he was naturally very proud.

From Blenheim we went to Eaton, where we found Granny Olivia, Poppets, Helen and Lettice Grosvenor, and our old friend Lord Kenyon. It was during that stay that Shelagh quoted in my visiting book, "A woman is more often influenced by what she desires than by what she feels." It is too true; and the pity of it is that she is not really infallible and sometimes desires unwisely.

In May we were to have been in London for King Edward's Coronation. As every one knows he had a terrifying illness and the ceremony was postponed. We therefore went home and had a quiet time at Fürstenstein with only cousin Charlotte Reuss, Jare Moltke and Gottfried Hohenlohe in the house. Hansel was just two years old and was a perfect darling, and

[1] Now Countess of Lauderdale.

[2] Died (or killed) January 8, 1915; his son, born December 1, 1914, is now the 21st Earl of Shrewsbury.

he and I and his nurse used to spend hours together in the woods.

I would never spoil my children as some of my German friends spoilt theirs. From the moment they were born I made up my mind that they must be brought up to do what they were told *at once*. Of course I hated it when it came to the point, but I stuck to my resolution, and Smith, the English nurse, who was with us for many years, helped me enormously. I was much criticized for this, one lady going so far as to hint to a common friend that I did not care for my children, as they were kept so much in the background. I could have killed her. This, if you please, was because the children did not appear at one of my dinner-parties at which she was present!

Even when Hansel was very small Hans and I liked to have him with us as much as possible—he would walk or ride beside us, asking questions all the way and wrinkling his little forehead and opening his eyes wide to make me understand and realize every word he said:

"Mummie, what makes the daisies grow?"

"They come up wild with the grass, darling."

"But who planted them there?"

"No one: they have always been there, when Daddy was a little boy, and even when his father and his father's father were little boys."

"Are they seeds, Mummie?"

"Yes, darling."

"Who put the seeds in the ground in the beginning?"

"The birds dropped them in pecking about."

"But where did the birds find the seeds, Mummie?"

So at last I laid the whole thing on the shoulders of God. This silenced his little questioning spirit as it has silenced many a grown-up person. Often I think children put into words the very questions that must always remain unanswered, no matter how much knowledge and experience we succeed in acquiring.

As soon as King Edward began to recover, we were told that the Coronation would take place in August, and Hans and I arrived in London in July in time to be present at Shelagh's first big ball at Grosvenor House. Every one was there, but Queen Marie of Rumania (then Crown Princess) eclipsed them all in beauty and fascination. Astride a wild horse at Fürstenstein in Rumanian costume, or on a public occasion wearing a crown and all her Orders, she is equally a Queen. I have heard her accused of being theatrical; but she accurately gauged the somewhat primitive taste and ideals of the Rumanian people and has given them exactly the sort of Queen they wanted and could understand.

I remember a delightful party at Lady (Arthur) Paget's at which Mary Garden sang and Jeanne Granier recited. It was given in honour of the Crown Prince and Crown Princess of Rumania, and included Prince Frankie of Teck,[1] Lord and Lady Warwick, Mrs. George Keppel, and Shelagh and Bend Or. It was a terribly full season. I escaped to Keele Hall for a breath of air and found the Hope Veres and Maurice de Rothschild with the Grand Duke Michael and Sophy. The Grand Duke wrote in my visiting-book: "If I am fated to be unhappy, I will labour to hide my sorrows in my own bosom and you shall always find me a faithful and affectionate friend." That is an implied promise which the Grand Duke has always kept.

That season I heard the first performance of Massenet's *Manon* at Covent Garden; Mary Garden sang and looked the heroine to perfection. In July I first met the young Duke Adolphus Frederick of Mecklenburg-Strelitz at a dinner Shelagh and Bend Or gave for the Duke and Duchess of Connaught, their daughter Princess Margaret, the Crown Princess of Rumania and the Tecks. I do not think the Strelitz boy was staying at Grosvenor House, though in August

[1] Died October, 1910.

he spent Cowes Week with Shelagh and Bend Or aboard their yacht.

I sang at a great many Charity concerts and in the middle of July presided over the German stall at an enormous Coronation Bazaar in Regent's Park in aid of the Great Ormond Street Hospital for Sick Children, of which my distinguished publisher, Sir John Murray, is one of the two Vice-Chairmen, Lord Warrington of Clyffe being the other. Queen Alexandra, who was our Patron, and a crowd of Royalties came. My stall, which was decorated with daisies, was a most attractive one. The Emperor sent me three hundred pounds' worth of Dresden china. The first day I was mobbed and it took me over an hour to get from the Park gates to my stall. I have always had in England what is, I believe, known as a "good Press." Indeed at all times English newspapers and journalists have been chivalrous and helpful. They have been curious, but never impertinently so, nor have they ever indulged in the annoying half-truths for which a certain type of American journalist is well known and disliked. To advertise the Bazaar, I suppose, my name had been much in the papers; public curiosity was aroused, and the consequence was a reception that was both embarrassing and flattering in its English warmth and spontaneity.

On the 21st Ursula, Shelagh's first child, was born; naturally she and Bend Or would have preferred a boy, but the dear baby was so sweet and lovely that they speedily forgot they had wanted an heir.

We went to Newlands for Cowes. There was a large party: the Crown Prince and Crown Princess of Rumania, Ellen Kilmorey, Prince Frankie of Teck, and General Sir Arthur Paget. We went for several cruises in the Emperor's new yacht *Meteor*. She proved very disappointing.

On August the 9th we attended King Edward's Coronation in Westminster Abbey. We sat in the King's private box, which was quite full, but I can remember only Sophy Torby. For this historic ceremony I wore my favourite blue, with a cloth-of-gold train, my diamond and turquoise crown and of course all my Orders. Patsy wore white with a high diamond and pearl tiara.

III

In the autumn we had a series of parties at both Fürstenstein and Pless. One, quite an amusing family one at Pless in October, was for the young Crown Prince William of Prussia, who, when leaving, broke into doggerel and wrote in the Visitors' Book:

> Always happy, no distress,
> When I visit Daisy Pless.

This was more polite than poetic, and as the sequel will show, it was not even very truthful.

I had often seen the Crown Prince in Berlin, but really knew nothing about him, as this was his first visit to us. He was only twenty at the time. In view of what has happened since I think it is worth while recounting most of what took place during this visit. It gives the key to the Crown Prince's character and has a bearing on after events that had their share in making history. I wrote in my diary:

October 18, 1902. Pless.

The Crown Prince arrived at half-past one. A tall, fair boy, clever eyes and forehead, a rather receding chin, mouth of little character (at present), long nose; very nice, with a quiet dignity. Takes a great interest in life; at present the active side of it, and his youth and spirit rebel at the restraint put upon every little action. I laughed at luncheon when he said, "I do love England and am furious at not being allowed to go there now with my father, and at not going to the Coronation; but papa would not let me go again [1] because he says I flirted too much. And mama was furious when I showed her a tie and waistcoat some English ladies had knitted for me."

---

[1] The Crown Prince visited England in January, 1901, and, with his father, was present at Queen Victoria's funeral. On that occasion he was made a Knight of the Garter.

I sympathized very much with the poor Crown Prince. Had I not myself often felt like a neatly tied-up parcel that was bursting within! I think he instinctively understood this, because he confided in me a great deal. At that stage of his career he just wanted some understanding person to play with; he was bubbling over with youth and high spirits; we therefore avoided a formal party and had only a few of his young personal friends from Bonn, where he was then at the University. I sang; we danced; played games and behaved like the children that most of us really were. The Crown Prince told me one day that his aide-de-camp had said he should not dance so much with me. With whom was he to dance? The other boys! I was very angry and told the poor lad he ought not to allow his aide-de-camp to say such a thing. A remark of this nature might be necessary concerning a "lady" in the Wintergarten,[1] but was insolent when made concerning myself. A real fire came into the little Prince's eyes, making him look for the moment as if he squinted, when he said, "I know." I determined that this third-class Court official should be made to realize he was dealing not only with a German Princess, but with an English gentlewoman and must recognize his proper place and keep it.

When the Crown Prince left we travelled from Pless as far as Breslau with him in our own private train and dined on board the train. I had a terrible headache and lay down in the aide-de-camp's compartment, not caring to do so in my own, which had been placed at the disposal of the Crown Prince. During dinner we had a good talk and I found the Prince really clever and broad-minded. I quote from my diary:

He thinks for himself about every subject and will puzzle things out. He does not accept word for word everything he

[1] Perhaps the best-known music hall in Berlin, where the "ladies" are not always ladies.

MY GRANDMOTHER, LADY OLIVIA FITZPATRICK.

may be told. He is broad-minded even on religion, which surprises me, as the Empress is a strict Lutheran and the Emperor even believes in *eternal* damnation! I got a letter from him this morning; it is so nice and youthful I must copy it here. It has a large daisy painted by himself on the top of the note-paper.

His English in those days was really very bad:

DEAR PRINCESS DAISY,—

After our nice drive in the train last night I have a feeling that I must write to you. I can't tell you how much I enjoyed our talk and it was so kind of you to listen to all the bosh I was talking. I only hope you weren't too much bored by it. You left your Taschentuch (I can't spell the word) in the compartment so, following the example of my brother,[1] I pocketed it and your comal (is this right?) too. Your anticamnia I will send you. Please *do* send me the name of your scent. I like it so much and the Taschentuch won't last longer than a fortnight. Don't forget the photo.

Yours for ever, W.

This was followed by a post-card also signed "Yours for ever."

On receiving these I determined to wait for some days and later write him a nice, quite sensible letter telling him not to do such things. Here it is:

DEAR SIR,—

I must ask Your Imperial Highness to forgive me for not answering your very nice and kind letter before, but I have thought over the reply for some days, and long to write just what I think. Do not be cross, Sir, but you are so full of understanding that I think you will forgive me and perhaps appreciate my courage. I will not give you the name of my scent for by now I am sure you have already got the name of someone else's, and my handkerchief is in a drawer mixed up with so many others that Your Imperial Highness does not know one from the other! It is not a sin on your part, it is not even flirting, Sir (you said you could not go to England because you were supposed to flirt). It is not really true. You are only young, Sir, and that is not a fault; it is a charm

[1] One of his brothers when staying with us a little time before had appropriated one of my handkerchiefs.—D. OF P.

envied by all and I hope you will keep it for many, many years —the charm of youth. And also some illusions, for, when they are all gone, the earth seems very bare and cold indeed.

But this, Sir, is what I pray you to do. Keep your thoughts and little stories in your own mind and heart. Tell no one. This is a hard truth, Sir—but some people to whom you might write about scent and pocket-handkerchiefs would show your letter and talk about you just because you are the first Royal Prince in Prussia. In England I know you wrote and sent post-cards (too many) and the recipients did not feel it such an honour! Some only smiled and, although they did not really know you, I was sorry, and cross as well, to hear them speak about it. But, Sir, in spite of this, many smiled with pleasure to see you and spoke so well of you and of your shooting and Your Imperial Highness was most popular everywhere. Sir, will you ever forgive me for writing like this! It is only because I see in you that you are, and will be, worthy of your noble parents. If I thought you otherwise I should not take the trouble to tell you the truth; but you are sharp and clever and see things as they are and you are anxious to know the world. Sometimes this knowledge brings pain and disappointment; but everything has got to be faced, carried through well and with a brave heart and hand unto the end.

You have a good brain and enjoy thinking; then think kindly and not crossly, Sir, of me and understand that I write this letter only to tell you of little things which I know to be true, just because I feel that I am a faithful subject of their Majesties, and therefore truly desire to hear the name of the Crown Prince used only with respect; or, if anyone smiles, it will only be in appreciation of his actions and words.

Tell your Aide-de-camp that he need not be horrified if he happens to catch sight of this English letter; it is all right —there is nothing nice in it, I am afraid.

God bless you, Sir, and keep you safe and well always. I send you my photograph to plead for me. Your Imperial Highness's obedient servant,

DAISY OF PLESS.

IV

In November Hans went to America as the special representative of the Emperor to some celebration organized by the New York Chamber of Commerce. One would have thought that the German Ambassador to the United States would have done just as well, seeing that the British Ambassador, the late Sir Michael Herbert, represented King Edward. However, just then the Emperor was making a great fuss of the Americans and had a short time before sent over his brother Prince Henry of Prussia on a special mission to popularize Germany and German products in the United States.

I wanted very much to go with Hans, but it could not be arranged and I was greatly disappointed as it would have been such a splendid chance of seeing the United States, a thing I have always longed to do. Also I would have seen everything under the best possible auspices. I had never given up the idea that Hans should return to diplomacy, and had got Prince von Bülow to promise to give him the Vienna Embassy. This Hans would have liked, and the Austrians, who are charming, would, I know, have welcomed us. However, the appointment was never made—I do not remember why—but I find quoted in my diary at this time the injunction, " Put not your trust in Princes."

In America Hans was a great success. President Roosevelt received him specially at the White House and went out of his way to express admiration for the Emperor—whether sincerely or not Hans could not say. In public Hans made it his special business to refer pointedly to Prince Henry's recent visit and the Emperor's cordial feelings towards Americans, which indeed were quite genuine. And how we all laughed at home when I received an American newspaper which announced at the top of its voice that Hans desired to succeed Dr. von Holleben as Germany's Ambassador in Washington " because his English wife, who was the most beautiful Royalty [*sic*] in Europe, valued Americans." It went on to describe poor Hans in language so personal as to be intolerable, patronizingly ending by saying he was " a splendidly built man, over six foot high, and quite handsome." Then, at a guess, added, "he bears himself like a seasoned veteran" (Hans had been quite ten minutes in the Army). Best of all was the ending which declared, "there is grace, ease and gentle breeding in his every movement." I would have loved to cut this out and send it to the Emperor, but my husband's sense of humour was not quite equal to allowing me to do so!

When Hans came back we went as usual to Chatsworth for Christmas and the New Year and the huge, comfortable house was nearly full. There were Princess Margaret and Princess Patricia of Connaught; of course dear Louise Devonshire and the Duke, Dolly of Teck and Meg, Violet Mar and Kellie, de Soveral, Theo Acheson, Juliet Lowther, Mr. Balfour, Lord de Grey and Gladys, Evelyn Cavendish,[1] Molly Sneyd, Sir Douglas Dawson, Harry Stonor, Evelyn Fitzgerald, Cyril Foley, Hedworth Lambton, Ettie Grenfell,[2] Francis Mildmay and Maudie Warrender. Needless to say there were theatricals. I did a musical monologue by Liza Lehmann called *The Eternal Feminine*, and also appeared with Muriel Wilson, Frank Mildmay and Leo Trevor in a one-act play of Robert Marshall's entitled *Shades of Night*.

V

In March, 1903, I went to Newlands, and remember it so well because Poppets had just got his first motor-car! What excitements we had and into what danger we ran quite unknowingly as we tried it! From Newlands we all went to Ruthin. It was mostly a family party, including Granny Olivia, Gladys Deacon, afterwards Duchess of Marlborough, Charlie Wood and Gerald Cadogan. We went from there to Eaton to

[1] The late Lord Lansdowne's daughter, now Duchess of Devonshire.

[2] Now The Lady Desborough.

meet the Prince and Princess of Wales (King George V. and Queen Mary).

A most amusing event was the great fancy-dress ball which Mrs. Adair gave in London in May. The hostess was magnificent in her Delhi Durbar dress; Frances Warwick was a lovely and imposing Semiramis, Princess Hatzfeld was Queen Esther, the present Lady Londonderry a picturesque peasant, and I went in a very striking and effective dress but not very comfortable for dancing in.

In my recollection the outstanding event of the season was a small ball at Buckingham Palace when King Edward and Queen Alexandra were perfectly delightful; the flowers were simply gorgeous; Queen Alexandra was radiantly lovely, and the King looked both handsome and imposing in knee-breeches with the Garter. If, as a Ruler, the King arrived late on the European stage, at least he arrived with great distinction. The reality behind the appearance was to make itself felt later.

From June 24 to 29 we were at Kiel. For some reason or another the Emperor did not arrive at the beginning, which was awkward, as there was a visit from a United States Naval Squadron. On the 24th there was a ceremony at which Hans and I represented the Emperor and Empress. Ten thousand people visited the United States flagship *Kearsarge* with Admiral Cotton commanding the Squadron, and the United States Ambassador in Berlin, Mr. Tower, on board. I remember a dance a day or two later on the flagship in honour of the Emperor at which I danced with Captain Charles Hussey, then United States Naval Attaché in Berlin and who, after the War, became Naval Attaché in London.

The Emperor was very anxious to advertise Kiel, and once asked us to come there and make it like Cowes—as if that could be done in a week! He said I should have a lovely cabin on the *Hohenzollern* and that everything would be done exactly as in England. My husband and I arrived and found the most awful little cabin and nothing for my maid, but we got this put right afterwards. Having in mind the delightful social activities of the Royal Yacht Squadron at Cowes, I asked the Emperor if he would come and have tea with me one day at the Imperial Yacht Club and I would arrange a party of German, English, American and other nationalities from the yachts. He said: " But nonsense, how can I do that sort of thing; I and Bülow came here for serious work and not for drinking tea." As the Emperor had asked me to make the effort, I was naturally annoyed and answered, " Your Majesty has plenty of time to drink *beer*." This was a fact, for during the whole of Kiel week one could never get a man, married or single, to join us for dinner or to come out in a boat, or, in fact, do anything that was sociable—they all had to go to what were called Beer Evenings at the Kiel Yacht Club. Princess Henry of Prussia, a charming woman and a sister of the Czarina, once gave a party (for the women whose husbands were so employed) at which we played Up Jenkins and other childish and unamusing games—because there was nothing better to do!

I thought when I left, that one might just as well try to make a cow into a donkey, and then try and make the donkey bray, as to try and make Kiel into a second Cowes. The unique prestige and social charm of Cowes is not something you can buy at a Woolworth Store.

Speaking of Kiel reminds me that it was there I discovered the one occasion on which women are of any public importance in Germany. During the yacht races there they counted as " hands," which is not the rule in England or America; of course, only a certain number of " hands " are allowed on a boat while she is racing. So at Kiel we hardly ever even got a sail.

I enjoyed Kiel considerably more when King Edward and the Emperor were there together. The King was so different in those surroundings that I wanted to laugh. The Emperor tried to make himself as agreeable as possible in a loud voice; and the Empress with her hands crossed on her tummy smiled kindly backwards and forwards like an india-rubber doll. But the whole thing was middle-class and terribly boring; the men no doubt enjoyed the sailing and inevitable beer-drinking, but the women had an odious time.

VI

For a long time I had been terribly troubled and upset by the insanitary state of many of the towns and villages in Silesia and felt that I could bear it no longer. They were intolerably bad. People lived in hovels with no "conveniences" of any kind. There was a horrid custom of placing such "cabinets"—mere shelters—as existed, upon the banks of streams and rivers, thus polluting the washing and even the drinking water. I had a famous bacteriologist down from Berlin and engineers from England, and did all I could to make myself disagreeable to the local authorities. At Kiel I took the opportunity of discussing it with the Imperial Chancellor, Prince von Bülow. He asked me for details; these I sent, receiving from him the following reply dated from Norderney, the Prince's summer residence on the North Sea:

NORDERNEY, 9 *August*, 1903.

DEAR PRINCESS,—

I have read with great interest your detailed letter, so *charming* in spite of its sad contents, which forms a valuable completion of the intelligence received from you at Kiel, and dealing with the horrid state of affairs in the towns situated near Fürstenstein.

Your suggestion that part of the sum granted for the flooded territory of the Province of Silesia should be utilized to effect changes in the bad conditions which you rightly expose, can unfortunately not be carried out, because this money is intended to benefit only those who have suffered by the flood.

But I will gladly see to it that an official inspection is made locally and I hope that we shall succeed in doing justice to your meritorious suggestions, which are proof of your humane sentiments. My wife thanks you very much for the very kind greetings and returns hers to you.

I am, Your sincerely devoted, BÜLOW.

In the autumn we were at Gopsall with the Howes, where we had some quite harmless Charades. A stupid American newspaper correspondent got hold of a garbled account of these from, one supposes, a drunken servant or some such source. No sober person could have supplied material for the vulgar head-lines and extracts which appeared in a New York newspaper. "Princess Henry of Pless a Romeo," "Lady Sarah Wilson in Kilts," "Marlborough's Aunts in Armour and Kilts"! As an example of American journalism of that time part of the account itself is, perhaps, also worth reprinting:

Lady Howe was dressed as a Knight Templar, with a long black cloak, with a white cross, a two-handed sword, bright steel armour and helmet. Her sister, Lady Sarah Wilson, more daring, appeared as Prince Charlie in kilts, and made a very attractive, well-shaped young man. Princess Henry of Pless made an extremely graceful though over-tall Romeo. It was generally voted that she would make the fame of any chorus, her nether extremities are so "divinely" shaped. But historically the success of the evening was Mrs. George Cornwallis-West, formerly Lady Randolph Churchill, who came as a roistering Spanish cavalier. She wore black silk tights, doublet and hose, a dark crimson velvet cloak trimmed with gold; had a sword, a great diamond blazing in her black sombrero, with its drooping feathers; diamond buckles on her pretty shoes, and a black moustache, waxed and ferociously curled like the Kaiser's. The ladies were at first rather shy about entering the room in their unaccustomed but most becoming costumes, and shrinkingly tried to hide their legs behind the skirts of their lady companions. But this feeling soon wore off and everything went as gaily as possible. It was odd to see what appeared to be men dancing with men partners. The affair was not to be talked about, it was understood, but it has come out nevertheless, and excites the greatest interest.

This, and much else far more lurid, was cabled to New York and, if you please, copyrighted throughout the world. The only amusing notion in the whole effusion was the idea of Sarah Wilson in "kilts." Why anyone should be supposed to wear several at a time only writers in newspaper know.

Other American papers devoted front pages to even more ridiculous accounts of an affair that never happened, illustrating their nonsense with portraits of Lady Sarah Wilson, Jennie and myself.

A true and much more amusing incident had, however, happened at Alloa House in October while we were staying with Violet Mar and Kellie and her husband. We produced *A Pantomime Rehearsal.* In the cast were Mr. Trevor, Charlie Wood, Lord Shaftesbury, Lord Frederick Hamilton, Muriel Wilson, Lady Feo Sturt, Miss Gerard, Mrs. Arkwright and myself; we had great fun and none of us quarrelled. But something too dreadful happened to me. Just as I was going on to the stage I half tripped over what I thought was some of the cord of the electric lights. I did not take any notice. But when I came off again, Muriel Wilson, who had been just behind me, said, with a sympathetic face, "My dear, *how awful* for you," and gave me a little bundle of silk and lace. It was not my petticoat! She had seen something hanging down, and as it was too late to stop me going on the stage, she gave it a little tug and down "they" came. How on earth I could have stepped out of them without knowing is not really a puzzle, because, when acting, I always forget all about myself.

All my life I have been the victim of the over-enterprising and uniquely inexact descriptions of the American "society" journalist. In May, 1903, he surpassed himself (if he was not a she) in silliness by putting into circulation a ridiculous and annoying story which has followed me ever since. As I had it for the hundredth time in a Press cutting of a few months ago I will here take the trouble deliberately to contradict it, as it may possibly have caused annoyance elsewhere. After paying me some fulsome compliments and describing a visit I had just paid to Paris, the article said :

> It is bewailed on all sides that the Princess dyes her hair. Originally it was coal black and then she was the Irish type, with deep blue eyes and raven hair. But she succumbed to the fad of "copper coloured" hair.
>
> Princess Henry is a sister-in-law of Mrs. Cornwallis-West, formerly Lady Randolph Churchill, and she and her American sister-in-law get on famously. The Princess vows she adores Americans, and most of the New York hostesses have had the satisfaction of entertaining her. Every one knows, however, that her social position will be delicate, when the present Prince of Wales is King. The lovely Princess Henry is the only woman of whom the Princess of Wales was ever jealous, and the hostility of the future Queen to the other woman is well known. When Princess Henry, formerly Daisy West, went to London eight years ago, she was "monarch of all she surveyed." Victoria's grandson, although married, was in her train of admirers, and, flattered by the royal attention, Miss West did not discourage the Prince. However, the snubs from his royal relatives brought her to her senses. She sent the Prince about his business and was married to Henry of Pless, an aristocrat without a great fortune. The Princess of Wales has never forgiven the beauty the sleepless nights during her husband's devotion to Miss West.

The blatant inaccuracies in this effusion are almost too absurd to contradict. I had ceased to be Miss West not eight, but twelve years before it was written. During my brief social life in London as a girl King George was in the Navy. I never once even saw, much less spoke to him! And to crown all, His Majesty was not married until nearly two years after I was! When I was supposed to be doing all this I was living quietly in Germany, completely absorbed in my new life. The description of Hans, heir to one of the richest men in Europe, as "without a great fortune" was just absurd. These things might not matter if, once in print, they were not again and again served up as something new and startling.

I dare say this or similar rubbish is in my dossier in a score of newspaper offices and, in spite of this contradiction, will only make a final appearance after I am dead.

In the early part of September we went to Klitschdorff to my sister-in-law Lulu and her husband, the Prince of Solms-Baruth. There was a large family party, including my father-in-law and his second wife Mathilde (the Dowager Duchess and Princess of Pless). The occasion was the marriage of Lulu's eldest girl to Prince Othon of Salm-Horstmar.

I was extremely lucky in all my "in-laws." No one ever had a better, truer, or more faithful and loyal friend than I had in my sister-in-law, Lulu Solms, and I am happy to say still have. She has a noble character and her friendship is a perfect thing. I shall have more to say about it later.

VII

In January, 1904, we were again at Chatsworth. There was a very large and typical party. As it was the first one at which King Edward and Queen Alexandra were present after their succession, I will describe it. I went there regularly every year, each visit being practically a repetition of the one before. Princess Victoria, with a fascinating Scotch terrier called *Mac*, accompanied their Majesties. Then there was Mr. Balfour, Sidney Greville, the Gosfords, Mary Elcho, Charlotte Knollys, John Ward, Lord Howe, Mensdorff and several others. Of course we acted a play; it was *Cinderella* by Harry Trevor, and Mrs. Willie James, Muriel Wilson, Hedworth Williamson and myself were in the cast. Muriel and I were a huge success as the Ugly Sisters, parts in which we each caricatured ourselves.

When staying at Windsor, Sandringham, or in a country house with the British Sovereigns, there was very little etiquette. At Buckingham Palace, where I once stayed, there was inevitably a little more, but at Chatsworth the Sovereigns were simplicity itself. One curtsied when saying good morning and good night, but on no other occasion. For the performance of the play there was just a little ceremony. The King entered first with the Duchess of Devonshire and the Queen with the Duke and took their places on armchairs in the centre of the first row. The house-party entered in a procession, more or less according to precedence, and seated themselves as they pleased: similar procedure followed the performance. Queen Alexandra always enjoyed Chatsworth enormously, and I have visions of her stealing into a back seat to watch the rehearsals, pretending she was not there and we humouring her by pretending we did not see her.

In the spring I went to Paris and spent some weeks —all the time I could spare—studying singing under Jean de Reszke. What a wonderful teacher and attractive man he was! Mixed up with my recollections of this period and of him are visions of Paris in all the glory of May; nor must I forget the amusement we derived from the racing at Longchamp—and, of course, clothes.

In the summer Hans and I went to Ireland for the wedding of Madge Brooke, Auntie Minnie's girl by her first husband, to Major John Sharman Fowler. We stayed with Lord Dudley and beautiful Rachel at Vice-Regal Lodge. I was always devoted to Rachel, one special bond between us being that we were married the same year. There was naturally a great gathering of the clans. Granny Olivia was, by general consent, the belle of the party. Then there was poor Adèle Essex, John and Evelyn Ward, the Lurgans, Murrough O'Brien and Victor Corkran. Sibell Grosvenor and George Wyndham lent Minnie the Chief Secretary's Lodge in Phœnix Park for the reception; the honeymoon was spent at Holly Mount, Pat FitzPatrick's delightful place in County Mayo. I think it was then that my brother-in-law Fritz became engaged to Nancy Roche, Lord Fermoy's very good-looking daughter. I stayed in Ireland for a little with Patsy and Poppets while Hans went to Lowther to the Lonsdales for the Twelfth.

Later we all met at Loch More; Shelagh, Bend Or, brother George, and Charlie and Lily Coventry. From Loch More we went to Dunrobin, where lovely Millie Sutherland was a perfect hostess. Of the party there all have escaped my memory except Edie Castlereagh (now Lady Londonderry), Constance Stewart-Richardson, and Sir Alfred Fripp—now king of the Froth Blowers.

In September we had a shooting party at Fürstenstein, which included Count Sternberg and his wife Fanny; she is a daughter of Heine Larisch, who used to hunt in Leicestershire in the old days, and she and I were, and are, close and warm friends: Lord Edward Gleichen, Neil Menzies, Mar and Kellie and Violet, Lord Lonsdale, Cecil Banbury and Oscar Herren were also there.

In November Shelagh's second child and only son was born at Grosvenor House. Every one was delighted, and no one more than I, because having a boy each seemed to draw us closer together. I could not be in London for the event because we had a huge shooting party for the Archduke Franz Ferdinand and his wife the Duchess of Hohenberg. I liked her very much indeed. She was born a Chotek, filled a very difficult position with conspicuous success, and was heart and soul devoted to her husband and her young family. The party included Prince Miguel of Braganza, the Sternbergs, the Löwensteins, Hansie Larisch, Hansie's younger brother Fritz, who was in the Austrian Diplomatic Service, and his dear wife May, Ernestine Thun-Thun, Siegfried Clary and Count Vico Voss.

On December 17th Shelagh's boy was christened with much ceremony at the Chapel Royal, St. James's, the sponsors being King Edward, Katherine Westminster, Granny Olivia and George Wyndham. He was given the names Edward George Hugh.

Thus ended a very full and happy year. I was delighted at the fulfilment of Shelagh's hopes which seemed to me a good augury for certain hopes of my very own.

CHAPTER FOUR

1905–1907

AT the end of January, 1905, my brother-in-law Fritz Hochberg married in London Nancy Burke-Roche, daughter of the second Lord Fermoy. This event pleased us all because Nancy is a charming person. Fritz, who from our first meeting was my sincere friend, adored England and hunting and wanted to spend most of his time there: Nancy, as befits one who comes of a famous hunting family, was a keen horsewoman; and everything seemed propitious.

I wanted my second baby to be born in London; and we took a furnished house in Bruton Street for a short time that we might be near doctors and friends. I have always believed in "keeping on my feet," as the poor people say: I therefore went about to the very last moment. The week before Lexel was born I sat in the stalls at the theatre with my husband, and one night dined at the German Embassy with Metternich, Poppets and one or two friends being there; this was after having in the afternoon driven Poppets and little Hansel about London. King Edward twice sent word to say that I was doing too much and ought to rest—but I knew more about it than he did. I did not look in the least a fright and saw no reason why I should not go out to quiet little dinners, and gave some of my own at Bruton Street.

On February 1st my second boy duly appeared. I do not know if the cause be at all that he was born in dear old London, but he is incurably English and loves London better than any other city in the world. The ceremony of his baptism took place at the Chapel

Royal, St. James's, and his robe was covered by a Brussels lace veil that Granny Olivia had worn when she was married and that Shelagh and I had also worn at our weddings. King George V., then Prince of Wales, Queen Alexandra and the Crown Prince William of Prussia were the Royal sponsors, the others being Granny Olivia, Patsy and brother George. Consequently the poor mite was weighed down with the names Alexander Frederick William George Conrad Ernest Maximilian—is it any wonder we called him Lexel! The old chapel was beautifully decorated with my favourite flowers, arum lilies and marguerites. Hans represented the Crown Prince and was of course at the door to receive Queen Alexandra, who looked lovely. Lexel was baptized with water from the River Jordan; I took him from the nurse and myself handed him to Queen Alexandra; he bears hers as his first name and, formally, is always addressed as Alexander I had now two handsome sons, and was as happy as a woman could be.

When Lexel was five weeks old I went to beloved Newlands by the sea; Hansel, who had been at Eaton with Shelagh, joined us and promptly fell in love with his little brother.

As always happened at Newlands, I had a wonderful time. Hans was with us as often as he could, but he had to rush to and fro as he had to attend meetings of the House of Lords in Berlin and the Provincial Parliament in Breslau. About the middle of March I had a nice letter from the Emperor telling me that the sanitary improvements in the Silesian towns for which I had fought so long would be carried out and the necessary moneys granted. I was delighted and, in my happy English home, felt comforted to know that the people would at least have clean water and be relieved of the terrible smells that invaded their homes. I had got my way at last and what some of my German friends called my "obstination" had resulted in some practical good. When I make up my mind to get a thing I generally succeed. Were I a great statesman

RUTHIN CASTLE, NORTH WALES.

or business man this would be called tenacity; as I am a woman it is only stubbornness.

After a short spell in London with Hans, doing theatres and seeing old friends, I went to Cannes to stay at the Villa Kasbek with the Grand Duke Michael Michaelovitch and smiling, kindly Sophy Torby. I had Hansel with me, also Lexel and his excellent nurse Smith who had been with Princess Frederick Leopold of Prussia for eleven years. I was particularly interested to find myself just then amongst so many Russian royalties. The Russo-Japanese War was drawing to a close; Russia had lost prestige, and the Czar and the Imperial family were much criticized both at home and abroad.

I remember a dinner-party at the huge villa of the Grand Duchess Anastasia of Mecklenburg-Schwerin, my host's sister; she had staying with her another brother, the Grand Duke George[1] and his wife, who was born a Greek Princess, and several others. It was there I first met her daughter Cecile, whose engagement to the Crown Prince had just been announced. The marriage was to take place in June and the Princess was therefore much in the public eye. I found her not only lovely, but charming as well, and in due course she became my kind and faithful friend.

Before the evening was over I began to think the Grand Duke George was quite mad. He shouted at everybody while we were playing Bridge after dinner, denounced Germans and English, and generally behaved in an astounding fashion. I thought all this particularly rude as his sister Anastasia had married a German; dear Sophy—one of the nicest women who ever lived—was a German; his niece was going to marry the future Emperor of Germany; and I was an Englishwoman married to a German. The Grand Duke George had two daughters, one of whom afterwards married William, the only son of Nancy Leeds—but that was after she had become Princess Christopher of Greece.

[1] Shot in Petrograd in January, 1919.

I am afraid that, before the Great War, many of the Russian Grand Dukes were a law unto themselves. This did not help them or their caste when the Russian Revolution came. One would have thought, had they been men of character, strong will and perception, that the fiasco of the Russo-Japanese War would have served as a warning and awakened them to the dangerous position of Russia, not only abroad but at home.

During my stay at Cannes I had a long talk with Helen Potocka (Betka's sister). Her husband was then Governor of Warsaw. His life had been threatened; they also threatened to burn his mills, and all the schools in Warsaw were closed; she and her sons had been sent by the Count for safety to the Riviera. He blamed the Czar and the Grand Dukes who would listen to no warnings and scoffed at the spirit of chronic rebellion that brooded over Poland. They considered such a state of affairs normal and believed that Poland could never stand alone and therefore nothing that happened there really mattered!

Here I will copy one or two extracts from my diary.

April 6, 1905. Villa Kasbek, Cannes.

This afternoon I drove with Sophy and then walked nearly the whole way home—humming to myself. When I am alone on a glorious day I seem to recognize no individuals. I had to walk half the way on the Croisette as the tide was high. There were many people but they seemed of no account to me; I felt as if they were in one world and I in another! All I saw was the intense blue of the sea and sky; the red and white sails of the little boats and, on the distant island of Saint Honorat, the peaceful monastery nestling there.

After tea Sophy took me to see her old father-in-law, the Grand Duke Michael-Nicolaievitch, who was held up while he stood to receive us: he had a fine old face, but was quite an invalid—the infirmities of old age. I spoke to him of Fürstenstein and he suddenly remembered the name and said that his mother the Czarina[1] had some photographs of it which he remembered as a child. She had been near there at some

[1] The wife of Czar Nicholas I., who was born Princess Charlotte of Prussia.

watering-place. I told him the watering-place was Salzbrunn and that his mother had given Vater, when he was a child, a cart and four horses and a box of little silver toys which were in daily use by my boy Hansel.

April 11, 1905. Villa Kasbek.

. . . Two nights ago the Grand Duchess Anastasia gave an evening party for the Grand Duchess Cecilie, who leaves soon for Germany. There were crowds of people. The Grand Duchess of Hesse and her unmarried sister[1] came with the Grand Duke Kyrill in his motor. They are coming here this afternoon to spend the night. The Grand Duchess and the Grand Duke are certain to marry although he will probably have to give up most of his fortune and live abroad as it is against the laws of Russia and the Russian Church to marry a divorced person, even though it was she who divorced her husband.

There was the further complication that the Grand Duke of Hesse and the Czarina were brother and sister, and the Czarina hated the very idea of such a marriage. However, the two people chiefly concerned were really in love and romance triumphed, since four months later they were married at Tegernsee, near Munich. They now have three children and are intensely happy.

My diary records nothing of great interest between my visit to Sophy and my arrival in Berlin in the first week in June for the wedding of the Crown Prince. He was then just twenty-three and, being fair, he looked very young and immature. But let me quote what I wrote at the time:

June 6, 1905.

For the wedding we had to be in the Chapel in evening dress at five-thirty. The Grand Duchess Cecile looked very nice and graceful in silver, only her crown was too much over her nose. Her mother, the Grand Duchess Anastasia, looked handsome, cold and proud. And no wonder, after what the papers said of her. . . . Ah! what cowards! And about a widow whose daughter was just going to marry their own Crown Prince. I felt so sorry for her. The Emperor looked ill, I thought, and the Crown Prince looked as if he ought rather to be learning his letters than answering the marriage

[1] Now the Infanta Beatrice of Bourbon-Orleans.

responses. Princess Salm mentioned to me that the Bridegroom had told her a few days before how fond he was of the Duchess Cecile, and that he had never been anything to any other woman ! I smiled. And I wondered how on earth he managed. Poor girl, I pity her ! After the wedding there was a Court and we all " passed " the Emperor, then the newly married couple and the Empress. We were told to make only one curtsy. I took as much time as I wanted over mine, and they all said I did it best—at least the Grand Duchess Anastasia told Count Vico Voss so. . . . The Silesian papers said that " amongst the beautiful of the beautiful " (if you could only have seen some of them !) the Duchess of Aosta and I were the best looking. It is not difficult to be good-looking in Germany. We got home at nine-thirty and had a dull supper.

Even now the Duchess of Aosta is easily the handsomest Royalty at any gathering at which she appears. Like her brother the late Duke of Orleans, she is tall ; with characteristic good looks and a style of her own she combines much of the sweetness and inextinguishable charm of her sister Queen Amélie. I should add that on the Crown Prince's wedding day Count von Bülow was raised to the rank of Prince.

A few days after the Berlin Royal wedding my friend Princess Margaret of Connaught married Prince Oscar (now Crown Prince) of Sweden, one of the nicest Royalties in Europe. I was delighted because I foresaw for them a very happy life. What I could not foresee was that her position as a Swedish Princess would one day enable her to show me proof of a friendship so staunch and enduring that its like can seldom have been known.

A round of visits, and much entertaining at Fürstenstein and Pless occupied us to the end of 1905, when Vater celebrated his jubilee as Prince of Pless and the Emperor annoyed us all very much by creating him a Duke ! We were not even consulted ! The head of the House had long been known as Prince of Pless and did not want suddenly to become Duke of Pless : more particularly as the new designation was not hereditary, being only for Vater's lifetime. Hans was furious and so was I. It was as if the Emperor had said : " I will give your father a lollipop and, provided you are a good obedient boy, I *may* hand it on to you later." Vater could not refuse it, but neither Hans nor I accompanied him when he went to Berlin to offer his formal thanks to the Emperor. Never was a Court formality more formal ! The truth was that the Emperor had heard rumours to the effect that Hans had Catholic leanings and pro-Polish sympathies and had determined to snub him. As usual he did it, I will not say stupidly, but—due to his excessive impulsiveness, and neglect of any advice—ineffectively. Hans was always ambitious and would perhaps have liked to be Duke of Silesia,[1] but he had no desire for a mere change of prefix that signified nothing. I do not think the Emperor ever particularly relished the fact that the Principality of Pless, originally Polish, was inherited by the Hochbergs in 1847 when the senior branch of the Anhalt-Cöthen-Pless line became extinct. He would have liked to have thought that we had it by direct grant from a German Emperor or Prussian King.

Two extracts from my diary will explain my feelings about the Emperor and public affairs as the year 1905 drew to its close :

October 25, 1905. Fürstenstein.

I wrote a letter to the Emperor from Pless. He will probably be furious, but I do not care. I am so terribly disappointed in him. Six years ago he was looked upon as a paragon in every country. England asked : " What does the Emperor think ? " " What would *he* have done about the Boer War ? " In France the Royalists said : " We wish to God we had a Sovereign like yours." Russia looked at the German Ruler with longing eyes—and what not else. . . . Now Germany has not one Ally : she is isolated. While the King of England in the estimation even of his enemies is acknowledged to be the greatest diplomat in Europe. The Emperor has certainly played his cards badly. He is so terribly tactless, loud and theatrical.

[1] This would have been impossible, as the title belonged to the Prussian Crown.

Soon after making the entry just quoted I wrote to the Emperor about Anglo-German relations. He was coming to Pless at the end of October for a shoot, and answered that we could discuss the matter then. We did, very fully. My diary says:

December 1, 1905. Pless.

The Emperor left here this afternoon. He was very agreeable. The first night we had a long talk over the subject on which I had already written him and regarding which Prince Bülow, two days before I arrived here, wrote me a most flattering answer, saying my words were the echo of his own, and so on. Either England or Germany must be lying, and I cannot really make out which. I do not in the least mind saying to anyone what I think, and I had fully expected the Emperor to be annoyed at my letter: I even dared to criticize his speech from the Throne of the day before. . . . Every one here seemed to be surprised at its warlike tone. . . . I said: "Your Majesty can't let sleeping dogs lie. What was the good of again speaking of Morocco. In fact the whole speech will cause a great deal of criticism."[1] He did not resent what I said; only once or twice he got very excited and during our conversation about England he had tears in his eyes. His vanity is most terribly wounded, and besides, I honestly think he feels it. He mentioned many things he had done to please England: he had attended Queen Victoria's funeral; he had declined to receive the Boer Generals; he had sent a Guard of Honour to meet the King as he passed through Homburg after the Baccarat affair in England, and so on. He said that none of these things were remembered and that the Press and Lord Lansdowne's speeches[2] were most offensive. It is a very difficult question. The two countries are of the same race, yet absolutely different in every way. . . . A nephew on one Throne, the uncle on the other; both countries believing themselves to be in the right and both sincerely believing that each wishes to dominate the other in the eyes of the world. I am sincerely sorry for both. To the Emperor it is a bitter disappointment to be misjudged and

[1] The year 1905 was a very critical one for Anglo-German relationships; the Algeciras Conference sat from January to April; intense anti-British feeling was reported from Berlin in July.

[2] Henry, 5th Marquess of Lansdowne, K.G., British Foreign Secretary 1900–5. Died 1927.

to be disliked—and he wants always to be first. He is apt to rise to a pitch of excitement so difficult for his Ministers to control, that they do not tell him everything for fear of what he might do. The King simply dislikes the Emperor. I am sure he has no real and dangerous intentions towards Germany ; but he just shows his teeth when a German approaches him. There are great mistakes on both sides.

II

We began the year 1906 at Chatsworth, where there was the usual party for the King and Queen. I wanted to see the New Year in with Shelagh at Eaton and got permission to arrive at Chatsworth late.

Charles Hawtrey appeared in Lady Bell's neat little farce *Time is Money*, in which Muriel Wilson and Maudie Warrender were also excellent. I did a musical fantasy of my own composition called *The Lotus*. It was suggested to me by a Burmese love song. Harold Simpson wrote the lyrics and Charles Braun the music. Queen Alexandra liked it so much that she desired it repeated, which was tiring as it took an hour, and I had to change my dress three times.

King Edward, who had been ill, walked with the aid of a stick and shot whilst sitting on a chair.

One day the King asked me if I would like to go with him for a drive after lunch. I said : " Of course if Your Majesty wishes it, but I would much rather go for a walk with George Holford " (who was in Waiting). Afterwards all the women exclaimed : " How could you, Daisy ? " I replied that the King asked me, " would I like to " ; that I didn't like sitting four in a stuffy motor-car and that I had always treated Royalties like human beings and found they enjoyed it. From Chatsworth I returned to Eaton, where the party included the Marlboroughs, Chesterfields, Lyttons, Lord Mar and Kellie and beautiful Violet, and Lady Sarah Wilson. After that, London (the dentist), a few joyous days at Newlands where, on January 21st, I picked primroses in the woods and sent them to little Hansel at home. But I could not remain away from the children any longer and was back at Fürstenstein in February.

On my way home I stayed in Berlin; and I find this written in my diary:

When I think of what going back to Fürstenstein means *now*! Those darling beloved boys on the stairs to greet me and their noise and laughter and little pattering feet in the passages. It makes the first years of my married life seem like a dream, dreamed years and years ago, of home-sickness and longing. But even yesterday in Berlin when I went to buy a present of books for Poppets and was shown some with beautifully done pictures of English cottages and gardens and woods with daffodils, my throat felt stiff and my ears buzzed so that I had to shut the books. No one who has not been through it can realize what it is to leave one's own country. Even for the sake of husband and children it is impossible to forget. One can only try not to feel too much; and at all events one can and must learn not to show one's feelings.

At the end of March I went to Cannes and again stayed at Villa Kasbek with the Grand Duke and Sophy, and during my visit saw a good deal of the Grand Duke and Duchess Vladimir, the Grand Duchess Anastasia, the Grand Duke George, and the newly married Grand Duchess Kyrill, who was looking extraordinarily handsome and well. While there I heard that Hans had broken his leg in Vienna and I decided to join him at once. Vater was already with him and Hans was an excellent patient, very cheerful. I love Vienna and the Austrians; in my diary I find the following comparison of English and continental Society:

May 17, 1906. Vienna.

No one knows who has not lived here the difference between this society and the society of any other country in the world. England—free and easy, sporting, gambling, well-dressed, clean; making the best and knowing the best of everything, accepting morality or immorality in a philosophical way; no one wonders, every one is tolerant; they gossip, but chiefly from interest, not from malice. Austria—select and religious, the most sporting country in the world next to England; the women are good wives, good mothers, sometimes amusing, generally dull, happy-minded, kind-hearted; always "grandes dames." France—full of life and wit; letting things come and go as they will; the men and women, over-scented, over-dressed, full of exaggeration but refined and full of the knowledge of all that is beautiful and in good taste; each trying to outwit the other in repartee, clothes and popularity. Russia—silent, bearded, morose; accepting in her society those who are turned out of another; an atmosphere of Grand Dukes, cocottes and closed carriages. And then—Berlin! Good God! it's worse than all—bands and beer; shuffling feet in the Unter den Linden; no one seems to know how to walk; it is either a swaggering soldier stride, or a lurch backwards with the stomach out; the women trip without grace and without the knack of holding their skirts that the Frenchwomen have, or the determination to hold it out of the dirt as does an Englishwoman. Society is small, bourgeois and jealous. The Court is narrow-minded, theatrical, and domineering; and yet, how I am in it all!

While we were in Vienna I heard that an old friend, Prince Gottfried Hohenlohe, had been very ill with congestion of the lungs following influenza. As soon as he was convalescent I determined, after consulting Hans, to go to see him. The Austrians were never as absurdly narrow and conventional as the Prussians, but, like all nations, they had their own Mrs. Grundy. When I first went to see Gottfried—he was not married then—I took with me Prince Festetics de Tolna, who was a grandfather, and as the patient's priest brother Constantine was to meet us there I hoped this would be considered sufficient chaperonage.

However, having paid tribute to Cæsar's relict (who, one may be quite sure, spent a dull and immaculate widowhood) I determined to go alone a day or two later and have a good talk about politics in Russia and Austria. Being a diplomat, Gottfried was very unforthcoming before others. His brother had just been made Austrian Prime Minister, and he had grown a beard and looked like John the Baptist! I mean Gottfried, not the brother, had grown a beard, and this seemed to make a serious conversation inevitable.

No one can be frivolous with a man who has a beard like that of a Jewish prophet. This is what happened :

May 28, 1906. Vienna.

. . . Prince Gottfried was saying how the German feeling in Morocco was excellent—but—for England, not Germany ! And I see the truth of what he says (and he *is* clever as every one agrees). He says that Germany has made enemies of France, England, and Italy (the Triple Alliance is at an end [1]), and now there will be a Treaty between Russia and England, by which England, in signing, safeguards her Indian frontier ; she can also now come down on Turkey and if, for once, the Sultan on any subject should say " No," England will step forward and murmur, " Now, Russian Bear, growl," which will frighten the Sultan into saying " Yes," without giving any trouble to England except perhaps the sending of an extra man-of-war or two to cruise in front of Constantinople ; and this all comes from German policy in Morocco. Germany is now surrounded on all sides by nations with which she is not on the most friendly terms. And to think what power, personality and energy the German Emperor really has ! If only he had used it in the right way, he might have made Germany the most influential country in the world, particularly now that Russia is at the bottom of the ladder. Instead of which England, from across the seas, wins this race of the Nations for greatness and power ! Prince Gottfried is still Military Secretary in St. Petersburg, but has been laid up here for nearly two months with congestion of the lungs.

I was interested to be in Vienna for the visit of the German Emperor which was about to take place. In reality he was never popular in that city. The Austrians and Prussians are naturally antipathetic and always will be, and the old Austrian Emperor can never really have liked being compelled to act as fag to his parvenu brother-Emperor. If the Austrians disliked the Emperor William II, the Hungarians hated him. My diary says :

The German Emperor is coming here much to the disgust of the Hungarians who think he is against them. And even the Austrians do not seem to be very pleased or flattered by

[1] This was substantially true, although the Alliance was never formally denounced.

his visit. They all say: "Why is he coming? He never does anything without a motive."

It is strange how that great man, full of thought and energy, has personally "come down" in the world's opinion. No one seems really to care for him, or trust him now. *How far* a charming manner, a little dignity, and *tact* can carry a person! And of these three qualities he owns none; and that I think is the reason why people absolutely fail to understand him. I pity him, as even to himself some day he will stand forth a disappointed man. His ambitions not realized—and, hardest of all, to be "misunderstood." Whether he is good—or rather evil-minded—I cannot yet make out.

The Emperor's visit was brief and only semi-official. Therefore there was not much state or formality. The following reference to an Imperial dinner-party may be of interest.

The Archduchess Otto to whom I refer was born Princess Marie-Josepha of Saxony and was the mother of the young Archduke Karl who afterwards became Emperor. Poor lady, she now lives outside Munich in very reduced circumstances and bears her hard lot with great dignity and resignation. The Archduchess Frederick was born Princess Isabelle of Croy. Her husband was a brother of the Queen-Dowager of Spain and uncle of King Alphonso XIII. Their eldest daughter was my dear friend, Princess Salm-Salm—whom I so often refer to in my diary as Christa.

June 5, 1906.

. . . The night before leaving Vienna I drove to the Palace of Schönbrunn with Lily Kinsky to dine with the two Emperors; only very few women, about twenty in all. Princess Montenuovo, Princess Kinsky (whose husband is Chamberlain to the Emperor), Princess Fürstenberg, Princess Metternich (the old one), two or three ladies-in-waiting, two Hungarian ladies, Betka Potocka, and one or two more. I stood by Countess von Bülow, the German Ambassadress, when the two Emperors entered, but no introductions were necessary as the old Austrian Emperor talked to me at once and asked about Hans. I told him Hans was pleased to be laid up in Vienna where he had so many friends, rather than in Berlin where there are always few people, and that he and I were so fond of the Austrians ; he nodded his old head and was delighted. The German Emperor was also very affable and full of enquiries. And the wife of the Archdule Otto who, I once thought, could not open her mouth, talked like a waterfall. The second Archduchess was Christa Salm's mother with all her other daughters, charming, unspoilt girls.

The dinner was a magnificent banquet off gold plate ; beautiful orchids on the table, banked in the corners of the room and round the doors of the dining hall. After dinner we listened to a famous *Gesangverein* composed of men (of all ages—some had grey beards), but all the voices together were very fine although a little monotonous after a while. The evening was over early at ten, as the German Emperor left that night.

From Vienna I went to Budapest for a few days with Betka Potocka.[1] We had a marvellous time and were fêted till I thought I would die of fatigue. The city and its inhabitants are perfectly delightful

When I got back to Vienna I found Hans convalescent. We had a few hectic days racing, dining, dancing and going to innumerable parties. From Vienna we went to Fritz and Nancy at Halbau to recover ourselves a bit

After this a few quiet weeks at Fürstenstein spent in fishing, and in receiving visitors such as the Kinskys and the Salm-Salms. Then on a comfortable boat to England with the children for a bathing holiday at Newlands.

III

In June I was in London and, amongst many other dissipations, I went to an interesting Ball at Apsley House where Princess Ena, now Queen of Spain, created a sensation by her fresh beauty and charm. I remember this ball so well because at Ascot King Edward said he considered it an impertinence Metternich not being there " as the Queen was there and all the other Ambassadors." I answered that Mensdorff (the Austrian Ambassador) was a much younger man

[1] Betka was the daughter of Prince Antoine Radziwill, and had married Count Roman Potocki.—D. of P.

and the American and all the others married and had wives and daughters, whereas poor Metternich was old and a bachelor. But it did not help much as just then the King was out of humour with everything German.

For one of the Newmarket Meetings we stayed the night with Edith Wolverton: a very nice house and charming people. I lost forty-eight pounds at Poker which, had they known it, would have horrified my German in-laws. Hans enjoyed himself enormously.

That month there was a State Ball at Buckingham Palace for the Japanese Prince Arisugawa and his Princess. The Duchess of Sparta, the Emperor's sister, was there, and I remember Winifred Portland, who was of course Mistress of the Robes, looking strikingly lovely. I wore a dress of gold tissue, my diamond and turquoise crown, the blue riband of the Order of St. Theresa of Bavaria, and tried to avoid looking as if long residence in Germany had turned me into a dowd. I think it was on that occasion that Queen Alexandra admired my cloth-of-gold dress very much and was horrified when, in answer to her question, I had to confess that the train alone was worth over four hundred pounds. She said she could not possibly afford such a sum. Fortunately I was able to defend myself by telling Her Majesty that the material was a gift from one of the great Indian Princes and had appeared on my back again and again in different forms. Indeed I have it now and it is as good as ever. All the same, dear Queen Alexandra, bless her, was the only person who ever took the trouble to make me understand that it would be a very wicked thing to pay such a sum for a Court train.

That season I sang a great deal in public and several times was fortunate enough to have Mrs. Claude Beddington as my accompanist. Easily one of the most decorative figures in London, Mrs. Claude is a first-class musician and an artist to her finger-tips. She was a great friend of my mother, has the same "little name," "Patsy," and she is a friend of Shelagh's. Every one who sings knows the cold shivers that go down your back during the first bars played by an indifferent accompanist. Tosti was of course inimitable as an accompanist; he was my first teacher and I had been spoiled in my youth by having him accompany me often; Jean de Reszke, too, was most sympathetic, understanding and *helpful*.

In the early days of July I went down to Colchester to help with a concert for the 16th Lancers, Guy Wyndham's Regiment. I sang Massenet's *Elégie*, D'Hardelot's *I Hid my Love* and, as an encore, the then inevitable Tosti's *Good-bye*. Mrs. Claude Beddington played my accompaniments beautifully and Olivia, Guy's girl, presented me with a lovely bouquet.

Count Wolff-Metternich, the German Ambassador in London, was a perfect old dear and, as he was a bachelor, I had always a *pied-à-terre* at the Embassy. Egged on by me he decided that year to give a great Ball and asked me to be hostess and receive the guests, Hans acting as my Master of Ceremonies. I determined not to have a dull Ball, with nothing brilliant except the Orders and Decorations of the elderly wearers, and think I succeeded. The essentials of a successful Ball are beautiful women, plenty of men, a fine house, a good floor, lovely flowers, perfect music, perfect food and wine, a good hostess and—good luck. To this one must add a sprinkling of Dowagers, Diplomats and Royalty, and the thing should go. I had wonderful flowers everywhere. The great terrace overlooking St. James's Park was fragrant with them and all went well. Metternich was delighted and, better still, had the pleasure afterwards of paying the bills—of which there were heaps and heaps.

As the occasion was German I wore my wedding Crown as a Countess of the Holy Roman Empire, and my Orders. But how nice it was to kick them all off when it was over, get into slippers and a dressing-gown and have a cup of tea by myself in my own room.

That season in London was an extremely full one. I was constantly dining out to meet the King and Queen

NEWLANDS MANOR, HAMPSHIRE

or the Prince and Princess of Wales. On these occasions—indeed always in England—I was sent in before the Duchesses and this used to upset me. Especially so when, as sometimes happened, I was sent in before an old friend like the Duchess of Devonshire.

I remember specially a dinner-party given by the Prince and Princess of Wales at Marlborough House because it was the only time I met Sir Henry Campbell-Bannerman, who was then Prime Minister. I found him both gallant and charming. I was wearing a train of the Indian tissue of which I am so fond. After dinner the Princess of Wales noticed it and said she had always wanted some but they never made enough of the same pattern for a dress. Besides, the material for a whole frock would cost eighty to a hundred pounds and that she thought was far too much. I was interested to know that her ideas about dress were even more modest than those of Queen Alexandra.

In the first week in July I was on my way back to Fürstenstein and spent a night or two in Berlin where every one was agog about the impending birth of a child to the Crown Prince and Crown Princess. On July 4, a son appeared at the Marmor Palace near Berlin. My diary for the next day says:

July 5, 1906.

. . . Princess Salm told me all about the Crown Princess; how the Empress had sent a professor (doctor) to see her, but the Crown Prince not being there she did not allow him to examine her as her husband had given strict orders that even if her pains began, no doctor was to be called until he was sent for and had arrived in the house! Nor would he have a special doctor or nurse (the Empress wanted an English nurse), but he would only have the nurse and doctor from Potsdam. Well at any rate, although he is as obstinate as ten mules, the Crown Princess had a son yesterday, and all is going well. I have just written to her, and to him (he wired me to Fürstenstein) and to the Emperor, and shall write asking Countess Brockdorff to give my respects and congratulations to the Empress. *How* proud the Crown Prince must be when ten months ago he had scarcely ever seen a woman—or so he says, and did not know, until Prince Salm (and she also) explained to him, what Nature had meant men and women to do.

I was again in England in August for Cowes and stayed with the Duchess of Manchester at Egypt House. I think that was the year that King Edward came ashore from the *Victoria and Albert* one night to play Bridge. He did not want any fuss, brought only one Equerry and they hired a crazy cab to drive them to Egypt House. The driver did not know where it was and took them to the wrong place. It was quite dark and the Equerry got out and rang. A window upstairs was opened and two outraged old ladies peered out demanding what all the noise was about. The King shouted up that he had come to play Bridge with the Duchess of Manchester. The angry ladies declared they knew nothing about either Bridge or Duchess; that he was drunk and if he did not go away quietly at once they would telephone for the police!

When I was in London in July, Soveral motored me to see Hampton Court and the lovely gardens. We then hired a man to punt us down the river and lunched tied to the banks of a side stream. On the way back we ran into a Regatta at Kingston, but could not watch it as I had to be back in time to dine at White Lodge. This excursion was to be kept a secret, goodness knows why; but Soveral never would let one lady know about another. Above all, the King and Queen were not to be told. One day at Cowes, to Soveral's horror, the two sons of Princess Beatrice began: "Oh, we saw you at the Regatta the other day——" Soveral hushed them up, changed the conversation quickly and Queen Alexandra, being deaf, did not hear. For such a careful diplomat he was sometimes guilty of bad breaks. Nothing is more stupid than unnecessary secrets. One day he and I went into Cowes and he bought two brooches with the King's yachting pennant in enamel; one he gave to me and the other he later on gave to the Queen. We were racing in the *Britannia* a day or two afterwards when the Queen showed me hers and then exclaimed : " Oh, you have one too." To tease her a little I could not resist saying : " Yes, ma'am, Soveral and I bought them together in a shop at Cowes."

IV

I need not go on describing parties and social functions in England and Germany because, after all, one is very much like another. I must, however, give a short account of one of the parties we had at Fürstenstein for the Imperial Army Manœuvres, as they were considered very important occasions and a great fuss was always made about them. That particular year, 1906, they took place in the middle of September ; the Duke of Connaught was present and looked very fine in a German Hussar uniform. Our chief lady guests were his nieces, the Crown Princess of Rumania and her sister, the Princess of Hohenlohe-Langenburg. Then there was the Emperor's sister, the Duchess of Sparta (afterwards Queen of Greece), whom her brother had never forgiven for joining the Orthodox Church three years after she married ; Mildred Chelsea (now Mildred Meux), Arthur Coke, General Sir Laurence Oliphant, Sir Ian Hamilton and Anthony Drexel. The manœuvres gave every one an excuse for dressing up, and all the Germans certainly availed themselves of it. Poor Hans went about day and night wearing a tight Hussar uniform with boots and all his Orders : anything more ridiculous-looking cannot be imagined. We had over thirty people in the house for several days. There was a Rumanian and a Greek lady-in-waiting, whose names I never succeeded in grasping ; Fritz and Nancy Hochberg, Patsy and Poppets, Sir Seymour Fortescue, General " Billy " Lambton, and Counts Esterhazy and Apponyi from Hungary.

Winston Churchill was there but not actually in the house, being the guest of the Emperor at the hotel belonging to my husband in Salzbrunn ; he came over twice, and people were always coming to lunch or dine. I remember thinking that, like the Emperor, Winston was pleased at the opportunity of dressing up and secretly admired himself in the tight jacket of, I supposed, the Oxfordshire Hussars. The only men who can wear a Hussar uniform with dash and effect are the Hungarians. The Duke of Connaught lunched at Fürstenstein the day it was announced that the Emperor had made him a Prussian Field-Marshal, and we all drank his health.

We went into Breslau each day by special train to watch the manœuvres. They ended up with a grand ceremonial Review for which we all put on our best smiles and best clothes. My diary says :

The Duchess of Sparta left before the Review at Breslau, and the other two Princesses were not very pleased with their reception by the Emperor and Empress after the Review. The Empress does not approve of the Crown Princess of Rumania ; and I thought that her displeasure might be reflected on me when we all went to see her but, to my astonishment, she was very nice and agreeable and talked more to me than to the others.

I rode twice at the Manœuvres ; they lasted only three days ; the last day was great fun : I had a general pass for all my guests, and Count Eulenburg and the Prince of Lynar, who were of course in uniform and staying with us, took us everywhere. On the last day we had lunch in a hollow within a few yards of the Emperor and his suite who were all standing on a high hill.

Later the Emperor saw us and wishing to know Sir Ian Hamilton and Sir Laurence Oliphant, descended from his heights and spoke to us—he came to the side of my horse and kissed my hand. I was the only lady there at the moment and he talked a little to me and then to the two Generals.

In the afternoon our party watched in the motors to see him pass—I remained on my horse as I knew he would be pleased to see me and the English guests waiting to see him ride by. And so he was, for, to our surprise, he stopped his train of followers, came across the road, called me Daisy and said good-bye and spoke to Poppets whom, as I reminded him, he had met at the christening of Hansel.

It was on this occasion that the party was christened " The Merry Wives of Windsor " because none of the three Royal ladies had their husbands with them !

V

I had to be in England by New Year, 1907, for a huge party at Chatsworth : the King and Queen and all the usual Court set and a nice mixture of people with brains. Princess Victoria has never become much known to the general public. In spite of her reserve, fastidiousness and natural shyness she is full of fun and cheeriness and can be a great asset at a house-party. Some Royalties are enough to extinguish any gathering, however well chosen, as I have sad cause to know. But the right sort are a godsend and certainly help to make a party go. Dear Charlotte Knollys was in Waiting on the Queen and Sir Fritz Ponsonby (whose wife was Ria Kennard, one of the noted beauties of those days and still easily one of the handsomest women in London) was in Waiting on the King and, as always, was an ideal guest. Then there were Lord and Lady Desborough, Lady de Grey, the Acheson girls, their parents Lord and Lady Gosford, Mr. Evan Charteris, and George Holford. Mr. Balfour was urbane, smiling, amused, and took a surprisingly intense interest in everything that went on. Somehow one does not expect a great philosopher, statesman and writer to be human ! As for dear Alice Keppel, she was inimitable. What spirit, wit and resilience that woman has ! My diary summarizes the party well enough—much better than I might do from memory :

January, 1907.

The acting at Chatsworth on the 5th of January was a great success. I came last on the Programme for better effect, and I sang three songs in costume, with acting and a cinematograph in between, to enable me to change without too much rush. My first song was out of the *Mikado* and I wore a brown wig and looked much nicer than with my own stupid yellow hair. Then an American coon song in a beggar frock and big pale blue felt hat, and a short dance with a red cotton umbrella. And for the last, a French song, *Il Neige*, by Bemberg, in a new white tobogganing dress from Fürstenstein, a white hat with a bunch of red holly in it, some mistletoe on my white fur muff, and high red boots ; I had fir trees round me covered with cotton-wool and small white paper fell over and around me while I sang, so it was a very pretty snow effect, if not quite original.

Throughout the visit the King was in a very good temper (except about the treatment of his nieces by the Emperor and Empress when they were in Breslau with me. I knew he would hear of this). He shot well too, and the weather was fine, sharp and crisp, with a little snow. The Queen was as charming and sweet as ever and gave me a dear little fire opal and diamond brooch for Christmas : she is a darling. It was the same party as usual, only Soveral was furious ; he was rather the man out, which as a rule he never is ! The Queen played in a Baccarat tournament after dinner, and we had to play to please her. Soveral generally went down and smoked a cigar alone in the smoking-room, and, after the Queen had gone to her rooms, I played Poker with Violet Mar and Kellie, Maudie Warrender her sister, Pocklewski from the Russian Embassy, Lord Dalmeny (Lord Rosebery's son) ; Lord Elcho, Lord Desborough and Muriel Wilson played dominoes with Lady de Grey.

From Chatsworth we went to Eaton, where we found Bend Or and Shelagh just back from a trip to South Africa ; they had May Roxburghe, Violet Powis, Adèle Essex, Lord Kenyon and some others with them.

I was very seedy all that winter and spring and could not face the cold of Silesia.

February and early March I spent at Newlands and Bournemouth, leaving on March 21 for Beaulieu on the Riviera, where the children and I had a wonderful time. We saw heaps of friends and relations. George and Jennie were staying near by with Adèle Essex and in April Jennie and I and the Duke of Marlborough made a fascinating motor-trip to Avignon, Arles,

Carcassonne and back to Beaulieu. The French provinces can be wonderful in the spring.

Otherwise life on the Riviera was pretty much what it always was—and continues to be. I give an extract from my diary which is of interest because it tells of the first time I heard that unique artist, Chaliapine :

March 23, 1907. Villa Espalmador, Beaulieu.

Am sitting in the hammock with lots of cushions and a fur rug, as there is no sunshine and it is very windy but I am shaded by bamboos and a big palm tree. The sky is grey. I only hope that if it does rain it will come down and be over before Hans arrives to-morrow morning as I want everything to look its best for him, so that he won't be disappointed. He was to have arrived to-day but he could get no places in the train.

I dined at Monte Carlo last night for the first time. Mr. Drexel gave the dinner ; the Duchess of Devonshire, poor old dear, very cheerful and very rouged ; Emily Yznaga (Consuelo Manchester's sister), Mr. and Mrs. Derek Keppel and Lord Charlie Montagu. Mr. Drexel and I went to the Opera after dinner ; of course they dawdled over coffee so the doors were shut when we arrived ; but I gave my name and looked very imploringly and the head man let us on to the stage in a funny little box with wire in front like a cold meat house that one sees in the gardens of small houses—only I should not have *kept* very long if I had remained there—as it was very hot. I did not go into the Rooms—and although I was longing to make a little money I didn't believe I should be able to stand the atmosphere. I am still very hoarse and my nose is always as if I had a cold in it—I cannot call out, and I have not sung since Chatsworth ; my voice has quite gone. I am *so* longing to be well. I think it is easier to be really ill than to go on in this half state as I have done all the time since January—except the month of February when I was really ill at Newlands.

The Opera last night was excellent ; the young Russian, Chaliapine, sang ; he is a marvel and the most extraordinary actor as well, although his part in *Il Barbiere di Siviglia* was not much for him to do ; but even there one's whole attention was centred on him. Mrs. Clayton (Jeanne de Fougère) that was . . . took me right behind the stage afterwards as she wanted to see if Chaliapine would sing at her house in Cannes.

He was introduced to me; he is extremely tall, and had on an artificial nose and chin, and dirty old clothes (dressed as a priest) and such dirty hands. He has his baby here with him aged two. I did not like to ask about his wife, as she might be dead, divorced, or only be his "maîtresse." He must be, I imagine, in his private life, a graceful and dignified man. He gave us the flowers he had in his hand. He is only twenty-six. What his face is like I cannot imagine as his get-up was terrible; and last year I saw him in a ghastly piece in which people were sent to be burnt and tortured in the religious wars! And there his acting was simply astonishing.

On our way back to Fürstenstein we stayed in Paris for a few perfect days. Hans was delightful. I bought clothes and went to a very magnificent party given by Princess Murat, at which we met the Grand Duke and Grand Duchess Vladimir and many old friends. We all wore tiaras and our smartest frocks. Prince Murat is of course the head of the Imperialist party in France and the Murat's more formal receptions have something of the atmosphere of a Royal party.

I had an Englishwoman's idea about the duties attaching to my position in Silesia; Hans had those of a German; that is to say, they never agreed. Once at Pless when Patsy was there I wanted to sing to her after dinner. Hans objected saying: "Nonsense; did you ever hear of the Queen singing after dinner?" "No," said Patsy, "because she can't; but the Princess of Wales[1] is a beautiful pianist and often plays for her guests after dinner."

Poor dear Hans; he had little sense of humour and no sense of proportion whatever—comparing me to the Queen of England.

However, I am nothing if not persistent, and by 1907 I had worn down his resistance a bit. He never at any time encouraged or supported my various activities; at best he just tolerated them. Poor dear, to have really understood me he would have had to be "made over" as the Americans say. I understood

[1] Queen Mary of England.

him and his standpoint well enough, but I just wasn't going to "stay put." This is how it happened:

June 14, 1907. Fürstenstein.

My first concert: I hope it will be a success. I would have had it years ago only Hans would never let me sing, because: "German Princesses don't sing in public." But lately he has become more sensible. I am just reading a book, *Fräulein Schmidt and Mr. Anstruther* by a Countess von Arnim, an American, I hear, married to a German; it is deliciously written as are all her books, particularly *Elizabeth and her German Garden.*[1] How I wish I could express in writing all I sometimes feel, it would be almost a relief to be able to put it quickly on paper and the very reading of it afterwards would do me good showing me perhaps how stupid, dull or ungrateful, how blind or exaggerated or hopeless my thoughts were; it would be like trying on a dress that one thought fitted, and then having to take in or let out the seams; and for certain to take off a lot of the trimming, the little lights and colourings to our thoughts that, to our conceited minds, make them interesting, whereas they would be far more wholesome and less troublesome if they were perfectly plain!

July 22, 1907. Fürstenstein.

The "moment suprême" of this week has come and gone successfully, being the concert which took place last Saturday the 20th in Salzbrunn for my cripple school and the poor round Waldenburg; such a concert has never been given in Breslau,[2] I think not even in Silesia, where the largest sum of money ever taken has been from three hundred to five hundred marks! Two years ago here they made four hundred marks, I think, and were delighted—I have made nineteen hundred marks. There was not even any more standing room available, and the front seats cost six marks, in spite of the Director in Salzbrunn telling me they were far too expensive and that no one would take any. The stage and the hall were decorated with white lilies and crimson rambler roses from Fürstenstein. "Les artistes" included Fräulein Steigermann,

[1] It had been stated repeatedly in the English and American Press that I was the author of this charming book.—D. of P.

[2] Breslau is the third city of Prussia (the first, commercially and educationally) and one of the four or five largest in the German Empire.

a charming little lady and a great swell who came from Leipzig, for nothing. Fräulein Suttes, who knows her slightly, asked her, and I was to pay her expenses ; but when she left she would not take a penny saying she had been so happy here and it had been a real pleasure. She sang charmingly with all her medals on from Kings and Emperors, which of course greatly impressed the audience. Then Count Pückler-Limburg sang ; a Mr. Verlohe from Freiburg played the 'cello *very* well ; Mr. Gerlach, who was taking a cure in Salzbrunn but who comes from Breslau and is a professional, recited, also for nothing. Schimmel, a young man, a baritone, sang, but as he asked for it and I had already engaged him, I had to pay him a hundred marks. Then the orchestra played ; and I sang too, my voice is really very good now. Every one was radiant and delighted and although I had an awful headache and was in bed all the day, I sang well and was not nervous when I saw what a full and smart house I had to please. The Hatzfeldts came to stay, also their second (married) son with his little Japanese wife (her father is a Japanese and her mother a German), the Strachwitzes, Gottfried Hohenlohe and Fritz, and old Countess Pückler came with her husband.

I was planning an early autumn party at Fürstenstein and wrote to ask the Duchess of Sparta. She had been so nice and tactful at the party for the Manœuvres the year before, in spite of the fact that her brother the Emperor was not very cordial ; and she had left before the Review in order to avoid the possibility of anything like an awkward moment in public : I therefore felt a little guilty and wanted her very much to come again. I think in writing a book such as this, one must do one's little best to set down anything, however slight, that seems to place historic characters in a true and correct light. During the War no story was more assiduously cultivated than the false one that the Queen of Greece was very anti-English, that she drove her husband and Greece into the war against England, indeed acting throughout as the Emperor's agent. There was not a word of truth in this. Like all the daughters of the Empress Frederick, she had a real affection for England. Whatever the influences and considerations were that caused Greece to side with Germany, the Queen's personal feelings and wishes had nothing to do with those causes.

The following letter from the Queen (then of course Duchess of Sparta) and other similar incidents recorded in this volume go to prove what I say:

THE ESPLANADE HOTEL, SEAFORD, SUSSEX. *July* 14, 1907.

DEAREST PRINCESS OF PLESS—or Daisy, may I say,—

What will you think of my very rude behaviour! How can I ask you please to excuse my not having answered your very kind letter before, for which heartfelt thanks.

I received your letter whilst still in Athens. Since, we have been a few days in Paris, then at Friedrichshof with my sister; now here in my beloved England the one place I love to be in most. We remain here till the beginning of August when we return to Greece. Unfortunately there is no question of our being able to come to lovely Fürstenstein this year, as I would love to do! There is not time left. How lovely it was last year, and I did enjoy it, and never forget your great kindness. How I should like to see it again, and the new garden. The weather has been too terribly cold here and we had fires in the rooms to keep warm; it's somewhat better now, though not like summer, which is all the better for me, and so bracing.

I like this little quiet place so much, it does me so much good. To-morrow I go up to London for a few days! Old Metternich gives a dinner and ball on the 22nd, how I shall miss you there! You had arranged it all so beautifully last year, do you remember? I hope you are quite well again by now and have recovered from the cure.

Do please come to Athens whenever you can and stay with us, we should be so pleased to have you. With renewed thanks for your kind invitations and hoping you will excuse my late reply.

With best love and many compliments to your husband,

I am, Yours sincerely, SOPHIE.

VI

My dear father-in-law had been unwell for some time, but no one anticipated serious consequences. It was therefore a shock to me when I suddenly heard that he was dangerously ill. I was devoted to Vater in every way and my grief was deep and sincere when he died at Albrechtsburg Castle, near Dresden, in the beginning of August 1907, aged seventy-four. In politics he was a free Conservative and sat in the Reichstag for a few years in the 'seventies; but his political activities were chiefly centred in the Upper House of the Prussian Diet, of which he was a member for more than forty years.

In his early days Vater, as I always called him, was in the Prussian Regiment of the Garde du Corps, but retired when he married Countess Marie Kleist, in 1857. This lady was the mother of Hans, Fritz and Conny. She died in 1883, and in 1886 he married Mathilde, Burgoine and Countess of Dohna-Schlobitten, who had a son and daughter by Vater, Willusch and Anna. She and they are happily alive and well.

During the Franco-Prussian War Vater was head of the Volunteer Ambulance Corps with the title of Royal Commissary and, when the war was over, he remained at the head of the Corps for more than twenty years. He was Grand Chancellor of the Order of the Black Eagle for many years. In 1873 he became Grand Master of the Royal Hunt, and held that position until his death. He was also Grand Master of one of the least known Orders of Knighthood in Europe, that of the White Hart of St. Hubert, the insignia of which the Emperor always wore when hunting. The Order dates from Frederick the Great. Not many people were given it because it was looked upon as more or less a Hohenzollern family affair.

The account I have preserved in my diary shows what a feudal funeral was like in Germany twenty-one years ago. The ceremony was in two parts; the arrival of the body at Freiburg from Dresden, and the actual funeral two days later:

August 16, 1907. Fürstenstein.

It is seven o'clock and pouring rain; it has been like this all the day. I left Berlin this morning with Hansel at 8.0 and got here at 2.50, just before Mathilde and Anna, Lulu, Aunt Anna Reuss, and Heine Reuss arrived. An hour later Hans and his brothers, and brother-in-law, Fritz Solms, got here.

All the head Jägers, some of the head miners, Staff, Foresters, Servants and Deputations walked up from Freiburg behind the carriage (an open hearse) which carried dear Vater in his coffin.

As all the other mourners arrived at Salzbrunn station they did not see the preparations in Freiburg; these included a lovely arch under which Vater was carried, all the miners and soldiers lining the streets. I do not know to what Regiments the soldiers belonged, but some wore white and red plumes flying from their hats and some cocks' feathers. The Emperor has ordered a squadron of Cavalry from Pless and salutes will be fired from the Linden Allée, because Vater was a Cavalry Officer for some time.

Mathilde is marvellous: she only cries a little, she even smiles. Lulu is also grandly reserved and quiet. I marvel and am astonished at their self-control and suppression of feeling.

When they carried in the little plain coffin covered with green Jäger cloth into the billiard-room (the plain coffin and Jäger cloth in accordance with Vater's wish) I cannot think how Mathilde could hold herself so; the clergyman said a few prayers, and then we went out. If it had been Hans who had died, I could not have stood it; I should have wished to be alone with my dead in the room and with the hateful miserable feeling that he lay there fastened down—I cannot even feel him, he has left me for ever—— Oh! it would have driven me wild. But then I am emotional and often exaggerated. I despise myself in a way. When I think of dear Vater's face, his kindness, the little jokes he loved, the little shoots he used to arrange for me at Pless, I am more than miserable. My dear Hans arrived so wet after the long walk from Freiburg in his uniform and Ribands. Mathilde talks of Hans all the time, saying what a dear and what a help he has been. I was grieved that he got to Dresden just two hours too late to see Vater alive, but it did not really matter as Vater just tried to get up out of bed and then fell back and died an hour later quite quietly; he never opened his eyes afterwards or spoke, and, the day before, he knew Hans was coming and was pleased. The morning of the day he died he seemed to be better. It is strange that Hans's mother died too in much the same way in her sleep in bed.

The billiard-room has been turned into a Chapel, arranged very nicely, hung in black, and big silver candlesticks have been put there. To-morrow a lot of lilies will arrive that I ordered in Berlin and I shall make a great big cross to hang behind the crucifix, and put some amongst the palms and white hydrangeas.

Later.

It is now eleven o'clock; all the women of the party have gone to bed; the men are still downstairs in the big salon, talking. It has been a strange evening to me and I cannot well explain it or put my impressions into words. It is the first time, God be thanked, that I have ever worn mourning or been near death or attended a funeral, except as a child; then, I remember, Patsy was away, and in great excitement I ordered for myself on my own responsibility a black dress with mauve bows; I was about ten. . . . Now there is death in the house and by the way we all seem to behave one would really think that Vater had gone on a shooting journey, or that he was quietly in bed. We all ate dinner; we even made conversation during the meal and laughed. After dinner I heard quite a long and happy laugh and this was Mathilde with Hans and Uncle Bolko, and some of the others. I also pretended and did my best to change their thoughts. I told stories to Vater's brother, Uncle Bolko, at dinner, travelling experiences I had had—all about Heiligendamm and the island of Rügen. After dinner I laughed with Lulu about Garsul the famous doctor who sees spirits and knows at once when we are going to die and if one has any disease, and things like that; in fact this evening seemed like any evening except that we all wore black dresses. My maid Marie was very surprised that Lulu or Mathilde wore pearl ear-rings, and Anna a mauve pendant. I think that in every country the middle class take more pride to be in absolute mourning than we do, it is perhaps a sign of their wealth, and possibly they like to show they can afford to buy much crepe and black ear-rings and chains, as Marie, and Friedrich the housekeeper, have now done. . . .

August 17, 1907.

It is eight o'clock and I have just come upstairs, the men have nearly all gone who came for the funeral—they left by special train. The Crown Prince (present instead of the Emperor who was busy saying good-bye to the King of England [1]) leaves only at eleven, and stays for dinner: we dine soon now.

---

[1] King Edward visited Berlin in August, 1907.

It has been a beautiful sunny day and only at about half-past seven as we left the Mausoleum did the sun set, and the sky was pink behind the castle; going we walked in a line of fours behind the coffin, and then we ladies drove home. It was all beautifully done; the whole avenue lined by miners in gala uniform and the head Foresters behind the coffin; they also lifted the coffin on to the hearse and carried it into the vault, and we followed. Mathilde walked with the Crown Prince, Hans with Aunt Anna Reuss, then Lulu with Uncle Bolko and I followed with the Duke of Schleswig-Holstein. At the end of the ceremony they blew the *Jagd vorbei* in broken strains and that was the most touching of all, as Vater loved shooting so much. Then they fired cannons and sounded *The Last Post*. The squadron from Pless could not come, it was too far, so the Emperor ordered a squadron of Cavalry from Schweidnitz. It has been a touching, and strangely peaceful funeral (perhaps it is always so at funerals, but then I have never been to one before); I mean, the prayers and the choirs; and sometimes the silence was never broken even by a sob. I do not know how they kept back their feelings. But all the time one felt somehow as if Vater was somewhere near us. I felt no dread in the vault, or fear. . . .

I can always, thank goodness, see the funny side of things and have generally been able to laugh and cry at the same time. The first time I saw my mother-in-law after Vater's funeral I made an awful *faux pas*. A woman relative who was present at the funeral wore a quantity of large red stones which, somehow, struck me as odd. So, without thinking, I blurted out to Mathilde: "Oh, my dear, why *was* she covered with carbuncles!" Of course I meant the precious stones of that name, whereas Mathilde and every one present thought for a moment I meant those horrid lumps people sometimes have and which, although I believe very painful, are somehow always considered rather funny and vulgar. I am quite sure my Granny Olivia would never have allowed anyone above the rank of under-housemaid to have carbuncles. But times have changed; I met a Royal Highness the other day who not only had them, but seemed quite proud of the distinction.

August 23, 1907.

I said to Hans that we ought to make out clearly what we had a year to spend and if at the end of the year a larger sum was cleared, as this year when there is one hundred and fifty thousand pounds more than last year, some of it could be taken and used on pictures, extra trains, yachting, and anything else he liked (such as doing up and repairing buildings, cottages and so on), but that the living and general expenditure ought to be kept to one sum. He said we could spend from thirty-five to fifty thousand pounds a year on household expenses. I said there was a slight difference between the two sums ! Now Count Vico Voss and Gottfried Hohenlohe (with whom I dined last night quietly at Borchardt where we did not see anyone) says this is quite absurd, that it is much more likely to be two hundred thousand a year.

Well—somehow I can't realize it all, I don't even think about it, and I only hope that whatever Hans does will be right and in whichever way he thinks I could be of use, I shall help him with all my heart, poor old boy. I think he felt his Father's death very much as he really loved and respected him, and I feel sure intends to do all as well and rightly as possible. But it is difficult I think to find one's absolute self-confidence at once, and later on when one knows the map of all the business and how all its machinery is worked the self-confidence must be there, otherwise the *Verwaltung* will laugh and do whatever it likes, and we shall find ourselves ruled by our own employees. The way a big property like this is managed abroad no one in England has the smallest idea. The people getting wages from Hans are if anything over nine thousand souls ; there are five thousand miners alone.

Dear Vater ! It is quite extraordinary what he has done for the property which he held for fifty years. . . . He was truth itself, honest and noble, lovable because he was always so kind, so appreciative of anything that he felt was right and in anybody who he felt was trying to be and do good ; I am thankful indeed that he has left everything in such perfect order, and thought of every one. The will though will only be opened in a fortnight.

VII

I entered on my new duties and responsibilities suffering from a grievous sense of loss. Vater was an

MY HUSBAND, HANS HEINRICH XV.

unfailing friend; a friend such as one cannot often hope to meet with in a lifetime.

It was said that he left four million pounds sterling. I do not know if this was so or not, but, at his death, a tremendous burden of responsibility fell upon my husband. . . . Mutan, our head agent, managed the property marvellously, and though during his life we sometimes grumbled a little at our lack of means, we always knew that everything was being done with a view to future prosperity. It was a property most difficult to manage as the net income for our use fluctuated from thirty-five thousand to over one hundred and twenty thousand pounds a year. The addition of a shilling a ton to the price of coal gave the estate an extra twenty thousand pounds a year. On a bare statement this sounds a great deal of money, but out of it large incomes were paid to Hans's stepmother Mathilde the Dowager Princess, the brothers and sisters, and with the state we were accustomed to maintain, the places we had to keep up, and our hospitals, homes for aged workpeople, pensions, and other charities, there was not so much to spare as one might suppose.

A dear old bell, that hung in the Gateway Tower at Fürstenstein and rang every night at ten o'clock, fell the night Vater died. After his death everything seemed to go wrong. A year or two later my husband conceived the mad idea of adding to and partly rebuilding Fürstenstein. The whole place was on such a huge scale that the actual alterations cost something like fifteen thousand a year, not counting all the antique furniture and fittings that were put in. There were over fifty beautiful Renaissance mantelpieces. When the alterations were begun Hans was told that even with a hundred men working all the time the work could not be finished for six or seven years. In August, 1914, it was not nearly done. It has been a millstone round my husband's neck ever since it was begun; I always hated it, and had a feeling of foreboding about it.

Managing both Pless and Fürstenstein was such an enormous undertaking that we were, inevitably, very much in the hands of our large staff. Things were well done, but it seemed to me that the spirit of the whole thing was terribly wrong. When a new miners' hospital was being built the details were considered by the officials as too trivial to interest the *Herrschaften*. As for " the Prince," he was only asked his opinion on very large financial questions. I tried very hard to alter this, and to make all the people, the agents, miners, woodcutters and all their wives and children realize that the officials and staff at Fürstenstein and Pless, and even Hans and I were there to advise and help, and that we were always interested in everything that concerned them. But it was an impossible task, the old bad ways had gone on too long for us to be able to break through them. Socialists and others who used to talk so glibly about the Czar " making reforms " have no idea how hard it is to " make " anything, or how much harder even it is to " reform " it once it is made. Were Socialism or any other " ism " established as long as capitalism it would have developed far more numerous and intolerable evils than the existing system has. I say this because Socialism is based on a strictly disciplined organization and, although individuals may often be harsh and overbearing, organizations and systems *always* are.

At this time my own dear father wrote to me:

My darling Daisy,—

Your letter was most interesting. The ceremony, sad as it was, must have had a stirring effect on all present. Few men can expect to die so universally loved and respected. I only hope, darling girl, you and Hans may long enjoy the fruits of so much wisdom and prudence and care and thought, and be the benefactors to all those many dependants on so vast an estate who will look to you for assistance and advice.

I am very philosophic about gossip nowadays, but when one is young one resents it. My diary shows that I was very annoyed about something the Prince

Consort of the Netherlands was reported to have said about Hans, I am sure I don't know why I was annoyed, because what he said about anything was of no importance:

September 3, 1907.

. . . I lunched with Count Stumm-Sierstorpff; he always impresses on me that he is my friend and tells me all the gossip; the latest being that that little ass Mecklenburg, husband of the Queen of Holland, told the Emperor the other day that it would be years before Hans could really stand on his feet, as his debts were enormous! Why, he scarcely knows Hans! He (Count Stumm) told me to-night that people are talking about my going about with footmen in red livery. I had told Hans that I thought the servants ought to be in black, that I did not think black on the hat and a black band on the arm was sufficient; but he said it was impossible to put all the servants and the stables in black and that it was never done in big houses. Well, I am sure I don't know, but I suppose I shall be blamed for this, and it will be called English.

VIII

In November I went to Eaton for a large house-party but can remember only Jimmy Alba and that very remarkable man the late Marquess of Villalobar who was for so long Spanish Ambassador in Brussels. In October I was at Newlands, where we had much talk of the forthcoming visit of the Emperor and Empress to England. They were to pay a State visit to Windsor and, at its conclusion, the Empress was to return home and he was to take a house somewhere in the South of England and have a good rest. Metternich, whom I liked very much, took his social and ceremonial duties too lightly and suffered from the great disadvantage of having no wife to entertain for him, or family to represent him at these numerous less important social functions which are, nevertheless, invaluable as a means of making a Diplomat popular and his work for his country effective. I find the following in my diary:

October, 1907. Newlands.

I dined and lunched with Soveral, very full of news and even more important than usual, as the Queen of Portugal was arriving and he was going to Boulogne to meet her. Metternich was away hunting (which rather annoyed his Secretaries, I think, as there was a lot to do in preparation for the arrival of the Emperor and Empress the day after to-morrow); yet he only got back Wednesday! I dined with him one night, and the last two mornings I got up early and had breakfast with him in my dressing-gown. He is such an old dear and so lonely—he was very pleased. We talked of all sorts of things. . . .

After the Emperor has been to Windsor he will spend three weeks quietly in England and rest after all his troubles and scandals in Berlin![1] He is ill too—Hans says with his throat. I hope to goodness it isn't! Poppets is going to offer him this house but Metternich thinks it will be too small as he wants a lot of bedrooms, his Suite is so enormous.

Hans saw the Emperor in Berlin and the interview was very satisfactory. . . . He said Hans was always to come to him for friendship or advice (I wonder how much of this promise he will keep), and he sent me his best love! I shall write to Eulenburg and tell him of Poppets' offer in case the Emperor cares to accept it.

One of the mornings I came down early to have breakfast with Metternich we were afterwards sitting in his room having a gossip while he smoked a cigarette. Suddenly, without any warning, through a half-open door we saw a footman showing into the ante-room a British Cabinet Minister. I fled and, in my haste, dropped my very gay mules, brocaded, with gold soles and linings. It seemed hopeless to try to recover them, so there they squatted accusingly on the hearthrug while Metternich and the Cabinet Minister solemnly discussed, presumably, serious matters. I am afraid that the German Ambassador's well-known reputation as a confirmed bachelor may have suffered in the British Cabinet. It was a lesson to me never to run away (when you are innocent), and I have sometimes

[1] The Moltke-Harden-Eulenburg Round Table scandals, exposed by Maximilian Harden in the *Zukunft*.

thought that it would make a good central incident for a one-act play or a short story. As a sequel, for example, the British Cabinet Minister trying to identify the Ambassador's secret *chère amie* and obtain from her important information would be diverting. I present the idea to Mr. Edgar Wallace.

However, to return to the Emperor. He did not accept the offer of Newlands; as we surmised, it was too small. Instead he took Highcliffe Castle in Hampshire and made a lengthened stay there, enjoying a complete rest and change. During his visit he went over to lunch at Newlands and Patsy's letter describing what happened is so charming and natural that I must give it in full:

MY DEAR LITTLE SWEET DAISY,—

Your letter and the darling boys' photographs—they arrived this morning, such a pity they were late; but your wire came in time and I read it to the Emperor who was perfectly charming, kissed my hand quite hard twice. It was a lovely day and he planted a tree. While he had his coffee Lehrhammer and Kitty Johnson sang for him—but unfortunately he had not time to go into the garden; he wanted to, but Harry Legge [1] followed us and told him time was up, that he must go on to Beaulieu as he had promised. He seemed to be enjoying his rest so much, poor man. The first he has had for twenty years!

He says he sits at Highcliffe with his hands in his pockets and never opens a paper. When I said I would not be a King for all the world he replied: "Ah yes, you're right; if I could have chosen my life I would have been a country gentleman and quite content with a home like this." I think he is looking very ill, that same *blue* look that his sister [2] has.

The Emperor said: "I had a long talk with Hans Heinrich. I asked him two questions both of which he answered to my satisfaction. I know he thought I would make him a Duke, but he has got to prove himself the grand man his Father was." I replied: "I know he will, Sire, but up till now he has not had much chance." The Emperor then said: "Now he and Daisy will work together for the interest of their people."

---

[1] Colonel Sir Henry Legge, specially attached to the Emperor.
[2] The Queen of Greece.

I told him how lovely Promnitz was, and how you loved it, and how early you got up in the morning, and how fond the Jägers were of you. His great trouble is whether or not you and Hans will put bathrooms in Pless, and not give him that *horrible* dreary suite of rooms again which always gives him the blues! I said, "Well, Sire, you go to Fürstenstein, you won't get the blues there and you'll find plenty of baths!" I then said, "Daisy is doing up all Promnitz and Hans is putting in baths." He also complained bitterly about the rooms he has at your sister-in-law's [1]; "no carpet—and did you see my bed! I am sure they always think I want to skate in those rooms! And the horns! everywhere! It is awful!"

I roared laughing.

Do you know the rooms, Daisy? Next he said, "I always said your daughter had brains and"—bowing to me—"so she ought to have." I made a curtsy, and replied: "Ah, Sire, she has far more brains than me; look at her scheme for draining those rivers; and you should see the interest she takes in her places and everything."

"Oh, yes, yes, I know; I am watching her and I take a great interest in her." "But, Sire," I said, "you can't expect them to do at once all that the old Prince did. He was a richer man; look at what Hans has to give his brothers and sisters." "Ah! but that was all arranged by the Father of Hans; it does not come out of income." "Pardon me, Sire, but I think it does, but—but of course you know best."

You see, Daisy, I did not like to say much for I did not know what I should or might say. He then remarked that you ought to have a house in Berlin. I said, "Daisy has often talked about that and wants to give quite smart parties there." "So she ought," he said. "But, Sire, there again, the house is *not* theirs." "Oh, but that can be all arranged; the other brothers do not want it, or to go to Berlin." "Well, Sire, I don't know; but just you see more of my Daisy; learn really to know her, and you will find what a grand nature she has; and as for Hans, he is the greatest darling, I know, and if half the people I know were as happy as these two are together it would be well for them." He turned round in his chair and looked me straight in the face; "*I am glad to hear this.*" I said: "Yes, Sire, he is the best husband I know."

---

[1] Klitschdorf, Silesia, the home of my sister-in-law, the Princess of Solms-Baruth.—D. OF P.

There, Daisy, is our conversation and I hope I have said nothing I ought not to say.

One thing he said made me smile to myself. I said: "I am never so happy anywhere as I am in Germany at Fürstenstein; and as for Promnitz, it's the most charming place I have ever been in." "Ah, well, there we do not agree—but I am never so happy as I am over here."

God bless you, Sweet, Your PATSY.

He said the King [1] had often told him what a charming place Newlands was; but he had no idea it was so charming as it is.

I should explain that during the lifetime of my father-in-law we made Fürstenstein our principal home. Directly we were married Hans, who has a mania for building, put in bathrooms and other necessities and amenities. Vater adored Pless and Promnitz and would never allow anything to be altered.

We spent the autumn very quietly, dividing our time between Fürstenstein, Pless and Promnitz, at each of which there was necessarily much to do.

Like Patsy, I have always loved Promnitz. It is small, and architecturally it is picturesque without being impressive, being a sort of cross between an Elizabethan timbered house and a Swiss châlet. It overlooks a large, lovely lake and is surrounded by fine trees. When I first knew it the interior was German and dismal. After dear Vater's death (I would not touch a thing while he was alive) I had the walls done in light cheerful colours, bought plenty of comfy chesterfields and arm-chairs and much gay, pretty chintzes and brocades. At first the family were rather aghast, but soon they all came to like the changes. I was always happy there, because we never could have large parties as there was not room. Just the children and members of the family and most of our time spent out of doors shooting and picnicking.

We arranged all sorts of gifts and entertainments for the people at Pless and Fürstenstein for our first Christmas as heads of the family and had a quiet family

[1] King Edward VII.

Christmas party at Fürstenstein. At Pless it would have been too sad.

I found that trying to live in two countries was a very exhausting business. There were my parents, sister, friends and the home of my birth in England, the charm of London in May and June, the wonder of the English summer, the fascination of the great English country house in winter, calling me: on the other hand, my husband, home and children were in Germany and I had many duties and responsibilities, social and otherwise, to discharge in Silesia and in Berlin.

Whilst my father-in-law was alive and I was not reigning Princess of Pless a certain amount of freedom was possible, indeed desirable, as it would not have been good for either of us if I had sat at my mother-in-law's table all the time. Now that circumstances had altered, a great deal more of my time must be spent in Germany. I find that in the two years covered by this chapter I had been to England at least half a dozen times; the Riviera three times; Vienna and Budapest once; to say nothing of frequent journeys between Fürstenstein and Pless and several short stays in Berlin. Fortunately I am an excellent traveller and love travelling.

Now, however, I must make up my mind to be *fürstlich* for long periods. It is an odd thing in life that what it gives with one hand it so often takes away with the other. Now that my husband had succeeded I could spend money, alter things, assert my own will far oftener, but with this freedom came new claims that tied me more than ever to surroundings amid which, try as I might, I had never quite succeeded in making the home of my heart.

CHAPTER FIVE

January, 1908–February, 1909

IN January, 1908, we were at Eaton, our small happy party including the Duke and Duchess of Roxburghe, Lord Mar and Kellie and Violet, Edith Villiers, Joe Laycock and Uncle Lindsay FitzPatrick.

Vater's death and all the resulting business at Fürstenstein and Pless during the autumn had tried both Hans and myself very much and we resolved to have a really good holiday.

I joined Shelagh in Monte Carlo at the end of January and set about the dismal business of hunting for a villa that " would suit everybody." Of course it was quite a futile quest because that sort of villa exists only in one's imagination. However, I found the Villa Cynthia at Cap Martin and there we settled down. Many people find the Cap too windy and the sea there too rough ; but I just loved it and so did the children. And was I not almost next door to Villa Cyrnos and the dear, fascinating Empress Eugénie with her mellowed and unchanging loveliness, like an ancient ivory which, as it grows old in years, grows ever younger in finished grace and beauty.

Silly gossip, so far as I can make out, is one of the greatest curses in life. One is never free from it, and in the cosmopolitan set in which I lived for so many years it was particularly prevalent. Nearly everybody had a feud on somewhere, and most people were always engaged in trying to improve their standing at Court in London, Vienna or Berlin. I always tried to keep clear of intrigue, and gossip unadorned by laughter or wit merely bores me ; I was brought up to consider it the special prerogative of the housekeeper's room and the servants' hall. Moreover, as a family we were all very careless (perhaps too much so) of what people thought or said about us.

One day the Prince and Princess of Saxe-Meiningen, accompanied by the Prince of Lynar, came to luncheon. The Princess, formerly Princess Charlotte of Prussia, was the Emperor's eldest sister and, of course, sister to my friends Princess Adolf of Schaumburg-Lippe, the Duchess of Sparta and Princess Frederick Charles of Hesse. The Princess had a pathetic face, not very well made up and which yet somehow reminded me of her mother the Empress Frederick. I had seen something of her while her husband commanded the troops at Breslau, but did not know her really well. After luncheon, when we were alone, she began :

" Daisy, I am very hurt and angry with you."

" With me, but why ? " (As I scarcely ever saw her I couldn't think what was coming.)

" Why did you cut me ? You stood for at least five minutes by me the other day and cut me dead."

The idea that I should cut the eldest sister of the German Emperor seemed so absurd that I laughed and asked how on earth such a thought could come to her.

" Yes," she went on, " and the Grand Duke Michael always cuts me."

And then the band played.

" Anastasia says I mustn't mind, he is mad," she went on.

" Well, perhaps he is, just a little ; we all are ! " I murmured.

" You know it ? And the awful things he says about you which all get to Berlin ? "

" About my dressing up in uniform—and combinations—and riding on a man's back ? "

" Yes ! my dear, he said that—and that you held a lighted torch."

" Well, Madame, if I dressed as they say, and did this thing, it wouldn't much matter if I held a torch or a night-light ! "

And then I told her the truth; that I had put on Hans's busby and coat and cloak on the top of my own skirt and blouse, and that Shelagh had done the same with Prince Salm's coat, helmet and sword. I added that I had spoken to the Grand Duke Michael about gossiping, indeed had a real row with him last year on the subject.

Then Princess Charlotte began talking about wanting to be friendly with Sophy—having known her years ago, and so on. So I tried to put it all right by saying that I knew Sophy very much wished to see her; that *she* imagined it was Princess Charlotte who didn't want the meeting. (I remembered Sophy did tell me something once but I have forgotten.) Anyway, I knew I was on the right tack as both the Grand Duke and Sophy were only too ready to be on better terms with Germany and the Emperor—and if they could gain this through a friendship with one of the Emperor's sisters, all the better.

In turning over my old diaries it is rather interesting to note that very often I can recall a small matter far better than so-called big ones. One event which happened that spring is as vivid in my mind as if it had taken place only yesterday. I never could bear to be defeated, and have often looked on in astonishment while great strong men allowed some silly convention to upset important plans. I think lots of wives will appreciate that I had the best of the following encounter.

We had ordered the motor at nine-thirty in the evening to take Hans to the station at Mentone as he had to be in Berlin for a very important Polish Bill in the House of Lords; he had been so full of this question for months and every vote against the Bill was of value. There we stood waiting and no motor came. Servants fussed, making believe they were doing something. Nothing happened. At last I said to Fulwell the butler: "Go next door to Madame Stern" (we had been introduced to her at the Carnival) "and see if she will lend her motor."

Hans shouted: " Rot. I won't hear of it."

Then I stamped: " Don't be so idiotic; she won't mind, every minute is valuable." I nodded to Fulwell and he was off.

I then turned to the groom of chambers: " Telephone to the Cap Martin Hotel to send at once a motor or carriage." The answer was that they had none.

Fulwell came back: Madame Stern was at Monte Carlo, the motor also.

Then I thought of the people who had just gone into the third villa up the road, and I said to Hans I would go there, but this was really more than he could bear: " Do you think that you, the Princess of Pless, are going to run about begging for motors—to people you don't even know?" (I knew them quite well by sight.) " Come in at once," and he pulled me into the hall. " You'll never see me in this infernal place again," and he turned to get a cigarette.

I said nothing, but slipped a white fur coat over my evening frock and in a pair of thin satin shoes flew up the road to the villa. It was quite dark, and there was some distance to go; the first gate was locked; I went further and found a little gate unlocked; I rushed up, rang the bell and could hear the servants talking. A lazy-looking French footman at last opened the door; I told him to go and order a motor (I knew they had one as I had seen them in it in the morning), but he walked away and did nothing; then the butler came —I explained—and he hesitated to go upstairs.

" *Ses patrons—Monsieur et Madame—étaient au lit.*" I said I did not care: " Go and wake them." Up he went. Again I heard voices; time was flying. I then went half-way upstairs myself and called:

" Mr. Kingsley, Mr. Kingsley!" (I heard later that his name was Kingland.) Out he came on the top landing, a pair of naked legs and slippers, a flannel dressing-gown and a bald head.

He only said: " Come up and see my wife," and then hid.

Up I went; she was in bed. I again explained.

She hurried off her maid to wake the chauffeur. I panted " Thank you " and flew.

I followed the maid to the garage—all darkness. At last we found the car; the butler lit it, while, through shut doors, I bribed the chauffeur to hurry:

" *Venez, venez, je vous donnerai vingt francs.*"

" *Mais qu'est-ce qu'il y a—mon Dieu—mon Dieu—un peu de patience.*"

" *Non, non,*" I screeched, " *je vous donnerai quarante francs.*" At last we got the man out. He didn't know where the station was—then I found that the footman did, so I bundled him into the car:

" Put on that coat " ; there was one hanging there. He was speechless with fury, but got in.

When I got back to Hans there was still ten minutes to catch the train, but fortunately no time for explanations. We started; the lamps would not stay lit; the chauffeur took the wrong and most curving road to Mentone; at last we got into the town along the tram-lines; I saw in the distance what looked like a station; the car began to bump about—it felt as if we were in a ploughed field. I made the footman get out saying: " *Où le footman peut aller à pied il faut suivre avec la voiture.*" I told him to implore them to keep back the train even a moment. He went. Soon we came to a closed wooden barrier across the road: I tore out—and myself lifted the wooden top—and the car passed through on the right road that led to the station. When we got there (it was the wrong entrance) we clambered over the place where the luggage was laid out for inspection.

There were just two minutes before the train was due to leave. I shouted breathlessly: " Where is the Berlin express," and they answered: " *Pas encore arrivé, Madame : dix minutes de retard.*"

I sat down to recover and Hans too, poor darling, both of us with a very happy smile. I had got what I wanted and so had he. He kissed me good-bye and said: " Well done, Daisy, that's just the wife I want."

He forgot how he had tried to prevent my going to the Villa and how furious he was even when I returned with the car. What pleased me most was not that the train was late, but that we had got there just in time even if it had been punctual. Hans went off quite happily, convinced that he had done it all. Men are like that.

In March I stayed for a few days with dear Sophy at Cannes. I had spoken to her about what had happened when Princess Charlotte came to luncheon; as a result the Princess accepted an invitation to stay at Villa Kasbek and I was really going there to meet her and do my little bit towards consolidating the happily renewed friendship.

During my stay I told the Princess exactly what Hans and I thought of the wicked Polish Expropriation Bill which the Prussian Government were trying to pass. In many cases it meant people being forced to give up their ancestral homes, often the very land containing the graves of their fathers. And all just because they were Poles. Princess Charlotte absolutely agreed with me and said she did not dare to go to Berlin just then as she would not have been able to control her feelings about the matter and would inevitably have got into trouble for expressing them.

The idea of a nation situated as Poland then was uniting to overthrow the Governments of Prussia, Russia and Austria was of course fantastic; yet it was one that haunted so-called statesmen. For years Prussia alternately cajoled and oppressed the Poles and misgoverned that portion of Poland incorporated in the German Empire. Throughout the reign of William II., the Polish question was second in importance only to that of Alsace-Lorraine. Pless was formerly, and is now again, in Poland, and both Hans and I were always sympathetic towards the Polish people and their aspirations. Indeed my husband's pro-Polish activities were not always acceptable to the Emperor, and were sometimes used by ill-disposed persons to try and do us both harm. The wicked

THE CASTLE OF PLESS.

Polish Expropriation Bill was passed [1] in spite of all Hans and his friends could do and I was glad that by making my husband catch that train I had assured at least one extra vote against it.

Another day the Grand Duchess Anastasia came to see me. We had a long talk about herself and I gave her some good advice, most of which was, I fear, entirely unacceptable. However, she was by then very happy about the Crown Princess Cecile and herself looked younger and happier than I had ever seen her. She was a very charming, but very unwise lady.

And now we were to have our real change by paying a long-projected visit to Spain. Shelagh, Hans and I started off for Madrid leaving Ursula and the boy, Edward George Hugh, with Patsy and Poppets at Ruthin. We expected perfect weather and, as always happens, we were disappointed.

The three days we spent at Seville it did nothing but rain ; one did not expect that in mid-April so far south.

My diary reminds me that, much as one loves and longs to travel, the most wonderful thing about it is how it intensifies one's love for England. If all the English were made to live abroad for a time how they would all adore their own land :

April 25, 1908. Seville.

I have been feeling a bit sad to-day, having just heard little [2] Shelagh talk of London and the season, her Polo week at Eaton, her big homes and her hunting, her joy in feeling that she is going to visit the house of her birth and to be with friends of the same feelings and race. Even George, with whom everything is not quite as he would wish it, has his little home near London, his friends close to. And I—I stand away—apart from it all, apart from them, and have to make and live my own life which I honestly do with the greatest interest and much love ; I love my garden in Fürstenstein and my little *Schwarzen Graben*, or as I prefer to call it, *Ma Fantaisie*—but

[1] On September 27, 1908 : this law, however, was never actually put into execution.

[2] A term of endearment much used by the authoress and her family ; the Duchess of Westminster is tall.

my soul—what I cling to—what I put out my hands to and wish to draw nearer me and hug—is the little island called England. This isn't nonsense or exaggeration, it is the sentiment born in my girlhood of dreams and romance—lights of gold and silver, a sky of stars, a world of sunshine; it is all that I have left buried there, and whose grave I stand over now when I go back home. And in passing by I have to try and pick up my stick of courage and go forward in a land across the sea, and think of my sons who will wear Prussian uniforms, and the busy life I want to lead and the good I hope to fulfil and——

Spain was wonderful and disappointing—as nearly all places, things and people are—and oh! the Spanish trains. All the same, everyone who can should visit this ancient country with its fascinating and unique combination of Moorish and Spanish civilization. Seville and Madrid most people know; yet Burgos, Granada and many smaller places are far more interesting. My diary gives only one entry under Madrid, as most of our time was wasted over social affairs. We stayed with Jimmy Alba at his beautiful and hospitable home:

April 29, 1908. Madrid, Palais de Liria.

Impossible to find even one moment to write. We arrived here from Seville hours late. The wheels of our carriage got hot so we had to bundle out just when we were comfortably settled and get into other carriages which they put on and which were hard and uncomfortable.

The next morning Hans insisted on my leaving cards on the Mistress of the Robes, the Duchess de San Carlos; then he went to the German Embassy and I came home. After luncheon we drove about the City and then went to watch the Polo. It was quite a good game; the little King, who only started to play lately, sits very well.

Shelagh and I watched the Holy Week processions through the streets and found them tawdry and boring. As for the Spanish spectators, they were not a bit reverent and appeared to treat the whole thing as a carnival.

The King, Jimmy Alba and lots of men we knew,

all bearing great names, walked one day in the Procession dressed, I think, in the costume of some mediæval Order of Knighthood.[1] Anyhow, they wore odd-looking feathered hats and long cloaks. Shelagh and I knew that the King, Alba, and several others were going to play in a private Polo match immediately after. In a Catholic country this sort of mixing up of sacred and secular appears to be the general custom, whereas we Protestants never dare think of God and worldly affairs at the same moment—at least we must rigidly act as if we didn't. I used often to wonder what really were the thoughts lurking behind the smugly severe faces in the Lutheran church at Pless on Sundays!

One evening we went at ten o'clock to the Cathedral for some ceremony the name of which I have forgotten. The place was packed, every one standing. We remained only a short time as to stay was quite out of the question. The men surrounding us on all sides pressed as close as ever they could and began pinching us in a manner quite impossible to describe. At last I turned to one and hit him hard on the face. Count Vico who was standing near thought I had suddenly gone mad. I rather enjoyed the prospect of a row, but the man did nothing, merely kept brazenly staring at me while, for the moment, I felt quite murderous. I was not at all sure that he was the right man, but I determined to punish someone.

After I got back to the Riviera I jotted down in my diary a few more impressions of Spanish weather and Spanish Royal hospitality:

May 10, 1908. Cap Martin, Villa Cynthia.

It seems years since I left Spain; and all the time as I sit here close to the sea in the hot sun, and hear the birds, and the doves cooing, and the precious boys playing, it makes me wild to think I spent a whole month away from them, and I have to leave again in four days. Of course I am very glad

---

[1] Probably the Order of Calatrava, one of the four great military Orders surviving in Spain since the days of the Moors.

to have seen Spain and all the lovely Renaissance architecture which I love. We lunched at the Palace with the King and Queen, and the King showed us everything—stables too, which are badly kept; and I never saw such a mass of decrepit-looking horses; he requires English help over this.

The lunch was at the Palace La Granja [1] (I can't spell it). It poured all the time, and the fountains which are magnificent and which were turned on, poured all over the paths which soon became like rivers. The Queen gets a baby next month so was not feeling at her best, poor dear.

The day I left we went to the Escorial Palace; it was lovely, one of the two fine days we had. We went in Alba's car and one of the King's cars which he lent to Prince Alexander of Battenberg.[2] The King could not come himself as he and the Queen had to open an exhibition of pictures. . . .

Much as I enjoyed our Spanish visit I found it very tiring. The trains and roads were so bad. Shelagh went home direct from Madrid. Hans, Count Vico Voss and I travelled back to Cap Martin from Biarritz by motor. As soon as I arrived at the Villa Patsy and Poppets joined me: I was really very ill and could not see strangers. The Empress Eugénie and one or two intimate friends came regularly; otherwise we were alone. Poppets painted all day and looked fifty. In June nearly every one has left the Riviera and it is at its very best. My diary gives an impression of how we passed the time:

June 4, 1908. Cap Martin.

Villa Cynthia still, although I am writing in the garden of a little villa up above us belonging to the Empress Eugénie, where she puts young bachelors when her own villa is full. She has lent us the garden all the time as it is nice for the children to play in and cooler than by the sea. The garden consists simply and deliciously—of only a green field with olive trees and tall grass full of wild flowers; a goat lies munching under a tree, and cocks and hens strut and scratch about and little birds with different voices are making musical conversation on every bough.

---

[1] The spelling is correct. [2] Now Marquess of Carisbrooke.

I have been out of bed and living on the balcony and in this garden for the past three days ; I have practised my guitar and have found out a lot of chords and can sing all the simple songs to it now ; it quite amuses me, and it is a good guitar which Hans bought me in Spain. Workmen are driving by in carts and singing !

The evenings are too divine—fireflies amongst the trees and a new moon, reflected in a perfectly calm sea with the lights of Monte Carlo glistening in the distance and making long bright shining spaces in the still water. And the frogs croak away in a solemn rhythm, the monotony of which I find soothing and homely ; in the evenings it is the only sound one hears. And then I have taken my guitar and begun to sing ; and Patsy who has stayed with me all the time remembers lots of tunes and all the old Irish melodies of Thomas Moore which Sir John Stevenson,[1] who was Granny's grandfather, set to music, much of it I believe at Headfort. Then there is my precious baby, Lexel . . . in a blue pinafore and a blue cotton hat the colour of his eyes ; there is nothing in all the world and surely nothing in Heaven to compare with " one's own child," and the kiss of his little mouth !

The last thing I did before leaving Cap Martin for Germany was to write to the Empress a long letter about the Silesian lacemakers. They mostly worked in their own homes and the middle-men who purchased their lace underpaid and sweated them frightfully. I wanted to establish a voluntary selling organization, staffed by ladies, to distribute the work direct to the shops in Berlin, London and elsewhere, and I wanted the Empress to give me her practical support in breaking down the frantic opposition I was sure to arouse. Every one, I realized, would be against me and would make endless difficulties.

When the time came to go home, as I had been so unwell, we decided to have one of our special coaches sent down from Germany so that I could travel direct and avoid the fatigues of the ordinary trains.

[1] Thomas, second Marquess of Headfort, born 1787, married in 1834, Olivia, eldest daughter of Sir John Stevenson, who composed or arranged much of the music for Moore's *Irish Melodies*.

June 8, 1908. In the train to Fürstenstein.

We left Mentone yesterday at three, and get to Freiburg to-morrow at the same hour. This is a very comfortable saloon, and I have a bed in it from Fürstenstein; besides this double carriage I am in, there are two very nice little bedrooms and other small compartments with beds in each. I have baby and Smith, a nurse, and a massage nurse with me, my maid Marie, two housemaids, two footmen and the groom of the chambers; so it really is not much extra as far as expense goes, the difference being on their tickets, first-class instead of second. And if I had gone via Paris and stayed at the Ritz, it would have cost more in the end, and it is really less tiring to get the whole journey over in one stretch. But the French officials are furious; they told the agent at Cannes who wired about it for me that they never expected the saloon would be so big, and so on. The result is now we have been dawdling all the way, and stopping at every little station and sidings. They soon found they had to put on an engine to shunt us about—instead of horses. We are two hours late and have missed all the restaurant connections, and I don't believe they want to get us on. We are in a siding now at half-past two, surrounded by open-eyed furious-looking French officials.

I think the French peasants are very happy contented people; they live on their own plot of land which yields them nearly all they want to support themselves; the country is rich and prosperous. And to think of the Empress Eugénie passing and travelling through this divine country—a dethroned Queen—it must feel very tragic, almost brutal, poor woman. She came so often to see me when I was ill, and is a darling.

While I was being lazy at Cap Martin with the children a delightful event took place. Gottfried Hohenlohe, to whom we and all his friends were so devoted, married the Archduchess Marie-Henriette of Austria. At that time I hardly knew her, having only met her once, on the occasion when we dined with the two Emperors in Vienna a year or so before. The young Archduchesses were there with their mother the Archduchess Frederick; I thought them all fresh, unspoiled and charming, as indeed the sisters of dear Christa Salm-Salm were bound to be. We asked Gottfried and his bride to a shoot at Promnitz in

September; he came, but she could not, as she was not quite well just then. However, Gottfried's prophecy that we should get to like her as well as Christa turned out to be quite true.

It is curious how things change. In 1917 Gottfried's little niece Princess Françoise of Hohenlohe-Schillingfürst married the Archduke Maximilian, brother of the unlucky Emperor Karl. They now live mostly at Starnberg, quite near Munich, and have two boys who, after the children of the Empress Zita, are next in succession to the Hungarian throne.

II

In June King Edward and the Czar met at Revel. The meeting caused a great deal of discussion and some uneasiness in Germany. The Emperor affected to consider Russia negligible and, at the same time, wanted her as a friend. In fact, just then and indeed right up to the Great War, whether inspired and directed by the Emperor or not, the policy of Germany was a vacillating one and, therefore, inevitably offended friend and foe alike. We know now that both "Willie" and "Nicky" were busy abusing King Edward behind his back. The King saw far more clearly than both Lord Lansdowne and Sir Edward Grey whither German diplomacy was leading. He used every gift he possessed—and they were varied and unusual—to strengthen his country against the day of trial, and this service alone should secure for him a high place in history. I do not know if the King and the Czar discussed the recent annexation of Bosnia and Herzegovina by Austria. One of the greatest moral blunders ever made, it was the initial cause of the outburst of the Great War, and will have consequences that will reverberate through all future history.

It always interested and astonished me to note how much more truly King Edward was appreciated abroad than at home. Foreigners sometimes perhaps overestimated the extent of his direct interference in international affairs, but, in England, even by men like Lord Balfour, Lord Haldane and Lord Oxford, he was consistently underrated. There is a "serious" English type of mind which, in spite of its brilliance, can never appreciate the fact that a man or woman can love life and gaiety, and yet handle serious things seriously and with great success. Yet in history there are many examples to bear out the truth of this.

People who live but little outside England and who are continually surrounded by those who share their political views nearly always minimize the imperiousness of geographical necessities. England and France simply had to be friends, and in 1914 England simply had to back Belgium and France or disappear for ever from the stage of European politics. This, in turn, would have led to the downfall of the Empire, because not one of the proud young Dominions would have remained part of an Empire that had traded its honour and its glorious past for a mess of pottage and called the bargain peace.

A letter from my friend Prince Gottfried Hohenlohe, written at the end of June from St. Petersburg, puts the situation amusingly and well. I might add that Monsieur Izvolsky, who was by no means a statesman of the first rank or a sincere friend of England, was succeeded in 1911 as Russian Secretary of State for Foreign Affairs by his own Under-Secretary, Monsieur Sazonov, a much abler man, who, realizing the military shortcomings of his country, was sincerely devoted to Peace, and who, as it happened, remained in charge of the Russian Foreign Office until the beginning of Russia's downfall in 1916. Prince Gottfried wrote:

Did you read about the *entrevue* at Revel? It *is* amusing how England—of course it is only the King—knows how to get everything he wants. He wanted to be friends with Russia and he knew awfully well how to manage Izvolsky, the Russian Minister, who is a fearful snob and likes *de poser en Anglais*. It really makes me laugh after all that the Emperor of Russia told me about, I mean *against* England. I wrote to some

Russian ladies asking if they had already little *Saints Edouards* in the corners of their rooms. As you know, the Russian must be always putting some new saint into the corner of the walls—ceilings and so on.

"The Grand Emperor" had of course to make a speech at Döberitz—I suppose because it was so hot! At least I try to excuse all the nonsense he talked by the awful heat. Why always talk? I don't think it means strength if one has always to talk about it. An old proverb says that a horse shoe only clatters (I mean makes a noise) if a nail is missing, and that is quite true. Revel was in fact a bluff, meant to make Germany, especially "William the Great" feel uneasy—and that just that happened so quickly, was the great success. It would have been so much wiser to keep quiet and smiling—*comme si de rien n'était et comme si—ce qui est du reste vrai*—neither England without an army, nor Russia without army, navy and money, nor France in its complete disorganization, could seriously think of hurting Germany in any possible way. But he must speak *et se démener—c'est plus fort que lui.*

After Spain and the Riviera I greatly enjoyed a stay at Fürstenstein, but, as I was still feeling the effects of the illness I had gone through at Cap Martin, I decided early in July to go to Wildungen in Hesse to do a sort of cure and have a quiet holiday with the children all by ourselves. It was a delightful and exhilarating time, amidst quaint villages and picturesque scenery. The Empress and her younger children were at the Palace of Wilhelmshohe, near Kassel. It was only some thirty miles away and she asked me and the children to motor over and spend the day, which we did. The Palace is very fine and was the residence of Napoleon III., when he was a prisoner-of-war in 1870, and there he and my dear Empress Eugénie met for the first time after the downfall of the Empire. My diary describes the visit:

July 29, 1908. Wildungen.

Yesterday I went to see the Empress, taking Hansel and Lexel and Smith. The Empress remembered she had seen Smith before and asked if she had not got another name. I said Thirza, and then she recollected Smith had been eleven years with her sister Princess Frederick Leopold. But she never said " Yes, my nephews are nice," not a word about them. Smith tells me there was always great jealousy between the two sisters about their children. The Emperor is in Berlin; no one else was there but the two little grandsons, the eldest Wilhelm, aged two, and the second one Ludwig, only nine months. Baby Lexel had a gala day; they all kissed him and said he was a darling; his eyes were like forget-me-nots and he ran about and picked flowers where he oughtn't to have done. Nothing could have been nicer than the Empress was—but—what a silly woman she is! Clothes and children are really her chief conversation and the only thing she thoroughly understands. Just herself and one lady-in-waiting and I and the children; she had on a chiffon dress with a long train and a large ugly hat covered with feathers. The same sort of dress she wears for lunch on the *Hohenzollern* at Kiel—instead of a smart, plain yachting frock. I wore an embroidered muslin dress and hat, Baby Lexel his blue pinafore (or tunic) to match his eyes and Hansel white drill. They all say Baby is like me and I feel as if this is a great compliment—as it is not a bit true I know. His hair is much lighter and his eyes bluer—and he has the sweetest smile. He said his poetry that he had learned for my birthday. Little Hansel was very shy and never said *Majestät*—but simply " yes " and " no," and kept his mouth open all the time! I felt really at one moment when he spoke in a whisper with his hat in front of his mouth that I would like to go up and give him one shake. The Empress asked me what I wished to do about the lace industry in Schmiedeberg. I told her (it is too long to write here) and I hoped and imagined she would give me some ideas or advice. But she never made a single proposal, only " it interests me very much and I shall be much obliged if something could be done to help the poor people." For a woman in that position I never met *anyone* so devoid of any individual thought, or agility of brain and understanding. She is just like a good, quiet, soft cow—that has calves and eats grass slowly and then lies down and ruminates. I have never really *talked* to her before. I looked right into her eyes to see if I could see anything behind them, even pleasure or sadness, but they might have been glass. She kissed me at leaving and stood on the steps to see us off in the motor! I thought of the time I had called at the Palace in a motor to leave cards about five years ago in Potsdam but had *not* gone up to the door; they only saw me from the windows, yet there was a great deal of talk. And when I wrote a furious letter to the Mistress of the Robes, Countess Brockdorff, and said it was a public road and that I could not have come in a sedan chair or a *Rollstuhl* and that the sentinel on duty let me in; she answered: "Yes, dear Princess, of course you were not in the wrong, but the truth is the Empress does not want the Emperor to see too much of them for fear he will want one!" (A motor.)

Now of course he has great yellow ones all over the place decorated and painted on every corner with beautiful eagles with outspread wings and crowns on!

I sent the Empress this morning a post-card photograph of me and the two boys done in Wildungen; Hansel wrote on it in German that they both sent Her Majesty their humble thanks for a lovely afternoon and hoped they had both behaved well; then Baby signed it—I held his hand—and I signed too.

July 29, 1908. In the Train.

We have had lovely days in Wildungen; we went fishing several days and caught lovely fish in the river with a fly. One day we sent Smith and Baby home early and Hansel and I stayed out; we had brought supper with us—hard-boiled eggs, cold ham, compôt-salad and bread and butter; we began eating by the river but the mosquitoes were so awful we had to move away into a cornfield, which was a little better. We were both so happy. I too felt like a child, as we had promised to be back by eight, not later, for Hansel to get to bed at the right time. And we did not get home till half-past nine and I could not be *fürstlich* and pretend it was the motor, as I thought it wasn't right to tell stories whilst Hansel was present! The day before yesterday we went to a new place, to a better river indicated by the doctor, and I caught seven nice trout in half an hour; they wouldn't rise till half-past six, it was too hot. Two mornings we spent with a charming old clergyman and visited the Hospital and two "homes" and then went to see his wife, who was delighted. I sent toys to the children, and chocolate and cake to the old women, and cigars to the men; they were all charmed and sent me flowers this morning before I left. I bought a present for each Sister and sent a photograph of myself and the children to the clergyman.

Oh! to think I shall be in England to-morrow morning; I am pining to get there, I wasn't there all last summer and only a fortnight last January. To see the sea and little Newlands and true friends, my comfy bed at the Embassy (the children go to Grosvenor House) and I to dear old Wolff-Metternich the Ambassador. We stay with Robin and Juliet Duff for Cowes, which will be delightful; they have taken a house on the Island.

We had a perfect time at Newlands and Cowes, whence I went direct to Eaton, leaving the children by the sea with Patsy. Somehow Newlands was the one place where I never felt any sense of disappointment. My visits there were always as perfect as I had anticipated they would be. Next to Newlands I enjoyed my visits to Eaton more than anything and, while there, I was of course within easy reach of Ruthin.

Shelagh had an enormous party for a Polo Tournament. There were Sibell Grosvenor and George Wyndham, Edie Castlereagh, Lettice Cholmondeley, Margaret Crewe, Peñaranda, Villavieja, Lords Wodehouse, Shrewsbury and Rocksavage, Captain E. D. Miller—in fact all the noted Polo players. Then there was Lord Hugh Cecil by way of contrast. There were thirty-five or forty people staying in the house, therefore I cannot possibly remember who they all were. But it was a perfect visit as Shelagh is a marvellous hostess and always made things go. Did some lurking secret dread make us all greedily snatch enjoyment to the utmost in those fateful years immediately preceding the War?

August 16, 1908. Eaton Hall, Chester.

Oh, diary, diary, I have been here one week, one happy week, laughing and feeling younger than I have felt for years. This has been the nicest time I have ever spent here and tomorrow I leave for Harrogate, to spend one night with Patsy, who is doing a cure there for rheumatism; and two nights to Gladys de Grey for grouse shooting. Robin and Juliet will be there; Gladys de Grey is Juliet's mother.

I have been riding here on a pony—we have all ridden polo ponies belonging to the men who have been playing; this has been a Polo Week and there have been six teams about ıere, all the men staying in the house and the ponies in the stables; we have been thirty-six every night for dinner. One day we rode in a gymkhana, lots of races of all sorts, taking apples from posts and throwing them into a bucket of water, then riding in and out between posts, and so on. We danced and played Poker in the evenings. Young Rocksavage[1] is the most beautiful man you can imagine, but with all that very manly; he is like an old picture, every feature, even his hands and his teeth are perfect; and all the men say he is beautifully made. Well, Constance Richardson tried to charm . . . in every way; at night she danced with very little on, short chiffon skirt and bare legs and feet—like Miss Ruth St. Denis the new dancer in London and Miss Maud Allan. I thought I would try once and see if I had any attractions left and I found I had; I talked and walked with each man in turn. . . . Jack and Shelagh teased me and I enjoyed myself and tried to make myself look nice and I felt young and frivolous just for one week. It isn't much, diary dear, for I am really not so very old. And I am never frivolous in Germany, nor do I laugh and make silly jokes and amuse them all, as I do here. I don't know why—but oh, it's all so different there.

I was going on to the de Greys from Eaton and on the way stayed a night at Harrogate which, according to my diary, does not seem to have made a very good impression on me:

August 19, 1908. Harrogate.

Came here from Chester for one night to see little Patsy and go to-morrow to the de Greys to Studley Royal—quite a comfortable journey, three hours from Manchester, to which place I motored from Eaton and missed the train by five minutes. Hedwig, my maid, had gone on with luggage, cushions and money, and I had not a penny, so borrowed five shillings from the guard of the train. Had dinner with Patsy in her little sitting-room (she is at a lodging-house, not bad) and afterwards we went to the Hotel to hear a thought-reader who was very poor. Met Frankie Teck, and Helen Vincent; they also are doing a cure. It is a horrible cold windy town and smells of sulphur everywhere. The drinking place is dirty and stuffy, and the baths dark and overladen with furniture and plush curtains, and the rooms look like

[1] Now Marquess of Cholmondeley.

compartments in a railway carriage. I should never dream of taking a cure at an English watering-place. Harrogate seems very badly managed anyway!

Gladys de Grey was of course the late Lord Pembroke's sister and remarkably handsome, clever and distinguished-looking. Her husband, who was also charming, was a marvellous shot. His father, the first Marquess of Ripon, who died in 1909, did the honours of his lovely Yorkshire home with that somewhat old-fashioned courtesy that has always appealed to me. He treated one as being entirely human and feminine, yet with a goddess somewhere not too far back in one's ancestry. I shall always remember him showing me Fountains Abbey which is perfectly situated in Studley Royal Park. Nothing could exceed the moving beauty of this truly marvellous ruined Abbey. There is a great open emerald green valley with a silver stream loitering, and, towering upwards against a distant background of magnificent trees this unbelievably beautiful soft grey tumbled mass of frozen history.

III

In the autumn we were greatly looking forward to a visit from the King and Queen of Spain at Pless. It had all been discussed when we were in Madrid in the spring. I had a large, and I hoped, interesting and amusing party asked to meet their Majesties, and Hans had provided some good sport. Here is a letter about it from the Queen:

MIRAMAR, SAN SEBASTIAN, *September* 20, 1908.

DEAR PRINCESS OF PLESS,—

As my husband is dreadfully busy just now, he has asked me to write and thank you for your kind letter, which he received this morning. We are both looking forward quite enormously to our stay with you, and all that you have arranged for us to do sounds too delightful. I think Alfonso wrote to you the date we could arrive, but alas! we shall not be able to stay longer than two days as we have to be at Barcelona on the 19th or 20th October. Isn't that too odious?

Another thing I want to tell you quite privately, and that is that Alfonso strained his side rather badly at Polo and the doctor said he must not ride for some time or he would not get it right. Therefore it would be very kind of you if you could arrange something else instead of the hunting. I hope this is not asking too much. Au revoir, dear Princess of Pless.—Believe me, Yours very sincerely,

VICTORIA EUGÉNIE.

And now I must give one glimpse of a small shooting party at Promnitz, which I liked best of all my German homes. It was not often we could have them there as it was too small—or seemed small after Fürstenstein and Pless. Looking back, we appear to have been able to put up a good many people. The stag-shooting there was particularly fine. Hans once told me that every stag cost between three hundred and four hundred pounds. It seemed absurd and yet some of our guests used to shoot three or four. My diary says:

September 27, 1908. Promnitz.

Sophy and the Grand Duke Michael left only to-day. Baron von Reischach came two days ago and also left to-day. I was very sorry to say good-bye to Sophy and M. He really behaved beautifully; I never knew him so nice and quiet. He said nothing nasty about anyone, and we did not quarrel once. He was most affectionate! Just as much as Sophy would have stood, I think! He keeps on asking me to call him "Mich." so at last I said I would do so only when Sophy called my husband Hans! The great excitement was the moment when he asked Hans to *duzen* him. Hans found great difficulty in doing it! He told me it was awful at the station to-day when they had to kiss each other on each cheek at parting.

I have always been convinced, and still am, that the more the great ones of the earth meet each other the better, and, in my own little way, I have ever done all I could to make such meetings possible. Of course the ordinary people should meet too, but that is not so easy. English, French and German politicians have always sat at home far too much, and still do so. I know that at present it is the fashion to consider Royalty as an obsolete and useless institution. Like every other institution in an imperfect world, it has its drawbacks. But the history, traditions and family connections of members of reigning Houses at least saves them from insularity and, quite often, gives their views and opinions on any question a positive real value—a value which may, quite possibly, transcend their intellectual attainments. Just as the children of a "horsey" family seem very often to be born with an intuitive knowledge and understanding of horses, so Royalties from their birth seem to have an uncanny flair for public affairs. Why, an accurate knowledge of their own family history and relationships is in itself no mean apprenticeship to history.

I knew the Queen of Spain and the German Empress had never met and, with such thoughts as these in my mind, I wrote to the Empress as follows; she had just been staying at Klitschdorff with my brother-in-law and sister-in-law Fritz and Lulu Solms:

PROMNITZ, *September* 28, 1908.

DEAREST MADAME,—

Will Your Imperial Majesty forgive this letter which is to say what an enormous honour and pleasure it would be to us if you would come to Pless from the 14th of October till the 17th. The King and Queen of Spain are coming then quietly after their Vienna visit. There will be only two small shoots as it is not possible to arrange a good pheasant shoot so early in the year. But I hope to arrange a nice little party.

Please, dear Madame, do not let it be said "The Queen of Spain has not yet paid an official visit to Berlin." She has had a baby each year; besides, the King of Spain *has* paid his official visit to Germany.[1] The King is so young and so brave in character. And all the time in Madrid I thought often how he reminded me of the Crown Prince in many ways. He loves riding and shooting and life in every way. I do not know if he is a great friend of the Crown Prince,

[1] November 6, 1905.

MY FATHER-IN-LAW, HANS HEINRICH XI.

but I am sure they would like each other very much; and the more the important and great people in this world like each other, the happier nations become and the brighter the future: I am sure of this. Dearest Madame, forgive me saying this; and only to you.

I hope Your Imperial Majesty had a nice time in Klitschdorff. Here it has been divine, and marvellous stags. Sophy and the Grand Duke Michael only left to-day. I was very sorry to say good-bye to them. I hope the two little grandsons are well and that you had a very happy summer. May I send my humble remembrances to the Crown Prince and the Crown Princess.

I have the honour to remain, dearest Madame, with humble affection, Your Imperial Majesty's obedient servant,

DAISY OF PLESS.

While the Spanish Sovereigns were at Vienna the King was hurriedly recalled to Madrid because of some political crisis about which I have forgotten; the visit to Pless did not therefore take place. We were dreadfully disappointed. At a ball at the Spanish Embassy in Vienna the night before they left, the King was talking in German to one of Charles Kinsky's sisters and saying what a disappointment it was to him not to be able to visit Pless, and how much he had been looking forward to the shooting. He suddenly looked hard at her, saying, "Do you speak English?" When she replied "Yes," he seized both her hands in his and said: "This is how I feel—damn!"

Very soon after this, when on our way to England, we spent a few days in Berlin, staying at an hotel, as the big ugly house in the Wilhelmstrasse was closed. The house was a gloomy place, and as, in Continental fashion, all the members of the family had a right to use it, we never spent much money doing it up or cared to stay there.

At the Opera in Berlin it was the custom for the Emperor and Empress and all the Royalties to walk in the Foyer during the intervals and hold a sort of Court. One night, soon after our arrival, we were doing the customary promenade when the Emperor came up to Patsy and me, looking, I thought, rather wild and mad. "Well," he said, "why didn't the King of Spain come to Pless?" I answered that he had important business and was obliged to return to Madrid for a Cabinet meeting—"as once Your Majesty had to hurry back to Berlin and leave your stag-shooting, and as the King of England once hurried back to London in the middle of a Newmarket Meeting."

"Nonsense! England was the reason he didn't come! If there is ever any bother or misunderstanding it always comes from England"—and he glared at me.

"But, Your Majesty, how can you imagine for one moment that England cares whether the King and Queen of Spain come to Silesia or not?"

There was a silence.

Then he looked at my tiara and said: "So you have got your fan on your head again." This was an old joke, so I laughed and said something about His Majesty forgetting nothing. I meant this to be nasty, as I knew of many things he would have liked to forget if he could.

Then I added: "Your Majesty seems to be in a cross mood to-night."

Patsy, who from shyness was sometimes laughably tactless, then said: "When will Your Majesty come to England again?" This fairly drove him away. He made a sort of pirouette on one leg and almost hissed out over his shoulder:

"I shall come when I am wanted." He did not hear the polite whisper about his being always wanted with which Patsy tried to mollify him.

We were contemplating a party at Pless in November for the Emperor and I wrote to my brother-in-law, Conrad Hochberg, to ask him to come. The Emperor could be very disagreeable if he did not approve of anyone in any way and he of course considered he had a perfect right to regulate every detail of one's private life. Conny's answer declining my invitation throws light on this side of the Emperor's character:

SCHLOSS DAMBRAU, OBERSCHLESIEN, *October* 22, 1908.

. . . Besides, I am sure my company would not be a success; I know for certain that the Kaiser disapproves of my living in England a great deal; the last time I met him in Pless when Vater was alive he only said good-day and good-bye to me and never another word to me between, so that I felt a very useless member of the party; he only would do the same thing again and would give me unasked advice about my being in England instead of Dambrau, which I certainly would not swallow. Moreover, I would like so much to give him a bit of my mind, which I could not do either, so on the whole it would only be unpleasant and awkward. . . .

At the end of October (1908) the Emperor gave his famous interview to the *Daily Telegraph*. It created a most extraordinary fuss. Bülow disclaimed responsibility and indeed went so far (in public) as to extract from the Emperor a promise that in future he would be a good boy and not go about upsetting apple-carts. Now there is, in the good sense, quite a lot of the woman in the Emperor; he never forgot a slight and he could be feminine in his malice when anyone humiliated him. From that moment Bülow's fate was sealed and his master only awaited a convenient opportunity to get rid of him. That I did not believe the "official" account of what took place my diary proves. As a matter of fact Bülow made the mistake and the Emperor was made the scapegoat. It was the Jameson Raid telegram episode of 1896 all over again[1]:

December, 1908. Berlin.

I stayed in bed to-day—except just getting up to go to the dentist, and to see the Crown Prince who came to the hotel

[1] There are good reasons for believing that Baron Marschall von Bieberstein, then German Foreign Secretary, inspired—if he did not actually draft—the Emperor's telegram to President Kruger; certainly he was the author of its immediate sequel, the Note to the Powers asserting that the continuance of Boer Independence was "a German interest."

and sat with me for an hour. He telephoned eleven, but arrived at a quarter to eleven ; so I opened the door in a pale blue dressing-gown and said : " Sir, if I wait to put on a dress it will take ten minutes so may I come like this." He laughed and seemed quite pleased, so in I went. He talked of his father and the senseless way the Order of the Black Eagle was thrown about ; furious now because some little Japanese Prince had just been given it. I answered : " I do not know the Japanese Prince in question, but the worst use the Emperor ever made of the Black Eagle was to give it to the Prince of Monaco. It puts His Majesty in a false light towards France and the whole of Europe." Then I repeated what the Emperor had said to Patsy and me about the King of Spain and England, adding : " Sir, *I* don't mind, it may have been in fun ; but what is the use of saying such a thing to two Englishwomen, one of whom lives in England and who might naturally repeat it when she goes back there." The Crown Prince said : " Yes, my father speaks too quickly ; he is too outspoken."

Well, we talked for an hour and I really found him charming. . . . I wonder *now* what he thinks about the famous *Daily Telegraph* interview which has just been published,[1] the draft of which the Emperor gave Bülow, and Bülow forgot to look at and gave it to A., and A. gave it to B., and so it went on until, like the illustration in the *Fremden blatt*, it got to the charwoman.

I won't enter upon politics now, except to say that I hear on good authority that Bülow *did* read it, and deliberately allowed it to be published ! One asks oneself for what purpose, and one can only think that he and the Emperor want a war. . . .

IV

Nineteen hundred and nine was a horrid year. At the end of January I went to Paris to get some clothes and from there to Cannes to stay for a few days with Sophy and the Grand Duke while I again searched for the ideal villa. It is quite hopeless trusting to agents, or even to friends. No one except oneself really knows what will " do." If one goes regularly to the Riviera one is eventually compelled to buy a villa,

[1] On October 27, 1908.

or hut, or something to live in. No one could go on suffering the agonies of scouring around every year. I know people who season after season take horrid, expensive, uncomfortable houses in preference to wearing themselves to death searching for something better. Ultimately Hans took a villa at Mandelieu on lease and I bought land near by at La Napoule with the intention of building one there to suit myself.

Berlin, indeed all Germany, was at that time agog about the approaching visit of the British Sovereigns. The following extract from my diary bears out what I have said elsewhere concerning the Duchess of Sparta ; it also throws some more light on the *Daily Telegraph* interview and its unfortunate consequences. It was common knowledge in Berlin that a day or two after the interview appeared Prince von Bülow went specially to Potsdam to extract from the Emperor a promise of greater reserve and discretion in dealing with public, and more particularly foreign, affairs. The subsequent announcement in the *Imperial Gazette* that the Chancellor enjoyed the " continued confidence " of the Emperor only made every well-informed person smile :

January 26, 1909. Cannes, Villa Kasbek.

Coming upstairs I find a nice long letter from the Duchess of Sparta full of England and her love for it, " the most beloved country in the world," she writes. She also spoke of the cruelty, and ingratitude of the German nation towards their Emperor, and so on (which is true to a great extent).

Bülow has behaved disgracefully, but of course now the Emperor dare not part with him, but *how* he must hate him ! And what a position the Emperor has put himself into ; his country has lost confidence in him ; his Chancellor apologizes for him ; and blames his master to shield his own carelessness in allowing a document to be printed without his concurrence (but I know he saw it) ; and now he can (for the time being) dictate to the Emperor.

But the Emperor ! Take him as a man he is impossible, he has no manners ; he cannot choose his friends. In little ways that perhaps don't even count—and yet farthings go to making pounds—he is bourgeois, and loud, and yet has sometimes the charm of youth! The other day, the 19th of January, Hans and I went to Potsdam for the ball given by the Crown Prince and Crown Princess. I would not have dreamt of going only she wired herself asking us, and ended up, "Please do say yes, love, Cecile." She is really so charming and natural and unspoilt that without seeming rude I could not refuse.

I saw the Emperor in the distance after supper and made him a little bow from the other end of the room. He beckoned to me, calling with his finger and then pointing to the floor. At first I did not move, refusing to believe his manner which was as if he was calling a naughty child to come and stand before him. But at the third time I had to go, or the whole room would have noticed I stood in front of him two yards away intending that he should come to meet me (which the Empress did, she was really very nice) but he never moved a foot. At last I went up to him and he began asking me a lot of stupid questions. I looked at him and said:

"When Your Majesty shakes hands with me I will answer," which he then did. As he had been talking to the Duke of R. (a conceited little *Jäger* and nothing else), after a time of stupid badinage I left him saying:

"I do not want to disturb further this *serious* conversation." He looked rather shy, as with the Duke of R. not even a Shakespearean clown could talk sense.

I went to a Court before leaving Berlin. Princess Lichnowsky was there; she is handsome, I think, and I like her, but I know all the Court people won't. They will think her rude because she is almost too natural; and she doesn't care a hang for anyone or anything! [1]

I badly wanted to organize a Charity concert in Berlin during the visit of the King and Queen of England and make it a great success by getting them to be present. Of course I had to ask the Emperor's permission first. This he would not grant, even though Sir Edward Goschen, the British Ambassador, went to see Count Eulenburg, the Lord Chamberlain,

[1] Prince Lichnowsky's appointment as German Ambassador in London was announced in October, 1912, in succession to Baron Marschall von Bieberstein

and assured him that Queen Alexandra had already let me know she would like to be present if it could be arranged. However, I determined to have my Concert even if I could not have the presence of the British Sovereigns.

The season in Berlin begins in January and ends before Lent. Into these few weeks had to be crowded Courts, parties by all the Royal Princes, the Ambassadors, all the great Country families, the Plutocracy, the Services and a thousand brilliant entertainments of all kinds. That particular Season was of course noteworthy because of the visit of King Edward and Queen Alexandra, for whom sumptuous preparations were made. For once I really wanted to be there.

Sir Edward Grey, his Foreign Minister, did not accompany the British Sovereign. Nevertheless, the visit was regarded in Germany as having political as well as social importance. My own opinion is that all such visits, indeed all intercourse between the King and the Emperor, however outwardly friendly, had negative results because the King thoroughly distrusted his nephew. Perhaps there was, in addition, an inherent antipathy. King Edward, naturally genial, human and unassuming, hated the Emperor's pose and swagger, which, by the way, was largely assumed. When the Emperor unbent he could be most human and interesting and it was of course well-known that with his own cronies he could be very unbent indeed.

We gave His Majesty and the Queen a magnificent welcome. My diary makes it clear that even in efficient Germany intentions and results are not always equal:

February 9, 1909. Berlin, Hotel Bristol.

To-day was the "great day," the arrival of the King and Queen of England, a bright sunny day; but they have a funny way of doing things here. The Procession was bad; the carriages did not keep equal distances, the horses of one being almost in the legs of the footmen standing behind the preceding one so that the poor men kept on turning round to see when they would be bitten. Then when nearing the Palace, the horses in the carriage of the Empress and the Queen refused to go on, and both ladies had to get out and get into another carriage ![1] In Salm's squadron, or one of the squadrons guarding the carriages, two of the horses got frightened and the men tumbled off and the horses galloped about among the others.

Then none of the Serene Highnesses were asked to dinner to-night; all the husbands went, but we all stayed at home and we are only eight. Christa Salm-Salm, Hedwige Arenberg, Princess Biron, Princess Donnersmark, Princess Lichnowsky, Princess Löwenstein, Princess Fürstenberg, and myself. (All these women have fine jewels and would be a credit to any Court.) Ossy Löwenstein, who often stayed at Sandringham as a girl when still Countess Kinsky, Hedwige who came all the way from Brussels for the occasion, and Christa whom King Edward always treats as an Archduchess—which of course she is—and I, an Englishwoman. Naturally every one is cross and says what strange behaviour asking the husbands and not the wives—a thing never done in Germany! The King will be the first to wonder at a State Banquet with scarcely any women, only those being asked who are *Palastdamen*, the ones who have the right to wear that big enamelled locket ![2] And after all, as Hans says, one's position ought not to be determined by the post one holds at Court. *Berlin will never be a smart social centre.* The Emperor and Empress have no ideas how they ought to behave. To-morrow there is the Opera and the evening after the Ball; of course to these we are asked *en masse* with every one else! But there has been no special politeness shown to any of us.

Hans has just come back from the Banquet, and says that Eulenburg told him he had asked the Emperor about inviting the wives of the Princes, but that the Emperor had said it wasn't necessary! *Eh bien!* Hans stood at the door and on passing with the Queen to the supper-room the Emperor said, on purpose loudly so that *she* should hear: "Where is Daisy?" Hans answered:

"Your Majesty knows she was not invited!"

The King on passing with the Empress also said to Hans: "Where is your wife: why is she not here?" to which Hans answered:

"She was not asked, Sir."

---

[1] The Master of the Horse, Baron von Reischach, was reprimanded for, and greatly chagrined by, this incident.

[2] The Official Badge worn when on duty by the Ladies of the Household of the Empress.

I am sure the Queen saw my letter to Charlotte Knollys, her lady-in-waiting and companion since years, in which amongst other things I said, on purpose, as I knew it would be repeated: "None of the Princesses are asked for to-night—all we can do is to go to bed; in this country only the men are wanted!" I felt sure the King and Queen would ask; that's why I wrote to Charlotte. The King will be angry as I am English, and Christa is first cousin to the King of Spain; besides the whole idea is ridiculous and rude.

February 10, 1909. Berlin, Hotel Bristol.

Just back from the Court Ball, much the same as most balls, only I did not dance; as is customary here all the square dances were already settled as to partners and they had only one or two waltzes, which they "hopped," and of course the minuet and gavotte; most of the girls ugly and badly dressed and the men in their uniforms looking ridiculous. Those old-fashioned dances want to be *en costume*. Every one was very agreeable to me, and the Empress talked and laughed quite nicely. I sat at the King's table at dinner (Hans says that the Duchess of X. and all of them were furious). At the King's table were Lulu (Hans's sister), Princess von Bülow, Hedwige Arenberg and Ossy Löwenstein; Lord Crewe, Max Fürstenberg and some old gentlemen. The Empress and Princess von Bülow sat on either side of the King, who talked to me over the table as did the Empress. This will also cause jealousy, I don't know why. I am so seldom in Berlin, and if only they knew how little I care about it all. It all comes to me so naturally, I take it for granted.

I had been standing for some time as all the seats of the Serene Highnesses were occupied; only one was empty next to Princess von Bülow (the wife of the Chancellor). I said: "I am so tired, does it matter if I sit here so much higher up than my position allows." Princess von Bülow said: "My dear, sit down, it does me good to look at you, you are nice, and lovely, and lovable," and she really meant it. She was born Princess Marie Camporeale, an Italian, and is charming. Princess Victoria (Vicy, the Emperor's sister), talked too, and said how nice it was to see me, how she hated Berlin, that it was an impossible town to live in, everything was stiff and false and so on. I said I thought perhaps it might change, but I personally had given it up as a bad job.

Presently the Emperor came marching towards us in step with the gavotte they were all dancing, staring, and looking furious. I made the same sort of face, and said: "I suppose Your Majesty intends to dance with me." Princess Vicy said to him: "Oh, what a face." Later, as he again passed us in the dance, "So you are of course wearing that silly lily again." I nearly always wear lilies at Court, and once for fun I said they were the emblem of peace between England and Germany!

The little Queen (Alexandra) waved to me once from a distance, much to the surprise of the good Germans; and then suddenly how very polite all the people became! Just because they noticed the Empress and the Queen being intimate and friendly—they are such snobs. Perhaps I am a snob to write about it, but as I have to dress up, wear Orders and be a *Fürstin*, it is just as well for the sake of the money I spend on my clothes that the result should be satisfactory; and after all there is so much of this in the silly life I lead that I have to write about it.

The Official luncheon to-day at the English Embassy for the King and Queen was very good; all or most of the Ambassadors and their wives. Rita Reischach (who is specially in Waiting on the Queen), Irma Fürstenberg, Christa Salm and Natalie Hatzfeldt were the other ladies with their husbands. The King sat between Princess von Bülow and Christa Salm; the latter he particularly desired should be placed there in order to show the people here that they ought to give her her proper precedence. The little Queen kissed me when I made my curtsy; and the King said after lunch he would have liked to have had me next to him but it was better as it was.

The King and I talked together for an hour, I think because he didn't feel well, so he didn't want to have to make forced conversation. He was furious at all of the Princesses not being asked last night for dinner and hoped I would tell the Emperor, which of course I shall. We sat on rather a low sofa and he would smoke although he coughs badly. Suddenly he coughed and fell back against the back of the sofa and his cigar dropped out of his fingers, his eyes stared, he became pale, and he could not breathe. I thought: "My God, he is dying; oh! why not in his own country." I tried to undo the collar of his uniform (which was too tight), then the Queen rushed up and we both tried; at last he came to—and undid it himself. I then made him sit on a higher seat, but he would not let me move from him. I persuaded him to see the Doctor I have had here each day, and who made me inhale this morning with a special machine; it did me good, so the King saw him to-night. And he told me later it had done him good too and that he is seeing him again to-morrow. Please God, this dear, kind, able Monarch is not in for a serious illness!

V

Directly the visit of the British Sovereigns and my concert were over I returned to the South of France with the children. Shelagh and Bennie had just lost, with great suddenness, their only boy, aged five years, and this made me feel more than ever what a sinful waste it was to be attending Royal ceremonies and going about in Society when one could be quiet in a sunny garden watching the spring come and the children play. Patsy and Poppets joined me at the Villa I had taken near Monte Carlo. I find in my diary an entry made after I arrived there, which gives further details of what happened in Berlin:

February 20, 1909. Monte Carlo, Villa La Vigie.

I arrived here on the 15th alone with the children in an ordinary train, not in a "Luxe" as we had our own private salon from home. To-day is the 20th. I feel as if I had been here ages; as I have felt lonely in the cold and wind (to-day was the first warm day) thinking of poor little Shelagh and Benny whose dear little boy is dead. He had an operation for appendicitis and died two days after. It happened the day of my concert in Berlin, Saturday the 13th, in the morning. I knew he was seriously ill; they wired me, but I could not possibly put off the concert; besides I prayed all the time I sang that God would spare his life; and they were all so surprised; those who knew I sang said: "You never sang better; what was it?" And those who didn't know said: "But why didn't you tell us you sang, it's extraordinary we never knew it." So I answered: "You haven't heard because this is the first time I have sung in Berlin. I am always told that German ladies and Princesses do not sing in public, and my husband would not let me."

Countess Brockdorff and a lady-in-waiting came, especially sent by the Empress! The Crown Princess also came and everybody in Berlin. I made five thousand two hundred marks, which was very good, and the rooms looked so nice with lots of flowers and two sofas and some arm-chairs from Fürstenstein (which I had brought to Berlin for my suite in the hotel) were put in the room where the Crown Princess had tea.

I sang as one item *When the Birds go North Again*; my father loves it so. One part goes:

For every heart has its sorrow, and every heart has its pain,
But a day is always coming when the birds go north again:
'Tis the sweetest thing to remember if courage be on the wane,
When the cold dark days are over—well, the birds go north again.

It is a song of Hope and I prayed all through it for the darling little boy of Shelagh's whom I really loved with his laughing brown eyes and dimples. Hans had a wire in his pocket even before the concert began saying the little spirit had gone, but he didn't show it to me till afterwards.

It is so true and beautiful that I feel I must write here a bit of a letter I received from Shelagh soon after I arrived in Monte Carlo. It can do no harm; indeed it would do anyone good to read it. Shelagh was so brave. But how I wish that little boy had lived. I have often thought it might have made an enormous difference if he had:

NEWLANDS, *February* 22, 909

. . . We have been struggling with innumerable letters every one, all my friends and even perfect strangers, have written me such charming letters. That little boy, Dany darling, was just sent us from God to shed his little light over all, people who knew him and people who didn't. These little balls of love must do good in the world even they only come for such a short time, but oh! what a big blank he has left in my life; I feel as if the world had grown suddenly dark, and I am groping to see and touch a little light. Bless you little Dany darling. Love to dear old Hans and kiss to you and Patsy from

Later on Shelagh and Benny came down in their yacht and joined us. We felt that for a bit we must all be together. Of course we were very quiet and spent a great deal of our time with the children—Ursula, Hansel and Lexel.

The darlings were one little playmate short.

CHAPTER SIX

April, 1909–December, 1910

THE seizure, or whatever it was, that King Edward had while he was in Berlin caused me and others a great deal of uneasiness. I had known him for many years and realized that his life was not a good one. His Majesty perhaps smoked too much and did too much ; moreover, the political situation at home and abroad worried him a great deal. Those who knew only the gay, social figure, or the kindly tactful Sovereign were unaware of how seriously he took his kingly position and responsibilities. The situation in Ireland, too, a country for which he had a sincere affection, was very perplexing.

Personally I think the King's great flair for foreign affairs arose from the fact that for thirty years he had watched the eddies of international politics from a position of great eminence divorced from direct responsibility. A gregarious creature, he went everywhere, saw every one, and *listened*. The European Press, and even British and foreign statesmen and diplomats, saw in his Continental visits nothing but social jaunts, whereas they were, behind the façade of amusement, serious missions.

These, and similar reflections, lay behind everything I did during that sad spring on the Riviera after the death of Shelagh's boy.

I find that virtue consumed me throughout 1909 even to the extent of causing me to keep a very full and regular diary. I am therefore going, as far as possible, to allow it to tell the story of what happened. However hurriedly and imperfectly written, it at least records accurately what I did, and it reflects truthfully what I thought at the time; which is by no means saying that it necessarily represents what I think now.

April 6, 1909. Monte Carlo, Hotel San Salvador.

Yesterday I wrote a long letter to the Crown Princess in answer to a nice long one from her asking for news of the Riviera, and telling me about their sleighing expeditions in Potsdam this winter; she says that they were not allowed to go again to St. Moritz because of all the shocking things they were supposed to have done there. So now they have done similar things in Potsdam and sleighed in small sleighs only made for two! She is really *so* nice and full of that "worldly understanding" which Germans as a rule so conspicuously lack.

All these Dreadnoughts which Germany and England are now building, one trying to build quicker than the other, and the suspicion and bad feeling between the two countries must come to a head somehow. I dread the moment when the King of England may die. This is also the reason why I do not care for Hans building that enormous wing to Fürstentein. A war would impoverish Germany, destroying commerce for the time; the woods in Pless, owing to the horrible *nonne*, will soon be worthless; and Hansel's expenses will some day be enormous when he has to keep up so much. Then there will be succession duty.

April 20, 1909.

After Hans left I went to Cannes for three days and stayed with Sophy and the Grand Duke Michael. I talked and sat with the Grand Duke Alexander-Michaelovitch, who is supposed to be dull and a bore, but we discussed India, Russia, shooting, missionaries and religion. No wonder he doesn't care to converse much with his own brothers who are like spoilt uneducated children: his wife is sister to the Czar and very nice.[1] Sophy wanted me to stay on but my only desire was to get back to Baby, and the villa and bathe!

Marie Hope Vere told me afterwards that my ears ought to have burned; after dinner the day I left they all agreed that the evening was nothing without me! One evening in Sophy's little private golf house, I said to the Grand Duke Alexander what a glorious day it had been; he answered:

---

[1] The Grand Duchess Xénie-Alexandrovna.

"Yes; but two suns are too much for anybody." I couldn't understand and remarked:

"How do you mean two suns, that up there is the moon."

"I mean you—you are the other sun, all sunshine!"

Early in May we were back in Fürstenstein which can be perfectly wonderful just after the last snow has gone. Silesian winters are extremely cold, and coming there in May from the South was like having two springs in the same year:

May 20, 1909. Fürstenstein.

Yesterday a telegram arrived from Buckingham Palace asking Hans and me to stay with the King and Queen at Windsor for Ascot. We hesitated for a long time before accepting as we could have made the excuse of Hans having to represent the family at Willusch's [1] wedding which is fixed for June 17. Our real reason for not wishing to go being that we both were looking forward so much to a lovely month in Fürstenstein. I really could have cried, although of course I am pleased to have received the invitation—but I wish I had not to accept it! Besides, I have no clothes! I can't go to Vienna now, as people are coming here on the 24th and 25th, and there is not time either to make them or try them on. I really can't get Ascot dresses in Breslau; and we cannot arrive in London before Sunday, the 13th, and have to be in Windsor on the 14th.

June 6, 1909. Fürstenstein.

. . . The children are very well. The next few days there is a lot to be done as all the relations come on the 8th and 9th to celebrate the four hundred years' ownership of Fürstentein by the Hochbergs. There will be an enormous dinner of over two hundred people and a garden party, and the great ball-room has to be cleared—which is a nuisance.

Hans and I went this morning to the Mausoleum and I took a big basin full of lilies of the valley for Vater's tomb. Hans agrees that it would be nicer to have the inside gates open and have air there and take all the crêpe off the altar and arrange it nicely. And I want to have a great big coloured window and make the whole thing more like a little chapel into

[1] My husband's stepbrother, Count William Bolko Emmanuel Hochberg, who married Countess Anne-Marie von Arnim.

which one can go sometimes and say prayers and feel peaceful; so I shall arrange this, and will make it lovely. . . .

June 10, 1909. Fürstenstein.

After dinner at half-past nine the whole place was illuminated, and Bengal lights were lit at the *Alte Burg* and on the *Riesen Grab*, and then eight hundred miners came carrying torches and led by their own band which took up a position and played while they marched past. It was a *Fackel-Zug* or torchlight-procession, and as they marched like soldiers it was a beautiful sight.

After it was all over I rushed upstairs and put on a short skirt and brown stockings over my pink ones, a coat, and a chiffon over my head; they twice sent up Frau von Pohl[1] to tell me not to do it, but Fritz, my brother-in-law, was ready to go with me, and after all it is my house, and I am really old enough not to give way to them in such little simple things, so I sneaked out; and it was lovely; we walked to the *Riesen Grab* and the house stood out through the mist with all its lights and illuminations like a vision castle. We stayed out about half an hour.

I thought they would all be furious with me and treat me like a disobedient child, but they were very nice and seemed very pleased to see me again!

Afterwards Mathilde and Anna came to my room to see the tiara which Hans and I got for Willusch's fiancée and were delighted with it. It is beautiful but I would much rather it was for little Anna's marriage. . . .

Fritz and Uncle Bolko talked about the new building; they also are very unhappy about it and I want them to-morrow to talk to Hans and persuade him to make Vater's old rooms broader and build on there and not undertake this enormous work—and improve this house as much as he wants to. But it is quite big enough, and surely as he grows older he will want rather to see his friends than to fill the house with mere acquaintances; and then all the extra expense for Hansel later on. I feel it isn't right. . . .

I think Hans has been very silly in telling Fritz Solms that if he had the chance he was to hint to the Emperor that should he be offered the title of Duke he would dislike it very much unless it was attached to another territorial designation. I quite agree; but all the same it would have been better for

[1] My lady-in-waiting.

him personally to tell the Emperor this when a suitable moment came.

It was my strong feeling that while I was at Windsor I ought to try and do something practical to relieve the growing tension between England and Germany. I knew King Edward disliked the Emperor personally, and that the Emperor felt this to be the case although he did not definitely *know* it. At the same time I realized that the King was much too big a man and much too good a diplomat to permit his personal feelings to influence his actions on serious affairs. It seemed to me that if I could take to Windsor a nice message from the Nephew to his Uncle it might be helpful. I therefore wrote to the Emperor as follows. The reply, unfortunately, has not been preserved, nor does my diary say anything about it:

SIRE,—

I write this letter to give utterance to thoughts which keep me awake at night. When I was in England last, I said to Mr. Balfour: "Tell me honestly, is there a treaty between England and France that is known as the *Entente Cordiale*?"

He answered that it could not be called a treaty; there was nothing on paper, nothing signed. I then lamented this incomprehensible feeling of distrust between England and Germany. He said:

"Do believe me, I think of it from morning till night. I would do anything to find a real reason, but whatever England does Germany attributes it to enmity in some form or another."

Oh Sire! I have lived in Germany all these years, and I am English born; I know the faults of both countries and I hear far more than many people, even diplomats. In Germany people talk openly before me and to me, for they know I love the country and my boys are German and will serve in Your Majesty's army, and they look upon me as a German; in England they speak as they would not speak before Count Metternich or any German, as they think of me as English.

How *can* one country truly know what another country thinks and believes? How are Emperors and Kings to hear the truth? They scarcely ever do. The people to whom they talk listen to every word they say and answer nothing, and

OUR HEAD FORESTERS AT PLESS.

A SEMI-STATE CARRIAGE AT PLESS.

go home and tell their wife and children: "The Emperor said this and that," and are delighted.

The fact is, English people are too conceited; Germans too touchy. What care and tact I have to use continually! If I say something or judge something, they at once think I am measuring by English standards, when I was simply judging by my own brain, and not thinking of England.

I enclose a copy of a letter from a friend of ours who was in Fürstenstein this summer, and which has appeared in most of the English papers. Sire, there was a time not so long ago, when no Englishman would go to France, when France was England's bitter enemy; during that period an Englishman would have been glad even to possess an old glove of Your Majesty's, and this attitude will come again. In families the nearer the relationship the more frequent the quarrels; so it is now between Germany and England. Born an Englishwoman and as one who mixes with many different classes of people in that country, I beg Your Majesty to know and believe that Germany is looked up to in many ways. I also beg Your Majesty not to be too proud when the time comes to put out your hand to my land and say, let us be friends and when we do knock up against each other on the high seas of commerce, let there be no bruises.

King Edward is more of a King than anyone in England ever anticipated. Now that his diplomacy has been so successful the whole country adores him; indeed the feeling of loyalty in England is extraordinary. I often see the King and never in all those years has His Majesty ever said one hard word against anything German; in fact he advised me to learn the language well, to get to know the people, to take interest in the country, and so on. And he meant it; one must not forget he is more than half a German, and in all differences between the countries he has thought: "The German Emperor is my nephew," and this fact has given him often a pride which Your Majesty cannot understand and probably will not believe; he has had Your Majesty in his heart and I know this. The same blood flows in the two countries: it cannot and must not surge up in enmity.

I shall see the King in England very soon. Cannot I bring one word of peace? Not to put in papers, nothing to be delivered officially—just a word of friendship.

English people *en gros* are good sorts, and forget easily. They are not revengeful, they do not turn round now on Germany and jeer at any defeat in Africa. It is such a happy island and so prosperous. They are not always thinking of and criticizing their next-door neighbour, and if once Germany and she could shake hands there would be a great wave of joy over England and a burst of hurrahs, and Your Majesty's reputation would be held by the people even higher than it used to be, while the words I have so often heard would be repeated: "My God, the Emperor is a grand man."

Oh Sire, forgive me: Your devoted subject,

DAISY OF PLESS.

II

We duly arrived at Windsor and I can imagine few things more delightful than to be invited there for Ascot. One sees the racing in the most comfortable way, meets all one's friends (and enemies), makes—or loses—a little money, and all without any fatigue or bother. My diary provides a pretty full account of what happened:

June 18, 1909. Windsor Castle.

Quite sad that to-night is the last night here. To-day is Friday and we arrived on Monday and it really has not been long. I was afraid at first it might be stiff and boring but it is not only a magnificent palace but a charming house to stay at—everything most comfortable and the servants so obliging. Hans and I have breakfast together in our own sitting-room, and at a quarter past twelve have to be ready for the races; before that, and after the races, one could do what one liked; dinner is at half-past eight or a quarter to nine. We always got back very late so I was only able to rest the evening of the one day the Queen and Princess Victoria did not go, as we went in motors and therefore got back sooner. After tea I took a walk with Soveral whom I consider to be almost a dangerous fanatic in his feelings against Germany, the danger to England, and so on.

To-day I did not go racing as the Queen asked me to go on the river; so she and Princess Victoria, Princess Murat, Mrs. Standish (a charming elderly lady, French by birth, who is here with her niece), Soveral, Mensdorff the Austrian Ambassador, Sir Harry Legge, in Waiting, and Lord Anglesey, young, about twenty-eight; all went on a steam launch from here to Cliveden; we left at one o'clock and got home at seven ; frightfully sleepy, and I must say it is tiring to sit facing one another and trying to be amusing and agreeable for six hours with only the meals for a break. We had lunch and tea on board. At Cliveden all the ladies were landed on one side of the river and the gentlemen on the other. Soveral arranged it ; it was most extraordinary and very pointed ! I felt quite shy afterwards, as we simply stopped, I think, for this purpose. The weather has been perfect all the time, just warm enough. For the two Royal Procession days I drove with the Princess of Wales, Mensdorff and Prince Murat.

The Queen is so full of charm and graciousness and the King such a good friend. One day coming out from dinner with him, he asked me (à propos of the stern countenance of a new portrait of his) if I was not afraid of him. I didn't quite know what he would have liked me to say, so I simply said : "Well, Your Majesty, I have never done anything wrong." Then he said : "No ! No ! I am too much of an old friend for you to be afraid of me."

I had to sing nearly every night—with the orchestra. Soveral and the Queen sitting always side by side ; he speaks distinctly and she always hears him. One night we danced. All my clothes have been a great success and Hans said I was the best dressed woman at the races. All very simple and draped ; one day a big bunch of pink lilies and my scarab turquoises. Then I twice wore Fritz's gold coat which made a great effect and looked lovely. They have all been so nice to me and all my friends so pleased to see me.

June 21, 1909. Newlands.

Dear, dear little Newlands, a mass of rhododendrons and roses. The sun comes out at intervals, but it is not warm and is inclined to rain.

I motored here after the Consecration, in presence of the King, of the Colours of the Territorial Regiments in Windsor Park just in front of the Castle. It was very badly done—most people said so—and not one man on parade could really march. All the Lords-Lieutenant were invited—but not their wives who had worked to get the subscriptions together to buy and embroider the flags ! The Lieutenants all stood together in one corner. I said to dear old Sir Dighton Probyn (who used to be with Queen Victoria) that, to begin with, the whole thing ought to have taken place in Hyde Park or somewhere like that, as publicity is essential if they want to raise a Territorial Army. A private ceremonial like this was absurd ; also,

Russian woman and her brother from the " Empire " danced. At midnight we drove home and I was very glad as I had started the day early and had left London in time to motor Mrs. Vanderbilt and Marquess Pallavacini (Hungarian, and dances well) down to Cliveden for lunch; the Connaughts were there. *We* were over half an hour late, but it did not really matter. After lunch at intervals during the rain (as the weather lately has been *awful*) I played tennis with Princess Patricia, Marquess Pallavacini and Lord Herbert. I laughed at myself playing tennis, but they said it was excellent. Anyway Princess P. can't play and she knows it.

I went to the Opera on Tuesday with Shelagh, which was very nice; I asked Poppets, and Shelagh asked Hansie Larisch. I got to London only on Monday—and to-day is Monday and here I am again at Newlands. It seems weeks since I have been in London.

Every one talks of the possible invasion of England by the Germans. Some believe it, and some call it hysterical rot (which it is); but as Metternich himself often remarks, what he says makes no difference to this talk; those who want to believe it won't believe otherwise.

I much enjoyed the visit to Cliveden as the Astors are delightful hosts and the house, cooking and surroundings are perfect. I first knew Lady Astor when she used to hunt in Leicestershire, and I always liked and admired her. She is very sharp and witty and has that unusual combination—to be found only, I think, in Americans—a cynical mind and a sentimental heart.

In July I went to a great Ball given by the Whitelaw Reids at Dorchester House. What a palace in which to entertain! The King and Queen and all the Royalties and Ambassadors and their wives were present, also the Crown Prince of Sweden and my dear, dear friend the Crown Princess. Shelagh, too, was there and looked lovely. We all made a great point of being at my sister-in-law Jennie's play, *His Borrowed Plumes*, which was produced for a charity. I went to a State Ball at Buckingham Palace and, for the last time, danced in the Royal Quadrilles. I believe they are now given up.

For Cowes Week we took Lisburne House and enjoyed

it so much, in spite of the fact that Hans had broken his thigh the previous hunting season and was still walking on sticks. It was dreadful for him, but he was so good and patient. While in London we had consulted Sir Alfred Fripp, who said he was to walk about and use the injured leg as much as he liked. But at Cowes the Queen kindly insisted on sending Sir Frederick Treves to see him, and he said that Hans was doing far too much and must lie up with his leg as high as his shoulder! Hans much preferred Sir Alfred Fripp's advice and followed it.

When there was no wind a cruiser towed the *Britannia*, with all of us on board, round the Island. The King of Spain kindly lent us a fifteen-metre boat, so, dividing our time between it and the *Britannia*, we saw all the racing. It was very hot and we bathed a lot. Once when I was bathing Queen Alexandra and Princess Victoria drove along the road by the edge of the sea. They saw me and waved, so I walked in the water as near as I could to the car and Princess Victoria snapped me; she loves photography.

III

In the autumn we had the usual shooting parties at Fürstenstein or Promnitz. I remember only one well because poor old Prince Christian of Schleswig-Holstein, who was riding a stout pony, dropped his false teeth in the stubble and everything had to stop while we searched for them. At first no one could make out what had happened to him; it seemed as if he was going to have a fit, as he slithered off his pony, fell on his knees, made loud muttering noises and began delving in the ground. It was as if he had suddenly been seized by some dreadful remorse, or a new and disagreeable sort of illness. Of course his great fear was that someone would step on and smash his eating and talking implements. That incident, and quite alarming stories that I have heard about ladies who somehow lost or mislaid their wigs, have made me determine that if ever the time comes for me to wear false teeth and a wig, I will have several sets of each—if one does have " sets " of wigs. I should add that the wretched Hansel was delighted with the poor Prince's predicament and seemed to imagine it was arranged specially for his amusement.

The following extracts from my diary describe typical days in our life in Silesia before the War. They give glimpses of existence in great country houses like Primkenau in Silesia, Castolowitz in Bohemia, and Lancut in Galicia (formerly Austrian and now Polish)—not to mention two very uncomfortable nights in an hotel in Breslau. They also tell of the new hotel we were building in Salzbrunn, and the many difficulties I had to contend with in adjusting the English and German points of view about sanitation and other matters :

October 17, 1909. Fürstenstein.

Had a busy day ; started at a quarter past ten for Striegau, about ten miles away, to lay the foundation stone for the monument to be put up in memory of the Austrians and Saxons who died at Hohenfriedberg.[1] It wasn't very impressive ! Somehow Germans with fat tummies, white evening clothes and top hats in the daytime always make me more inclined to laugh (or cry), as it often looks like a funeral. I tapped on the stone with a little hammer and each official personage said something. I only prayed to God that the souls of the dead soldiers were at rest and in peace. And as I left I put two little tuberoses from the bouquet they gave me, against the stone and the mortar ; I felt I was putting them on a grave. We got home for lunch bringing General von Woyrsch with us. Hans of course had to make a speech during which he said : " and the Emperor joined with the King of Saxony and the Emperor of Austria "—then he stopped dead ! As usual just a little over-anxious to do everything according to etiquette, he did not know which name he ought to say first, whether that of Austria or Saxony ! And then an old man prompted him ; it looked rather as if he had forgotten under which Sovereign the men had lost their lives. I thought it strange that neither the battle nor Frederick the Great was mentioned.

[1] The battle in which Frederick the Great defeated the Austrians and Saxons on June 4, 1745.

This afternoon Poppets and I went to see the new Miners' Hospital. It interested him very much and is certainly marvellously built and arranged, and the head doctor, Müller, is a distinguished and charming man. It is a beautiful building, high and clean, all white tiles inside, and everything in the way of machinery, baths, instruments and equipment of the very latest kind. We saw several sad cases, it makes one so long to help, and yet one feels so powerless. One poor man was bandaged right across the eyes and sat up like a child and played with my hand when I told him I would look after him in the future, and, for the present, do all I could for his wife and children. Several men had lost their legs; another one's back was broken, and he will probably die. I am of course sending books, wine and fruit, and shall put up a library, and arrange some outdoor games for them to play, such as Bowls, Ninepins, and so on.

From Fürstenstein we went for a few days to Lancut, in Galicia, where charming Betka Potocka was a most gracious hostess. When I reached Fürstenstein from there I wrote a short account of the visit:

October 25, 1909. Fürstenstein.

We returned from Lancut on the 23rd as Minnie and Guy Wyndham arrived on that day and Poppets had to leave here yesterday, the 24th, for London. The darling, I hated parting with him, he was so happy and well, all the time, and enjoyed and took an interest in everything; he really is a marvel, and looks about sixty, instead of seventy-six. Minnie and her handsome little gipsy-looking daughter Olivia arrived from England very well, and Guy from St. Petersburg,[1] more cheery and talkative than I have ever known him.

The three days in Lancut were great fun and every one so pleased to see me; I suppose because my face is cheerful and my nose turns up; they did all they could to make me stay longer. And really this year people have been so extraordinarily pleased with me that I forget how old I am and feel twenty (and look it, so they say). I played tennis there, much to Count Voss's amusement and sarcastic smiling, as he recognizes only very serious play. Then we shot, and people, as is usual abroad or so I always think, shot much too low and

[1] Colonel Guy Wyndham, C.B., was Military Attaché at Petrograd from 1907 to 1913.

six beaters got shot in their bodies. One, they said, was dead! And I thought he was too, when I saw him, lying with his head on the ground; but later he recovered. It all comes from this infernal counting of how much is shot and how much each gun gets. It is absurd. It always makes me furious when I see men shooting into a cover! And in some places at birds that come out right in their faces!

When we had several engagements close together in Breslau we often found it less tiring to sleep there for a night or two. But on the occasion now described it would obviously have been more restful to have gone home:

October 27, 1909. Breslau Hotel, Breslau.

I went to the Bazaar this morning at twelve. There was scarcely a soul there, but this afternoon more came, and I made seven hundred and fifty marks, which is supposed to be enormous, as all the other stalls made less! I had the *Schiess Cude* or shooting-gallery, but I can't help smiling when I think of London where I have made five hundred pounds at my stall alone. Minnie and Guy came with me this morning and left for England this afternoon. Hans goes back to-morrow to Castolowitz and I am to take Hansel there with me on Friday. I am in bed now; and shall put this away and huddle up and go to sleep, while all the Silesians are dancing. As I said to Hans, I feel more at home with Hungarians or Austrians; they seem truer and more natural: some of these people are funny.

October 27, 1909. 4.30 a.m. Breslau Hotel.

I am going to move to a bed in another bedroom and am writing while my maid gets it ready, as I cannot sleep a wink; the electric trams go by just under my window, and all the traffic, and people talking and shouting, make it impossible to sleep. Have you ever listened to the traffic of a town in the dark, or late in the evening, with a faint light burning in your room? It is almost sadder than sitting near a fire when the embers are red and there are no flames, and you make pictures to yourself of caves, and hell—and heaven! But listening to the sound of a town, rolling on and on and on, brings back all the past years to one—things one has seen, and done, and said, felt and thought; happy days, and disappointments .... London faces, and days of crisp frost, and skating weather;

every feeling of mankind, good and ill, passes by with the roll of the traffic in a big town ; now I can see in my imagination the people hurrying along the pavement and across the street ; and nearly all are to be pitied. In fact we all are to be pitied ; so many of us try our best, and our best is so feeble, and is such a waste of time, compared with what we could do with our lives if circumstances allowed it ; every woman with a husband, children and houses is tied. (I don't write homes, because houses become sometimes merely hotels.) Such a woman has to live according to the position she is almost paid to fill. (And if the situation happens not to suit her she cannot give notice and change it.) If the woman is content to appear nice to herself in the glass, and make friends of (mostly) fools, have furs and diamonds, and forget her soul, she may be happy, but not otherwise.

My readers already know of my dear friends Count Sternberg and his wife Fanny. I loved going to their splendid yet friendly home. They have never changed and I still go there almost every year. In those days Castolowitz was in Bohemia—the nice old, friendly name. Now, on the map, the country is uncomfortably named Czecho-Slovakia :

October 30, 1909. Castolowitz.

We have just dined in two rooms, twenty-four in each. I tried to make polite and interesting conversation but it bored me ; so I came here to write. Soon I shall have to go back and dance, and then I shall sneak quietly away and go to bed. Hedwige Arenberg is here, and Ejie Windischgrätz, both content to sit on a sofa and talk to any man who comes to them ; I don't know how they do it. I cannot waste three minutes upon people who are absolutely indifferent to me. It is a sign of old age coming, and yet Count Hiene and all say how well I am looking.

Little Hansel rode beautifully to-day, they all tell me, and Hans is so proud of his boy ; every one talks of him and what beautiful manners he has. It always amuses me when they all tell me this, even English people, as I never bother about my children's manners ; good manners come naturally to them. Now I suppose I must go back to the drawing-room and smile !

We shot duck this morning ; the weather is divine, so hot !

This autumn has been perfect, to make up for the very wet summer I suppose! Is there a "making up" I wonder, in another world, for all the sufferings poor people have had here! No dismal roads, no hard pavements, no horrible houses for them, but rest for tired feet, and aching hearts. . . . I hope so.

November 21, 1909. Fürstenstein.

After Church I saw the ground plan for the new Salzbrunn Hotel, which will have the roof on in a fortnight. I spoke with Keindorff, our General Director here, and the architect, and Herr von Pohl. I am going to do the whole thing myself, including linen and silver and china, as I feel I can do it cheaper than they would with their enormous ideas, and Hans is pleased to let me do it, and seems quite proud of me.

He agreed with me afterwards and was surprised at the way I took the proposal to order the carpets, for instance, at our own *Warenhaus* in Waldenburg. Keindorff said we would get them twenty or nineteen per cent. cheaper. Then I boiled over and said that if we did things like that of course the town of Waldenburg could be (as they are) against us. Vater had built this store to do good for our miners and workpeople by enabling them to buy at cost price. The question had already been raised in the papers about the Fürst von Pless's "dry goods store," and Hans had told the Emperor (in fact written to say) that he did not build it, but that Vater did to benefit the miners and workpeople only, and we gained nothing by it. But of course if we did what the General Director and the others suggested it would be contrary to what I considered to be right. Keindorff was much surprised and shut up. . . . Then, after I had seen designs for Louis Quinze music-rooms, Louis Quatorze drawing-rooms, a big oak dining-room, and similar absurdities, they promptly showed me a sketch for a corridor and the parterre with one closet and bathroom at one end. I ordered the accommodations to be repeated at the other end, as well as in the middle. They argued about the unnecessary expense as the people wouldn't use them! But I said the people they *hoped* to attract by all this splendour would want to use them, and my idea of an hotel, particularly an hotel in a health-resort, was first the sanitary arrangements and then the Louis Quinze decorations.

After lunch we had another talk about expenses. The money for this hotel is being borrowed, over a million marks at four and a half per cent. When the hotel does pay, they say, it can pay only two and a half per cent.; the rest must be made up by the outside fees from the guests and the extra sale of Salzbrunn water outside Silesia. My idea is that the whole thing is an absurd mistake; the hotel ought to have been built more of wood and tiles with nice Heidelberg balconies, to cost twenty thousand only, and five thousand to furnish, to begin with.

I feel there must come a financial crash if we go on wasting money like this, and I almost enjoyed the idea as I walked with Hansel yesterday thinking what a relief it would be not to have so many parties; a small stable and nice simple liveries with no silver braid; no gala liveries for the servants in the house; fewer servants outside, no *Garde Förster*, and so on.

I drove a little way to the station with Hans to-day and I hated the dressed-up grooms, very expensive black horses simply for station work, and a Jäger behind with plumed hat. I felt like a *nouveau riche*. I hope in time Hans will at any rate let me have some of the horrible shiny silver taken off.

Diary dear, don't you understand, it is wrong to advertise one's riches and power in the faces of those who have not got either. To do things in a quiet dignified way is quite another thing.

Here is a description of a visit to Primkenau, the Silesian home of the Duke and Duchess of Schleswig-Holstein. The Duke (Ernst Günther) was a brother of the Empress and very popular. He died in 1921 and, as he had no children, was succeeded by his cousin, the second son of Prince and Princess Christian. His wife, Dora, was born a Princess of Saxe-Coburg and Gotha:

November 18, 1909. Primkenau.

I arrived here from Halbau at half-past seven and came to bed with a headache. I really couldn't be bothered to dress for dinner and make conversation. Besides, I *had* a headache. After dinner the Duchess and her giggly though very pretty lady-in-waiting came upstairs and sat by my bed. The Duchess is really much better than she was, though she does always come and feel one's clothes and sniffle at one. She has a pretty figure but an ugly face. Young Albert of Schleswig-Holstein, the only son now of Prince Christian, was downstairs in the hall; I never liked him. Then a Count Reichenbach, Count Vico Voss, a Duke of Saxe-Weimar (I have not seen him)—and I don't know who else. . . . I shall be the only lady visitor in the house and shall go out with the men to lunch to-morrow.

November 24, 1909. Pless.

I met Hans and the children in Breslau on the 21st and we came here together. Leaving Primkenau the Duchess took me to the station in the morning at nine; she was dressed in black as it was *Toten Sonntag* and she was going to church; she had on the most awful old cape and hat, and looked like an old lodging-house keeper. Poor dear, it was very kind of her, I am sure, to take me to the station and get out of the carriage (she gave me a bouquet of flowers before I started); but I hope she does not think I shall do the same for her when she comes here! Unluckily I told Hans (as a joke), and he said, of course I never did the right thing; I ought to go to the station and meet all Royal Princesses! Awful idea—my life as it is, is half wasted in saying silly things to silly people I don't care about.

When I got to Pless I felt very desperate and thought of myself as being not much different from a bit of movable furniture ready to be brought out when required and that must have new covering put on it at intervals; to be gilt and grinning when an Emperor visits us, as ours does to-day.

Mathilde and Anna arrived this morning, Lulu and Fritz Solms just now; both delighted at the idea that the Emperor is coming to us; they all seem much excited about it—I am not. If he is nice I shall be pleased; if he is dull I shall be bored and shall probably show it. I shall, however, propose to him something in a nice way—and that is, at all costs to befriend England, and, if possible, to put on paper for King Edward or the English Government a declaration that Germany has no intention of attempting to take any possessions or colonies from England. I shall also urge that as soon as the present British and German shipbuilding programmes are completed, England and Germany should agree to construct no more ships for a long period of years. I could say so much and I will say it.

November 30, 1909. Pless.

"I could say so much and I will say it," are, I see, my last words. Well, I did say it! And on the very first night as the Emperor sat by me at dinner. He began: "A nice state your country is in! What are they doing there?" and that sort of talk. We discussed this atrocious present "Socialist" government[1]; then the Navy; I told him that in almost every way England wished to copy Germany, her Army, Navy, Old Age Pensions, factory, mining and labour legislation, Insurance, and so on. . . .

I pointed out that it was natural for a great country like England, which up to now had always been first, to be annoyed at suddenly finding another country excelling her in almost all things. . . . The agitation in England against Germany was largely a ruse of those who desired to see more men become soldiers and sailors. And then I discussed the idea of a ship-building agreement, and the English fear of invasion. . . . He said that the idea of invading England was the absolute greatest rot; what would Germany do with England? what would she want it for? Besides, it would be perfectly impossible. The wisest and best thing England could do would be to make a treaty with Germany. Then I said: "Your Majesty, that's all very well, but you surely can't make a treaty about nothing." . . . He said: "My dear child, it could be done."

I spoke afterwards for a long time with Herr von Jaenisch, Minister in Darmstadt, but who always travels with the Emperor; he did not either see how a treaty was possible!

I had dreaded the four dinners and four lunches, sitting each time by the Emperor, not knowing what on earth we could talk about, but it all went off beautifully. We shot two days.

The Emperor enjoyed the lunches in the nice big tent, and really the Egyptian patchwork inside and the white cotton roof through which the light shines is most effective, and throws a nice warm red light over everything.

On Sunday we went to church. One day we motored to Promnitz for tea. Every one came except Mathilde and Anna, and Lorrie Larisch. It was a glorious afternoon, the sunset pink over the crisp white snow, and the moon rose full on the opposite side of the lake opposite the house; it was all still and white and not a bit cold. We had a homely tea at a big table, and I had had all the woods, through which we passed on the way home, lit up with red, green and white Bengal lights. I drove with the Emperor and took Hermann Hatz-

---

[1] Mr. Asquith's Government, April, 1908, to 1915.

feldt with me, going—and Heine Larisch in his place, coming back. . . .

In the evenings we talked—or rather the Emperor did. I never met a man who can remember such millions of things at the same time, even Irish stories (one of Patsy's oldest ones) which I suppose he heard in England—he repeated it in German—I nearly died with laughter. And then he half acts while he tells the stories ; one evening he went on from eleven till a quarter to one. And then at tea-time too he keeps on till nearly dinner-time. At least, all this happened here, but they all said that in other places he always left the room at once after tea, and sometimes did not even come to tea ! They had never seen him in such good spirits, and I really think he went out of his way to be nice. I sang standing on the staircase—the band from Salzbrunn accompanied me and played beautifully ; every one was astonished. Then the *Gesangverein* from Gleiwitz[1] of eighty women and a hundred men came one evening and sang for forty minutes in the big marble ballroom ; it was very fine.

Altogether, diary, the party was more than successful ; the last night, at dinner, Fritz Solms began to cry and look funny. I did not dare to look across at him ; and Hans asked me if I had noticed, and when I said, " Yes, what was it ? " Hans said he was so much affected by the whole thing being such a success ; and he always cries when he is emotional. Lulu wrote this morning and thanked me for having asked them. Anna also wrote and said that she and Mathilde thanked me for such a happy and *gemütliche Zeit*, adding : " It really all seemed like a sort of fairy enchanted house."

Everything went well and every one was happy. The last night we danced informally ; at least I and the girls did, and the Emperor came and looked on. Lulu, too, danced once or twice ; it was all just for fun, as we made even Prince Hatzfeldt dance : and he is a respectable grandfather. The orchestra was on the right-hand side of the top staircase, so it could not be seen, and Hans said therefore the dancing and the light looked very nice. In the party were Prince and Princess Fürstenberg, Prince and Princess Hatzfeldt, Prince and Princess Solms, Mathilde and Anna (my mother-in-law and her daughter), Heine Larisch and Lorrie—Count Larisch could not come. Then there was Frau von Jaenisch ; I asked her as her husband had to come with the Emperor ; and then

[1] A town some twenty miles north of Castle Pless.

several Gentlemen in attendance on the Emperor. Herr and Frau von Pohl were most useful and helped us enormously. The horses all went beautifully, and the servants, twenty-six in all at dinner, dressed in their gala uniforms looked really splendid.

The Emperor thanked me for everything and said the improvement to his rooms was really marvellous. He at once said he wished we would paint the dining-room pale green or cream white, instead of the awful black and chocolate colour it is now. The last night at dinner he laid a little case on my knee, and when I opened it I saw a bracelet with his miniature (rather bad) surrounded with great big diamonds on a gold curb chain. I really did not know what to say, I was so astonished. He said: "Don't say anything—put it on." Then he held my arm while I stretched it in front of him to show the bracelet to Mathilde who sat on the other side of him. I am surprised none of the other women were jealous, as he has been here many times in the old days, and never gave Mathilde anything; neither did he ever give anything to Lulu, or to Nathalie Hatzfeldt, both of whom have received him in their houses.

He was so nice to the children too, and the last night sent for them both without my knowledge. To my astonishment, when we were all assembled for dinner—all the *Oberförster*, General Director, Secretaries, and others—the door opened and in walked Hansel, and Lexel in his *dressing-gown*. I jumped up, but the Emperor said: "I sent for them," and he gave Hansel a pencil in gold, and Lexel a gold whistle; it was really too nice. Then, as we went in to dinner the children ran upstairs; of course Hansel went ahead and Lexel trying to be as quick fell on the stairs three times: the Emperor laughed and enjoyed it and said: "If the Empress were to see that she would preach to you for an hour; she always thinks a child can do nothing for itself and must always be followed and helped up, which is nonsense."

The Emperor left at eight a.m. I had said good-bye the night before but I got up as a surprise and went down to his sitting-room after he had left it (in my blue silk kimono and a gold Indian shawl) with both the boys, and waited for him to come in and say a last good-bye, and I really think he was sorry to go. I had a basket of flowers put in the train for him, with a *little* picture in it of Hansel and me, and on it I wrote: "A god-son and his Mummie, 1909."

Now I must go to bed; to-day is December 1st and to-

FÜRSTENSTEIN, SILESIA.

morrow a lot of people arrive to shoot, which is awful as I shall be alone. Hans leaves to-night for one of the Emperor's shooting places, and as the Emperor goes there himself and this is the first time he has ever asked Hans, he did not like to refuse. And the Duke of Holstein and his wife are coming!

December 1, 1909. Pless.

I wired the Queen of England for her birthday to-day, and she wired back: "I thank you and your dear Hans for kind wire for my old birthday." We looked up in the calendar and find she is sixty-five. It really seems *quite* impossible; she does not look a day older than fifty, and has a lovely figure and a straight back, and fresh red lips that are *not* painted, as one sees they are always moist. And I have seen her at Cowes in the pouring rain, and she certainly is not enamelled —and all that nonsense as the people say.

IV

By the middle of December we were at Eaton where Shelagh and Benny had a large party to meet the King and Queen. It included, so far as I can remember, Violet Rutland and her girl Marjorie Manners (now Lady Anglesey), dear Constance Shaftesbury, Alice Keppel, Lord Essex, Sir Fritz Ponsonby, Jimmy Alba and Soveral. But I must go back a little and let my diary tell what happened:

December 14, 1909. Eaton Hall, Chester.

Two days ago in London the Queen sent for me to go to Buckingham Palace at three o'clock, but I was in bed, far too ill with a horrible headache. I wrote to her explaining and she again sent for me the next day—to call before I left for Chester. I did not get the message till I came in to lunch, so I ate in a hurry and drove quickly to the Palace, as I did not want to miss my train down here. She was very sweet and looks so young. She saw me all alone, having come out in the middle of lunch; we talked a little—about the Emperor's visit to Pless and so on. Then I went with her into the dining-room; most homely, no ladies or gentlemen-in-waiting. Only the King and Queen of Norway (formerly little Princess Maud); her husband very good-looking, and the sweetest little boy, their son; and dear Princess Victoria. I was very sorry to have to hurry off so soon as I wanted to hear lots of things!

In London I had a little quiet serious talk with Metternich, and told him what the Emperor had said to me at Pless. Metternich makes me rather angry (I was staying at the Embassy). He is never there and I don't believe ever reads a paper; he takes a quiet sleepy view of everything—and things seem to me to be looking bad. And Soveral, the Portuguese Minister, is a firebrand against Germany.

The King talked to me after dinner last night. Here, and in Germany, they say it is impossible to find out what His Majesty really feels about the present policy of the British Government: but it was not difficult for me to find out last night as he asked me what I thought! I told him, and he said: "Yes! Yes! disgraceful, disgraceful!"[1]

I did not tell him that the Emperor had said that England must give up the idea of the two-power standard in the World's Navies! But I did tell him that the Emperor had said the best thing would be for a treaty to be made between England and Germany, and that his one desire was for peace and prosperity. The King thought for some time and then answered with a laugh: "Yes, and what would France and Russia say?"

I could not help replying: "France, I imagine, Sir, could only be delighted to be one in such a treaty and feel at rest, seeing that if there was a war between Germany and England, it would be France who would be the greatest sufferer, as the war would take place on her fields and in her towns and nowhere else. Germany is not going to risk losing any ships by coming to invade the English coast; she will march to England via France, as that country is in treaty with England."

"Well," he said, "we must keep the peace somehow."

There are two reasons why I shall never forget that talk and the party at Eaton. It was King Edward's last visit and throughout he was most kind and considerate. Then a happy little incident that took place will always remain fragrant in my memory as an

[1] Although her diary does not specifically say so, the Princess is no doubt referring to the late Lord Oxford and Asquith's Irish Home Rule policy, and the Socialistic experiments of his chief supporter, Mr. Lloyd George.

example of King Edward's warm nature, kindly heart and simple homeliness.

I was sitting next to him at luncheon one day when he asked: "What are you doing this afternoon?"

"Oh, nothing very amusing, Sir; motoring over to see my Granny at Brynedwyn: it is not far from here."

"Of course; quite right, too: I will come as well." I was startled for a moment, wondering what on earth I would do with the King for a whole afternoon at Granny's little cottage. Then, having gained time, I said:

"Alice Keppel is coming, Sir, and I doubt if there will be room?" But the King was not to be put off. Some of the party thought the whole expedition sheer madness. However, we three started. When we arrived I hurried ahead to prepare Granny a bit. She had just come in from a drive. Her bonnet was crooked, her lovely white hair all blown about and her nose red. The idea of seeing the King did not at all amuse her. She asked why he had come as she had nothing particular to show him.

However, the King was delightful, though he started badly by sitting down uninvited in Granny's favourite chair. He made outrageous love to the old lady and in a few minutes they were both flirting desperately. Granny never could resist flirting and neither could the King. Indeed Granny, who could have given points even to the flapper of to-day, would start a flirtation with St. Paul under the very eyes of the Deity!

Granny's father, when he was Lord-in-Waiting to Queen Victoria, was a particular favourite of Her Majesty and his daughters had naturally been a great deal at Court. Gossip, whether rightly or wrongly I don't know, had it that the Queen thought Granny unduly lively and attractive.

The King said: "Is it true that my Mother sent you away from Court for trying to flirt with my father?"

"I can't quite remember, Sir; most likely I wanted

to flirt with your father: he was a very good-looking man—besides, all the Coburgs inherited a roving eye. How humiliating it would be for a man to think that no woman ever wanted to flirt with him."

"I doubt, Lady Olivia, if that is a form of humiliation on which either you or I could pose as an authority."

The King admired very much some photographs of Patsy and of Granny's sister Mary whom he said he remembered well. We had tea and a delightfully cosy afternoon.

It was so nice, too, at dinner at Eaton being able to assure "anxious inquirers" that the King had enjoyed himself and the expedition been a great success. We are all human. I didn't want the King with me a bit, but have no doubt some members of the house-party thought Alice Keppel and I had "managed" the whole thing and they would therefore not have been sorry to think that the King had been bored to death, as they naturally did not feel flattered at His Majesty deserting them for the whole afternoon.

That was the King's last visit to Eaton, and I like to remember how he voluntarily gave up so much time to going to see an old woman and how successfully he made her feel that even if youth had fled, her attraction and charm remained.

V

From Eaton I went to Newlands, where I found the Grand Duke Michael, Sophy and Zia Torby. It was only a glimpse I got of them all because by the 9th I had to be home for a visit from the Crown Prince and Crown Princess. This is what my diary says about it:

January 17, 1910. Fürstenstein.

The Crown Prince and Princess were delighted with everything and propose to come again in June. We met them with two open carriages each with four horses, postilions, outriders and footmen in full dress. The whole of Freiburg was lit up, and all the school children and *Kriegerverein* lined the streets. It was very windy but the Crown Princess was delightful and did not mind a bit. As they arrived in the evening I had on a toque and a white fur coat over my evening dress. She said she was pleased that the Duke of Sparta was here, but I do not know whether she meant it. They left after dinner on the 12th and motored to Glatz in our motors which went well.

In the morning Hans had shown them all over the place, stables, horses, new buildings and so on. I did not get down till twelve o'clock, I had such a bad headache. Then we were all photographed and after lunch we had a paper chase; it had thawed, so we could not skate. Pat FitzPatrick, Hansel, and Dick Wyndham (Minnie's youngest boy) were hares, and most of us were hounds except the Crown Prince, who was not quite well and drove with Hans. Before we got to *Ma Fantaisie* for tea we were caught in a sudden and fearful snow-storm; when we arrived we all took off our coats and dried them in front of the fire, but little Hansel has had a cold ever since, poor little chap. I had a tent there for the tea, which was brought in, so somehow we all found room in the little cottage. I drove home with the Crown Prince, he would have held my hand if I had put it under the rug; and in my sitting-room which I was showing him in the morning, he quietly took my arm.

Before dinner I sang. I think they were very sorry to go. I will copy two telegrams from the Crown Princess, one she sent to Christa Salm, which Christa sent me to see, and the other I got direct from her to-day. The party was only the Stumm-Sierstorpffs and Wuthenaus (she is sister of the Duchess of Hohenberg, probably the future Queen of Hungary), the Duke of Sparta (the Duchess could not come), the Prince of Lynar, Marquess Pallavacini, besides Pat and his wife Grace, Minnie, and Shelagh. Shelagh had to leave on the morning of the 12th; I took her to the station in spite of guests and "crowned heads." . . . I am sorry to say she is disappointed with her villa at Nice. The 13th and 14th we shot again; all the guests stayed on. On the 11th, I forgot to say, we played Hockey on the grass as there was nothing else to do. Lynar and Pallavacini played well; all the children played too; *and* the Duke of Sparta, who was sick when he got home!

To-morrow I finally settle about the hotel at Salzbrunn. I spent the whole of the 15th in Breslau about it, and on the 19th I go to Count Pückler in Hirschberg to talk about the

Silesian lace industry; I meet Hans at Hirschberg station at half-past two, and we go on to Berlin for a fortnight; a Court, dinner-parties, and so on. On the 21st we dine with the Crown Prince and Princess.

January 27, 1910. Berlin. The Emperor's Birthday.

Just back from the gala Opera—the Overture and the second act of *Rienzi*, which I had never heard and which did not strike me at all as Wagnerian; it is so much lighter than most of his work. After the Opera there was the usual "Foyer" which was full of Royalties, every one very nice to me, saying I looked younger every day, and so on. The Crown Prince and Princess wishing they could come back with me to Fürstenstein and toboggan, and have fun. The Emperor said he had to get up and begin to receive congratulations at seven this morning!

The Crown Princess of Rumania and her husband are here; she is supposed to flirt with our Crown Prince and at luncheon at Christa Salm's the other day spoke of the time, a few years ago in Breslau at the Manœuvres,[1] when the Empress was not at all polite to all the Princesses, and the Crown Prince was not allowed to go near her! And now since he was in Rumania for the christening of her last baby all has changed! I think some understanding about a *railroad* was arrived at; for the sake of diplomacy and commerce much is often forgotten—and too much often remembered.

What have I been doing since I last wrote? Well, I have been to a Court. We had dinner with the Crown Prince and Princess, a nice little party and music afterwards; they wanted me to sing, but all the music that the professional had with her was too high, and I had none of my own. Grusfeldt played the 'cello. The Crown Princess is in some ways as charming as a naughty child and *won't* wear mourning for her grandfather,[2] her excuse being that "Wilhelm hates black." I faintly suggested white, pale mauve and grey, but she was wearing blue and pink roses and looked very beautiful. He went about looking very happy.

Then Hans and I dined at the Palace, to our astonishment quite alone—no party; only the Empress and her daughter, the Emperor, and the usual in-Waitings. The Emperor was

---

[1] See page 124.

[2] The Grand Duke Michael Nicholaievitch, who died at Cannes on December 5, 1909.

three-quarters of an hour late and kept us all waiting. He had been to a big men's meeting commemorating the battle of Höhenfriedberg and of course they all drank to the health of Frederick the Great. So at dinner I said:

"Your Majesty must indeed praise Frederick the Great for the possession of Silesia; it is the biggest gem in the Prussian crown."

To which he haughtily answered:

"Yes, and if it wasn't for Frederick the Great you would not now be in Fürstenstein."

I could not understand the sense of this, so replied quite truthfully and naturally:

"But, Sir, Fürstenstein belonged to the Hochbergs centuries before Frederick the Great was born; the only difference to me would have been that instead of being in Berlin, I would now be in Vienna!"

He looked and said nothing, or I might perhaps have added: "But I am more than glad to be in Berlin instead, and a subject of Your Majesty's." So I said nothing either, only smiled right *at* him!

Soon after dinner the Empress showed me her picture by Laszló, which is very good but not flattering; then she guessed I was going on to the Italian Embassy and made me leave in time for the cotillion. I must say she was charming. I told her about the lace in Hirschberg, the new hotel in Salzbrunn, my cripple school and so on. In spite of Frederick the Great the Emperor was very nice at dinner; we talked of all sorts of things, even about the new bathrooms in Pless, and his rooms there.

Then the day before yesterday there was a big reception at the French Embassy, in honour of the French picture exhibition, lots of people having come over from Paris on purpose—but not the best people! The Emperor and all the Royal Family were there. I sat next to Prince August Wilhelm[1]; he looks about twenty, and is twenty-three; he has just married his first cousin, a Holstein; he does not shoot, but plays the violin I believe. I have promised to dance the cotillion with him at his brother's ball (Prince and Princess Eitel Friedrich's). This ball is a fearful bore, but Hans insists on my going, although he will not be here; he has to go to Vienna for three nights about some exhibitions of wild animals. The two buffaloes the Emperor shot at Pless are being sent there stuffed. There are some fearful dinners coming on, and some

[1] The Emperor's fourth son.

stupid balls, and two Court Balls, and so on, and I *wish* I were in Fürstenstein.

Irma Fürstenberg gave a big supper to-night after the Opera and a dance afterwards. All Berlin is supping here.[1] To-night, the "tiara" set, and the "hat" set are staring at one another, but I really couldn't face it all and start making more stupid conversations—which I did for an hour at the Opera House. So in spite of all their faces of astonishment, I am up here and now in my bed, having had a cup of hot soup and a leg of cold chicken ; as my maid went out I *picked* the leg, with my teeth and said :

"Marie, I couldn't do this downstairs, could I?" And she looked quite sad as she replied :

"Oh, Your Highness, and just to-night when it seems you look extra pretty and every one wants you ; I am most sorry."

"But, Marie, these two warm bottles are much more comforting than two ugly silly men whom I should have had to sit next to downstairs."

There I sat with a foot on each warm-water bottle in the bed (it is bitterly cold outside).

Before leaving Berlin I duly held my sale of Silesian work at the Hotel Esplanade. The Empress allowed all the Princesses to come (with their husbands in attendance of course) : this was a great honour as the etiquette was that they never entered an hotel. Her Majesty received me afterwards and was extremely charming. When writing (after I got home) to thank her for being a Patron I told her I was expecting a baby and she personally wrote a very nice letter with a "God bless you" at the end of it. She was a thoroughly good, kindly woman.

From Berlin we went direct to Monte Carlo which Hans always loved. Personally I think it is a boring place as there is nothing to do but gamble, gossip and eat. I like an occasional gamble but cannot bear spending my days and nights in the Rooms or at the Sporting Club. As for food and gossip, one is everywhere surfeited with both.

I must say I like Bohemians and Bohemian society.

---

[1] The Hotel Esplanade.

I dare say it is as boring as any other when one knows it well ; but to me it had always the charm of novelty. Moreover, one can say (more or less) what one thinks and that one could never do in Court Circles in Berlin :

The other night at Nice, Muriel Wilson, Millicent Cowley (she was Lady Hartopp) and I dined with Monsieur Bernstein, the author who writes plays for Sarah Bernhardt ; he looks like a long sick worm, but is very clever ; he asked all the cosmopolitan society left in Nice : dear old Baron Plessen and another nice German boy—I forget his name—the Duke of Elchingen (Princess Murat's brother), a Marquess something else, and two Poles whose names I can't remember or spell—one I had often seen. When he was introduced he sat down and I thought he was mad, and kept Plessen close to me. He began in French :

" *Toute la semaine j'ai souffert, depuis que je vous ai vue ; vous êtes pour moi la plus belle femme que j'ai jamais vue.*"

I laughed and thought it would be silly to get up, so told him :

" *Je ne crois jamais aux compliments.*"

" *Je le sais, je le sais*—but you can always know that once you made a man *presque fou et misérable.*" I merely said :

" *Presque fou ! Je vous aurais cru tout à fait fou.*"

Muriel danced and I sang—even French songs, and a coon song. All the men went on their knees round me begging me to sing again *Vous êtes si jolie*, which they swore I sang without any accent. The middle-aged enormous fat curly-headed Pole is a musician and he paid me marvellous compliments, and said I had all the " tricks of the art of singing." I said the " tricks " were not taught, they were natural to me.

Anyway at supper they were all delighted and Bernstein said they all talked of it afterwards. He sat next to me and began to sing a part of *Faust* and at the end he said :

" *Eh bien, qu'est-ce que Marguerite a dit ?* " I answered :

" *Eh bien, j'imagine que si Faust a continué comme cela pour longtemps, il a diablement embêté Marguerite.*" He was furious and changed seats with Charlie Wood (dear Gordy's brother) who then sat next to me. I said :

" I feel there'll be a row."

We were all tired. At last I said to Monsieur Bernstein :

" It is after one, and my poor footman and chauffeur have been waiting since eleven-thirty." He turned round and said :

"*Eh bien,—et nous—est-ce que nous comptons pour moins que vos domestiques? Vous pensez plus à vos domestiques qu'à nous.*"

So I answered:

"*Oui, c'est naturel; mes domestiques, je les connais depuis plusieurs années—et vous, je vous connais depuis quelques minutes.*"

From the Riviera I went to Fürstenstein for one night just to arrange about the garden of the Salzbrunn Hotel. From there I travelled by night to Pless, using our own private saloon and sleeping in my own bed —a luxury I always appreciated. We stayed at Pless for a short spell, Hans and Hansel hunting three times a week. Prince Lichnowsky motored over twice to go out with hounds and to lunch.

There was a squadron of the 11th Uhlans quartered in Pless; Hans wanted the officers to hunt, but they were too frightened. Then General von X., commanding the 6th Army Corps, the Colonel Commanding the Regiment stationed at Neisse and several A.D.C.'s and Staff Officers all came to inspect the poor little timid squadron and stayed with us for two nights. They shot roebuck and ate and drank a lot. The old Colonel went out, missed three times and knocked his eye so badly with the edge of the telescope fixed on the rifle that we had to send for a doctor and have it sewn up. Count Vico Voss shot three roebuck and I shot one.

The second night the Inspecting General was at Pless we gave a dinner-party. All the neighbours, people from the towns and their wives. Frau von Pohl came from Fürstenstein to help. She told them all what to do and posted me as to how many children each one had, what their principal interest was and little things like that. Cousin Adelaide Taylour was also a great help, as she "gets on" so well with every one.

When we got rid of our Generals Hans and I went to Vienna for a few days. It was a very easy journey from Pless; the city in May was glorious, and the people fascinating and Hans and I both loved it.

Before we left Fürstenstein I had heard of King Edward's death, my diary will tell how:

May 23, 1910. Vienna, Hotel Bristol.

The one terrible moment that came as a great shock to me was when I was alone at Fürstenstein and Hans in Breslau. My maid came in with my breakfast and the news: "They say the King of England is dead; the English huntsman has had a wire from his wife in Bremen." I tried not to believe it and wired to the Embassy in Berlin, and got the answer that it was true.

The shock I may say has passed, but the feeling of a sudden dark cloud and great change will remain for very long, I am sure; in fact for me the whole face of England seems changed, only my own homes remain the same. But London—Court Balls—Cowes Week—and so many other things are so closely connected with this dear, dear King that I don't feel as if I should ever want to go near them again; and as Hans said: "You will go there to see your parents, and I to get my breeches and that's all."

And lately I had met him so often and so intimately! Last year in Berlin, then Windsor for Ascot, and dinners and so on in London, Cowes Week, and then this December at Eaton, and his visit to darling old Granny. As well as a great King he was the kindest gentleman and truest friend one could ever hope to meet. He was so human, so full of sympathy and understanding; he attracted even dogs and children to him. Although I was devoted to my father-in-law, I was more self-conscious and less natural with him than I was with King Edward. I wrote to the present King, and to the darling Queen Alexandra, and Princess Victoria, Soveral and Alice Keppel . . . poor dear, she was his friend and confidant since so many years. At any rate when the King was dying and unconscious the Queen sent for her and herself led Alice to his bedside. I say God bless her for it. I find this natural somehow; but few women would have done it. The King had had several fainting fits, like the one he had in Berlin whilst sitting on the sofa next to me, but of course lasting much longer. He died peacefully.

I feel (and am not the only one in England, so Cousin Adelaide tells me) that on the top of the King's serious illness in Biarritz, to come back to be dragged into the middle of a political struggle verging on Socialism and to see his country falling towards a blind pit of darkness ; the anxiety it caused him and a wish perhaps for hurried speech, was quite enough to give him a shocking fit and so kill him. I wrote and said more than this to Mr. Asquith. A copy of this letter is with the other copies of special letters, and their answers. He is the present Prime Minister. I know it is an awful thing to have done, but what do I care, what does it matter to me ?

The King passed away four years before the outbreak of the Great War which he had long dreaded. His end was hastened and his last moments embittered by the prospect of fratricidal strife between England and Ireland, the uprising of a fierce and vindictive spirit of Socialism and by the cynical attempts of his own Government to destroy the Second Chamber, which in England, more than in any other country in the world, is the one barrier against hasty and ill-considered legislation. As I was not in London at the time, my father sent me the following account of a very sad, but interesting historical occasion :

NEWLANDS MANOR, LYMINGTON, HANTS, *May* 21, 1910.

MY DARLING DAISY,—

I came down here from London after witnessing one of the most remarkable sights it is possible to imagine. I mean a population of millions of people mourning its King. The number and demeanour of the masses of human beings in the whole three miles of the funeral Pageant was most amazing —all uncovered and silent—one and all felt they had lost a friend as well as a Sovereign. The effect on the popular mind will do wonders for monarchical institutions and this alone will entitle King Edward to everlasting gratitude. Queen Alexandra bowed her thanks and she behaved throughout with splendid courage. George V. looked very regal on horseback, which surprised some people, and the Kaiser in his English Field-Marshal's uniform very imperial. I had a chance of an official ticket but I preferred going to Brooks' in St. James's Street, where just above the level of the street one had a fine view of this historic scene. The Grand Duke Michael who was riding recognized me : he was amongst the minor Royalties.

You are right in supposing that the anxiety caused by the political situation had much to do with the late King's desire to return instead of waiting in the South till we had got rid of the piercing east winds then prevailing in England.

It is said poor Mrs. George Keppel was not recognized by the King when she went to the Palace—he was too ill.

People are of course speculating even now what the new Court will be like and they anticipate a good deal of change. I know the new Queen better than I do the King—and have a high opinion of her good sense and courtesy. It is said the King is a bad linguist which, if true, is unfortunate.

Shelagh is wonderfully well: Benny runs down to-day till Monday. He is out with his Yeomanry. Patsy is fairly well.

I hope you are all flourishing and I am always your ever loving

POPPETS.

VI

To carry on as usual after the loss of our dear ones causes us to feel somehow a traitor to the dead; to fail to carry on makes us a traitor to the living. In the beginning of June I had to be at Fürstenstein to receive the Archduke Karl, who, unknown to himself and to us, was heir to such a tragic destiny:

June 3, 1910. Fürstenstein.

We arrived here yesterday, it was very hot and to-day it is pouring and windy and there was thunder all the morning. Our Crown Prince arrives in half an hour, at half-past six. The little Archduke of twenty-two arrived half an hour ago; he is the Archduke Otto's eldest son, and will be Emperor of Austria one day, unless the morganatic children of the Archduke Franz Ferdinand and the Duchess of Hohenberg are accepted as Royal; she is charming and will anyhow have a right to be proclaimed Queen of Hungary; indeed most people in Austria already look upon her as their future Empress.

I really could not sit downstairs for a whole hour now and make conversation, so I showed the Archduke to his room and said that as he had got up so early I was sure he would like a little rest. They all laughed when I came downstairs and said I had told him to go to bed like a child—his Aides-de-camp went upstairs with him. He and the Crown Prince will both go out shooting each day; dinner is at nine so it will give me time to have a quarter of an hour's walk and a rest.

To-morrow is the unveiling of the *Denkmal*, or monument, in remembrance of the battle of Hohenfriedberg. We leave at half-past ten. In the afternoon there is to be a drag hunt. Then there will be a day's racing in Breslau. Thank goodness I feel well, but I do not wear my pretty clothes as I shall wear mourning for our dear King as long as England does. I got the nicest letter from King George this morning, so genuine and full of affection. It is amongst the other letters I keep in case anyone will ever care to read them. I was not able to make up a smart party now, every one being away in Vienna for the Derby week. I asked every nice and good-looking woman I could think of, but none could come! There are here now only Count and Countess Herberstein, Prince and Princess Metternich (she is a beautiful woman and has brought a pretty niece with her), and Cousin Adelaide Taylour, who is always such good company.

June 12, 1910. Fürstenstein.

I really could not write before; I have been enjoying a few peaceful days since the Crown Prince's party broke up. It went off very successfully. One evening I had a very clever reciter and the next evening the band came and played and I sang with it, and the Crown Prince and one or two men danced. I, too, danced three times; as Fritz, who was here, in one of his most charming and agreeable moods said, I really showed nothing of my sadness. I set them all going and then sat down. We had the Royal Pavilion at the Breslau Races and served a big tea to all the "Silesian nobility." It was a fine sight! The Crown Prince left at six-thirty; all the others stayed on for dinner. Hansel and I drove back in a motor from seeing them off and I felt very pleased to find myself alone in an empty house.

I drove through the town with the little Archduke in a state landau escorted by outriders, Jägers and so on, and three other landaus with four horses followed; the whole thing made a good impression, and I must say the horses and carriages are beautiful—but how much I prefer my little *Schwarzen Graben*. . . .

Hans left five days ago for Berlin; he had to receive the Emperor and Empress at the opening of the new race-course as he is now President of the Union Club. He writes to-day that he sent for Freytag to do a lot of correspondence à propos of the Polish question, as he is trying to arrange that the Polish nobility shall give the Emperor a big reception, for the first time in history, when he goes to Posen.[1] Of course this would be grand and diminish the bitter and exaggerated feeling that the Germans now show against the Poles. It is all being done secretly and no one knows of it, except of course the Emperor! Hans had to go to see the Chancellor and other Ministers about it.

I have more than once mentioned my sister-in-law, Lulu (Louise) Solms and said what a kind staunch friend she is. I used to go to her in all my difficulties and she never failed me. With a good brain and a strong character, she is my ideal of a real *Christian gentlewoman*. I had poured out some trouble or another to her and this letter which I received in reply will give a much better idea than I can of the fine woman she is. And then her quiet keen sense of humour—so un-Germanic. Rosy is her daughter, a lovely girl, who married Prince Otto of Salm-Horstmar. I suppose I was depressed as one sometimes is in such circumstances. But apart from any temporary causes such as the state of my health, I suffered from a feeling of deep foreboding which I could not throw off:

KLITSCHDORFF. *June*, 1910.

DEAREST DAISY,—

Thank you so much for your dear letter. I'll tell you first of all, my dear, a truth to which Rosy, in her wisdom, arrived in no time which is this: That men are childish silly things, that think themselves cleverer than women, and are, and stay childish with their "bigger brains" and all their superiority. And then they are so vain.

Well, Rosy tackles hers quite nicely, but it made me laugh when she told me quite seriously her discovery. I think we are apt to forget so often that they are big babies, and as we can't slap them as we would little babies, we have got to get round them by flattering them and admiring them.

I think this whole building in Fürstenstein also, is only vanity of Hans, because really you never can want all those rooms to live in. Perhaps once or twice a year he will fill

[1] To impress and influence the Poles the Emperor had built a fine Royal residence in Posen and had appointed Count Hutten-Czapski, a Polish noble, as its Lord Warden.

them with guests, but most of the time you don't want them, and you might quite well do without them. I quite understand he wants to do up some things, and alter here and there, now he has more money, but I think the building a mistake, only to think about the servants you will want, to keep the thing going, and thinking of the future for Hansel, when everything will be more expensive than it is now, and no income growing in the same way as the expenses. But I think one thing, dear, if you wanted to stay at home Hans would let you, and I think he would by and by feel himself, that he too wants rest and quiet. If you simply tell him: "I'm going to stay here quietly with the children during summer," he can't force you to go to Vienna, or Paris or anywhere. I know he likes to go to the Riviera in spring for a few weeks, and naturally you want to go and see your father so long as you have him, but why are you continually moving from Fürstenstein to Pless and vice versa?

My parents used to come to Fürstenstein in spring and my mother stayed there till autumn, when she went to Pless. Naturally Vater went to Pless for a fortnight and so on, but everybody knew that the *family* was at Fürstenstein. I really believe, it has a good influence on everybody, husband included, to know there is a *Mittelpunkt*, where they can come and rest, and get advice and be petted. I am quite sure it is a mistake of the Empress going away herself the moment the Emperor's back is turned, it puts everything in unrest, and makes him lose the feeling of "home."

You say you have dark days before you, dear, thinking of the possible loss of your parents. But think how happy you are to keep them so long. It is a sorrow I never can get over, that my Mother did not see my children, and did not see my life arranging itself. What delightful times I have got with Rosy seeing all this! And she missed it, Mother I mean, though I think she sees and knows. I pray to God, for all of us, but particularly for your parents, you won't die first, as you say. I don't think there is anything more unnatural than the grief of parents seeing their grown-up children die!

I don't think, getting on with your letter, it is true what you say about Hans, he was *very much* in love with you when you married, and he used to tell us all your many graces and accomplishments, of which you had seven or nine, if I remember rightly, including sculpturing, painting, and singing. And when we came to England and saw you, we naturally all went

MYSELF AND MY ELDEST SON, HANSEL.
From a portrait by Ellis Roberts.

down before you. I believe every one of us has his pack to carry and I suppose it is all right.

I should be ungrateful grumbling, having so much, but naturally I would have arranged my life a little differently, had I had the arranging of it, when I think and remember *what* I thought life would give me when I was young. I read somewhere of somebody having the blues, somebody old like me, and walking out in the woods, in autumn, seeing the leaves drop quietly to the earth, and saying: This is God's goodness, to let the old leaves drop and make a covering for the young ones coming; so it is with life, I can't ask anything more for myself, but God in His bounty still to use me to shelter those to come. So I'll gladly shed my leaves on Faleusec or whatever place you get your baby at, if I can manage it, dearest, only I am not sure if I can, as perhaps we'll have guests here, and I can't leave. Yours,

LOUISE.

At the end of June Shelagh's second girl, Mary, was born at Eaton. I spent my birthday in England and on July 30 was present at St. Mark's, North Audley Street, where the baby was christened, I being one of the sponsors. I was at Newlands for Cowes and from there went to Eaton for Shelagh's Polo week. We had good weather, good Polo, good company and therefore of course a good time. The chief guests were the King and Queen of Spain, and the King not only played Polo hard, but found time to go to see the Spring Hill Beagles. Others in the party were the Castlereaghs (now Londonderrys), Lord Shrewsbury, Reggie Herbert (Pembroke), and George Wyndham.

On September 23 my youngest son, Conrad Frederick (whom we called Bolko) was born at Lichterfelde, near Berlin. The Crown Prince was his godfather. I was terribly ill; indeed I have never quite recovered. For a long time they thought that I would die.

I find amongst my letters one to my mother from dear Madeline Wyndham,[1] the delightful old mother

[1] The late Honourable Mrs. Percy Wyndham of Clouds, mother of the late Right Honourable George, and Colonel Guy, Wyndham.

of George and Guy. It was written about six weeks after Bolko was born:

CLOUDS, EAST KNOYLE, SALISBURY. *November* 10, 1910.

DARLING PATSY,—

My deepest thoughts and prayers are with you in this fresh anxiety, but I do hope and believe your darling Daisy with her wonderful spirit and pluck will soon win the fight against those terrible clots. . . . She is so strong in herself and young. And God will save her (she is so good) to live and make better the world with her sweet goodness and gentleness. Minnie will be so grieved to hear of this fresh attack, but I have known people get through worse attacks of these clots, and get quite strong after it. God bless you and darling Shelagh, Yours lovingly,

MADELINE WYNDHAM.

A week or two later I received this from Patsy:

November 26, 1910.

MY LITTLE DANY,—

How strange you should write that God and good spirits are very near one? For all my prayers have been, "Oh Almighty and Powerful God, send a dear gentle loving spirit to my Daisy, to guard her through the night and day, and please send one to me too, God."

My Dany, this is so like you—I copy it from a book of mine:

"Love, redolent with unselfishness bathes all in beauty and light. The grass beneath our feet silently exclaims the meek and gentle shall inherit the earth—pure unselfish love like sweet flowers sends its sweet breath to Heaven, glances into the prison cells, glides into the sick chamber, brightens the flowers, beautifies the landscape, blesses the earth—makes the little children smile—and helps the weary-hearted."

That's what my Daisy will do with her beautiful nature and God will make you strong and well, my darling—and yes, a happier time is before us now. God will be with us and help us. If we could only realize—God is all powerful—is ever present and He is good—so there is nothing to fear. Good night, my most precious one,

PATSY.

CHAPTER SEVEN

1911–1913

THE visit to Nice not doing me as much good as we had hoped we decided to make up a small party and go to Egypt. I wanted to stay in Khartoum and, from there, go further south, so I wrote to Lord Kitchener who was then His Britannic Majesty's Agent and Consul-General in Egypt, for help and advice. There was not much time to work out plans but he wired to Sir Reginald Wingate, the Sirdar of the Egyptian Army and Governor-General of the Sudan Provinces, who was most kind.

The complete change of scene and climate had its effect and, in spite of the sophistication of travel in Egypt, did something to satisfy my incurable love of wandering. Hans could not get away, so there was only Shelagh, Benny and myself.

By the end of March I was back at Cimiez, above Nice. Here are two entries from my diary:

March 22, 1911. La Pastourelle, Nice.

On the 19th we all dined in Monte Carlo—Shelagh, Oscar Herren, Poppets and Gerald Paget, who are all staying with us here. Stumm-Sierstorpff gave the dinner at Ciro's and there was a *Bataille de fleurs* towards the end of dinner and all the people threw flowers at each other; it was quite amusing, but somehow I have not "come back to life yet" and the music, and the people, and the noise and laughter only jarred on me, and sounded sad and far away. I was the last woman to leave our table, and, as I walked through, the people stood up—I carried a stick and I expect lots of them knew I had been very ill—and they pelted me with flowers. I had to shut my eyes and hold on to the chairs to feel my way through the restaurant. I sat next to old Nimptsch at dinner and he said I looked more beautiful than ever before, and younger; I am glad if this pleases other people; as for myself I really do not seem to care!

I used to love to meet the Empress Eugénie and her friends. Several times she had staying with her old Madame de Pourtalès. She was still very handsome with lovely features and to see these two famous beauties side by side was like stepping back into another century. Madame de Pourtalès had been very kind in recommending Bagnolles in Normandy to me for a cure. She had also promised Patsy to give me the name of some lotion for my leg. Passing the door one day I thought, in my impulsive way, that I could stop and ask for this without paying a formal call. I was untidy and tired and did not want to be seen. This is what happened:

March 26, 1911. La Pastourelle, Nice.

This afternoon we went to have tea at Mentone at the tea-shop where, on previous visits, we have often gone with the children; the head woman was so pleased to see me, and said how sorry she was to hear that I had been ill, and that they had all wanted to send me some flowers but had not known where to send them. I thanked her, and meant it, for the nice thought.

On our way back we stopped at the Empress Eugénie's to ask Madame de Pourtalès for the name of the stuff to put on my phlebitis leg, that she had told Patsy about when she and Shelagh went to Villa Cyrnos to call on the Empress. When we arrived we found a lot of people at the door, so I tried to hide in the corner, not being in the mood to see them. We sent in the message hoping they would think that a footman had come to ask. But unluckily, one of us had been seen and out they all came, including old Madame de Pourtalès, about eighty. She got into the car to talk to me; I had not seen her since King Edward's last visit to Paris. Then her daughter got in and asked me to come to Paris, saying she would arrange all sorts of fêtes for me. I could quite well have got out of the car, but pretended I couldn't. Then the Empress suddenly appeared and I felt an awful fraud; and she also climbed into the car and sat and talked to me; she is eighty-four, and looked very well and is always so dear and nice, just like Granny. Then we drove away and they were all very sorry for me not knowing I had got out at Mentone and had a large tea!

Here are extracts from another letter from my sister-in-law, Lulu Solms. It is so characteristic of her and gives a glimpse of her delicious humour and happy domestic life. "Our Princess" is of course the Emperor's sweet only daughter, Princess Victoria Louise, then aged nineteen; the Prince of Wales was then only seventeen:

. . . I haven't heard anything from you for ages, which is my fault, as I didn't write. Duke Ernst Günther was here the other day and said you looked lovely, and just eighteen! Well, I don't look eighteen or fifty either. I look like sixty; I've grown fat and grey. And my Fritz thinks me quite good-looking still; but naturally a man wouldn't know, being married so long. . . . Do you go to England for the Coronation? . . . Do you believe the Prince of Wales is going to marry our Princess? He is so young; but they hint at it in the papers. I don't believe it. . . .

We remained the whole spring and early summer at La Pastourelle which had a lovely big garden for the children. I determined to be well enough to attend King George V.'s Coronation. In due course I did so, and sat on the right of the altar amongst the distinguished foreigners, only a very few having been invited. I had a perfect view of this significant and moving ceremonial:

June 23, 1911. Grosvenor House, London.

So many months I have not written, but everything seemed to weigh too heavily on me to bother to take paper and pen. I have had a very happy Spring in England. I went to dear old Ruthin which was looking lovely, and Patsy and I went to Llanarmon which was also looking beautiful and I fished for trout in a lovely river.

I got back to Pless the first days of May, Baron Nimptsch and Oscar Herren coming too; we stalked and boated, and celebrated Hans's birthday on the 23rd of May instead of the 23rd of April; but unluckily it poured with rain. Then we went to Fürstenstein; little Patsy came for ten days and we cut down trees at the *Daisysee*, which was a great success, to show up some fine old beech and birch. Count Vico Voss came for a day or two and we fished there together. He is not very well, or very happy, poor dear. Then we were suddenly asked here for the Coronation; it was very nice of the King, as no foreigners were invited (like last time) except of course a heap of Royalties.

The Coronation was a superb sight and the King dressed in flowing robes of gold. After he had taken off the long ermine-trimmed overmantle in which he arrived, he looked like the picture of a Byzantine saint or prophet. His regalia was so heavy he could scarcely walk. But all the time I felt sad, as I could not help thinking of the late dear King whom one really knew intimately and loved, and who was always so kind and pleased to see one. . . . I wrote to Queen Alexandra as soon as I got back; she remained at Sandringham.

The Crown Prince and Princess (German) are having grand receptions here. I heard from her this evening, delighted with it all. I have to play hostess for Wolff-Metternich at the Embassy on Sunday. No one else is invited to dine as he has no room; there are twenty-four German royalties alone. I don't know what I shall do with them after dinner!

Every one is *so* nice and pleased to see me well again, but although I arrived here only five days ago, it seems like five weeks, and I shall be glad to go with little Shelagh peacefully on her yacht on the 30th to steam up the canals of Holland.

The echoes of the solemn music of the King of England's Coronation had hardly died away before the Emperor astonished his true friends, Germany, and the World, by sending the German gunboat *Panther* to anchor before Agadir—the key to Morocco. Every one sensible had thought that the Algeciras Conference of 1906 had once and for all settled the situation there, as Germany had then specifically declared that she had no special interests in Morocco.

I was terribly distressed both by the political situation in England and the disquieting look of European affairs. In August there was a large party at Eaton for the King and Queen of Spain and, while there, I had the following letter from Lord Rosebery:

MENTMORE, LEIGHTON BUZZARD, *August* 6, 1911.

DEAR PRINCESS OF PLESS,—

I see you are to be at Eaton this week, and so I know an address to which I can write my apologies for not having answered your letter in the Spring.

The fact is that it perplexed me a little, as it urged the concession of Irish Home Rule, which I have no power to promote, even if I had the inclination, which I have not. Those who have the power, i.e., the Ministry, have also the inclination; so that you need not fear.

While I was deliberating, I saw in the newspapers that you had left for the Riviera, but without giving your address. So I bided my time till I should know it.

I hope too this explanation leaves me blameless! And that you are all right again. Yours sincerely,

RY.

From Eaton I went to Bagnolles in Normandy to do the cure recommended by Madame de Pourtalès, and while I was there Hans did one in Marienbad. The children passed the summer between England, Ostend and Klitschdorf. From Bagnolles I wrote to the Emperor as follows. I really could not resist doing so. It was said at the time by many in authority, and I for one believed it, that the plan of sending the *Panther* to Agadir originated with the Foreign Secretary, Herr von Kiderlen-Waechter, and was carried out in spite of misgivings expressed by the Emperor as to its danger. Kiderlen's idea of course was to strike a blow at the *Entente Cordiale*. The blow failed and, as usual, the Emperor had to bear the blame.

SIRE, YOUR MAJESTY,—

The present moment in England is one of suspense and anxiety, also in France, from where I write. The First Person in England told me at Cowes (not privately, so I do not consider it wrong to repeat it to Your Majesty), that in May last, your promised word to him was that if further difficulties arose in Morocco a European Conference would be summoned. He said to me: "Is this calling a European Conference, to send a war-ship suddenly to Agadir?" I said: "Yes, it was absolutely right; it was a movement to bring things to a head and to force a Conference, so that other Powers should not go to sleep and then wake up some day to find Morocco a French Colony, while England looked on all the time from the corner of her eye ! "

Sire, even women may think, and feel things sometimes, and I *cannot* see war coming ; I will not believe it. But now at this moment I have met people here whom I have never met before who although naturally they wish the best for themselves and their country, England, all say, " Germany has our greatest respect." Well, if now (it is not too late) Your Majesty's Government calls this Conference all Europe will raise one voice in praise of Your Majesty, and will say, it is the Emperor who has kept the peace ; the Emperor has kept his word and called this Conference. It is the German Emperor who leads the world, and the Morocco question will be then settled once and for all in full agreement with the rest of Europe. And it will be Your Majesty who will have led the way.

Sire, war would bring disaster on all countries for years, and at a moment when German commerce is on the verge of completely triumphing—as indeed she is doing in all things.

And if war is made and lost by her, it will be her Emperor who will be blamed by all the German middle classes, talkers, merchants, tradespeople and socialists ; but if peace is maintained by a European Conference, the Emperor will be acknowlodged the greatest man in Europe ; and although Europe knows this now, its nations will then be only too glad to own it publicly, and " Peace " will restore " goodwill towards men."

God bless you, Sire, always.

Early in September Hans was in London. I wrote begging him to find out the feeling there regarding the possibilities of war. Of course it was an unfavourable time of the year as everybody likely to be in the least behind the scenes was out of town. Hans wrote: " There has never been any war without at least one of the parties concerned wanting it. That is simple enough. . . . Here at the Foreign Office they seem to believe that Germany wants war, which is of course nonsense." . . .

Was it ?

The Emperor was coming to Pless for a shooting party from December 1st to 5th. I determined to do two things : give him a good time and have some serious conversation. I had a cheery party: Mildred, Winifred and Anthony Alsopp, Olivia FitzPatrick, Bertie Paget, Alec Thynne and brother George.

The Emperor duly arrived. On Advent Sunday we all went to the Evangelical Church at Pless. The Minister, a dear, earnest man, preached a fine sermon on humility, broadmindedness and brotherliness, qualities which, presumably, the Emperor never for a moment considered that he in any degree lacked.

It would be ridiculous for me to claim that my letters to the Emperor and Baron von Stumm, and what I said to them both at Pless, had any fundamental effect on European affairs. Yet the mouse helped the lion, and the facts remain.

During his stay I spoke to the Emperor with absolute freedom and openness. It must be remembered that I had several marked advantages. I was not the Emperor's servant and he could not therefore lose prestige in his own eyes by listening to me or following my advice; I was English, and the Emperor always liked and admired the English; I was frank, outspoken and quite fearless and independent; last of all, I was a woman and when the Emperor really admired or cared for a woman he was far more influenced than he would ever have cared to admit. The Emperor simply could not do without feminine sympathy and understanding. Sympathy and the utmost devotion he always got from the Empress, but I doubt very much if she ever really understood him.

Whatever the worth of my efforts the Emperor in January let it be known that he would welcome private conversations and a frank exchange of views between Berlin and London and, as a result, the English Cabinet and Sir Edward Grey sent Lord Haldane on his famous visit to Berlin in February.

On December 6, the day after the Emperor left Pless, I wrote and invited Baron von Stumm, who was then in the Foreign Office, to visit us and I told him (quite privately) that by coming he might do work that would have valuable political results. The Baron came. We had long talks and, after his return to Berlin, he wrote to me as follows in very good English:

BERLIN, HOHENZOLLERNSTRASSE 8, *December* 27, 1911.

DEAR PRINCESS,—

May I wish you a merry Christmas and a happy New Year before you start for England? I hope you will have a smooth crossing. I was so glad you invited me to Pless the other day and I hope I succeeded in convincing your English friends that we don't entertain any hostile designs here against England, and that the most unfortunate situation that has arisen is due in the greater part to mistrust, without any foundation.

If you go to England, you can be of very much use in always insisting on this point, and in telling people how much the speech of Mr. Lloyd George [1] has been resented here, which came out of this mistrust.

As we agreed the other night, something positive should be done to bring about a change and the best way would be to come to some understanding of a political nature. It does not matter much on which question this would be the case. And I think it would be better, at the present juncture, not to mention any particular point, as this might be talked about and give those people who are always seizing every opportunity of making mischief between the two countries an excuse for again accusing us of nefarious designs and secret plans for injuring England's position in the world.

But I think, no harm can be done if you tell people that you know positively that we should be only too pleased to come to an understanding on some colonial or other question, where we could meet the wishes of England and at the same time ourselves get something, in order to be able to convince those that are always pretending England grudges us everything, that they are wrong. Once such an agreement was concluded, matters would improve very quickly. I feel sure of that. But something ought to be done to disperse the clouds that are hanging over us.

Hoping to see you and to hear from you on your return from England, I ask you to believe me, dear Princess, Yours very sincerely,

STUMM.

---

[1] In the City of London on July 21, 1911.

The outcome of the policy outlined in this letter was that Germany recognized the French protectorate in Morocco in return for a section of the French Congo; but it was not a victory for either Germany or Kiderlen-Waechter because even at the time popular opinion in Germany laughed at the "compensations" obtained from France.

Amongst the most attractive things about this queer, diverting, disappointing, yet delectable life of ours are its contrasts and unexpectedness. I received Baron von Stumm's comforting letter at Eaton where I was spending Christmas on, I think, the very day on which Shelagh acted beautifully in Mr. Dion Clayton Calthrope's vivid little play *Scaramouche*, in which she was not a bit overshadowed by the finished art of Mr. Norman Forbes and Mr. Basil Kerr, who played the two men's parts. George and I appeared in Alfred Sutro's *The Open Door*. While playing in it I could not help wondering if to avoid a European war there was still *The Open Door*. We had Madame Henriette Gautier to dance and Kandi's Viennese Orchestra to play. Shelagh, who is a brilliant hostess, made every one extremely happy. And while we acted and sang and played and went about our daily business forces of darkness were gathering that were soon to burst and drench in disaster poor stupid, floundering Europe.

II

In February, 1912, we made up a party which included my brother-in-law Fritz Hochberg, and again went up the Nile. An entry in my diary summarizes the situation, domestic and otherwise:

. . . Perhaps, though, things will change, when the German Emperor's mailed fist becomes a little more friendly, and the black eagle ceases to crow night and morning. On the whole, just lately, it has been crowing like a *nouveau riche* over the sudden glory and real power of its nation. I really don't mean this disrespectfully because Germany has well earned the respect and admiration of every country. But there are great faults on both sides. And she is over-busy advertising her power and excellence, and building a Navy as big as England's, which of course England cannot allow as her whole life—her food, her very existence—depends on her Navy. Without a Navy or with a defeated one, England would no longer exist, whereas Germany without one would still be Germany.

I was in London before I started for Egypt, in bed for four weeks, as my leg gave way and I could scarcely walk; and even now I walk very little and am carried about; but, thank God, I can ride, which I have not been able to do for three years.

All the time I was in bed in London I was receiving Official people, Diplomats, English people. I wrote to the Emperor and sent him a lot of newspaper cuttings—all friendly and reasonable towards Germany—but simply, and with reason, stating the fact that as long as Germany increased her Navy, England was bound to do the same.

Hans came with us as far as Cairo and spent two days and nights on this steam *dahabeeyah* which we have taken between us; then he went to Monte Carlo, and St. Moritz where the boys are, and to Berlin by the 15th of March to meet the Emperor.

I wrote and told Hans that I give the Emperor *two* years, and that if in that time he does not realize the greatness of his nation without the necessity for war—which he would simply make for the desire to have his name prominent in history—then though he might come to Hans's house, he would no longer see me there at any time, and never would I go to his Court again. And I do not say this because I am English. If Germany was in danger, or in a position in which the winning of a great battle would help her financially, or that the question at issue entailed her existence, I should then think she had a right to fight. But to make war, and shed blood, and make orphans and widows, for the sake of his own aggrandisement would in my eyes make the Emperor the greatest sinner of this generation!

All or most of the men who came to Pless with him in November said: "Try and keep him quiet; he is mad about the Navy and can think and talk of nothing else." Bethmann-Hollweg, the Imperial Chancellor, is against the Navy Bill. . . .

I told the Emperor it was always more dignified and gentlemanly to stick to a promise when once made. But he is vain and obstinate. . . . I said to two men in his presence:

"You are cowards and dare not tell the Emperor what you think." To the Emperor himself I said:

"Whom can you trust? Who tells you the truth? No one. You nominate your own Ministers, and if they do not agree with you or refuse to act more or less on what you expressly desire, they can only resign; Your Majesty disgusts them. And the gentlemen you shoot with, they will only agree with every word you say, for fear you will not visit them again." He was furious at first and said:

"What the English want is a good thrashing, and they'll get it if they don't take care."

I replied: "Your Majesty ought to pause and think; we are not living in the fifteenth century."

Then some of the entourage came to me in great excitement and said: "But you are one of *us* now; you are not writing to England; you will not repeat what the Emperor has said in a moment of excitement."

I laughed and, with the idea of giving them all a good fright, said:

"If I chose I believe I could make England declare war in a week. Now her Navy is strong enough to beat yours, and her best time to fight is now. But I'll wait perhaps. As, for the present, I *will not* believe in war, it would be too sinful a course; but when the time comes I shall go with those who have the best right on their side."

If England puts too many spokes in the wheels of Germany's progress on foreign shores and really tries to stop her, on ground over which England cannot pretend to have any right, then I shall stay still and say nothing. But if Germany deliberately annoys England, and tries for sheer devilry and conceited rivalry, to increase the taxation of both countries, rather than tend the poor and use the money for the good of the poor, simply for the sake of the Emperor being able to launch more Dreadnoughts during his reign, then I shall close my door to him and his policy. No one can conceive what I went through during the Emperor's last visit to Pless; the band playing, and women in diamonds, and Hatzfeldt [1] coming to me and saying: "Yes, I am afraid there must and will be war": (and he went that very night to Berlin to see the Chancellor). But every one in England and all future history will

---

[1] Paul Hermann, second Prince von Hatzfeldt, son of the first Prince, who was the predecessor of Count Wolff-Metternich as German Ambassador in London.

know, as men in power knew in 1912, *how* near war was: twenty-four hours made a difference.

There is a coal strike in England since I left, and Italy and Turkey are still fighting; China has become a Republic; in fact the whole world, externally and internally, seems in a turmoil.[1]

Brother George came with Captain Bertie Paget, Lord Alexander Thynne, and others to shoot wild boar—and got two buffaloes in Pless. Then we went to Fürstenstein for Christmas, when Lady Mildred Allsopp and her son and daughter came from Dresden too; she is Violet Mar's and Maudie Warrender's sister, so I knew she would be nice, and I asked her although I did not know her, as Violet wrote and asked me to do so. I could not bear the idea of her spending Christmas alone at an hotel in Dresden, where her children are studying; so they came and were very nice. The weather was like spring and we did a lot of riding.

One night we dressed up and had a fancy ball; Hansel of course as an Indian, and little Lexel as Cupid with a wreath of roses and arrows; he looked a perfect darling and they all loved him.

I had Eddy's daughter Olivia from California (Eddy is Patsy's youngest brother who settled out there years ago) to stay with me all the autumn, and till now. And her cousin Eily, daughter of Patsy's eldest brother Pat from Ireland; they are both nice pretty girls and Hans likes them; and I am blessed if Hansie Larisch [2] who is forty but seems like thirty, as he is so full of life and so nice (he never *did* have any hair), is not going to marry Olivia. She is turning Catholic, but is very happy and the wedding is to be in Pless on the 29th of April. She is only seventeen; but being dark and Spanish-looking seems older; she is such a dear girl, so natural and good and charming; he is lucky and I hope they will be happy.

But somehow I have begun backwards with my diary. The whole of the time the Emperor was at Pless was not taken up with politics. Apart from my own plain speaking (which he never seems to resent) he

---

[1] Italy declared war on Turkey, October 6, 1911; China was declared a Republic February 12, 1912; there was a Coal Strike in England from February 29 to April 6, 1912.

[2] Johann, 7th Count Larisch von Moennich, born 1872, married in 1912 Olivia, daughter of Edward FitzPatrick, Esq.

Given to me at Pless in anticipation of the birth of my second son.
(Sketch by the Emperor of the Stork coming to Daisy.)

was delighted with his visit and so was Hans, as it really went off beautifully. I am afraid I was the chief figure, but I had to be. One night I did the monologue which I have done twice already in the dear old past days at Chatsworth; it takes thirty-five minutes and all alone; and even Mathilde and Lulu cried; and they all loved it and rushed afterwards to kiss me, and said I was an artist. But this is not very difficult to be if one loves acting as much as I do; it all comes quite naturally to me. Then Betka Potocka recited in French to piano accompaniment. May Larisch did a sort of Greek dance to an altar of roses, just graceful poses. Mechtilde Lichnowsky sang *en costume* and Hansie Larisch dressed up some of the bandsmen as Neapolitans and sang in imitation Italian; Olivia danced with castanets, and two other girls did chorus.

III

I had never lost my faith in Lord Rosebery. It always seemed to me that his detachment from the more trivial side of Party politics, his independence, great wealth and intellect, and his silver tongue and magic pen gave him a unique position in European affairs and that, in a great crisis, he would be listened to as no other English statesman would. He had recently made an important speech in Glasgow and I wrote suggesting that he should follow it up with a series of addresses designed to make it plain to Europe that the Franco-British *Entente* was in no sense a challenge to Germany, and that the sole aim of British diplomacy was to stabilize the peace of the world. Lord Rosebery replied as follows:

ROSEBERY, GOREBRIDGE, MIDLOTHIAN, *January* 25, 1912.

DEAR PRINCESS OF PLESS,—

I am very grateful to you for your kind note. I am indeed uneasy as to our position, for we seem to be bound on the Continent by some invisible and formidable bonds. But as this is the settled policy apparently of both political parties it is not easy, perhaps not possible, to put things right. Anyhow I cannot. I have tried and found it a task both thankless and fruitless. And now I am, I hope and believe, definitely outside the political arena. Moreover, were it otherwise, I do not know enough. It is perhaps my ignorance which alarms me. I am not going south till the week after next, or I would gladly come and endeavour to cheer your rest cure. And indeed if I come I shall probably return the next night. But when I do come to London for good I shall be quite at your disposal. Believe me, Yours sincerely, RY.

My next task was to write to the Emperor. The letter is too long to quote in full. I said everything, repeating all the old points I had made so often. I tried to infuse my letter with sincerity, salt it with truth and sweeten it with a little necessary flattery:

. . . The English will be the last to declare war and this I can swear. Just see how they have changed lately, and every single blessed soul I see says: "Yes, of course we see and understand; Germany is perfectly correct and has a right to move further over the face of the world." They long for something to crop up, over which they can come to some agreement, either in Portuguese West Africa, or Persia, or anywhere. And this is, Sire, not only for political purposes but because of the enormous respect they have for Germany; and the, how shall I say it, sort of open-mouthed admiration all England has for Your Majesty as a man. Do you think I say this to flatter you, Sire? Do you think I want anything —or hope to gain anything? My ambition would be to live in a little cottage by the sea with my children and flowers, and never to go to any Court or enter Society again. Only I should be very very sorry never to see Your Majesty again. Do you think it was happiness for me that time at Pless—to have Your Majesty say things that you did not mean (more to tease me perhaps than anything), but I was and am honoured to have had Your Majesty's confidence, which I keep to myself. Was it happiness to me for someone also to come suddenly and sit next to me and say: "Yes, there must be war, I am afraid." And the band was playing and I had to laugh while I thought of the possibility of women being made widows—children made fatherless. Was it for this that God gave power to men? No: a thousand times, no. Sire, you know this and feel it too, for you are good.

The whole tone of the English Press has changed during

the last month, as the cuttings I send will show, and the Germans even have noticed it. And I hope the Gentlemen round Your Majesty have also perceived the change. I send Your Majesty some notices to read—and some speeches by eminent men which were made even in November last. . . . How well I know what all the people I speak with in Germany think . . . and to you they dare not tell the truth ; to Your Majesty they prefer to say " Yes," or even nothing, rather than argue the point ! . . . If only you would wait to increase your Navy Bill. . . . Why increase it just this year ? The very last thing on earth that England wishes is to make war. . . .

Sire, believe me—when I was ill last winter in Germany I foresaw so much—Your Majesty will laugh—but this is possible to some people, they feel it ; certain stars in the sky are only visible to some people. Well, only trust me for three years, and Your Majesty will not only be German Emperor, but Councillor of the World. . . . Look at your reception in London last May. The reflection of it was still in England when I came over months later. And then such a thing has never happened before as to cheer, at the Coronation of a King, another Royalty, as they cheered the Crown Prince and Princess all along the streets. The Crown Princess wrote to me and said : " We really might have been one of the family," and so England felt.[1] The present King is anxious about Anglo-German relations, but believes Your Majesty is his friend. . . .

What do all those Gentlemen whom Your Majesty brought to Pless know of the feeling in England, and do any of them really know Your Majesty ? I scarcely think one of them does, for it is the people round you, Sire, who want to keep the power in their hands and their agreed device is : " Don't tell the Emperor." Look at your own brother how he behaved five or six years ago, look how Bülow behaved. Where is their chivalry ? Germans are sometimes narrow-minded and suspicious. . . .

Don't criticize and wonder and be influenced by people who say : " Daisy is always in England." I know Your Majesty thinks women are meant only for Kinder, Kirche, Kuche, but

[1] The German Emperor was present at the Unveiling of the National Memorial to Queen Victoria on May 15, 1911, and was represented at the Coronation on June 22 by the Crown Prince and Crown Princess ; both the Emperor and the Crown Prince and Crown Princess received great ovations.

women have done good in the world. I am not ambitious for myself, but I want to see right always prevail: where right is there is peace. There is no hatred for Germany in England I repeat, and I have on purpose seen and spoken to people of every class. And I should be the first to know. There is a great respect and admiration—and uneasiness at Germany's challenge to England.

England is ready to stop building but must go on doing so as long as Germany does, and she has the money. Eighty millions is there to spend, so Winston Churchill told me, if this should prove necessary. England quite understands that Germany wishes to build, but only hopes that some day a sort of balance of building power will be settled upon. . . . And Your Majesty will lead the way, and it will not be by agony of death, or making the young corn-fields red with blood, and the world dark in misery and tears, but by doing good, and bringing strength and wisdom and religion to nations. And that is what God meant His world to do. Oh, Sire, think—and believe me. . . .

I have marked the most important things in the newspaper cuttings. Please let Count Sheile or Hans or Baron Plessen read them, perhaps quietly to Your Majesty if you forgive me, Sire, for having sent them. (Herr von Jaenisch will just miss out, I am sure, the passages I have marked; he has little courage.)

Sire, Your Majesty promised the Empress Frederick to be my friend. Then please do not repeat what I write—but oh! it would be good sometimes if only I dared tell Your Majesty the whole truth and *all* I hear, even in Germany. . . .

Just then I had another matter very much on my mind. At Pless in November (1911) when we were discussing Anglo-German relations the Emperor was very wroth with Sir Edward Grey. He complained that he had invited the British Foreign Secretary to meet him in Germany and had never received a reply. I did not know Sir Edward well, but we had corresponded and I was well aware of his great reputation for courtesy. Feeling sure there was some mistake I wrote him explaining fully. The Emperor's vanity, naturally enough, was hurt and until it was healed he would see nothing good in England. Sir Edward at once replied as follows:

FALLODON, LESBURY, NORTHUMBERLAND, *January* 28, 1912.

DEAR PRINCESS OF PLESS,—

I was away from home for a few days or I would have replied to your letter before this.

I have certainly never received any letter of any kind from the German Emperor; if I had received one I should not have been so discourteous as to leave it unanswered. I might not in my present position have been able to do at the time what he desired, but whether that were so or not I should have answered and should not have been open to any reproach of rudeness. Yours sincerely,

E. GREY.

As soon as my rest cure in London was over I went to Nice. I have always rather liked it. "Smart" people with money who have no position in their own countries turn up their noses and say it is common. I dare say they are good judges. I find it central for both Cannes and Monte Carlo and if one has a house at Cimiez or up in the hills it is healthy and charming.

In February Mr. Asquith's Government sent Lord Haldane to Berlin on a Mission of Peace. Many of my Conservative friends denounced this action as foolish and futile. I thought it sensible and politic and, as the following letter shows, Baron von Stumm [1] did not consider it futile. As the reader has already seen, the Baron's English is excellent:

ROME, VIA SARDEGNA 44, *April* 5, 1912.

DEAR PRINCESS,—

I was so busy, when in Berlin, that I found it impossible to write and answer your kind letter which you wrote me from Egypt. You saw in the papers about Lord Haldane's mission and though it is impossible, at the present moment, to say what the final result of it will be, at any rate it has gone very far in removing distrust that existed on both sides.[2] But one must not be too optimistic and expect matters to change very

[1] Baron von Stumm, during the War, succeeded Zimmermann as Chancellor.

[2] Lord Haldane arrived in Berlin on February 8; he had long interviews with the Emperor, Tirpitz, Bethmann-Hollweg, Hindenburg, Zimmermann and many others.

rapidly. Feelings are too deeply rooted in both countries. But they have decidedly taken a turn for the better lately. Of course the Canal [1] question is a very delicate one. If only people in England would believe that it is built for no aggressive purposes, but solely for defence, and that it has to be kept strong as long as we have to fear a combination of several Powers arrayed against us. But as soon as the improvement in the mutual relations begins to make itself felt in one direction or the other, the tension that exists as far as the Canal question is concerned, will subside.

I have heard of the work you did in London, and a very meritorious one it was. The Emperor received your cuttings and how much he valued them, you may infer from the fact that he sent them on to the Foreign Office. There they passed also into my hands, with your remarks on the margin. I may go to London in June, when I hope I shall also be able to achieve some good. But not on an official mission. All that the newspapers wrote about my paying one is nonsense!

I am here on a short holiday but shall be back in Berlin early next week. If you pass through Berlin, do let me know. Otherwise, I shall be delighted to spend a day or two at Fürstenstein, if I find it possible to get away. There is always such a difficulty on account of the work to be done. Believe me, dear Princess, Very sincerely yours,

STUMM.

The following is, in part, the reply I sent to the Baron. The passages I have left out are repetitive or unimportant:

FÜRSTENSTEIN, BEZ. BRESLAU, *May* 30, 1912.

DEAR BARON STUMM,—

I hope you are not, which would in a way be comprehensible though not reasonable, beginning to lose your patience and say: "Well, if there has got to be war, let there be war, we are all sick of this continual argument and discussion"; as neither seems to wish to help the other towards a reasonable and possible understanding. I think Doctor Delbrück's [2] article in the *Nord und Sud* the most dignified, clearly worded, patient, and reasonable letter that anyone could have written.

[1] Kiel.
[2] Minister of the Interior.

I really have no words to express the approval (if I dare use such a word) I feel for his letter.

Mr. Balfour's article is not worth discussing seriously. I never admired his political knowledge although his book knowledge may be immense; he dawdled over the politics of England and was never certain of himself; he always reminds me of a quiet old owl, who suddenly opens his eyes, looks very clever and intelligent, blinks, and then shuts them again. If one considers for a second one must see that things are in a very grave and sad state. I say grave, for whichever country won, if war was declared, I do not see what the victor could gain to any great extent that might make the horrible result of war worth the blood and money it would cost. I say sad, because England has no wish really to fight the Germans. I mean that Germany as a nation is looked up to with such enormous respect by England. . . .

The time for diplomacy has passed. I really am sorry for any German Ambassador in England who takes up a new post at the present moment unless he does it with enthusiasm and a determination to win. I know that Baron Marschall von Bieberstein [1] as a diplomat has done wonders, but I hear he is rather deaf and speaks scarcely any English.

I enclose in this an article (written as a letter) . . . I ask you if some big man in Germany could not publish it under his own name in the *Nord und Sud*, or any other paper or magazine to be translated into the English Press.

One of the important persons for Baron Marschall to try to influence is Winston Churchill. I met every one I could in London in January and February, while I was doing a rest cure in bed (it was not much of a rest). I got up from bed for Winston and he absolutely believes that Germany is intentionally a danger to England on the sea and wants to fight, and said so to me before a lot of people; as an argument he said Germany, to protect her commerce, need only build cruisers, not Dreadnoughts. What I answered you can guess; it would be too long to write down here, but even an English Admiral agreed with me.

Sir Edward Grey has been told things that the Emperor is supposed to have said against him; I do not know what, but he feels this. I do not think I know Sir Edward personally but we have corresponded. The Emperor in Pless last Novem-

---

[1] Baron Marschall von Bieberstein succeeded Count Wolff-Metternich in London in May, 1912, but died the same year.

ber insisted that he had asked Sir Edward to stay with him (he did not say when he had written) in the month of August and that he was still waiting for an answer to his invitation! I said that I was certain there was a mistake and that the invitation had never been sent or received and that I would find out. Of course it was as I said: no invitation had been received. Alas! it is a pity but one must realize that the personal feelings of those in high government positions, and the personalities of those occupying Thrones, have always and will always affect political affairs. People are ambitious and people are snobs. Sir Ernest Cassel and Soveral ought to be expelled—or go peacefully—to another world; but they both have the ear of England, and Soveral is a personal friend of the present King—whom I ventured to advise to learn and think and judge for himself and not to believe the foreign political ideas of Soveral. He agreed and did not mind my saying this to him. Cassel said to me at a dinner in January:

"You seem to have all gone mad in your country."

I only answered:

"I suppose you mean in your country" (as I believe he is a German).

I hoped the Order of the Red Eagle and his interview with the German Emperor would have satisfied him and kept him quiet. But I met him on purpose at dinner a few days after he returned from Berlin—every one most anxious to hear what he thought—and he quietly said:

"Well, I believe and maintain there will and must be war in the spring." I tried to, and did keep my temper and only smiled but I could have thrown a knife at him.

At dinner one night I sat next to Prince Louis of Battenberg. I honestly believe he is to be trusted (unless Winston twists him round his little finger), he is a Gentleman, careful, and his German blood is there. I believe one could do something with him and he is a great admirer of the Emperor, remembering every word he has ever said to him. I should like them to meet. He is entirely and patriotically English, but he has vision and understanding.

This is an idea I have[1]—women as a rule go too fast,

[1] ". . . I have always held it to be a very valuable by-product of all Councils that, apart from anything else, they bring Foreign Ministers into touch. I sometimes wonder how business got on in the olden days when the British Foreign Minister never knew what people he was dealing with." Sir Austen Chamberlain in an interview in Paris on his way to Geneva, March 4, 1928.

I suppose I do—but there is no time now for etiquette in politics; the smile and bow of an Ambassador will accomplish nothing.

It is time an individual came forward and spoke like a man. Would it not be possible for Baron Marschall von Bieberstein to assemble a private meeting, and have a "sitting" as they do in every Parliament, and deal with the whole English and German question as a *European* problem? Let the different Ambassadors attend, at least those of Austria, France, Russia, America (for Germany's future must lie in South America), Italy and Spain; then the heads of the Cabinet in England, in all about five I suppose, and five influential men of the *future* government of England, and eight or ten of Germany's most prominent men; the whole company need not be more than about twenty people. The German Ambassador of course, and Sir Edward Grey, would be the two who would speak, and deal with the different outstanding questions; each Ambassador would speak afterwards in turn (if they have anything to say), and then let each man stand up and say openly and truthfully what he believes, knows and feels to be fair and right. I would also propose to have two Bishops, one English and one German. My dear Baron Stumm, this proposal may sound to you womanish and theatrical, but I ask you to think that if a political matter of the interior policy of a country is worth all the meetings and sittings which last in England sometimes till three in the morning (as during the Home Rule Bill), is not a great and grave and solemn question like German and English Foreign Policy worth the thought of all the most influential men, and should it not be discussed together in private with locked doors? There are so many questions—Portuguese West Africa, Zanzibar, Agadir, the Monroe Doctrine, Mexico, Persia, Bagdad Railway, and so on.

It is no use dawdling on, one man speaking after another —his remarks travestied by the free Press of each country. The old ways and paths have been trod long enough; let a new idea be tried and let someone act. . . .

P.S.—Two things I must tell you; the best thing is to pretend to treat Soveral as a friend. He has been in London so long: Baron Marschall might speak plainly to him, as if asking for the friendly advice from one clever man to another. Now—I do not know what—but something must have happened; two men (not influential ones) have just suddenly come to me separately and said: "Don't quote me, but

Kühlmann[1] has been caught red-handed." . . . And they added "he is nothing but a spy"! If *they* heard this—all London did! I was in bed doing my cure so found out nothing further.

IV

In July Jennie Cornwallis-West, who had a genius for organization which is inherited by her son, arranged an entertainment at Earl's Court which she called an Elizabethan Tourney or Pageant. I was cast for the part of Princess Errant.

The big Hall at Earl's Court was laid out as the courtyard of a mediæval castle. Into this entered a procession headed by trumpeters and pursuivants heralding the four judges who were Lord Dudley, Lord Essex, Lord Shrewsbury and General Brocklehurst,[2] all dressed as Elizabethan courtiers. Then came Lady Curzon, who is extremely lovely, as the Queen of Beauty. She was carried under a canopy and surrounded by her ladies which included lovely Lady Diana Manners (Lady Diana Duff Cooper), Muriel Wilson, Zia Torby, Violet Keppel, Mrs. Raymond Asquith, and Victoria Sackville West. After she had taken her place on the throne I entered with an immense train which was supposed to be representative of the strange countries of the East. Prince Christopher of Greece looked extraordinarily handsome in a richly brocaded Cossack costume and cap shimmering with jewels and trimmed with sable. Prince Bentheim wore a long cloth-of-gold cloak over a white and gold uniform and both he and Prince Christopher were on white horses with handsome trappings. Then there was the Hereditary Duke Frederick Adolphus of Mecklenburg-Strelitz, Charlie Kinsky, Jimmy Alba, Prince Christopher's nephew, Baron von Kühlmann, Count Osten-

[1] Herr von Kühlmann was Secretary of the German Embassy in London. Whatever his activities at the time to which the Princess refers, he certainly, later on, under Prince Lichnowsky, his nominal chief, carried on a secret correspondence with the German Government which was inimical to the cause of Peace.

[2] Afterwards Lord Ranksborough, died 1921.

Sacken from the Russian Embassy, Lynar's brother —and I can't remember who else. My ladies were Nada Torby, and Paula Pappenheim who wore a most becoming robe of sheeny damask and a Juliet cap.

The newspapers and the public liked me because I rode the enormous horse belonging to the Drum-major of the First Life Guards and which has since been immortalized on canvas by Mr. Munnings. We galloped twice round the arena, and it was great fun. I took up a position near the Queen of Beauty; next entered the Knights who were to tilt. The Duke of Marlborough, in sombre black armour, Lord Craven, Lord Compton (now Lord Northampton), Lord Tweedmouth, Lord Ashby St. Ledgers (now Lord Wimborne). Mr. F. E. Smith (now Lord Birkenhead) could not come for some reason and was represented by his brother Sir Harold Smith, who was almost his double and who rode reasonably well. But the best horseman by far was the Duke of Marlborough. Many of the others when tilting had some difficulty in keeping their seats; he did so with ease, managed his horse well and dealt some really hard knocks.

The head director of the whole thing was Sir Frank Benson, who was really wonderful and very charming. Very wisely he let the chief person in each episode choose their own train; thus one had one's friends near one all the time and it was consequently very amusing.

Personally I thought the most interesting event was the *Ballet de Chevaux*. In this episode Shelagh looked superb and her splendid horsemanship was greatly admired. All the ladies in the Ballet were first-rate horsewomen, all lovely and mostly tall. There were Lady Londesborough, Lady Stafford (Duchess of Sutherland), Edie Castlereagh (Lady Londonderry), Juliet Duff, Sarah Wilson, Enid Chesterfield, Rosemary Leveson-Gower and Irene Denison (Lady Carisbrooke). It really was interesting to notice how well some people looked in their Elizabethan clothes. Jack Brinton looked quite at home in armour. They said Lord Craven's suit was presented to an ancestor by the King of Spain in 1560 and was valued at six thousand pounds. But I cannot think he was so foolish as to wear this. The other suits were, I believe, modern copies and cost about one hundred pounds to make: moreover, the old ones would never really fit. I forget to whom the Queen of Beauty gave the great gold cup, but rather think it was Lord Ashby St. Ledgers or Lord Winterton. The horses all belonged to the Life Guards and therefore were accustomed to music and noise and behaved beautifully. Mine was heavily caparisoned and was draped with ropes of roses held by pages, but he did not seem to mind a scrap. Everybody of course came, including Queen Alexandra, the Grand Duchesses Olga and George, Princess Beatrice and Princesses Helena Victoria and Marie Louise. I thought at first it never could pay; but it did. I was told eighty thousand pounds was taken and that as much as two hundred pounds was paid for a box and fifteen guineas for a single seat.

It was the last occasion on which I appeared at any great popular function in England, and it was perhaps not inappropriate that I should do so as *Princess Errant*!

V

While I was in London I got into touch with Lord Haldane, bringing to his notice some points concerning Anglo-German relations which I thought might have escaped him. I always found him helpful and anxious to do his best. He understood the German mentality in a way few other English statesmen have done. I disliked the Liberal Government of which he was a member. It seemed to me that it had worried King Edward into his grave, dallied with the possibility of Civil War in Ireland, mutilated the Second Chamber, let Lloyd Georgism loose on the world, and by the vacillation and apparent weakness of its Foreign Policy encouraged an aggressive spirit in high places in

Germany. Lord Haldane, I felt, would have been firmer could he have carried Sir Edward Grey and his other weak-as-water colleagues with him. It is as yet too soon to say whether a firm open front in England between 1912 and 1914 would have delayed or averted war. Nearly all responsible Germans think that it would have done. But I do know that it would have been a happier thing for the Liberal Party if before the bar of History it was able honestly to maintain that a policy of firmness had been tried and failed. Of course one knows all the arguments about the dangers of any British policy that might have encouraged an aggressive spirit in France or exasperated Germany. But my experience in life has been that it is uncertainties that breed difficulties and dangers. Fewer difficulties arise between individuals when each knows exactly where he stands, and, after all, nations are only individuals *en masse*.

The Emperor was due in Silesia the first week in September for the Imperial Manœuvres—the last that were ever held. I was feeling far too unwell to be there, so, after London, I went again to Bagnolles and from there to La Napoule. When the Manœuvres were over Hans wrote me an excellent account of the whole thing. Here it is:

FÜRSTENSTEIN, *October* 3, 1912.

. . . The days in Breslau with the Emperor were a great success, and so was the famous dinner here on August the 28th. . . . I had to appear at the Review of the Army Corps on the 29th, when I rode *Magnic*, who was a bit hot; I had also to attend the military dinner on the 29th too. The Emperor gave me the first class of the Red Eagle, which is a lot, as I got the first class of the Crown only eighteen months ago.

The next week we had some small manœuvres near here, where I went with the boys. One morning, when I motored out with them, we followed Infantry marching slowly, and a lot of men were lying in the ditches, some attended by others, as the heat was very great. Lexel said: "I think we are a bit late, because the battle seems to be already over." He thought that all those chaps lying about had been shot.

On Sunday, the 7th September, the Emperor arrived at Salzbrunn. I was put up too at the Grand Hotel. The King and Crown Prince of Greece also came. Then there were Fürstenberg, Lynar, Reischach, Lyncker,[1] old Plessen, and heaps of others whom you know. Everybody was speechless in admiration of the Hotel, and the excellent taste in which it was arranged. Of course I told them all that it was you who arranged it. The Emperor said that he had never seen such an hotel in the whole of his life. He made me a Lieutenant-Colonel. He drinks now only Marthe-Ouche at home, and told me that he would ask for it at every private house he was going to. At the Manœuvres I rode *Maroon* and *Patch*: they both went very well. I had them put up with the Emperor's horses in more or less the centre of the manœuvres, in a big tent. The whole thing was great fun.

One day after Manœuvres the King and Crown Prince of Greece and Max Fürstenberg came to Fürstenstein. The next day they came again with the Emperor. They were all very amazed at what they saw. I drove there with the Emperor and the King of Greece in a motor. Then we went to the stable yard, and from there to the new kitchen-garden, in which the Emperor took great interest and had an endless conversation with Cellarino.[2] At the Castle, Selle reported himself as new Knight of St. John in his gorgeous uniform in which he had to accompany us all over the building. The third and last day of the Manœuvres (September 10) we breakfasted at three in the morning, motored out at three-thirty, and came home to Salzbrunn for luncheon. In the afternoon I left with the Emperor for Kobier, from where we motored to Promnitz. There the Emperor was met by Hansel and Lexel, von Pohl, and all the Jägers in full dress. We had already dined in the train. There was no party at Promnitz. Only the Emperor with a small suite: Count Platen (Hof-Marschall), General von Chelius and Colonel von Martius, Aides-de-Camp, Treutler (Foreign Office), and the Doctor. We always dined alone. For luncheon I invited on the 11th, Lichnowsky, the 12th Stumm and the 13th Tiele. Pohl lunched every day. The boys took all three meals with us every day, and the Emperor was charming with them.

I stalked with the Emperor three times without any result, but in the afternoon of the second day (Friday), he shot the

---

[1] For some time Chief of the Military Council.

[2] I never saw or even heard of him!—D. of P.

best stag which has ever been shot in Germany. On Saturday morning he shot a grand stag too, and a third one on Saturday afternoon. Sunday morning we motored to Pless for church. When we returned we took a walk in the Park; at one there was a big luncheon, and at three we left for Solza. The party there were all the sons and sons-in-law with their wives, the Festetics, Clarys and Coudenhoves. Monday the 15th, we shot eighteen hundred pheasants that could not fly, and ducks that flew well. It is also a strong order to arrange a shoot for the 15th of September when there are no partridges! Tuesday the 16th, we motored to Grätz and Kuchelna (both Lichnowsky's[1] places). We arrived at Grätz in time for luncheon and in the evening at Kuchelna the Emperor left.

I went back to Promnitz. There I found Felix Aehrenthal and the Herbersteins. A few days later came old Dohna,[2] Bissing and Praschma. Sport was poor as the weather was bad and the stags did not run well. I only got two, but I will try and get a few more at the end of October. I came here with the boys and the Herbersteins on the 29th, and we are all very busy about the building.

The 7th of this month I have to go to Dresden for the wedding of Gobby Hochberg with a Schönburg-Waldenburg. She is a distant cousin of ours, her grandmother being a Hochberg, sister to my grandfather; she is of course a sister of that rogue who married Don Carlos of Bourbon's daughter, and whose marriage was annulled. . . .

While all this was going on in Silesia I was at La Napoule where Patsy and Poppets spent several weeks with me. From there we all returned to England together and went to Newlands. I wrote to Lord Winterton asking him to come to us there for a week-end and discuss politics. He replied as follows:

GRAVENHURST, BOLNEY, SUSSEX, 17.11.12.

DEAR PRINCESS,—

I hasten to write and thank you for a most interesting letter; my only reason for not replying before is that events in Parliament last week were so all engrossing and absorbing that one really had no time to do anything.

---

[1] Baron Marschall von Bieberstein, the German Ambassador in London, died September, 1912; it was officially announced on October 17 that Prince Lichnowsky was to be his successor.

[2] Richard, 2nd Prince of Dohna-Schlobitten, died 1918.

The information which you send in your letter is deeply interesting, and I would like to have full time to consider it in all its bearings on the general situation before I make any comments on it.

Certainly, your theories are largely borne out by events. I myself am much less Germanophile since the Balkan war. I always hated the idea of a war with Germany, but it seemed to me the only way out of an impasse. Now, I am much less certain of Germany's warlike intentions. But still the next few years will be the really critical time.

I wish I could come next Saturday, but I have to come here for meetings in my constituency every Saturday now. I don't know what the course of business will be next week in the House of Commons, but if I could run down for the day, I will send you a wire to find out if it will be convenient. I should so like to meet your husband and children. If you're in Germany in January or February, I wonder if I might come over for two or three days. The difficulty is that one scarcely knows three days ahead what political business there will be. But perhaps I might come at short notice, since I gather that you will be in Berlin, and I wouldn't bother you to put me up, but I could stay at the Adlon Hotel or somewhere.

There is one more thing I want to say. There will be distrust of Germany here so long as (apart altogether from armaments) German diplomacy seems to be always working underground. There is still a great dread here of Bismarck methods, and the feeling is that Prussian diplomacy has retained its subterranean characteristics while losing its genius and objective. Deceitful for the sake of being deceitful. You must admit that this was deplorably evident in the Kaiser's Near Eastern policy of some years back—and in Morocco.

Yours sincerely,

WINTERTON.

VI

Circumstances, inclination, my health, various things conspired to induce me to spend the spring of 1913 in England and I am glad now that it was so. One so often resents things at the time and then, afterwards, is glad that they happened just as they did. We need more faith, or vision, or something—I have never quite discovered what—to enable us to live happily, serenely accepting what comes.

[Rita Martin.

MYSELF WEARING THE PLESS PEARLS.

Hans was at Fürstenstein looking after his precious building operations, the boys were at their lessons at Pless, I was spending Easter at Ruthin and enjoying the society of dear Granny for the last time.

However, I had to be back in May for the marriage of the Emperor's youngest child little Princess Victoria Louise to Prince Ernst August of Cumberland. The Emperor had given the Prince the vacant Duchy of Brunswick and the marriage settled the old feud between the Houses of Prussia and Cumberland. The bride was the little girl about whom Lulu had written me saying it was rumoured in the German Press at one time that she was to marry the Prince of Wales.

If she had, I wonder, would it have stopped the war? Anyhow it was impossible, as the Prince was much too young at the time.

The wedding was really charming and the Emperor was obviously sorry to lose his only daughter, to whom he was devoted. The principal guests were King George V. and Queen Mary and the poor unfortunate Czar. I think that must have been the last time King George saw his Russian cousin.

I did not go into the Chapel as I would have had to stand. I watched the procession enter and then sat down under the shadow of the big staircase to wait for its return. Two men-at-arms crossed their swords for me to rest my foot upon. As I listened to the distant music I recalled how, soon after Bolko was born, the little Princess had sent me a big bunch of flowers with a card attached on which she had written: "Father and I have just stopped at this shop to send you these flowers with our love." It was entirely a love match and I hoped and prayed they would both be happy.

For the Court after the wedding ceremony I had made a special effort and put on all my best clothes in honour of King George V. and Queen Mary. I wore my cloth-of-gold train (the one which, without my knowing it, cost four hundred pounds), my best crown and jewels and of course all my Orders. As I could not walk well I carried a very tall golden stick studded from top to bottom with turquoises—somebody gave it me years before, I have ungratefully forgotten who: I think it must have been one of the Indian Princes as it is solid gold and Europeans do not give such presents. I will quote from my diary:

July 21, 1913.

. . . My reception at the Court was extraordinary, it really might have turned my head; but as it was, it only interested me; as I seemed to be standing beside myself, and watching. I really might have been a vanished queen that had suddenly returned.

The King of England was very nice. He had a fright once and looked at me quite close and grinned, as he had almost trodden on the Empress's dress. The Queen also was very kind. I was standing with one of her ladies, and the Emperor came up and began to tease me about Fürstenstein, saying he had to go now to the hotel at Salzbrunn, as I would go on rebuilding and made that an excuse for declining to take him in. He did it on purpose for, as I turned, the King of England was standing behind my back very much amused. The Emperor was of course referring to the fact that for the recent Manœuvres Hans had to put him up and all his Staff at our own hotel in Salzbrunn.

That year I had a bad fit of *Wanderlust* and decided to gratify an old longing by going to South America. I was sick of Europe and its policies and affairs and wanted to visit new lands, acquire new interests and meet new people. Fortunately my brother George was free to come with me, so, at the end of July, off we started on the Hamburg-Amerika liner *Cap Finisterre*. Of course we called at Lisbon—but my diary will best tell what happened:

July 31, 1913. On the boat to Rio de Janeiro, Brazil.

. . . We drove to Cintra, of which dear old Soveral used to talk a great deal, so I expected something beautiful. We went in two cars through a sandy bare country, not a tree, until we got to the simple village hotel where Byron wrote poetry; he must have had a hungry imagination to write *Childe Harold*, and so on, in those bare and hard surroundings! We were all terribly disappointed to find we had not time to go to the top of the hill on which the Palace of Cintra stands. . . .

We went to a little Palace in the town with some modern Gothic furniture in it and some white painted passages. But there were some lovely old Moorish tiles far prettier than those I saw in Seville, as all the old ones there can be, or have been, copied, but those at Cintra are quite unique. There was one design with a lily on the top, and one which was nothing but a dark green vine leaf. I tried to copy it, to have it done in some of the bath-rooms in Fürstenstein.

July 31, 1913. On the boat to Rio de Janeiro.

. . . God is good to me, and if sometimes I am lonely I have so much worldly good . . . then I must be thankful for all the friendship shown to me, and close my eyes and ears against sad sights and cross words, and wait quietly for the tide to change; and then repay all the kind looks and words I receive a thousand times, and make people happy and content, forgetting what is best forgotten. . . . For a woman to forgive is just the grandest thing in the world—but sometimes one is too conceited, and what they call proud, to forget oneself sufficiently to put out one hand, and with the other cover the wounds that have hurt. The thankfulness felt by those forgiven is like the relief from great pain, and they can face themselves and the world again—at least I should feel this were I greatly in the wrong and shown great forgiveness. . . .

August 6, 1913. Royal Mail Steamer *Amazon* for Buenos Ayres, Argentine.

. . . The Hotels in Rio were all awful. In the one we stayed at, my bathroom door wouldn't even lock, and I at last ceased to mind and only laughed at the idea of anyone happening to come in! The American Ambassador called one day, I did not remember him but he told me he had met me in St. Petersburg; and without remembering him I asked him to lunch, as I did also the German Consul, and Señor Francesco Regis de Oliveira, an old friend and now Brazilian Minister in London. They were all so anxious to be polite, that I had to show some gratitude. . . . Then one night Oliveira gave a dinner for me and asked every one he could think of, all the swells of Brazil. They all talked French, but anyway I had the most frightful headache and went home in the middle of dinner. I really would have stayed but I couldn't, and this shows me I should not allow myself to be entertained in Buenos Ayres. I have had enough of Society in the little Europe in which I live: here I have come for freedom and new ideas. George agrees. We shall stay there only ten days or so.

The one really farcical thing we did was to go to the big Race Day, their "Derby." I simply cannot picture it fairly for you. Try and imagine a rush of motors down a sandy path, dark policemen waving, and no one taking any notice; arrival amongst a mixed zoo, all dressed in fashionable dresses, girls and women, half Italian, half Portuguese, wholly Brazilian: powder on their faces and necks, rouge and lip salve by the pound. The motor stops, a long pale brown man is coming towards me to receive me! And I have to take his arm, put my hand on his dirty coat and walk up some stairs rather like a ladder: then I find myself in a room full of ugly people, all small, except two evil-looking tall ones in uniform. I turn hopelessly for George and see his head behind me high above the others. Oliveira comes shyly towards me and says something in French which vaguely sounded like "Monsieur le Président." I saw two wooden chairs upholstered in turquoise velvet, and on one of them what looked like a hungry monkey dressed for the first time in European clothes: he steps down and I say "Bon jour" to the President of Brazil. I then move as if I were treading on ants and beetles and weird little fat animals. I sit on one of the hideous blue chairs with ugly children close to me. A woman is introduced and she introduces another. Two are proud of themselves and can talk English, one through a mauve lace veil and the other in thick white lace. And I had thought they would all talk French. We waited and waited in the "President of the Jockey Club's" stand, and saw some of the most improper-looking females walking below, in worse than fashionable clothes. Then a roar of maniacs went up and the horses started. . . .

August 8, 1913. Buenos Ayres, Argentine.

It is ten-thirty and we have just arrived; you can guess the sort of arrival! People with cameras and flashlights. We were taken with great care down the most awful ladder and across planks from off the ship. There came to meet us the Brazilian Minister and nice Señor Ramos Mexias and his wife whom I had met in London; the latter has resigned office now although he was always elected without opposition Minister of the Interior. They both, and Señor Agrello, who was on the *Cap Finisterre*, waited one and a half hours for the boat.

My room is full of flowers, and I have promised to go to the Opera to-morrow with all my jewels on, but I have very few with me! And then there are the Races on Sunday! And I have agreed to dine with the Ramos Mexias on Tuesday. To think I had promised myself not to be entertained. And I had promised myself the seclusion of some quiet "Estancia" as I really do not care to go about in Society. I have not come abroad for that! And I know they will all rush at me and I shall feel such a fool. And already I saw in one of the papers that I was supposed to be the most beautiful woman in Europe, and they have had, I hear, a lot of my pictures in the newspapers. Well, I hope they won't be too disappointed; being fair, perhaps, will help me here where they are all dark. And my being a Princess is obviously the chief thing even in this continent of Republics, so I suppose as usual I must smile!

VII

I had a glorious time in South America and returned to Europe fully determined to go back there. Perhaps I shall—one day. I arrived in England in October for the wedding of Prince Arthur of Connaught to the charming elder daughter of the Princess Royal. Two days before the ceremony a terrible colliery disaster took place at Senghenydd in Wales, casting a gloom over the occasion. A public subscription was opened for the victims; the Royal presents were publicly exhibited to raise money for the fund and, thinking of Ruthin and all our miners in Pless, Hans sent one hundred pounds, and I fifty.

In the last days of November we were at Primkenau, the Duke of Holstein's place in Silesia, to meet the Emperor and Empress. I will quote from my diary:

November 29, 1913. Primkenau.

We got here yesterday to meet the Emperor and Empress. The Duke of Holstein, the host, is the Empress's brother and very nice. His wife is the daughter of Prince Philippe of Coburg who is here too; Philippe's brother is King Ferdinand of Bulgaria who married (secondly) a Reuss; she was about forty when she married (I had almost written to tell her not to do it) and is perfectly miserable now, as he treats her abominably. " Reuss " is like a thin small microbe of royalty, but it touches everything in Germany and, as Vater's sister married a Reuss, I suppose that is why every one here calls me Daisy, and the hostess makes me call her Dora ! And she is very nice when you really get to know her. Hans is pleased, so that's all right.

The Emperor insisted on my sitting next to him at lunch, and after lunch bent and twisted my felt hat about on my head—up at one side and down on the other. At any rate I kept the ball rolling at lunch. I again told him not to trust Cassel, and talked about the dinner in London after Cassel had been to Berlin to be presented by the Emperor with the Red Eagle (the only birthday Order the Emperor gave that year—and he gave it because I wrote privately to Baron Stumm in Berlin and said that Sir Ernest Cassel was dangerous and that he wanted a little plaster). Well, at that very dinner with Admiral Prince Louis of Battenberg on my right, two generals, a newspaper representative, diplomats, and so on, at a moment when war was quivering in the balance over Morocco and Algeciras, they as usual all turned to me (the dinner was given by Minnie Lady Paget for me, as I had just returned from Germany) and asked when will Germany make war ? I laughingly said :

" Ask Sir Ernest, he has just been in Berlin with the Emperor."

To my rage he said to them all :

" Well, I feel certain there will be war in April."

It was then the end of January. I could have thrown a knife at him. And I told the Emperor about all this as I think it is right that he should know, and begged him not to trust Sir Ernest, and he said he didn't, but was most surprised all the same. (I had told Baron von Stumm all this at the time.)

The Emperor leaves to-night and before he goes I shall try to talk with him about South America and Brazil and the rotten German Representatives that are there, and the stupid things they do, leaving undone the things they could and ought to do.

The year ended up with a party at Pless for the Crown Prince :

December 13, 1913. Pless.

. . . I spoke of old times to the Crown Prince, particularly about my unwelcome letters to him to keep him quiet; his letters of affection used to disturb me, wondering who might get them and read them before they were posted. I told him many home-truths, one being that he must never ask a hostess, as he had just asked me, to invite a lady to stay in her house to meet him. He wanted Lady X. and unfortunately wrote and told her so—thinking he would find me complaisant! We arranged (as I insisted) that if she has told every one in England, as I guess she will do, I shall simply say that the whole thing is her own invention and that the Crown Prince would never dare to make such a request to me.

It was too sad and extraordinary all he told me. So—diary, such is life—and every day I seem to learn something new, and it is never really anything happier. All the world seems full of restlessness, privately and politically. I spoke with the Emperor at Primkenau about the Germans and the great power and influence they might win in South America, if only they had wiser and better Representatives. He told me to speak with Herr von Jagow, Baron von Stumm and Wedel, which I shall do as soon as I get the chance in Berlin.

Prince Eitel Friedrich, the Emperor's second son, was at Fürstenstein to shoot; one night we were fourteen people to dinner in a room that held eight. Why we dined in such a small room I cannot make out. Here one does just what the Staff arrange, unless one is energetic and insists on knowing about everything.

I have several times spoken of my brother-in-law Fritz Hochberg. He had an unusual and interesting personality. Very few people understood him; perhaps even I did not, but I liked him. A few years before the War he developed an extraordinary enthusiasm for Spiritualism, New Thought, and all that sort of thing, and often tried to influence me. I neither affirm nor deny. All these things if they thrive and grow must have some root in reality. Christian Science, for example, is sometimes wrong; but it is often right. Is orthodox Christianity always right? I say let the bees gather honey where they can find it and let each human being have his or her own private beliefs. Spiritualism helped Fritz to live and, when the end came, it helped him to die. I want to preserve a little picture of Fritz and I feel that an intimate letter of his own, written with such evident sincerity, will do so much better and more truthfully than I could:

THE COTTAGE, GREAT BOWDEN, MARKET HARBORO',
December 5, 1913.

. . . I went straight to London to get some massage and treatment, which has done me a lot of good, and at the same time I attended some séances and went to some lectures, and went to see King.[1] I met some extraordinarily interesting people, you must meet them when you come over; and verily we are living in a wonderfully interesting epoch. And one is astounded at the cabbage-people being so satisfied in their cabbage-state, and not seeing the Lord's wonders surrounding them, and God's glorious kindness and patience. And we silly wights fret! And worry about all those trivial, small worldly things. There's a man, Harvey (in business and very rich), you must meet; I have already arranged to bring you together when you come to London after you've done your *Knicks* (reverence) like a good "slave-girl" or "sultana" to your Sovereign in Berlin.

This great work Sir Oliver Lodge has just joined, giving up his Oxford job for it. Just fancy, and realize what that means. And into this chain, you and I will come, as links—but, . . . it is wonderful. It is such a privilege. It is all growing into a huge brotherhood, round the whole world, and none of us will be lonely any more; it will be like a big loving family; and all the departed spirits helping and joining in. . . . So patience, . . .: there won't be any shooting parties, nor powdered footmen, or, if it pleases the cabbage-people, let them have them, what does it matter to you, to us? We carry each of us the shining treasure in us, to brighten up our lives, to shine on our way.

I had the most extraordinary experience, these last days in London. Perfectly wonderful. And my gratitude to God is boundless. Oh, darling, how good He is in allowing me, of all people, to help and serve in the big universal cause! Isn't it wonderful! It fills my heart with joy and gratitude. Father came, and Mother, Aunt Ida, King Edward, your little

---

[1] A medium, I think: I never met him.—D. OF P.

dead girl, all in broad daylight; and I'm sent over for Christmas as a special mission to you, just as I'm being sent at the end of March to Damascus, for what work there God alone knows. I don't worry. I trust. It will be all right. King . . . tells you to keep quiet mentally, not to mind, not to worry, just to let things blow over and to get to the Riviera as soon after Christmas as possible.

Let Hans have his people for Christmas, it will give him something to do, and you and I needn't join them, but can have quiet walks and drives and teas alone in the *Schwarze Graben*. I've such lots to tell you.

Have you read that charming book, *The Education of Uncle Paul?* Answer, please.

Don't think for one moment that I imagine you are lonely for one or another special, personal reason. Because I don't, and I know you aren't. It's just your great, *the* great human, natural craving for affection and being understood. Don't I know . . .? But does one ever get it, my dear child, from any human, mortal thing? I doubt it. They have so much cabbage-stalk left in them. And if once you reach the higher plane and knowledge, one doesn't want it so much.

The one condition I attach to my Christmas visit to Fürstenstein is that nobody shall give me anything, not even a small thing. Nothing please. I get already such a lot in being allowed to help you; imagine what a joy! Hans gave me that expensive kaleidoscopic camera and the thing to look into, for it, this birthday; so that has to count for many birthdays and Christmases, and I'm not going to give anything, as I gave him those two big glasses, which have to count, alas, for several Christmases. So please don't give me anything. I really actually dislike it. I'm much happier without presents. Give me lots of sweets and *Pfefferkuchen*, I just adore them.

If I were you I wouldn't even try to be alone with Hans; much better not. You'll both only feel the unpleasant (to say the least of it) gulf and emptiness between you, because you see, Daisy, you've gone on. Your horizon has widened, broadened; his has got narrower and is limited by his princely crown, Imperial favour, and . . . . So now, good-night. Trust and be at peace. We are all helping you over this, with loving and strengthening thoughts, and on the other side they're helping too. And wake to-morrow in a happy day. Yours,

FRITZEKINS.

Fritz, like all of us, had his faults and his weaknesses. But he was never hard, censorious or unkind. Better still, as he grew older, he grew kinder, more understanding, and more helpful. He was always kind and sympathetic to me, however tiresome I might be. He, Vater and Lulu were utterly reliable and faithful friends.

VIII

And now I think would be a good time to put down together in one place something of what I thought of the Emperor as a man. Apart from the Great War, William II. and the Empress Augusta Victoria, as the last German Emperor and Empress, will always rank as historic personages. No Hohenzollern will ever again wear the German Imperial Crown. They may again reign in Prussia, although that is very doubtful. I think there will be a King in Bavaria again where the Wittelsbach, an ancient reigning house compared to which the Hohenzollerns are mere parvenus, are intensely loved. Other of the more conservative and catholic countries such as Saxony, may desire one day to reunite ancient ties. But, have a Prussian at their head, No! The Prussians are disliked all over Germany, and the Hohenzollerns reigned only because they had succeeded in uniting Germany, making her into a great nation and a first-class power: now they have smashed their own handiwork to atoms and are therefore finished.

Of course I met the Emperor often, but hardly ever absolutely quietly or intimately. There were always people round us *listening*. I remember, years ago at Pless when some discord had arisen in the Press between Germany and England—I never saw a man more unhappy and affected than the Emperor was when talking to me after dinner. He said: "Oh, I am always misunderstood, there is no one living to tell the truth to me," and a tear fell on his cigar! I was at once touched and antagonized. The act of weeping into his cigar, so typically German, somehow put me off. Besides, he was such a good actor he could make himself do anything. All the same he spoke truly because, if he had chosen sound friends and advisers, he would never have made the sad mistakes he did, which were like those of a child who thinks he can run with the hare and hunt with the hounds. To my mind that was his political practice for a period of years. I used to feel very indignant with the men who would not help and protect their master. But of course he was a difficult master to advise or manage, being full of personal vanity and so sure of his knowledge of every subject. Indeed he was as " touchy " as an English nursery governess or a Socialist leader.

I had a new tiara which was really too high. I wore it at one of the Court Balls, and then sent it to Friedländer the jeweller to see if he could make it lower. A night or two afterwards at the Opera, after holding out to me his colossal right hand to shake, which was like giving yourself into the clutches of a bear, the Emperor said :

" Your tiara the other night was too high. It wanted sitting on."

" Yes, Sire, Friedländer the jeweller is sitting on it now."

" If someone doesn't sit on it I shall sit on you."

" That would be no good, Your Majesty, as I should always bob up again."

His tactlessness was appalling. Gottfried Hohenlohe was German Military Attaché in St. Petersburg. Once, when he was at Pless for a short leave, the Emperor said to him :

" You have a great friend in Russia."

" Yes, many, I hope, Sire."

" I mean that Grand Duke Boris."

" Yes, Sire, I like him very much."

The Emperor then turned abruptly away and, speaking to someone else, said : " He is not a fit man for any decent person to shake hands with ! "

Gottfried heard and fumed. The Emperor then

asked a few more questions to which Gottfried somewhat curtly answered "Yes" and "No," took up a paper and read a little, and then got up and left the room. Silence reigned. At that time there were many silly stories about the Grand Duke Boris, who is said to have taken a lot of women dressed up as nurses to the war with Japan—all sheer gossip to which the Emperor, above all people, should have paid no attention. He realized he had gone too far, and the next day out shooting he put his arm through Gottfried's. Then, Gottfried saw his opportunity and told the Emperor that his recent refusal to invite the Grand Duke Boris to the Manœuvres had made a dreadfully bad impression in Russia, and that the Vladimirs, and indeed the Czar himself, were furious. The Emperor was frightened and swore he had not said that the Grand Duke Boris was not a fit person to shake hands with. But of course he *had* said so, and in the hearing of a good many people. He ended up by asking Gottfried, when he went back to Russia, to "say something to put the matter right." The whole episode was characteristic of him. He wanted to be on the most friendly terms with Russia, and set about it by offering a positive insult to a Grand Duke because of an unfounded story which he had not even attempted to verify; he then denied the insult, and, when cornered, appealed to someone else to get him out of the mess.

While I was in Cannes in 1904 there was a crop of rumours about the health of the Emperor, who was yachting in the Mediterranean. When I heard that a doctor had been on board the yacht at Naples, and there was much talk of serious complications, I wrote to ask how he was. I left Cannes before the answer arrived: and this is what followed me through the post-offices of Cannes, Monte Carlo and Biarritz, to Paris: "Best thanks for letter. Never felt better in my life. Much better than those lying French journalists wish me to be."—Another characteristic example of his tactlessness, because of course the contents of the telegram was commented upon all over official France and, you may be quite sure, a copy at once reached the President and the Foreign Minister.

IX

There were some extraordinary ceremonies in Berlin. I remember once when I was in bed recovering from influenza Hans came rushing in furiously enraged because he had to go to meet the Emperor at the "White Stag" dinner. This was a sort of private club, and to gain admission every one had to kneel over a chair and tell a dirty story and be smacked on his behind with the flat of a sword by the Emperor. Then a chain of stags' teeth was hung round the candidate's neck, and he was a member. Anyhow, Hans was furious at having to go. So I got out of bed and put on a dressing-gown and went to keep him company while he was dressing, which meant cramming myself into the furthest corner and listening to him swearing at his servant, who as usual said nothing, but whose mouth stretched like a piece of elastic. You never could tell by that man's face if he were laughing, crying, or contemplating murder.

After awful excitement we got Hans hooked into red cloth and gold braid trimmed with unborn lamb. I remarked that the lamb was rather dirty, but Hans said it was good enough for Berlin! The uniform was Prussian, and I wondered what the Germans were coming to when they began to be careless about their beloved uniforms.

The men always wore uniforms, appropriate or otherwise. On one occasion the Emperor caused a good deal of amusement to some of his younger subjects by selecting the uniform of the Engineers to wear at the Berlin Motor Club dinner.

Once at Kiel the Emperor launched a new battleship. Of course this was a formal occasion and the men had to wear uniform. Hans had none with him, and so had to wear evening clothes and a top-hat out of doors on a broiling June morning. He was perfectly livid with rage and I am afraid I did not mend matters by laughing at him.

I was never bored by having the Emperor in the house. Of course it was a nuisance in many ways; that could not be helped. He generally wore the Prussian hunting uniform which is so well-known, and adored being photographed surrounded by the house-party (at a respectful distance) with his foot on a young mountain of buffaloes, stags or other big game.

His left hand and arm would be carefully turned away from the camera, or concealed in a large sable muff. It is not a withered arm as I have so often seen it described. The arm and hand are perfectly formed and healthy but they have never grown; they are the arm and hand of a child of seven. The left sleeve was always cut the same width as the other, but shorter. The little hand could just go into his pocket and there he usually kept it. The Emperor could not of course use an ordinary knife and fork; he had a special combined one which was always carried by his body-servant. With this instrument he managed quite well, but I have very often cut up his food for him, and this he never seemed to mind. There is an old superstition that body and mind grow to match; if the body is not quite symmetrical neither will the mind be. In my judgment there were large tracts of the Emperor's mind that matched his defective arm: they just hadn't grown up!

When he stayed with us he nearly always brought a large Suite, which, however, did not matter in the least, as Fürstenstein is the size of a town. In fact it is a town with its own Court-house, prison, military and civil administration, and so on. We always gave the Emperor and his Suite a whole corner to themselves. There was generally a Cabinet Minister in attendance, or else one or another of them would pay frequent visits. Of course the Emperor arrived in his own train at Pless station if he was coming there, or at Breslau if he was coming to Fürstenstein. He would be met

MY ELDEST SON, HANSEL.
From a portrait by Galli, painted in 1914.

by Hans (in uniform) and a gala carriage with postilions and outriders. (Our State Coach, fortunately, was used only when we went to Court in Berlin, or in London—when it was specially brought over for the purpose !)

I, of course, met the Emperor at the door ; the house-party would be assembled in the hall in rows, women on one side, men on the other like the sheep and goats in the Bible. The Emperor would greet every one, graciously or curtly, according to how he was feeling, and go direct to his rooms. Hans had special rooms built and decorated for him which he liked very much. He always breakfasted in his room (at what hour I never remembered to inquire), and came down to luncheon and dinner. These meals, especially dinner, were dreadful ordeals and tried me to death, which is not surprising as I began by being exhausted with hunger. It was all very well for people to say : " Why don't you have something beforehand," but one simply can't sit down to two luncheons and two dinners regularly for days on end.

The mornings were spent stalking or shooting. Luncheon began at three-thirty and went on for an hour and a half or even two hours. Dinner began at ten o'clock or even eleven o'clock. The men wore uniform, the women wore their smart clothes, the contents—more or less—of the family jewel chest, and tiaras, and both men and women Orders and Decorations. I loathed these meals. Throughout the visit the etiquette was oppressive. Every time the Emperor spoke to anyone, or even entered the room, every one jumped up, the women curtsying and the men clicking. As far as I could discover no one, except the Empress in the privacy of their bedroom, ever saw the Emperor in mufti. In my own mind I am quite certain that he must have had a uniform even for that private occasion. I must find out.

If the Empress accompanied the Emperor the procedure was much the same. I do not for a moment wish to insinuate that the Emperor was a tedious guest.

Far from it ; he was always delightful. It was the proceedings during his stay that were such a bore. To me, who had stayed so often in a house with English Royalties, those proceedings were of course fantastic. Yet I feel sure that most of the German guests, whatever they might say, secretly loved it. The Germans, and more particularly the Prussians, adore being ruled and kept in their places and perspire with satisfaction when they get plentiful opportunities for heel-clicking and hand-kissing !

I always took my own line with the Emperor, refused to be stiff or unnatural, and he never once resented it.

When the Emperor left he would, I understand, tip the servants with care and circumspection and drop ugly tie-pins on the more exalted members of the staff. These were highly prized although their intrinsic value was nil, being almost as economical as the medal of a minor decoration. The letter W. is not a pretty shape and when it is large and gothic, heavily crowned and very bright it is quite hideous. My butler has one of these very massive tie-pins which he insists on wearing on what he considers state occasions. The sight of it used to depress me, but now it quite cheers me up because it reminds me of all the dismal functions I need no longer attend.

The Emperor's clothes, as I have said, were often extraordinary. Gottfried Hohenlohe told me how he once came down to a dinner, at which no other Royalties were present, in breeches with the Garter in diamonds and rubies round his knee, a green coat, the Golden Fleece round his neck, and his own Order, the St. Hubert or whatever it is called, hanging somewhere about him. Once at tea at Pless, after shooting, he wore an evening shirt under a green coat covered and looped up everywhere with gold braid. I do not know why the green coat should remind me of another of the Emperor's rather tiresome failings—but it does. He would discuss his friends behind their backs. I think it was at this very tea that he began (in my absence) saying : " Daisy this " and " Daisy that." He declared that we were undignified and had played hide-and-seek on all fours in the dark. That during a game I had almost put out my mother's eye and that she had been nearly blind ever since. Also, that another of our undignified amusements was sliding down the stairs on tin trays. And all this to someone who, of course, repeated it to me within a few hours.

One of a Sovereign's greatest difficulties is to get people to tell them the truth. Most of us dislike the truth and hate people who insist on blurting it out. Truth, if it is served at all, is best served as a *Soufflé Surprise* and the *Surprise* should always be some little secret flattery we had always guessed about ourselves but which, until that moment, no one had ever had insight enough to discover and publish. This makes us like ourselves and the "truth-teller." No one disliked undressed truth more than the Emperor and yet—I must say it again—he always let my tongue wag as it liked, which indeed is the only way it will wag at all. If I cannot say what I want to say I just shut up.

The Emperor suffered from a misconception common to most of us. He conceived of himself as a much bigger man than God had made him. That he was sincere in his love and admiration for England I am convinced. A clever man—and the Emperor was extraordinarily clever—may deceive other clever men; he cannot deceive a woman's intuition. I think I have said before that my great love of my native country—allied perhaps to that lively sensitiveness to any criticism regarding it, which is not uncommon in youth—kept me continually awake to anything savouring of dislike, fear or criticism of England, even carefully concealed. The Emperor often criticized England; he always did so impatiently or petulantly as one often does when criticizing relations whom one sincerely likes and admires but who one feels are at times lacking in understanding or appreciation. That was the real grievance. The

Emperor felt that he was never properly understood or appreciated by either Queen Victoria, King Edward, King George or the British people. Feeling his own sincerity and believing in himself, he sought to force his personality on us. As an actor of ability in a favourite part will sometimes endeavour to win, by over-acting, the applause and admiration of an audience which he has failed to win by charm or subtlety, so the Emperor too often tried to dominate British public opinion by acts which antagonized or—worse still—merely bored or amused us.

The Hohenzollerns made modern Germany. The newly created German Empire of 1870 felt that, having laid low France, its traditional enemy, and emerged as one of the Great Powers of Europe it must proceed without delay to become one of the Great Powers of the World. No nation without a Fleet can achieve that position. After the fall of Bismarck the Emperor saw it as his mission, indeed his simple duty, to lead Germany to the summit of her destiny. As the Hohenzollerns had founded and built up, so they were to consolidate the Empire. This view of his duties and responsibilities was a perfectly right and legitimate one. No one grudged Germany the right to expand, or her desire for colonies for her superfluous and ever-growing population, a market for her industries and a Fleet sufficiently powerful to protect her rapidly developing commerce. Indeed, in another twenty years of self-control, by peaceful penetration abroad, and order, discipline and relentless industry at home, Germany would have come to share with the United States the rulership of the world. But when Germany sought to make Russia an allied vassal, Austria a subject nation, France an impotent nonentity, and England a second-rate naval power, she made the same mistake that other nations had made before her. What Philip of Spain, Louis XIV., and Napoleon the Great failed to do was hardly a suitable task for William II. England has never interfered on the Continent—

and never will interfere—until her own safety is threatened. Nor will she interfere anywhere in the world unless her Dominions or Colonies are threatened. England is too old, too proud, too secure—if you like, too lazy—a nation to be bothered about outside affairs of other peoples. But she will not be bullied, or intimidated, or hectored. It first amuses, then bores, and in the end exasperates us to have mailed fists shaken in our faces. Clanking swords irritate our ears after a time. None of these things, however, seriously upset us, and the Emperor's idea that Germany was being deliberately encircled by a group of hostile Powers led by England had little, if any, justification in fact. There was a great deal of the woman in the Emperor; he suffered from the fatal defect of being ultra-emotional and could easily bring himself to believe anything he wanted to believe. Such a man should have surrounded himself with strong, wise, cool-headed advisers and consulted them continuously.

I have in this narrative explained several times to what devices I had to resort in order to ensure Press cuttings reaching the Emperor personally. This was essential because he never saw an ordinary newspaper. There was prepared for him daily a newspaper printed in gold—can anything more hideous be imagined or more tiring to read! It was made up of excerpts from the Press of the World, suitable ones, of course, such as it was considered the Emperor might wish to read. Nothing else. A good deal of attention was paid to the American Press, a country in which the Emperor took a real interest, and the good opinion of which he was genuinely anxious to secure. This carefully edited *Golden Journal* was for years the only medium through which news of the doings and feelings of the outside world reached the German ruler!

CHAPTER EIGHT

1914

IN London, early in January, 1914, I dined with the Crewes at Crewe House to meet the King and Queen of England. I sat between the King and the Duke of Devonshire and His Majesty and I talked politics and affairs. During our conversation I said: "1913 has not been a very lucky year for you, Sir." "I am afraid," was the reply, "1914 does not promise to be much better."

The five years or so preceding August, 1914, were amongst the most brilliant and prosperous of modern times, yet anyone in the least behind the scenes was uneasy. This feeling of apprehension grew to such an intensity that King George's remark at the Crewe House dinner but voiced the feelings and opinions of every one who held any position of high responsibility in Europe. As Algernon Blackwood has somewhere said: "Everywhere behind the fun lay the fear.".

In spite—perhaps because of—this haunting foreboding, people, driven by some fiendish, overmastering fate, went on with their business, making money and amusing themselves: it was almost as if they dared not stop to look or listen.

Towards the end of January I was at Newlands, and Shelagh and I acted at the Bournemouth Winter Gardens and at Lymington. The performances were in aid of the Canning Street Hospital for Crippled Children. Shelagh and Mr. Arthur Bourchier appeared in a play by Tom Gallon and Leon M. Lion called *Pistols for Two.* I appeared in a monologue called *The Eternal Feminine*, by Lilias Eldon and

Liza Lehmann, which I had lengthened and adapted as a short play. I also sang and played the guitar.

From Newlands I went direct to the South of France. A year or so before, I had bought some land at La Napoule, a mountain with most lovely views over the Mediterranean and the Esterels ; about the same time my husband had leased a huge villa called Liberia at Mandelieu which almost adjoined my property. So there I went in February with the children, but without Hans who was with the Emperor ; and Granny Olivia, Shelagh and many other friends came and stayed with me. Hansel and Lexel caught whooping-cough and I had to isolate them in a small villa near by because baby Bolko has had something wrong with his heart from his birth and, had he caught the infection, it might have proved fatal to him. We all had ponies, rode in the hills, went fishing and picnicking. I had Poppets with me for a time, Cousin Adelaide Taylour, Jimmy Alba, and other friends, and I like to look back upon this last happy period we all spent together in France before the War. Indeed some kind fate ordained that from January, 1914, till the end of July the whole of my life should be comparatively calm and uneventful.

About this time every one thought brother George would marry Nancy Leeds. She was very much in love with him and made no secret of her feelings. I think it would have been quite a suitable match in many ways. I liked her as she was always kind and nice, and she was of course extremely rich. People said she began her career as shorthand writer to old Mr. Leeds and that he was so struck with her charm, ability and good sense that he married her. If so, he acted with wisdom and discrimination because she made him an excellent wife. She wanted, as they say, to get on socially ; she succeeded and I admired her for it. Afterwards, she married Prince Christopher of Greece, became a Royal Highness and filled a difficult position extraordinarily well. Her only son married Princess Xénie of Russia, the daughter of the Grand Duke George, who very sensibly has chosen to be known as Mrs. William Leeds. I hope poor Nancy, who died so soon after her second marriage, was happy in all her grandeur, but sometimes I wonder. Royalties are very nice to meet occasionally but difficult to live with, as from their cradle their attitude towards life and individuals is influenced by so many considerations that do not obtain elsewhere. Difficult as it is when the family is actually a reigning one, it is far more so when it is not.

But I have wandered away from brother George. In April, to every one's surprise, he married Mrs. Patrick Campbell, a very beautiful woman with a fascinating personality, and who is pre-eminently the greatest tragic actress on the English stage.

By June I was safely back at Fürstenstein, and I find this in my diary. It is a gracious little memory I would like to preserve :

June 3, 1914. Fürstenstein.

I and the boys have had supper at seven-fifteen in the woods. Oh the peace, alone with the children! We had only one servant and cooked crawfish, eggs, boiled potatoes and baked apples. I had hot soup sent down from the house. We also had brown bread with lots of butter on. I made the salad and sent to the kitchen for some little spring onions which I cut up and put in the salad and we ate them with delight because we never really had done that before! Had there been people in the house we could not have done it. I and the children would have had to change into evening dress and dine ceremoniously.

We had a lovely quiet June. I did not bother about politics beyond writing to Baron von Stumm to emphasize the enormous business and commercial potentialities of the Argentine and South America, and ask him to beg the Emperor to look into the matter and see that only competent and efficient German Representatives, alive to their great opportunities, were sent there. I had formed but a poor opinion of those I met during my visit.

Otherwise we had a restful time. Hansel, Lexel

and Bolko worked with their tutors; Hansel shot roebuck; we rode and picnicked in the woods, fished and in between had agreeable visits from my mother-in-law Mathilde, Vater's brother Uncle Bolko and his wife Aunt Leonorchen, Count Maurice Esterhazy, Aggie Barclay and various relations. Signor Galli was residing in the house painting all our portraits (not at the same time) and I began to learn Italian. The boys, particularly Hansel, gave up a lot of time to the fascinating pursuit of Hawking. It used to be cultivated a good deal in Silesia, but died out during the War, and, so far, has not been revived. The following extract from my diary gives another aspect of my life in Silesia and is interesting because it is the last entry I made prior to the War, the entry immediately following it being dated August 6th:

June 23, 1914. Fürstenstein.

. . . Now I am going with Hans and my cousin Aggie Barclay[1] to see the pictures by Silesian painters on view in the Picture Gallery in Waldenburg. When I return I ride with Hansel to the Kunzendorf Hospital for the presentation of chocolate and little presents to the patients. In the evening Hans and I go to the theatre in Salzbrunn as it pleases the people to see us. Yesterday I presented the Lawn Tennis Tournament prizes. One speaks of resting quietly at home but, in many ways, it is far more tiring than travelling or being in England, where one need only think of oneself, whilst here one must think of so many. Early this morning I had to see the head gardener and the chief secretary and now I must go and make myself look nice for the people in Waldenburg!

About the time I wrote that, perhaps that very day, I received a long letter and memorandum from Sir Arthur Crosfield concerning the industrial and political situation in Europe. The letter exhibits great foresight and statesmanship, and the problems with which it deals are even now agitating post-war Europe. It advocated a universal eight-hours day, the elimination of useless and wasteful competition

[1] Mrs. Hedworth Trelawney Barclay, a daughter of Richard Myddelton, of Chirk Castle, North Wales.—D. of P.

between nations, more particularly between England and Germany, and the adoption of a wide system of international co-operation. Sir Arthur, who has since done so much for the League of Nations, conceived of these industrial reforms as a preliminary step to a general military agreement tending to the reduction of abnormal expenditure on armaments, and to the consequent relief of the burden of taxation in England and Germany—a burden which is to-day greater than ever it was.

Sir Arthur rightly saw in Alsace-Lorraine the root cause of all the existing jealousies and the insane waste and folly of preparing for War. He had his own solution which he begged me to bring privately to the notice of the Emperor and the leaders of public life in Germany, and, if that failed, lead a public crusade in favour of the reduction of Armaments and international amity and co-operation—in fact, become a modern Joan of Arc—but unfurling the *oriflamme* of peace and not of war.

Briefly, Sir Arthur's idea was that Germany should return Alsace-Lorraine to France, receiving in exchange agreed tracts of French colonial territory, and, in addition, a large sum of money which, however, was to be spent by Germany only on social reform—not on armaments. This done, England, France and Germany were to ally themselves against Russia which Sir Arthur, again rightly, considered, on account of its reactionary instability, to be the great potential danger to the peace of Europe and the world—a peace to be guaranteed by the three great Western European Powers, who would be able eventually to range behind them the moral backing of the United States of America. Sir Arthur's words on this point were:

> Then would follow, as surely as day follows night, that alliance between France, Germany and England, with which in turn other countries would be associated, which would be a permanent guarantee of peace among the Great Powers of the world. Such an alliance would make it rapidly and increas-

ingly difficult for any of the smaller Powers to kick over the traces.

Armed with these arguments and this document should I have gone at once direct to the Emperor?

Had I done so, would it have been of any use?

History has made use at times of queer and feeble instruments. Could a frail Englishwoman, perhaps ignorant and ill-informed, certainly since years foreseeing war with her heart and feelings rather than with her mind, and moved by intuitions rather than by reasoned knowledge, have done anything effective to stem the tide of great and disastrous events?

I often wonder and, even now, I do not know. Does the very presence of Opportunity ordain that one should embrace it? Perhaps I ought, at any rate, to have made an attempt to see the Emperor. When one looks back, a most extraordinary thing about the years immediately preceding the Great War is that, although many highly-placed European personages were alive to the danger, no one did anything very definite to try to avert it. I think that the young of all succeeding generations will ask accusingly why we were so timid, inert and fatalistic.

I had personally many reasons for refraining from doing anything at that moment. First of all, Sir Arthur Crosfield, admittedly able and disinterested, was, like myself, a private person. He did not hold, and never had held, office in any British Government. Then, I had not seen the Emperor for five months. As I have said before, I practically never saw him quite alone. There were always people about him whose chief concern it was to ward me off or hush me up. I have always been careful to avoid boring men. All men hate the importunate widow type, and the Emperor was quite easily bored. I had a great belief in and respect for him as a man; I had little of either for him as a Sovereign. He was surrounded by incompetent people, and for this he must before the Bar of History bear the blame, because the Sovereign who was strong and self-willed enough to dismiss a great historic disinterested figure like Bismarck should have been strong enough to surround himself with capable advisers. I am afraid the real cause is that the Emperor was never big enough to face the truth, or to find and keep near him those who looked upon indiscriminate flattery as unworthy and unbecoming for them to offer and for the Emperor to accept.

It is true that the Emperor always listened to me with patience and with apparent respect for my opinions. But I was never misled by this. Had I been old and plain, frumpy, tedious and dowdy like the majority of the women he knew, he would have put me where, mentally, he put all women, that is, into a nursery, a kitchen or a waste-paper basket. If he reads these words at Doorn—and I am pretty sure he will because he is, and always was, very curious, too curious, to know what people said and thought about him—he will agree, and will realize that he never knew true from false, pinchbeck from gold, pregnant from trivial, and that posterity will remember him only as one of the great might-have-beens of history. He was an unfailing and loyal friend to me personally, and this I will always acknowledge most sincerely and gratefully. But he was not an unfailing and loyal friend to the best and highest that is in himself. In his secret heart he was always sincerely devoted to the cause of Peace. He was the Emperor and King, practically an autocrat, yet he allowed himself to be overborne, intimidated or perhaps even perverted by the wicked apostles of War.

There have been men and women who for good or evil have shaped history. It is as yet far too soon to apportion blame or to analyse and weigh the stupendous forces that swept the world in August, 1914, with the bloodiest, wickedest and most futile War that has ever been fought. Looking back, the one outstanding stark reality is its utter senselessness. A downright imbecility, it staggers the mind with its vast purposelessness. None of these things can be understood for many days to come. When the time arrives, it will not be found that William II. was a great captain who guided his own ship of state aright and steered a straight course before a Europe besottedly sailing to destruction; it will be written that he was a mere cork floating prominently for a moment on top of a wave which he never even dreamed was about to submerge himself, his dynasty and empire, and all for which they stood. Moreover, in the process the great Austrian and Russian and Chinese Empires as we knew them were to be shattered into pieces and that incomprehensible evil which, to cover our ignorance of what it is, we call Bolshevism, was let loose upon the world.

What exactly was it that happened when the German Empire went to pieces? Does anyone know? It is absurd to believe that all that followed November, 1918, in Germany, happened because a political agreement made only in 1870 proved futile. It is equally absurd to say it was because the Emperor and the Hohenzollern family disappeared from their place on the European stage. Something far more mysterious, profound and far-reaching was at the bottom of it all.

While I was considering Sir Arthur's sensible suggestions and hesitating how best to act, the Archduke Franz Ferdinand and his wife were murdered at Serajevo in what was then known as Bosnia.

The moment I had so long dreaded, the fatal moment when diplomacy, reason and common sense abdicated their natural functions, had arrived. The time for words had passed, and the earthquake action of war was at hand.

That summer I took a charming little house in Savile Row, London, a spot where I could rest between country visits, be quiet, see my friends and get away from the unending publicity of hotels. Lord Roberts, for whom I had an abiding admiration, had been stumping England on the issue of National Service. Naturally he had many hard things to say against Germany. He and I met somewhere and talked and, pursuing my policy of always trying to bring together leading men in every country, I asked him to come to us for a short visit in the autumn. This is what I wrote :

5 Savile Row, W., *July* 25, 1914.

Dear Lord Roberts,—

It was nice of you to write, but you did not enclose a copy of the speech you made in the House of Lords. Do be very nice and let someone send it to me with your photograph.

It will only be a small shooting party in November. Besides, I think the Emperor would like to sit with you in a quiet corner and talk. Indeed, the more one knows of him, the more one realizes how he likes peace, not only in a room to make conversation, but amongst the nations of the world. He will be interested about current affairs in England as, without himself perhaps ever stopping to think out the reason why it should be so, one realizes in speaking to him that his mother was an Englishwoman ; that he takes the most personal interest in the internal politics of England and, at the present moment, must be very sarcastic at the terrible state of things here. . . .

II

Thursday, August 6, 1914. Berlin, Hotel Bristol.

I see that my last words in my diary are " and make myself look nice for the people in Waldenburg," dated June 23rd : now we have the 6th of August.

On the 28th of June I left Fürstenstein for England, and am now back here at the terrible moment of a European war, and shall try to make myself look nice, but it will be to please all the tired and wounded men from the battle-field. I am trying to go as soon as possible to the South or East to nurse, wherever I am sent to. I went to-day to the biggest surgeon in Berlin and he was really so nice and surprised at all I could do in the way of bandaging, and so on ; in his presence I helped to put a plaster of Paris bandage on a man's leg, and also saw a little one who is recovering from an operation to his appendix, the wound being still open. I know the doctor thought this would upset me, but somehow I am not made that way. As long as I can help to ease the flow of blood by pressure of my fingers on the wound itself, or by holding a very tight bandage above the wound, as long as I can help to stop the blood, it does not affect me; but to go only to watch an operation would be quite another matter.

I go to-morrow at nine o'clock to a big hospital and have to dress as a nurse. Most of the women at this hotel will be in bed at that hour I expect, and no one need see or laugh at me, but I do not much care what anyone thinks; I can dress up for luncheon later if I have to.

It is hard not to be able to write or wire to England. My darling Poppets of eighty-two will be feeling it dreadfully; and Newlands, dear little peaceful Newlands, with all the flowers close to the sea where we have bathed, is in a very dangerous position so near Southampton.

It is really strange and sad to think, as my diary will show, how everything I prophesied has come true; I told Hans six years ago not to build at Fürstenstein, as there would be a war; and after my little baby Bolko was born I also told him that the new stables in Fürstenstein would be used shortly as a hospital; I could see wounded people on the *Wolfsberg* so clearly that I had even made seats for them; and they certainly will be in use in about two months' time.

I shall probably go back later to Fürstenstein and to Pless to superintend the hospitals, and there will be many, many wounded coming back to Germany, some to their homes and some as wounded *prisoners*. Thank God I am myself so well now and God certainly gave me back my strength for some reason, as four years ago I was quite sorry not to die, and I asked Lulu what on earth I was to live for if my life was to be a continuation of parties and society without any real rest or "home."

I was in England, as you see, for a month, and the day I left (I arranged to leave at three hours' notice) they all thought I should never get over the Dutch frontier. All this horrible situation has arisen so terribly suddenly.

I lunched on the Friday in London with the French Ambassador, Paul Cambon, the brother of the French Ambassador here in Berlin, who left only two days ago. Paul Cambon even thought that Austria and Serbia would fight it out alone and that no general European crisis would arise. I left his house—it was the 30th of July—to join Patsy at three-thirty and we went straight to the office to get my passage to Germany on a Hamburg-Amerika liner. I saw it announced in the office that the *Imperator* was not leaving Southampton for America. This aroused my suspicion and I went at once to the German Embassy; poor Prince Lichnowsky saw me for a short while. He was terribly distressed and pale and I had even to hide a smile when he said to me with his two hands stretched out: "Just look how things are after all I have done"; meaning of course that he had thought England and Germany had become such friends. Poor man, he really thinks he could stop a European war because they liked him in England, him and his dear wife. But about all this I will write you presently. I will finish my journey now. Lichnowsky gave me of course a *laisser-passer* and I left on Saturday morning, August 1st. We did not know whether the train would be allowed to pass the Dutch frontier, but the sleeping-car portion did so, although we arrived in Berlin six hours late.

The night before I left (Friday) a telegram came to Savile Row at eight-thirty to say the motor-car with Schulz the chauffeur[1] was to return to Germany at once. I was very surprised that no message came for me. It was one of those surprises which one remembers all one's life; and when I arrived here in Berlin there was still no message for me at the station and I had no idea where Hans was. So I told Seidel and my maids to stay where they were on the platform, while I went into the town to see what I could find out. All the motor *Droschken* were engaged, but I climbed on the seat of one next to the driver and put two marks into his hand. He perhaps thought I was an American. The Russians who had engaged the car objected and said they were going to the Russian Embassy, and after rather a fuss agreed to take me to the Bristol, but not until I had looked at the man straight in the face and told him that if he wanted to get me off the car he would have to call two policemen, as I was there and nothing would induce me to move; so they dropped me at the Hotel and I smiled my thanks a little sarcastically.

They told me at the office here at the Bristol that "der Fürst" and "der Prinz" were staying in the hotel but had gone to Potsdam, and gave me an address. I at once went off there, in another fiacre, to Hans's Regimental Barracks and saw our motor waiting there at the gates. I found them both at lunch, very surprised and not pleased to see me. Now I am settled here, as for the next few days I shall move nowhere,

---

[1] On Friday, July 31, the Belgian, Russian and Austro-Hungarian Governments ordered a General Mobilization, and a state of *Kriegsgefahr* was ordered in Germany. The London Stock Exchange was closed.

MY SECOND SON, LEXEL, AGED TWENTY-ONE.

and I shall never know all my life if Hans really wanted me to remain in England or to come back to Germany!

Hansel has just been in to say good-night to me. Such a big strong grown boy. As soon as Hans left Fürstenstein to come here to Berlin, the boy at once ran off, as in the old days when he ran away into the woods and camped out like an Indian. He wanted to join a Regiment and be a soldier. As he is only fourteen and a half of course they would not accept him; but I love the spirit of him, as it is just what I would have done if I had been a boy. In a way it is rather like what I have done now when they said I could not leave England, and I did. They also thought here of sending me back to Fürstenstein at once to do my jobs and play in the garden, instead of which I shall go off to the front as soon as I can with the Red Cross.

To-day I went to Potsdam to see little Anna [1] whose husband has gone to the front and Mathilde her mother who is with her. Hans said I was not to try to go, as I had no general pass for myself and some "Graf" and "Gräfin" had been shot at yesterday and it was a most dangerous thing to do. But when Hans left the hotel at three o'clock off I started. Wanot (my chauffeur) had his own pass, and besides there is a crown on the car. We were stopped six times by soldiers or policemen and we both smiled and I showed them the Emperor's miniature bracelet which I wore on my arm; then I shook hands with them. When we got to the Barracks we found two guards at the gates, but they let us pass. Many of the soldiers I saw were quite young and were due to leave next Saturday, and to-day is Thursday.

I have come to the conclusion that whenever I want to do anything I must just do it myself and ask no questions.

I hope that if the doctors from here let me go to the front, I can take Schwester Martha with me. She was going anyway by herself last week but will now wait and accompany me. She was the Sister who did night watch for me when I was so ill after baby Bolko was born and she knows all I suffered during that terrible time and which I am now glad I went through, as otherwise I should not have learnt all I know, and would not be able to go and nurse the wounded. I wonder when I shall dictate this book again. If I could take Helene Wagner, my little personal secretary, it would be of course very nice; I am going to try.

[1] My stepsister-in-law who, in March, 1913, married her relative Count Hermann of Solms-Baruth.

A Baron Kap-herr arrived to-day here to see Hans and me. He had been in the Hussars as the best squadron leader for many years, and then in Paris for many years in the German Embassy. He, too, is longing to work in the Red Cross, and kept on asking and begging me to try to arrange it. But first of all I must see what is going to happen to myself. Now I must go to bed as I have to be in the hospital at half-past nine and I must finish a letter to the Crown Princess.

While all these things were happening to me strange things were going on in London; things which I did not hear about for many months.

At midnight on Tuesday, August 4, three short days after I left London, Great Britain declared war on Germany. By eleven o'clock on Wednesday morning Prince Lichnowsky was having his last interview with Sir Edward Grey at Lord Haldane's private house in Queen Anne's Gate, where the British Foreign Minister was then staying. The Prince returned to the Embassy in time to receive the King's trusted servant Sir Frederick Ponsonby, who came personally to express His Majesty's regrets that he could not receive the Ambassador to say good-bye—a spontaneous and unusual courtesy which the Prince greatly appreciated. While these events were taking place poor Princess Lichnowsky was walking in St. James's Park, weeping, and the workmen were busily engaged taking down from the doors of the Embassy and Chancery the brass plates bearing the Imperial German arms.

III

On August 19th Hans wired from the "Hauptquartier S.M. des Kaisers" that he was well, had a lot to do, and that it was very interesting. My two main personal preoccupations were how to get letters to and from England, and how best to find out about and help British prisoners-of-war in Germany. Through my ever kind and dear and lamented friend, the Crown Princess of Sweden, I very soon arranged to send and receive letters. One of the first to reach me from England was the following:

THE CLOISTERS, RUTHIN, NORTH WALES,
August 24, 1914.

DEAR PRINCESS OF PLESS,—

Mrs. West has just told me that it is now possible for letters to get through to you. I should like you to know that we are all thinking of you here in Ruthin. We have special prayers in St. Peter's which include all those tending the sick and wounded either our own or others—as you are doing. And we shall, next Sunday, ask God to take special care of you and yours. It is difficult for us to realize it all here in peaceful little Ruthin but our sympathy with you in this hour of trial is very sincere. It seems only a few Sundays back since you were singing in dear old St. Peter's.

May God bless and keep you and yours,

Yours very sincerely,
LEWIN PRYCE, Warden of Ruthin.

It was like a refreshing breath from the Welsh hills and brought me comfort and peace. There were some people left in the world who had not, thank God, gone stark, staring mad. Another early letter from the front was from the Marquess Pallavacini, my Hungarian friend whose brother was at one time Austrian Ambassador to Turkey. His description of the Hungarian troops is interesting:

BUDAPEST, *August* 28, 1914.

DEAR PRINCESS DAISY,—

By quite a wonderful chance I got your letter to-day. Very many thanks for your kind thoughts and wishes. I came up here three days ago with a special mission and am off to-morrow morning to the same seat of war in the South. We had some great fights down there, and I never dreamt of anything so good as our troops are. Their heroism and dash is simply appalling. Everything would have been wonderful, if the higher tacticians had had clearer heads. Anyhow I believe matters will be repaired and despite the fact that we have very few troops now left there, we will be able to give the enemy a thorough licking. And all the glorious fights, which are fought in France and Russia now will be a good help to us. The Hungarian soldier is something wonderful—every man is a hero in himself. It is a fine feeling to fight with such troops. . . .

Amongst the very first British officers to be taken prisoner by Germany was Ivan Hay of the Fifth Royal Irish Lancers, who was captured at the Battle of Le Cateau on August 26th. I wrote at once to Hans to ask him how I could find out about him and other British prisoners-of-war.

I was naturally terribly anxious about brother George, Percy Wyndham, Bend Or, and all my relations and friends. Hans wrote:[1]

GROSSES HAUPTQUARTIER, *September* 2, 1914.

. . . I am awfully busy, so I have very little time for writing. The English force has been beaten three times, once at Maubeuge, and twice at St. Quentin, close to Paris. And even before that a Brigade of Cavalry has been beaten. Lots of prisoners have already been made, but as they are sent at once to Germany and no names are taken, it is quite impossible to find out who they are. The fighting was, and is, very far from where we are.[2] It will be quite impossible to find out who is killed, wounded or made prisoner. As one hardly hears it about our own men, and only through the reports of their superiors, it is quite out of the question to find anything out about the losses of the enemy; especially when they have been beaten at different dates and different places. I would advise you to write to England if you can get a letter through by some neutral Embassy and find out if George has gone to the front or not. More they will not know in England either, because the connection of the Expeditionary Force and the harbours has been cut off, and naturally in England they will not hear what has become of their army. By all that I hear the English have been fighting very well and quite different to our other opponents. . . .

Hans's letter was not very helpful. So I set out to discover for myself what had happened to Ivan, and

---

[1] The Prince of Pless was A.D.C. to the Emperor throughout the War.

[2] Great Headquarters in the West were at Coblentz until September 1914, when they were transferred to Luxemburg and, later on, to Charleville.

I succeeded. I was not inclined formally to join any Organization set up to help prisoners-of-war because I was determined to do nursing. My intention was informally to assist all such organizations as far as I could and to concentrate on giving personal help to British prisoners.

It was very hard to know what to do for the best. The natural thing to do would have been to go to Fürstenstein, turn it and the Hotel at Salzbrunn into Hospitals and, when I had got them going, make my headquarters amongst our own people at Pless, do what I could for the wounded from the Russian Front, and, generally, visit, encourage and give practical help to Hospitals and similar institutions in my own part of Silesia.

I had no husband or near relative to advise me; moreover, Hans at first thought the War would last but a very short time and was averse to any large expenditure. By his orders, too, Hansel remained in Berlin where I could not leave him in an hotel by himself. Moreover, I soon learned that I was not wanted in Silesia, as it was too near the Eastern Front and already there were violent anti-English demonstrations in Breslau and elsewhere.

Owing to the friendliness of Princess August Wilhelm, the Emperor's daughter-in-law, I was enabled to start nursing at once at Hospital No. II. in Tempelhof, a suburb of Berlin. The head Doctor, Professor von Kuester, was an excellent chief and a kind, humane and able man.

Some extracts from another letter from Hans will give a good idea of what was taking place at the front and how the War looked to a German at Grosses Hauptquartier in Belgium on September 16th, 1914:

I have not written you for a long time, as I would not give you a shock about Hansel's joining the regiment, before it was settled, and now I am very pleased that he has only to join early next year and will only have to go to the front some months later. . . . Of course, it is an awful idea, to send such a young boy to the War, but I assure you that now every man and every boy is wanted. The losses, especially amongst officers, have been very great; that is the reason why they take them now so young. I hope that we will finish soon with France, but with Russia and England it will go on for a long time; with England certainly over the winter, and with Russia all next summer. We have no intention of having another war again for the next fifty years, therefore the peace must be so that there is no chance of recovery for our enemies, and naturally those terms they will not accept, as long as they have any possibility of continuing the war.

Everybody must understand that after such loss of lives as we have had, we cannot make a cheap peace. Even the German shipping world (mostly Hamburg people) who are losing the most during this war, have declared that the only thing to do is to fight to the very extermination of the enemies, because only this would bring a peace one could rely upon. If we followed Lichnowsky's advice, we would probably come to terms very quickly, but there is no question of it. So we must be prepared for a very long war. I cannot tell you anything about what happens here, except what you see in the papers, because we are not allowed to do so. When you get this letter, the great victory over the French will be probably already gained and then, I think, their armies will offer no more serious resistance. We are awfully busy, so I have very little time for writing. Several times I went by motor to see different armies. The country looks now better, the more we get into France. One does at least see some villages which are not destroyed. As a whole the people behave better, the more one gets into the country.

We get sometimes here English newspapers. It is incredible the gross lies they publish, and their morality seems to have quite changed. They praise the Belgian women for their bravery in pouring boiling water on the German troops when they entered the towns. A number of the *Sphere* has a big picture of our Petersburg Embassy being destroyed by the mob, and in the text to this picture they say that it was done as a revenge for the bad treatment of Russians in Berlin. Not a word of blame. Even *Punch* is just as bad with his cartoons and jokes. ("One ought not to say: Kaiser Wilhelm der Grocer (Grosser) but, Kaiser Wilhelm der Butcher")!

I cannot understand what you mean when you say that some Englishmen arrived in England with their hands cut off. They must have been cut off fighting, because, if they had been made prisoners, they would not be in England. About the famous Belgian neutrality the English make such a fuss about, it has now been proved that the forty-fifth regiment of French infantry went into Namur on July 30th.[1]

KILRONAN, BRIDGE OF ALLAN, N.B., *Sept.* 16, 1914.

MY DEAR LADY,—

Thank you ever so much for your letter; any news of Ivan is so welcome, as his letters are very irregular, and he says so little in them. Your "Daisy" wrote to me some time ago and I wrote to thank her but have had the letter returned. I don't know why as I sent it as she directed, so I am sending it to you to forward. I have been here "following the drum" for the last two months, and it is a very curious life. I long for my garden and my peaceful life. Please don't call me Lady Erroll. I remember the Bundoran days so well, in spite of the years that have gone. I think of you in a yellow Leghorn hat and yellow feather. I thought you the loveliest thing I had ever seen. With love, and many thanks for writing,

Yours affectionately, MARY ERROLL.

P.S.—I am sending my letter and envelope; perhaps you can tell me why it was returned.

At the end of September I had another long letter from Hans which is interesting as it shows how wrong a really well-informed German, employed on the Headquarters Staff, could be about England. The parts I leave out have to do only with historical parallels by which Hans reinforced his arguments. As always, he wrote in English.

GROSSES HAUPTQUARTIER, *September* 24, 1914.

. . . Perhaps you will have seen in the papers that Percy Wyndham[2] has been killed. About other Englishmen it is impossible to get any information. They say *The Times* has

---

[1] The French General Mobilization Order was not issued until August 1; from July 30 to August 3 the 45th Infantry Regiment was on the Meuse guarding the bridges between Givet and Sedan; on August 22 two Battalions of this Regiment arrived outside Namur and, with a Battalion of the 148th Infantry were the first French troops to reach the vicinity of the city.

[2] Only son of the Right Hon. George Wyndham and Countess Grosvenor, and stepbrother of the Duke of Westminster.

published a list of casualties but I did not succeed in getting a copy. In one of the illustrated English papers there were lots of pictures of killed or wounded or missing officers, but mostly in Line Infantry and Third Hussars; nobody you will know. Only one picture of Captain Grenfell, Ninth Lancers, and under it was written "saved by the Duke of Westminster." In about a fortnight or so, lists will be exchanged between the different governments of all the prisoners. So one will be able to see who has been taken prisoner, but no news will of course be obtainable about the killed. This will only be reported by the English regiments to England. Perhaps Hermann Hatzfeldt could procure you a list of the wounded English officers, so far as they are in our hospitals. It must be a dreadful time for you, my poor darling, and I pity you with all my heart. I know you are a good German, as far as your wishes for our victories go, because naturally the future of your sons depends upon the future of Germany. But, all the same, you must feel very much all the misery which is in store for your old country, and by which heaps of your relations and friends will suffer. As there is no doubt that the war between Germany and England will be carried on to the bitter end, even you can only hope for a most crushing defeat of the English, which would bring it to an end as soon as possible. But, after England once got into this mess, she has of course to fight to the last, at least, till she sees that there is no hope of a victory left to her. It is noticeable that the defeats of the English and the French make a great effect on her, and the English papers admit them all, more or less, but they don't say a word about our victories over the Russians. The reason is simple: the English public was taught to believe that the Russians would get sooner or later to Berlin, and that the fighting in Belgium and France had only the purpose of occupying a great number of our armies, to make the Russian advance easier. When the English public will hear of our victories over the Russians (and I hope there will be soon another one) they will understand that there is not hope from that side. A *great* victory over the French and English armies, which is going to happen at the end of this week or during the next, will also stop, to my idea, the sending of fresh English or Indian troops to the Continent, because England will realize that they would only mean a drop of water on a hot stone. Besides this, English armies have never fought by themselves except against Niggers and Boers, and in the Peninsula under Wellington, when most of their troops were Hanoverians.

It is useless to make the present Government in England responsible for this war. The Unionists have always been much more bellicose than the Liberals. The excuse that they were obliged by their Treaties to fight, will not wash either. Why did they make an *entente* with France, of which everybody knew, with their idea of *Revanche*, that they were only waiting for the right moment to attack us. This way is certainly not the way to secure the peace of Europe. And when Russia was mobilizing her army, England could have told her and France, that *she* intended to remain neutral, and then the two others would never have dreamt to begin hostilities. I am sorry to say it is England who wanted this war, especially for commercial purposes, and with the idea of defeating the German Navy, which she considered to be in her way. Remember the English history: England has always opposed diplomatically, and when this was not enough fought, that country which had the best fleet, so as to establish, and later on to keep, her supremacy on the sea. For the rest . . . always against the strongest Navy.

So, from the English history, it is logical that she turned now against Germany. But she made the mistake, that she underestimated our fighting power on land and sea. Especially the fact that the German Navy has grown quicker in size and efficiency than she could realize. Had she ever thought of this possibility she would never have handed us over Heligoland, which is now our strongest position against her, and without which our Baltic Canal would never have been possible. So, all this big war is practically the war between England and Germany. We always thought that the world was big enough for both of us, but England thinks it is not. And England means to fight to the bitter end. This is also why she has induced France and Russia to pledge themselves not to make a separate peace.[1] (I don't think France will stick to it very long.) England is afraid (and she is perfectly right there) that we could let France out cheap, and make *her* pay the piper. That is exactly what I hope we will do. And even you must agree with me, that no peace with England is possible, where a possibility of a rising is left. This would only mean a series of innumerable wars. And after this war, the biggest ever fought since the creation of the world, we want a long

---

[1] The agreement not to make a separate peace, known as the Pact of London, was made jointly by Great Britain, France and Russia on September 5, 1914.

and lasting peace, with no "balance of powers," which only leads to new frictions. Then England will have to mourn her supremacy over the seas, and, most probably, her World Empire (thanks to her idiotic policy about Japan), but for the rest, everybody will be happy again, and industries and trade will flourish in all countries, as they have never done before. So, you see, the general outlook is not bad. Let us hope that the end will come soon, because the sooner it comes, the more lives will be spared.

I quite forgot about Bolko's birthday. Of course, he is too small to have noticed it. I am so glad to hear that all the boys are well. Prince August Wilhelm was here yesterday. He had seen the Gardes-du-Corps two days ago, and says that all Lulu's [1] boys are well. God bless you, darling, a very big kiss, Yours, HANS.

Thousands of women will remember to have shared my feelings when I say that during those terrible early months of the War nothing gave me greater courage or support than the knowledge that many of our men relatives and friends went to the War with a stouter heart and a more enduring courage because of our affection and friendship. In peace time it may be different, but when war, danger, or opportunities for endurance and heroism come, man thinks of woman as an ideal and an inspiration. Even those stupid men who regard women only as toys find in the day of fierce trial that she is something more. From the first day of the War I received from every front messages, many of them mere mud-stained field post-cards, telling me that my mere existence helped. Here is a typical note, one such as innumerable women cherished—and still cherish:

I have just had my orders to join my Regiment and proceed to the front at once. You asked me to tell you if I went, so this is why I write these few very hurried lines. It is a queer feeling—to go forth and leave *everything*, when it is most probable one will never come back. In case, dear, we never meet again I wish you good-bye and may God always bless, take care of, and make you very happy. You and I have been

[1] My sister-in-law had four sons serving at the front.—D. OF P.

dear friends, I have loved that friendship, am the better for having known you—no man can pay a good woman a higher compliment.

The Empress's brother, the Duke (Ernst Günther) of Schleswig-Holstein, was a soldier and a gentleman. He had often been our guest at Fürstenstein and Pless, and we had continually stayed with him and Dora at Primkenau; he knew the English and had near relatives in England. Yet he could write the following letter! In fact public opinion in all countries was kept so much in the dark, popular imagination was so excited and gossip was so general, that many people were, like children, prepared to believe anything. I was glad to hear about Ivan and liked the chivalry of the Duke's attitude towards him, but the passages in his letter about the white flag upset me terribly. He wrote in English:

VASSEYS NEAR SOISSONS, *September* 28, 1914.

DEAR PRINCESS,—

I saw a letter yesterday, which you sent to the Ninth Army Corps about Captain Hay. I saw him at Le Cateau on the Belgian-French frontier, where he was one of the prisoners. He had the liberty to circulate, was quite well, told me his horse had been killed and he had gone bang into our troops and been made prisoner. I told him, we had nearly done the same thing the day before with three thousand English but had got away all right. He said if there had not been war, he would have been at Fürstenstein; I told him that I perhaps would have met him there. I gave him my card, as I had to hurry on and could not do more for him. I suppose he will now be prisoner somewhere in Germany.

I received after Château Thierry a shrapnel bullet on my girdle, but my binocular saved me. My motor was hit by ten bullets, was out of work for a day, but we got it repaired. Another day seven officers of my staff were killed and wounded round me, but I did not receive anything, so I was fortunate.

The bitterness against the English is aggravating every day. English troops put up a white flag and held up their hands and our troops advancing without shooting, they received shots from behind. Our troops also say that English troops killed off the wounded, stabbing them in the throat with the big knives every trooper has got; and we captured an Army Order of General French saying in case a white flag was shown it was not in all cases to be respected; it depended on what was the interest of England. This is very regrettable, because it will come to this, that no one will give quarter and all will be killed before they are captured. As I have so many friends and relatives on the other side I regret it very much. I suppose my cousin Gleichen is fighting against us. We were quartered in a château, where they told us an English general had been the day before, a nephew to the King; he commands an Irish Brigade,[1] and as we captured a good many Irish, I suppose it is he: perhaps also Teck.

The wrath was greater already in the beginning against the English than against the French as many believed that England would not fight us, and has been at the bottom of the whole affair. The English maps of Belgium, which we captured are from 1903 and 1904 for the use of the Army solely, so it is evident everything was prepared, even the ammunition accumulated in Belgium. It would be in the common interest, if you could give details about this evil form of war in an English paper, it might save much blood, much cruelty; the same about the dum-dum ammunition.

The Duchess of Sutherland is at Namur; she seems to have let herself be shut in with the troops, I have not seen her, and I was rather satisfied, because, true a friend as she always has been for me, perhaps she would have wanted things which I could not have accorded. I am rather astonished, that one lets her circulate with her ambulance everywhere, because I am sure that she will serve her country. It gave me a great shock to find that Countess X. in Brussels was very half-hearted in her German feelings. I wrote her a very hard letter; it is the first time in thirty years that we have taken an entirely opposite view. I am very glad, Princess, that you look after our wounded so nicely, you always have been so warm-hearted *und das Herz . . . klopft in der Stille*. Dora has also passed her examinations, she is going soon to the front. It is an awful war, so much more bloody than others; some regiments have lost nearly all officers.

I was not going to sit down under this, and wrote asking the Duke to come and see me the moment he

[1] Major-General Lord Edward Gleichen commanded the Fifteenth Infantry Brigade from 1911 till March, 1915. He was British Military Attaché in Berlin, 1903–6.

got to Berlin. Very soon he did so. I asked him to get me a copy of General French's Order. Needless to say he never succeeded. However, he was perfectly sincere in his belief and replied:

The copy of General French's Order I will send for to the front, as I am returning there from Berlin; letters take too long. The hour we spent at the Esplanade is heartening me all the time, you can make life sweet and you deserve not to be unhappy. Thank you so much for the trefoil of luck, I will keep it as a token.

Nothing could weaken my determination to do all I could for British prisoners in Germany. I was quite prepared to make myself a nuisance to everyone and, where necessary, to trade shamefully on the affection of old friends. As far as I could I would obey the regulations; if they got in my way that was their fault, and secretly I was quite prepared to bend or break them. The funny thing was—it often happens so in life—that I did not suffer for what I did (or was prepared to do) but for what I did not do. One of the small things I did was to get Duke Ernst to write to some old General requesting him to allow Ivan to communicate as often as possible with his mother, and to retain his badges of rank. In Germany a Royal Duke was always a safe card to play.

In December Robin Grey[1] wrote a long letter to Mrs. John Jacob Astor (now Lady Ribblesdale) describing his captivity, a copy of which he sent to me. It is written with great clearness and restraint, and as there were then and afterwards so many different stories about how prisoners-of-war in Germany were treated I will quote here his description of the conditions as he found them. He complains of shortness of water, overcrowding, vexatious regulations and the conduct of certain "bullying Jacks-in-office." The overcrowding was the worst because in Germany, as in England, no adequate accommodation for prisoners-of-war existed in the early days:

[1] Captain Robin Grey, Grenadier Guards, died May 15, 1921.

. . . And because they are on the ground floor the windows of these rooms may not be opened after dark. Sometimes at night the atmosphere is absolutely unbearable as you may imagine with twenty to thirty men all living, sleeping, eating and smoking in one room. And it is often made worse than it need be by the tastes and habits of some of our allies. Our food is brought to us three times in the day. At eight in the morning we have some coffee and a slice of brown bread and butter; at noon they give us a cup of soup and a piece of meat with potatoes and a slice of bread. If the quantity is not very generous, the quality is not bad and it is cleanly cooked. At six in the evening we usually have a sausage and some dry bread. In each prison there is a canteen where we can buy certain things to add or vary our daily ration. When we first became prisoners and even when we first came here the canteen was allowed to sell several things that enabled us to improve our fare considerably. But one by one most of these little luxuries have been *verboten*. First of all chocolate and cocoa, then all cakes and biscuits, then quite lately all jams, preserved fruits, pickles and so on, and rolls and white bread, and to-day we hear that no more butter will be allowed. To what extent this is due to shortage and the needs of their own people, or to what extent it is instigated by a desire to deny us anything we like, it is impossible to say. The great trouble about this place is that it is not suited for officers' quarters and that the accommodation is inadequate for the number of prisoners here. The exercise ground is very small; there are only four baths for about five hundred officers, fifty orderlies and fifty German guards; the latrines would be in hot weather, if they are not as it is, a menace to our general health; there is only one pump for us all to get our supply of water from, and that so situated as to make the water unsafe to drink. Of course here again we do not know what difficulties Germany may not have to find adequate quarters for the large numbers of prisoners she has taken. . . .

Here a few days ago an English colonel was cursed and called a *Schweinhund* because he had left a book on his bed; another was similarly abused because he did not jump up quickly enough when the Commandant came into the room. This sort of thing is bound to happen because nearly all those who have had charge of us have been and are of very inferior class and rank. Oh, it galls and enrages one to see British officers herded like sheep and shouted at by German guards with fixed bayonets; to see officers still stiff from wounds

A WATER-COLOUR PAINTING OF THE ROYAL PALACE OF LA GRANJA, SPAIN, WHICH I VISITED IN 1908.

Given to me by the King of Spain.

pushed about and hustled; to hear a gallant and courteous Colonel who wears the Victoria Cross insulted by a German Jack-in-office. But we are prisoners and I suppose must bear all this. . . .

And yet all these aggravations and irritations, the insults and indignities and discomforts are merely "the trappings and the suits of woe." The woe, when all is said, is that we are prisoners. Think what it means, the loss of liberty at such a time as this; the exile and the lack of news when all we hold most dear is in the balance; to be buried in this tomb when history is in the making. We are most of us average fellows enough whose talents and merits have hitherto fallen on an indifferent world. Now for the first time in our lives we are really needed; we are called and it is the call of our comrades, of our corps, and of our country. And we cannot go. You can never know how this forced inaction galls, you cannot imagine the continual gnawing regret, the bitterness of disappointment, the sense of failure where most we hoped to win.

IV

It now seemed to me that it would be a good thing for both England and Germany if I could get through to responsible people in England Duke Ernst Günther's story of the white flag and the dum-dum bullets. The bullets *canard* made a terribly bad impression. I felt quite sure it was not true; yet what could I say or do to prove it. It is quite, quite impossible ever to overtake and *kill* a malicious lie. That the English used dum-dum bullets always has been, and I fear always will be, believed in Germany. Only the other day I heard my own son Lexel say to Major Chapman-Huston: "Of course you used dum-dum bullets." So what is one to do!

What I did then was to write to Jack Cowans, Patsy and every one else in England that I could think of. I besought Jack to draw up and sign and get Lord Kitchener to sign a document denying the charges made in Duke Ernst's letter and promised to show it to the Emperor and have it communicated to the German Press. I was encouraged by those in authority in Germany to write this letter and to send copies to my mother and others. I was assured that my letter would go direct to London by *messenger.* I realized that this meant that there were German spies with access to and from England, and did not like it.

What object had the German authorities in view and why were they so anxious that I should write to England that they even went the length of assisting me to draft a letter to a member of the Army Council, and letters to my mother and to other influential people? I did not realize it at the time, but I did afterwards. They wanted to deny the violation of Belgium, and they wanted it denied in London by an Englishwoman.

The letter I wrote under dictation is too long to quote here, but is easily summarized. It insisted that English troops were in Belgium before I left London on Saturday, August the 1st; that Germany knew this or she would never have crossed the Belgian frontier; that in the absence of encouragement from England, France and Russia would have kept quiet; that in scientific warfare and organization Germany was far ahead of England, and that she possessed all sorts of new secret machines of the deadliest kind; that the use of black troops by England was a dishonour,[1] and that the price to be paid would be first the grant of self-government, and then of full independence, to India. The letter, above all, urged England to make an early peace, and declared that there was no shortage of men, or food, in Germany!

From the very beginning Germany realized that the "scrap of paper" incident would tell against her for all time, and with a foresight, care and patient industry which no one can deny her, she at once set about preparing counter evidence.

Hans's letter to me about Hansel proved that already Germany was short of officers, and Robin Grey's about

[1] "In the fighting in East Africa the Germans had 30,000 natives in arms."—Repington, Colonel C. a'Court, *The First World War,* Vol. I, p. 125.

prisoners' food restrictions that a food shortage was already foreseen—especially fat, sugar and flour, the Russian supply of which had of course already stopped.

V

And now there happened an incident, the effects of which followed me all through the War, bred dissensions between my husband and myself which have never been obliterated, and for which I shall never forgive Germany—or rather Prussia.

When the War broke out both my brothers-in-law, Conrad and Fritz, were living in England. Fritz had Minstead Manor in the New Forest and a hunting-box at Lubenham, near Market Harborough; and Conny a place in Somerset. Of course both left England at once, all their property was sequestrated and the usual silly stories about their being spies were circulated. Both of them, as these pages have shown, adored England, disliked and distrusted the Emperor, and lived in Germany as little as possible.

Fritz was in Berlin looking for war work suited to his very frail health and said to me one day: "Would you like to motor out to Döberitz, a prison camp about eight miles west of Berlin, and see the English prisoners?" I did not even know there were any prisoners so near Berlin, and of course I fell in with the suggestion at once. I asked, could we talk with them, and Fritz said "No." It therefore seemed to me little use going, but Fritz persuaded me, saying it was a lovely drive and that it would do me good to leave the Hospital for a bit. He called for me one afternoon at half-past four, telling me he had permission to visit the Camp and search for someone he knew who was said to be there, and off we went. When we arrived we passed a sentry at a gate and went into a big field where I saw a lot of men. I was in my Red Cross uniform, spoke to no one, did not even smile, and, I suppose, was hardly in the place ten minutes. Dead tired I went home and went to bed as I had an awful cold. A day or two later my mother-in-law said: "I hear you have been to see the English prisoners." Thinking that perhaps she also wished to go, I replied: "Oh, there is nothing to see and one may not even speak to them." To my intense astonishment she answered: "Mitzie Ratibor is furious and says they will take the Red Cross from you for having done such a thing." I paid no attention, never having taken the Duke of Ratibor very seriously. Subsequently there was much gossip amongst my friends, and this I ignored until I heard the story had been carried to the Emperor. Then I wrote to Hans and told him everything. He replied:

GROSSES HAUPTQUARTIER, *October* 7, 1914.

. . . I am very pleased that your visit at Döberitz was so, that nobody can find fault with it. I received letters from Christian Kraft Hohenlohe and Nimptsch, telling me the same. General von Plessen had written at once to General von Kessel about it, and his answer must arrive to-day or to-morrow. As it was General von Löwenfeldt (Stellvertretendes General Kommando des Garde Corps in Berlin) who told the whole story to the Emperor, you will understand that we must wait for a denial from the other military authority, General Oberst von Kessel, Oberst-Kommandierend in den Marken.

I am very sorry that such a useless fuss was made about such a trifle, but you can rely on me that everything will be put right. Of course your position is difficult, I mean, you must have feelings for both countries. So I have too, although I bundled out gradually of my English acquaintance since a few years when I realized that everything there was going from bad to worse. You asked me often why I dropped all my English friends, and why I would not go any more to the London season. . . . The reason was, that the people bored me because I understood that I had nothing in common with them, and that all their ideas were so utterly different to ours. When I was younger, and thought only of hunting and horses, of course I loved England and everything English, and admired and liked the good English sportsmen. But when I gave up hunting, I realized more and more that only the love of sports was the thing which had connected me with them (except of course family relations). Then I knew too, and have told you often, (I remember that it always made you angry), that the war between Germany and England was sure to come sooner or later. And this idea makes social relations always a bit difficult. It gives me an uneasy feeling to have to treat people as good pals when one knows that one has to fight them some day. And this war is not like a football match or a game of Bridge, when one shakes hands again after it is over. The hatred between the two countries will be immense, and last much longer than we shall live. And the politics between them, after the war, will still increase it. . . . I don't tell you all that, darling, to make you sad, but to prepare you for the state of things, as they will be when the war is over.

Hans's next letter gives an excellent summary of current affairs, emphasizes and tries to explain German feelings towards England, and advances the story of my awful misdemeanour which, by now, had almost begun to assume the dimensions of an affair of State. I suppose I should have been flattered at my own importance; I was only irritated and bored:

GROSSES HAUPTQUARTIER, *October* 14, 1914.

. . . As I wired to you the other day, I have received all your letters and none are ever opened. I have not given the four-leaf clover to the Emperor, because I want first to get that stupid affair about Döberitz in order. I have insisted now on a straight declaration from the persons concerned, and when this arrives, then I will talk to the Emperor about it. But I would strongly advise you to leave him now in peace, and not to write to him any more, or send him telegrams. He is extremely nervous and it gets worse, the longer the war drags on. It is difficult to find another topic of conversation, because he seldom listens to anything else. If we could only persuade him to play Bridge, which we others always do when we are free. Old Moltke always used to play Whist (Bridge was not invented then) during the war of 1870. You never told me in your letters if you heard anything of George? Of course we here never hear anything personal except of our own men.

The publication in the *Norddeutsche Allgemeine Zeitung* of papers found in the General-Stab at Brussels, and which the fools forgot to take with them when they fled, are very interesting. I hope you read it. The Berlin *Continental Times*,[1] or whatever the paper is called, is sure to give a good English translation, which will be easier for you. I hear that at Antwerp some more material has been found, which will be published soon. It is no use, my poor darling, throwing the whole blame on the present English government. It was King Edward and Delcassé who were the real organizers of this beastly war. It is no use talking of it any more. But you will remember that I have always told you that this war was sure to come. . . .

I hear that Turkey is beginning to move, which will cause a rising of the Moslem population in India and Egypt. Perhaps this will induce England to finish hostilities. Have you heard that the Russians have been for a week or so at Lancut? Poor Countess Betka Potocka! I am afraid that not much will be left of the place.

We are here put up very comfortably. I have a charming little villa together with Prince Ysenburg. Very nice furniture, comfortable rooms, and a good bath-room. I have engaged a Bohemian housemaid (her mother does my washing) to come every morning and keep the house clean. When we arrived it had to be broken open, because the inhabitants had fled, like most of the population. It is best so, because where they had not already gone, they had to be turned out of their houses, as we could not share them with them. I hope, for our comfort, that we will stay here a good bit. Luxembourg was awful.

I cannot tell you any news, except what you know by the papers. Everything has to be kept so secret.

I have seen several times Aloys Löwenstein.[2] He is with his motor-car with the Bavarian Crown Prince. Prince Eitel Friedrich has been here, too, several days. He wanted a rest, because he had hurt his leg. Now he is all right again. Officers declare that his pluck is beyond description.

Now I must finish. Don't forget about the dentist. Write soon again and give me some news about what is going on in Berlin. Where is Zander Münster?[3]

A very big kiss. Yours, HANS.

My best love to Conny and other relations, if you see them.

---

[1] This publication, which had no status, journalistic or otherwise, was subsidized by the German Foreign Office during the War; it only published news favourable to the Central Empires. The Editor was said to be a renegade Englishman.

[2] The Prince of Löwenstein-Wertheim-Rosenberg.

[3] Prince Münster of Derneburg.

From the very beginning I had disquieting news of the Austrian armies. The Austrians and Hungarians were magnificent fighters—but they were never properly led. I had many friends and relations amongst them and knew. As early as October 20 Marquess Pallavacini wrote to me:

I am still always on the Serbian frontier. The war there is no fun. Rather disheartening. I wish the Germans would lend us a good General; we are in want of one. Perhaps your Emperor could help us, because our tactics are all wrong. It is a dirty war with very bad leadership. We only hope that things go all right in the North—it seems so now—and that will make everything easy in the South too. . . .

Towards the end of October I heard that gallant, cheery Robin Duff had been killed, and that brother George was with the ill-fated Naval Brigade at Antwerp under "General" Winston Churchill! The wretched Döberitz incident was still, so to speak, holding up the war and, apparently, Hans and other highly-placed officers had nothing better to do than deal with it. Hans wrote:

GROSSES HAUPTQUARTIER, *October* 26, 1914.

. . . At last the official report of the Commanding officer at Döberitz has arrived and I send it at once to you.

1. It says (on page two) that you approached a sentry, told him that you were *Vorsteherin* of the Red Cross, and had the right to visit the prisoners' camp.

2. Then it says that you were surrounded by a great number of the prisoners with whom you were talking.

Conny says that you got a permission from the *Kommandantur* to visit the camp, and that you went there to get news about George. That you only spoke to the German officers, but not to the prisoners, that you did not give any presents. Christian Kraft Hohenlohe and Nimptsch write too, that you did not speak a word with any of the prisoners.

Please write me a line at once (not a telegram), stating,

1. if you went to the camp with or without a permission, and, if with one, who gave it to you;

2. if you spoke to the prisoners and what;

3. if you gave them anything.

These are the three points that want clearing up.

Many thanks for your dear long letters, and the enclosures. As far as we hear, there are no complaints that German prisoner in England are not well treated. But people are furious about the treatment of the other Germans in England. Of course, it is impossible to know what is true, and how much is exaggerated.

Winston with his trip to Antwerp made himself really too ridiculous. Now the English men-of-war have been shelling Ostend. I hope they will do the same with Calais when we get there. It is rather an odd way of treating one's Allies, and the friendship between them will not be very great when the war is over. . . .

The Russians have been about a week at Lancut, but behaved very well, although there must have been severe fighting just there. They only took a little picture with them, and told the servants so, because it was written under it: *Chacun à son tour*. There must be a big battle going on now in Poland.

I got a very nice letter the other day from Lexel, and beautifully written. Endermann seems to do him a lot of good.

Now I must finish. A very big kiss. Yours,

HANS.

Upon receiving this letter I consulted Prince Hatzfeldt (Duke of Trachenberg), Count Schönborn and such other of my friends as were available. Feeling that the affair had gone too far to be hushed up or passed off by an official apology, we decided to demand an official enquiry. I therefore wrote in my best German to General von Plessen. Here is a translation:

BERLIN, HOTEL ESPLANADE, *October* 31, 1914.

To His Excellency Chief General von Plessen, Great Headquarters.

EXCELLENCY,—

My husband has sent me the Report which General von Löbell has made about me. This Report is false from beginning to end. As what I have already repeatedly written is not believed, I beg to request an *Official Enquiry*, in order that I may make a statement on oath, and be able to summon witnesses. I hope that a woman will not be refused what a man would be granted.

With greatest respect, THE PRINCESS OF PLESS.

Prince Hermann Hatzfeldt helped me to draft the letter. The formal signature was meant to indicate that I was going to stand no more nonsense. If "Great Headquarters" had time to start silly rows, then they had time to settle them. However, I was taking no chances, so I sent a copy of the "Report" and a copy of my letter to General von Plessen to the Emperor, and one to General von Kessel, who was always my friend.

General von Plessen's reply to my letter was so amusing (and so typically German) that I really must give a translation of it. No good German woman would of course dream of sneezing if she could get her husband to do it for her. The General conveyed this quite clearly in the suavest language. He was more polite than truthful and businesslike. My letter to him was not in the least "agreeable" and his to me was undated!

BERLIN.

YOUR SERENE HIGHNESS, MOST GRACIOUS PRINCESS,—

To your Highness's very agreeable letter of 31 October, I have the honour quite loyally to reply that I am not in a position to initiate an Official Enquiry as Your Highness wishes. I most respectfully submit that you should leave to His Highness the Prince, your noble husband, the rectification of this affair, of which I have received information in your letter, and that you will allow him to undertake the representation and the defence of his noble wife.

With the expression of my distinguished esteem, I have the honour to be, Your Highness's devoted servant,

PLESSEN.

I was determined not to be browbeaten by a lot of silly old Generals whom, before the War, one only received on sufferance and to whom it was nearly always a terrible bore to be polite. Prince Eitel Fritz, the Emperor's second son, has always been, and is, my kind good friend. A fine soldier and a chivalrous foe, he made for himself an abiding place in the hearts of the German people during the War. Amongst others I wrote to him telling him of the petty persecution to which I was being subjected. He replied at once, acquitting me of all blame except that I had perhaps been a little indiscreet. He spoke of the brotherhood of the trenches and—like many another fighting man in every country—wondered how people at home could be unkind to each other.

Poor Lord de Ramsey and his son Reginald Fellowes were in Germany when war broke out and were interned. I went a long way to visit them in some place near Eisenach as I realized how much it meant to prisoners to see a fellow-countrywoman. I brought every old newspaper I could lay hands on and found they even needed money until they could arrange to get some from England.

But even in prisoner-of-war camps many people in all countries succeeded, thank God, in remaining human. Ivan Hay wrote to me that Ober-Lieutenant Brandis, the Commandant of his camp—his mother by the way was an Irishwoman—was "quite the kindest old man and the nicest I have ever met"; he added "three poor old German women who work in the canteen here heard that it was my birthday to-day and brought me some roses and violets, an egg and some apples. It was really so kind of them. I had often carried pails of water to the kitchen for them but I never thought they would remember my birthday."

I love to think of this English, or rather Scottish gentleman forgetting that he was a smart cavalry officer and a captive and voluntarily undertaking menial tasks (if any work to help another can be called menial) for the womenfolk of his captors. And the beautiful manner in which these dear, humble German women reciprocated: flowers and food and fruit—to them at that time as rare and precious as were the frankincense and myrrh to the ancient kings. How glad one is even now to remember that war is not all beastliness. Because of those old canteen women I have been able to forgive Germany much. Nor are all Germans hidebound with red tape. As Barrie would say, kindness would keep breaking through, and Lieutenant Brandis even allowed me to send letters and books for Ivan under cover to him and these he would personally hand to Ivan unopened. It was the utter uselessness of being a prisoner that irked men so. Poor Ivan's joy when he was made postman to the British in his camp and the enthusiasm with which he dashed round with the letters! He longed to be allowed to go to work in a Lazarett, but that was of course impossible.

Friends everywhere were kind in writing to prisoners and trying to get their letters through with the help of one or other of the neutral Embassies or Legations. The King and Queen of Spain were indefatigable in their efforts for all prisoners-of-war, and never forgot their friends. I find amongst my correspondence at this time a message from Queen Victoria Eugénie full of sympathy and encouragement which, if I remember rightly, reached me through the Marquess of Villalobar, the Spanish Ambassador in Brussels. I had correspondents everywhere and it was a great comfort. I must now quote a letter from Mrs. Davis, a most kind American friend, as it gives a picture of life in London and a glimpse of life at sea and in New York towards the end of that horrible first autumn:

SEVEN EAST SEVENTY-THIRD STREET, NEW YORK,
November 8, 1914.

DEAR PRINCESS OF PLESS,—

A voice in London telling of German success and denying German atrocities was indeed a voice in the wilderness.[1]

No one wished to hear good of Germany, and every one urged me to tell you how impossible it would be even for you to think of returning to England. You and I who have known the calm, British nation could not believe it possible to arouse this bitter racial feeling against everything and every one German. It is bitter—bitter—venomous. Lady Paget, and Lady Essex promised to write news of Gordon Leith [2] and every one, to reach you through the American Consul.

---

[1] The reference is to my letters to Sir John Cowans and others.—D. OF P.

[2] Colonel Gordon Leith, C.B.

So many things were absurd. They thought every German of importance killed, even the Crown Prince, and that you were living at the American Embassy. No food in Berlin—merely death and destitution. Mrs. Leeds was too sweet and sympathetic, and wept at the thought of your being unable to return to England. She is a dear, true friend so call upon her when you need anything. Your Mother and Father both well she said. The Duchess of Westminster is in France, also your brother, George Cornwallis-West. The English are determined to fight until every German is exterminated. General Paget said even if it meant the extinction of a generation, the war would go on.

I saw Percy Fitzgerald's brother and heard all about his marriage to the Duchess of Sutherland. She has written a little book, *Six Weeks at the War*, which I will send you, and has now returned to do Red Cross Service. The streets of London are dark and everything closes at 10 p.m. The German manager, and every German employee had been put in prison, or on parole, so the Ritz was entirely under English management. A good English law makes it compulsory to accept English Officers and members of their families at *all* hotels at ten shillings a day each, including rooms and board. That should be introduced into Germany.

The Krupp people will have to tax their ingenuity and invent something to settle this dreadful war. You must tell Herr Professor at your next conclave. The bloodshed and slaughter of all the world is too dreadful! And the hatred makes one quite ill.

I arrived here yesterday after ten days of storm on a very poor boat. We were transferred to three different ships by the White Star Line, each in turn being withdrawn as required for transport or hospital service. There were interesting people aboard whom I knew, thank God! I gave Chandler Anderson a line to you as he was going to Berlin, and is arranging the exchange of German and English prisoners—man for man, rank for rank, which is fair and just. The Germans are well cared for in England; but prisoners there as in Germany need warm clothes and blankets. I urged Lady Paget, Mrs. Leeds and others to send such things via Mr. Lay [1] rather than to Red Cross Depôts. All such stuff can be easily and quickly delivered through the American Consuls in London and

[1] Mr. Howard Lay, Consul-General of the United States in Berlin.

Berlin; so if you wish to send anything to German prisoners do so through Mr. Lay to Mr. Skinner. Many asked about Prince Münster.

I have not had time to get in touch with American affairs, but shall try to see both Count Bernstorff and Mr. Dernburg. I go at once to stop a few days on Long Island, as people are still in the country.

These clippings from the morning papers may interest you. Of course, you see the English people are hounding all naturalized citizens, and I understand that Prince Louis of Battenberg was forced to resign. The spy craze has become fanatical, and no one with German affiliations is safe from suspicion.

Take care of yourself—charming person. Be careful what you write, as the Colloredo-Mansfeldt's letter to a friend was published in the London *Times*. Every good wish——

The next letter I must quote is from Hans:

GROSSES HAUPTQUARTIER, *November* 11, 1914.

MY DARLING LITTLE DANY WIFE,—

At last I had a chance of talking the Döberitz affair over with the Emperor. He understood everything and told me to tell you so. There was never a question of my not believing what you or your friends wrote about it, but, as a report from Berlin was asked for, one had naturally to wait for it. Your declaration proves now that the official report is full of lies. I was away for a bit the last days. This is also the reason why I could not see the Emperor sooner. *Entre autre*, I stayed two days at Brussels, from where I went to Antwerp. All was very interesting.

Lichnowsky, who was with General von Kluck's army, has now been transferred to General von Mackensen's Staff in Poland. Poor devil. I am sorry for him. But he is too silly. He keeps on telling everybody that he could have prevented the war, and that our Foreign Office is responsible for it. You can imagine that this theory has not had very pleasant effects for him.

It is no use my writing to you about the war (on land and sea) as you see everything in the papers. But I would like to know your opinion about the future, as far as England is concerned. To my idea, there can be no doubt that our successes on land and sea must have been a very disagreeable surprise for England. If they go on hiding their fleet, we shell their ports, and if they send her out, they expose her to our submarines. The exaggerated anti-German feeling (the concentration camps for the Germans in England, and the forced resignation of Battenberg, and the most appalling lies in words and pictures about Germany and German warfare), all that seems to me a proof of disappointment and weakness. One could compare it to people who, in a discussion, begin to get insulting because they have no more arguments. The declaration of the Holy War by Turkey, the rising of the Boers, and (at least) a certain unrest in India, as well as a certain difficulty with the food supplies to England, must also more or less affect them. The most prominent feature now, Winston, is daily attacked by several papers, mostly the *Morning Post*. I am sure that, when Parliament meets (I think on December 2), these attacks against him will grow in the Commons. As he is very vain, very unscrupulous, and intends to hang on to his office . . . he will not allow himself to be kicked out personally, but will drag the whole Cabinet with him, if he falls. Then we would have a new Cabinet and General Elections. The new Cabinet would perhaps be composed of Minorities and Labour Party men. And this might lead to Peace. Write to me, darling, what you think of this possibility, because you know England better than I do.

The other day, it was in a place in the north, I had to interview some English prisoners. In the middle aisle of a huge church there was straw put down, on which were lying about two hundred English prisoners, men and officers, *all* fast asleep at midday. New batches of ten to twenty or more were coming in every half an hour, and directly they were put into the church, they flopped themselves down on the straw and slept. This, and the surrendering of small quantities was a proof to me that the men were literally tired out. Till the evening there were about two hundred in the church. Most of them looked awful. People they would never have recruited in ordinary times, a sort of type one sees hanging around the public-houses in England. And in every batch of twenty or so, there were men of all possible regiments : Highlanders in kilts, Life Guards, Infantry of all denominations and a few Indians. I found one Indian who could speak English fairly well.[1] He was a Mohammedan from the North. He repeated the whole time : " We Mohammedans, the Turks and the

[1] The first Indian troops only reached the Flanders front on October 19, twenty-three days before the Prince's letter was written.

Germans are brothers. We don't shoot on the Germans, but the Germans shoot on us." Then he said that the English threatened to shoot on them (I did not understand if he meant in India or in France) if they refused to fight. But the most astonishing news that the fellow told me was that the Ameer of Afghanistan was marching with a big army into India and would soon be proclaimed Emperor of India. How could this man who had left India six weeks ago, have heard of it. It is clear that his English officers did not provide him with those news. . . .

Of course we felt bound to credit anything my husband wrote from Great Headquarters. If they didn't know there, from what source could one receive reliable news? This feeling caused me to be very upset by the following passages in the next letter I received from Hans. It is undated, but must have been written at the very end of November or the beginning of December because, after receiving his letter dated November 11, which I have just quoted, I had twice written, on the 12th and on the 15th, and had received no reply:

. . . To my idea, everything depends now on a decisive victory over the Russians. The enemy resistance on our Western front is only based on the hopes of a Russian advance. From the moment the French Government sees that the Russians are done, they will give in. The French are practically only kept in order by the English, who are dotted all over the line, as a sort of police. They fire on the French if they want to retreat or surrender. You will remember that I told you years ago of the possibility of the Green Flag and the Holy War.[1] Well, now we have it, and it might induce England too to ask for peace, so as to get her white troops free to quell the different rebellions. News which arrived from England says that the effect there of the Holy War is much greater than Germany had expected. Let us hope that all this will bring the war soon to an end.

I am awfully sorry about poor Robin Duff. The number

---

[1] On November 11 the Sheik ul Islam declared a Jehad or Holy War against all the Allies; two days later the Sultan of Turkey as Khalif declared a Jehad against all those making war on Turkey or her Allies.

of friends and acquaintances who have fallen on both sides is enormous. . . .

We are all very anxious about the news from Poland.[1] Up till now the big battle there seems to go very well for us. . . .

Alphonse Clary, only son of the Prince of Clary and Aldrengen, and one of our greatest Austrian friends, was then serving with the Austrian Army on the Polish front and this letter from him gives a graphic account of the very battle of Cracow about which Hans and the German High Command were so anxious. Alphy, who was a brilliant cavalry officer, says :

. . . There is a quite tremendous battle going on and I hope—when I come back this evening, to be able to write and tell you of a real . . .

November 25. I was called away and only came back to my rooms to-day, after having spent thirty-six hours out in the battle ; it was the most wonderful night one could dream of, but oh so terribly cold, and my heart melted for our poor soldiers who are out day and night. There was a terrible east wind blowing, a sort of gale, and one simply froze. Thank God we did some very good work and drove the Russians out of some enormously fortified positions. But one feels rather weary afterwards, and although it is quiet now, I keep on hearing the thundering noise of the guns and the rattling of the machine guns. But the thought of the wounded exposed to the terrible cold is so ghastly. Every infantry man out there is a hero. Oh, but the terrible responsibility before God for those men who wilfully brought this war upon unlucky Europe. You are so right to say that it is a war of jealousy ; and truly the *real* culprits are some vile merchants sitting in the city of London, who fear a new and prosperous competitor. And now so many of our dear English friends are paying the price for all that. So many friends have passed away in every country. I have lost my very best, Cary Schwarzenberg,[2] who was my cousin and with whom I was practically like a brother. I feel as if a bit of myself had gone, as he knew me and all my thoughts so well and was a very great help in many hard moments of my life. He leaves two little boys of three and

[1] The battle of Cracow began on November 15, and ended on December 2.

[2] Charles, Prince of Schwarzenberg, killed September 6, 1914.

MY YOUNGEST SON, BOLKO, AGED NINE.

one year and a lonely little widow to face all the hardness of life. But there is one good side of war—it brings out the very best of every human creature, it makes every one believe and trust in God again, because we all can see and feel what tiny little helpless puppets we are in life and how we all depend on God's mercy. And then it makes one see how ghastly a hollow so many things really are we used to aim at in life, how terribly uselessly so much of our time was spent. I think war makes every man so very much older and wiser. Then it makes me feel the value of friendship, and oh how I thank you for yours, dear friend, you have been such a star in my life and made it so sunny with your wonderful person and charm; you have the marvellous and rare gift of making every one happy by your presence alone; and often, when I felt weary and sad, when life seemed to be quite horrid, I only thought of you and felt that as long as your sun was shining on my path I could not be unhappy. . . .

On December 1, Countess Brockdorff, Mistress of the Robes to the Empress, wrote urging me to try to communicate with a relation of hers, Lieutenant Hans Werner von Helldorff, who was a prisoner-of-war at Abergele, in Denbighshire. It is near Rhyl and Ruthin. I must quote some of Countess Brockdorff's letter just to show what a close friend of the Empress was at this time being told about the way German prisoners were treated in England:

DEAR PRINCESS,—

You have got his address and wished to help him on. Please do not postpone your letter; he is ill, suffering from kidney, liver and bile—for want of air and exercise. The prisoners are allowed to walk in a place of fifty metres long and width. A short time you seemed not to think that there was cause to complain that *eight* officers are together in *one* room with only three chairs and three washing stands—for so long! Please add to this, the fact that they had often mouldy bread, meat already putrefied—too bad! Eighty-four officers in one house; the other night there was a fire on the roof and the hundred and forty men in the house—with one small staircase—seemed to have been in real danger.

But that could not be helped; but really the treatment they have to go through is a shame. And this poor Helldorff writes to his sister, Frau von Plessen, and to his other sister who is my niece, that he wished to be dead. Don't you think they could allow him a cure somewhere being actually a sufferer and ill? He *must* have some treatment, better food and exercise. He has written seventeen letters, only four arrived here. Please, dear Princess, do write for him. I fear you ought to try and write in German to a neutral, and let it be translated into English so that it may pass from Germany to England. It is all so sad. Yours very sincerely,

W. BROCKDORFF.

I would willingly write it for you in German.

All this time I had only bits and scraps of news from home. Patsy sent me messages in queer and weird ways that only she could have thought of. At first she sent quite a number through Mrs. Howard Lay and Mr. Laughton at the American Embassy in Berlin, until the American Ambassador, Mr. James W. Gerard, suddenly became terribly neutral and stopped it. One day in Liverpool Patsy went up to an American in the street and handed him a message written hurriedly on a dirty piece of paper, which somehow reached me. How kind people were—even utter strangers. She would tackle the most unsympathetic and unlikely people and beseech them to get a message through to "her precious little Dany." And nearly always she succeeded. She would beard anyone; the King, Lord Kitchener, Lord French—anyone. As for her friends in high places she just made them do what she wanted. Dear little Patsy, what audacity, what courage, what resource! Where her affections and those she loved were concerned she just went straight ahead, never counting the cost. At times this led her and her loved ones into many scrapes; but she was so single-minded she didn't care a scrap. And, after all, unselfish, devoted love and friendship is none too plentiful, and is worth all the wisdom and circumspection in the world.

George was still with the Royal Naval Division and not, as Mrs. Davis had said, in France. His wife, Stella Patrick Campbell, had gone to America to act and raise funds for the Allied Red Cross. Poppets was at Ruthin superintending all the County war work and carrying out the many war duties required from a Lord-Lieutenant. Shelagh was of course with her Hospital in France.

VI

I ought to say that quite soon after my unlucky visit to Döberitz and while the official inquiries regarding my conduct were going on, I received orders to leave Berlin at once. Of course I paid no attention, just went quietly on with my work at the Lazarett in Tempelhof, seeing my friends, writing to prisoners and so on. But I must tell how it happened.

I knew that, having refused to take the hint to leave Berlin, I was being watched and my correspondence opened. One day when I was out old General von Boehm left a card saying he would call on me later. During all this trying time my two best friends and advisers were Hermann Hatzfeldt and Clement Schönborn; Prince Hatzfeldt was head of the Prussian, and Count Schönborn[1] head of the Bavarian Red Cross. Clement was a splendid friend not only then, but later, and his daughter Marie Catherine is now the wife of Hansel my eldest son.

Directly I saw the General's card I said to Clement: "What fun; perhaps they are going to put me in Ruhleben."

When, later, the General called again I was very formal and this conversation took place:

"It is an honour for a lady to be visited by a General who must have so much to do: please sit down and tell me what it is you wish to say."

So there he sat with his pale face and no hair, and I knew that really he was quite nice.

"What I have to say, Princess, is not pleasant."

"Please, General, don't mind that; I am becoming quite accustomed to unpleasantness."

[1] Count Clement Philippe Erwin of Schönborn-Wiesentheid.

"I have to tell you that you must leave Berlin at once."

I picked up the telephone, remarking that I would call up the Reichstag.

"I would not do that, Princess, I wish to speak to you alone."

"Why, General? You find me alone; but I wish to have a witness present to hear what you are going to say. I will ask Prince Hatzfeldt; I am a nurse and he is the head of the Red Cross."

Hermann was not at the Reichstag; so I telephoned to Clement Schönborn who said he would come in ten minutes. I then said to the General that if he cared to wait in my sitting-room I begged to be excused and would rest in my bedroom. He said he would withdraw and wait downstairs.

In ten minutes he returned with Clement who asked him why I was being ordered to leave Berlin. He replied that he could not answer questions, but that it had to do with my correspondence and my visit to Döberitz. I requested the General to give me a written order to leave; this he did and then ceremoniously took his departure. Nothing would induce me to leave Berlin. To show this I left the Hotel and moved into a furnished flat where I slept with my pistol under my pillow. I never showed fear, even if I felt it!

What I did do was to sit down immediately and write to the Emperor as follows:

YOUR MAJESTY, SIRE,—

I thank Your Majesty for the wire received yesterday. I hold it in my hand now as a comfort, but not to show it—as General von Boehm came to see me and calmly said there was an order that I had to leave Berlin at once and remain in Fürstenstein till the end of the war. I go to see Countess Brockdorff this afternoon, and I shall remain in Berlin until I receive orders from Your Majesty or the Empress. I have been all these years Your Majesty's true subject not only by marriage but in heart and in every word I have ever said or written before and since this war, and you know this, Sire. I care for nothing at such a time; you can do with me what you wish, but nothing will induce me to leave Berlin where my children are, until these orders are confirmed.

I cannot be treated like a spy, being oh! so truly honest, without an examination and a reason given.

I await the orders of Your Majesty.

All sorts of charges were brought against me, mostly quite silly, but none the less annoying. One was that I had dined with Count Moltke, the Danish Minister in Berlin, and his wife, whom I had known since years. It appears, although I never knew it, that he had once served for a short time in the French Army and the Germans therefore distrusted him. Another was that I was constantly going back and forwards to England!

Meanwhile there was the consolation of my work at the Lazarett and for the British prisoners. No one worked harder for them than the dear old Dowager Grand Duchess of Mecklenburg-Strelitz, aunt of Queen Mary. The grand-daughter of King George III., and elder sister of the Duchess of Teck and the Duke of Cambridge, she was English through and through. I had been in communication about prisoners-of-war with her grandson who had succeeded his father Adolphus Frederick V. as reigning Grand Duke in June, 1914. His grandmother had sent me a list of British prisoners and asked my help. And he had been one of my Esquires when I was Princess Errant in the Elizabethan Tourney at Earl's Court in 1912! Little did I then think that the next time I should see him would be in Service uniform in Berlin in October, 1914. The Grand Duke wrote as follows:

NOYON, *December* 15, 1914.

DEAR PRINCESS,—

Many thanks again for your very kind telegram to Bruxelles. I would be so much obliged if you would kindly help me again to find out where a few other English officers are. I enclose my Grandmother's letter, in which she mentions the names. The *comble* of kindness would be if you would let the Crown Princess of Sweden know where the officers are. From here it is rather impossible to write to her. About Lord Gerald and Hugh [1] my Grandmother must have made a mistake, but meanwhile I have written to her. My thoughts are so much with you, dear Princess, and I long to see you again very soon. Here they are quite impossible to talk to! The delightful hours I had the pleasure of spending with you and your clever conversation I shall never forget. Please do send me a line to let me know if you are quite well and have had no new troubles; I hate to know you unhappy and cannot help you.

From here I have not much to say; we are in the same trenches and nothing much happens. There are four Lazarette here and I love to go and visit the poor wounded. At Chauny, a few miles from here, we have a German shop from Tietz and I can buy or order all I want for the wounded. It is my only pleasure to be of some use here.

Again many thanks if you would kindly help me; please return me my Grandmother's letter as I collect them all. With my best compliments, Yours very sincerely,

ADOLPHUS FREDERICK.

Here are some extracts from a letter of Patsy's started at the beginning of December in the form of a diary and sent to me as she had opportunity:

. . . I keep thinking of you with all your children in a little flat with daisies, and tending your Hospitals, and the dear brave wounded to care for. It is such a help to Shelagh too. But the cases of tetanus are the worst of all to watch, though she gives them a little chloroform every time the attacks come on. But sometimes she has cheery and amusing boys in. Just privates! She had two Irish boys in both with their right arms off and they did nothing but chaff each other and ask for the loan of each other's arms. Then I told you about the two dear smart men in Hans's regiment who, when she talked to them, weak as they were, tried to salute her and were so pleased and brave and grateful. They are getting well. . . .

There is one Irish song just makes me cry when I hear all the young recruits singing it—*It's a long, long way to Tipperary*. And I travelled down in the train the other day with a boy who had just come from the front—I don't know who he was—he says the Germans have learnt it and sing it quite beautifully, all the voices together. . . .

[1] Lord Gerald and Lord Hugh Grosvenor, sons of the first Duke of Westminster.

Granny is a marvel and her dear sweet, so tender smile is a great comfort to me.

Patsy, naturally, was doing what she could for German prisoners-of-war in England just as I was for English prisoners in Germany and, even in kindly England, it laid her open to all sorts of ridiculous suspicion and gossip. She, as she wrote, " did not care two straws," but it resulted in much annoyance to Poppets and eventually they stopped her visiting prisoner-of-war camps in Wales. People used to write begging her to try to get them some information about a relation. One list of names she forwarded me included that of Lieutenant C. W. Williams Wynn of the First Battalion Coldstream Guards, and son of a neighbour. I was begged to find out " if he was alive or dead." One would have thought such innocent activities justified themselves. But no. Ignorance is nearly always malicious; and what people cannot understand they will always suspect. Another extract from Patsy's epistle is rather amusing and shows the sort of tiresome difficulties with which she had to contend. Ursula and Mary were of course Shelagh's two girls and " Sibell," Bend Or's mother and George Wyndham's widow, dear Sibell Grosvenor :

RUTHIN CASTLE, *December* 12, 1914.

I opened the papers just now and there was my Daisy dressed as a nurse standing between two wounded soldiers.

Ursula and her nice little governess came over to luncheon yesterday. Sibell sent them in her car and Ursula was so loving with her grandfather. It quite touched him. Mary comes here on Monday. But I shall send her back to Eaton on the 23rd to be with poor little Ursula. They are supposed to spend Christmas with Benny. But Heaven knows where he will be. He gave Shelagh five hundred pounds for her Hospital and wrote to her. Oh, dear Daisy, if they could only come together. It's so sad for the children.

Daisy, if I could just peep in on you and the precious boys, how grateful I would be to God, if He would let me. I asked Jack and he says it is not possible. . . .

December 17, 1914.

My dear Daisy, we won't call it Christmas, but at this time of year our thoughts turn to long long ago days, when my little children used to stand outside my door and yell out "Christmas is here." Happy childhood with little presents worked by the eager loving hands. . . . I asked Jack if I could not get to you if only for one day. But he wrote me I must put it out of my head. That it's quite impossible. . . .

December 20, 1914.

It was such a comfort to get dear old Fritz's letter yesterday. He tells me writing through his friends reaches you quicker. I go back with Biddy for the first of January to her Hospital. I sent word to the Préfet at Nice that they might have convalescents of *any* nationality at your Villa.[1] He is very pleased. . . .

My early morning letters just come in and one from you, my precious darling. It is censored but I don't fancy much taken out, except something about your clothes; that has been half taken out I fancy, as I can't read it. . . . There is some writing in pencil at the back of one of the two printed bits that is quite impossible to read as it's all rubbed. I can read the word Fips and Florie, so I can put that together, it's about some scent dear Mother gave you, but I can't read the name Mru on the outside of the first sheet; you write in pencil: "Send Mrs. Lay's clothes to Mity." But where are her clothes? Let me know and I will see about them at once.

Biddy is quite wonderfully well; she comes to Newlands on the 24th for a few days, and I go back with her to her Hospital as she is quite alone, poor little darling. She was half hoping she might have had the children for a few days, but Benny wants them at Eaton and it is his turn.

George's wife Stella made five hundred pounds for her by one matinée out in America. Daisy, do you know I like that woman; she is nice to me, which the other one never was, and she worships George, and poor old boy, he is so different and loves soldiering again.

I have seen a lot of that queer mad Irishman who married Millicent Duchess of Sutherland[2]; he has all the fascination and irresponsibility of a true Irishman, all sunshine and tears,

[1] Our villa at Mandelieu had been offered to the French Government as a convalescent home and been accepted.—D. OF P.

[2] Dear Milly married Major Percy Desmond Fitzgerald, D.S.O., in October, 1914.—D. OF P.

like the Irish mountains. But I don't envy the woman he has married.

And I have been fighting so hard with the powers that be to get to you. I know someone who once lunched at Newlands would be kind and help me out there. But it's here that they would be horrid, never thinking it is just a mother's great longing to be with her child. . . .

The clergyman has got your letter and was so pleased with it. All, all the people, the poor ones in the streets come and stop me to ask for you, some of them just asking for "Miss Mary," people I did not know even knew you, quite poor tramp sort of people. . . .

December 28, 1914.

Christmas has come and gone, and we just let it pass and never noticed it or alluded to it. It passed in pouring rain and wind and it has rained ever since. Little Shelagh is very quiet, very gentle; dear old George very loving; Poppets just a little fussy—about nothing. But all our hearts go out to—my precious Dany girl. Biddy said "Poor little Dany, poor darling, she must be very lonely." George came and sat on my bed and said "Darling little Dany," and squeezed my hand. Poppets came up and just said "That dear child"—but his poor old eyes had tears in them. . . .

I had hoped to send you some tiny thing . . .

Pat and Grace FitzPatrick are at Ruthin with that wonderful old Granny, who is, thank God, just a happy child, singing to herself, sleeping the sleep of the pure in heart as she ever has been and not a pain or an ache anywhere.

Little Shelagh goes back to her Hospital on the 5th. I go to Ruthin. They are going to present Poppets' picture to the Town Hall, very quietly. It is a marvellous picture, thanks to your choice of an artist.[1] My darling, little Biddy gave ten pounds, and I told Mr. Denton to put you down for ten pounds, as I knew you would feel it dreadfully if your name was not there too, and I said some day you would be able to get the money through. They all, the magistrates, were so anxious to have your name.

I received one letter from Poppets about this time. I had let him know I wished to send a donation to the British Red Cross. The dear darling was always so

[1] Mr. Ellis Roberts, whom I afterwards got to make me a copy; it is reproduced in this volume.—D. of P.

wise and circumspect and wrote: "I don't advise your subscribing to anything. . . . It will be better to abstain from showing any sympathy for what passes outside your present surroundings."

VII

As for me, I remained quietly in my little flat in Berlin. I had a modest Christmas entertainment there for as many of the patients from the Lazarett as I could accommodate. A Christmas tree and a gramophone made things gay.

When the order to leave Berlin reached me I had, of course, to give up regular work at the Hospital, although I continued to go there occasionally and bring little gifts, tobacco, books and so on. At the formal conclusion of my service I received the following letter, which I prize enormously. It was of course in German:

Her Serene Highness the Princess Marie Therese of Pless, called "Sister Daisy," has, during the months of September and October, been working in the outer department of the Reserve (Garrison) Hospital, which is under my direction. With great sacrifice and love she has taken care of the wounded, and comforted and gladdened them by her cordial manner. Untiringly she endeavoured to cheer them up and to refresh them and to ease their sufferings.

"Sister Daisy" may be called a benefactress in the truest meaning of the word.

Professor Freiherr von Kuester. Berlin, Tempelhof. 25.X.1914.

The following letter from Marquess Pallavacini, who always wrote in English, gives another glimpse of how Hungarian troops were faring on the Serbian front:

Feldpost 30, 3. A.K., *December* 30, 1914.

Two of your very kind letters, addressed to the Feldpost 63, came to hand yesterday, very many thanks. It was kind of you to think of me for Christmas and I hope that sooner or later I will also get the "little funny things" you sent me, which was really more than gracious and thoughtful of you—and I don't know how to thank you.

As I wrote to you some time ago I was transferred to this Kommando about a month ago, so I not only had the luck to escape seeing our Serbian débâcle, but also to see wife and family for a few days in Budapest, during the Parliamentary sessions; and last not least, to serve under the most capable General we have. And, alas, we have only very few. The whole Serbian affair was only owing to the impossible and sinful leadership.[1] With some of your Generals and Hungarian troops we would have been in Nish by the month of September, and there would be no Russian army anywhere near our frontier. It is awesome what a lot of people have lost their lives for nothing, and owing to the same faults all the time.

Of course one can't lose hope and there is no reason why one should; I am pretty sure that in the end we will come out on the top—but at what costs!

Since last I wrote you I have been made Oberleutnant and got an Order—*Militar Verdienst Medaille*—for some Serbian affair. It is quite funny that slowly one gets quite a soldier and forgets having been anything else. But Christmas was not a very cheerful affair. I hope we will all have better days next year. I send you all my best wishes for 1915 and hope that everything you wish for will come to fulfilment. I often think of you, what hard times you must live through now and believe me to be, dear Princess Daisy, yours ever sincerely,

PALLAVACINI.

I will close this account of the fate-filled year 1914, by giving the gist of the Official Report upon my visit to Döberitz. It is a characteristically German production, tinged unconsciously, as so many things in Germany are, with humour:

REPORT ON LETTER IIB. NO. 15762 OF THE 14.10.1914.

DÖBERITZ, *October* 17, 1914.

Through a letter of the Chief Command of the 5th of September, 1914, and through Press Notices and private letters to the Commandant, it was known to the Command that the Princess of Pless had visited the Prisoners' Camp. According

[1] The Austrian forces were routed by the Serbians at the battle of Kolubra, December 3–6; on December 15, Serbian forces reoccupied Belgrade and the (second) Austrian invasion of Serbia came to an end.

to the Press Notices and also according to the private letters addressed to the Commandant, the Princess of Pless is said to have distributed chocolate, sweets and flowers among the prisoners. In some letters and newspapers it was even stated that she had delivered a lorry full of partridges, and so on, to the prisoners.

The investigation ordered by the Command into the matter resulted in the following:

"An elegant lady, in nurse's uniform with white arm-bands and red cross, approached the sentry in the company of a gentleman, whom the sentry described as the Prince of Pless, and stated that she was the Princess of Pless and Chairman of the Red Cross and that she had the right to enter the Prisoners' Camp. Whether she distributed, as has many times been stated, chocolate and sweets to the prisoners could not be ascertained by the investigation. It was only remarked that she was surrounded by a large circle of English prisoners with whom she conversed. These prisoners also accompanied her and, to judge from the gesticulations, they were asking something of her, upon which, again to judge from the gesticulations, she indicated that she had nothing further. The visit was only a short one. She can only have distributed a small quantity of sweets, because a packet with her or with her conductor was not observed."

The "lorry-load of partridges" which I was said by the newspaper to have smuggled in—presumably under my petticoat—made me laugh, but my real comfort that Christmas, was the compliment, the true compliment, the writer of the Report unwittingly paid to Englishmen. Such a statement from such a source at such a time, did me more good than I have any words to describe. I thought to myself, "So that is England—and they *know* it." The translation of the concluding words of the Report is as follows:

Enquiries of the prisoners as to whether the Princess conversed with them for a long time and gave them sweets, met with a negative result. The English prisoners are very close, and do not give information about anything which could injure their country or their countrymen.

VON LÖBELL.

CHAPTER NINE

January–June, 1915

FOR the moment I had successfully defied Prussian militarism by remaining in Berlin for two months after I had received General Löwenfeldt's order to leave it in three days. At first I thought it politic to give out that I was ill, but I very soon dropped that fiction, received my friends and went about as usual in a quiet way. My greatest grief was that I could no longer work at the Tempelhof Lazarett. The Director, and every one concerned, would have loved to have had me, but, in view of the military order of banishment, to go on working in a Military Lazarett was clearly out of the question. However, I continued to go there at intervals and bring presents of gramophones, cigars and cigarettes, sweets, fruit and newspapers to the wounded.

The military party, which eventually ruined Germany, was doing its best to ruin little me. The first rubber was mine; but that was only because I had powerful friends outside the military caste (with which indeed I had never been intimate) and, for the moment, the Emperor was still a power in the land. It seems ridiculous to compare my position to that of the Emperor. But is it? Straws show the way the wind blows. The military party in Germany had already determined to dominate everybody and everything. I was but a tiresome fly to be brushed aside as (in a few weeks of course) they were going to brush England off the earth. They forgot just two things: that the tiresome fly was an Englishwoman, and that England meant Englishmen. As for the poor Emperor, for the time being he was useful and therefore must for a little while longer be allowed to indulge in the delusion that he was powerful. When no longer needed he also could either be cast aside, used as a figure-head if one were still required or, in the almost impossible event of failure, sent into the wilderness as a scapegoat.

There were, and I suppose there are still, those who wanted the Emperor to suffer personally. Let them be satisfied. I do not know at what moment during the War he realized that, far from being the All-powerful, he was the merest pawn in the most fate-filled and gambling game of chess that has ever been played. He is a man of acute sensibilities, and when he did realize this, his anguish must have been intolerable.

At the beginning of the War I started out with a threefold determination: loyally to do my utmost for the country of my husband and children by continuing my, perhaps feeble and useless, but certainly lifelong and sincere, efforts to do everything that might make for peace between England and Germany; and to nurse Germany's sick and wounded; and to do everything in my power for British and Allied prisoners.

Not until the beginning of 1915 did I begin clearly to realize the hatred, suspicion and jealousy which were directed towards me personally on all sides. In the civilian hospital in Berlin (where I worked on trial for a short time before I went to Tempelhof) I was one day washing a man's leg, so filthy that the dirt came off like little pieces of black skin, when I was roughly informed by one of the Head Doctors that it was unnecessary for me to do such work. This having no effect I was then told to hold, while it was being dressed, a horribly diseased hand, too revolting to describe. The way these two and other similar incidents happened made it clear to me that the authorities were trying to get rid of me. They thought that, being a Princess, I was not in earnest and, being an Englishwoman, I was not to be trusted. They therefore tried, as a brutal Doctor had once tried before in a hospital in Silesia, so to overwhelm me with disgust that I would run away. But that type of German

THE CROWN PRINCE AND HIS ELDEST SON, PRINCE WILLIAM.

knows little of women, and nothing at all of English-women.

I now realize with what conceited indifference I started to work in Berlin, never imagining that anyone would object. I had lived in Germany so long that though the War almost tore me in half, it did not occur to me that people might hate me or doubt my loyalty. I closed my mind to the rights and wrongs of the nations and only saw the terrible suffering.

When people put their chins in the air and half-close their eyes it doesn't frighten me; but the little spirit in me hides itself. Why is it that no one ever can be, or dares to be, quite natural? There is something secretly antagonistic in us, and something so private that no one can help us, or come really near us.

It is so tragic that there are no two people who really know each other—who can frankly look into each other's souls—who know from minute to minute just what passes through each other's minds and hearts, for it is as impossible to explain one's thoughts and feelings as it is to describe a perfume that pleases one. But it is comforting to smile frankly and sincerely at people, as I can now, who smile back in tenderness and affection, not in forced thanks for champagne and the opportunity of shooting roebuck and pheasants.

However, the most intolerable thing I had to suffer then and afterwards was the delay in receiving my correspondence, the knowledge that all letters were kept back until they were read—or suppressed—and the unending spying and watching. I was never secure a moment, hardly dared to use the telephone, and could only speak intimately to my friends behind the locked doors of my bedroom—and not always then!

I had of course, as I have said, made ample and efficient arrangements for sending letters to and receiving letters from England, and that annoyed and mystified the military authorities most of all. They never quite succeeded in making out just who was behind me or how I got so much of my own way. Those "friendly critics," on whom we can at all times rely, of course went about saying that I brought most of my trouble on myself. I dare say I did, but I have never found that reflection particularly comforting or inspiring: it always seems to me one for the coward rather than the courageous. I dare say I ought to have buried myself in obscurity during the War and never so much as said Bo to a German goose, much less Boo to a German General. But that is not the way Englishwomen are made. It certainly was not the way Daisy Cornwallis-West was made, and long years of trying to be Daisy of Pless had not, I am afraid, modified her to any great extent.

Patsy had not heard from me for a month and was naturally most uneasy. Her letters were reaching me, but she did not get mine. On January 8 she wrote me from Ruthin. "Nancy" is Mrs. Leeds, who was afterwards Princess Christopher of Greece, and "Jack" is General Sir John Cowans, the British Quartermaster-General throughout the Great War. "Walter" is Captain Walter Brooke, of the King's Own Yorkshire Light Infantry, Aunt Minnie's son by her first husband:

Lady Crewe writes me she has written to you and also given your address to some of your friends. I lunched with dear little Nancy on Tuesday. She is so genuinely fond of you, my Dany. She cried when talking about you, and dear old Jack said such nice things about my Dany. Every one is thinking of you and all so so nice. . . .

I left this off yesterday so as to tell you about Dads' Presentation. A large lot of the County Magistrates were there, over a hundred in all I should think. Sir Watkin Wynn made a charming speech saying such dear nice things about Poppets. Then Dads himself spoke so well—a long speech on his forty-five years' experience as Lord Lieutenant, and giving some good advice to the younger men under him. . . .

Oh, my Dany, how I wish I could send you cuttings out of different papers, about Christmas at the front. All the dear Tommies, on *both* sides, going and singing together and playing games, just like happy children. Little Walter, Minnie's boy, wrote home and told us it was quite true; one of the Tommies on the other side just stood up and said: "Let us play to-day." And the dear Tommies they did play, and all sang songs and then hymns together. It seems so hard that little harmless *nice* things said on both sides, such natural things, should be censored in the newspapers.

My readers will remember that from his birth little Bolko had never been strong and all this time in Berlin he was under medical care. Fürstenstein, to which they had ordered me, was quite impossible with a sick child. It was too far from anywhere and one was not allowed even to use the telephone to Breslau or the telegraph to Berlin! I therefore decided to take Baby to Meran in Austrian Tyrol. I considered it courteous to write to Countess Brockdorff, Mistress of the Robes to the Empress, and asked her to tell Her Majesty of my intention. The Countess, who was always my good friend, replied:

DEAR PRINCESS,—

I fear you will think me very rude, but I *could* not come even to say good-bye. I have been absent lately, to see a nephew of mine, who is wounded, and you may say for my excuse that I am more in a hurry than ever—and very busy—and not allowed to dispose over my time.

But I am anxious that you shall *not* think that I am without sympathy for what you are going through.

I hope you will soon feel more at rest in Meran—and that the children, especially Baby, will be your comfort, seeing them improve in Meran. This *very* great but hard time will pass over—and we all have to take and carry our charge.

May God grant a happy *Wiedersehen*, Yours,

W. BROCKDORFF.

5.1.15.

Thank you for your dear Mother's kind note you copied for me.

And here I must say just a few words about this dear German who was such a good woman and a great lady. A little later I wanted to interest the Emperor personally in a British prisoner-of-war. I asked the Countess to forward my request under cover of a letter from the Empress as otherwise I knew that it might never be allowed to reach its destination. She replied:

" I don't know, dear Princess, what the Emperor will say—but I shall of course do what you wish, and send him the paper. You *are* a good kind-hearted advocate ! " I knew of a sad anniversary in her life and sent her some of my favourite lilies. She wrote : " Resurrection : Redeemer : Peace and Glory : That's what the lilies say to me. I felt just lonely and sad when they were brought to me—it is a memorial day in my life. I thank you for your kind thoughts. . . ."

But I have never wanted for good, true women friends and, I hope, never shall. Rushing off from London in such a hurry—I did not even bring my clothes—everything there was in a mess. Bills to be paid for the house in Savile Row, linen and personal belongings to be stored, chattels I had hired to be returned and so on. Nancy Leeds was a perfect brick, and, being an excellent woman of business, did everything in the most satisfactory way. I must pay this tribute to her dear memory.

When I got to Meran I found the Emperor's youngest son, Prince Joachim, there on sick leave. He had stayed with us several times at Fürstenstein and I knew him well. He and I, accompanied by his A.D.C., would go for walks together and he would sing aloud nigger songs in English. I begged him not to, as I would be blamed. When he met a woman with a face that was not ugly, or one in a smart hat, he at once stopped and talked to her. They knew who he was and were pleased and flattered.

One day he came to me in a furious rage saying : " What do you think ? They dared to cut my mother off the telephone to-day from Potsdam, because we were talking English ! " I replied : " My dear friend, what else can you expect ? After all, she is the German Empress, and I am only an Englishwoman, and even I would not have dared speak in English on the telephone." I had to console the poor boy, who got dreadfully excited. About a year later he married a Princess of Anhalt, and in 1920 took his own life. I never heard the reason why. He survived the War but, like so many who went through it, he could not survive its consequences.

The tales that were circulated about me at this time now seem very amusing. One was that I had an English head-gardener who died and that I sent his corpse to England and that in the coffin were letters containing all the latest and most secret news of the German Army on the French front. Being a first-rate gardener he was of course Scottish and very much alive, and his name was Todd. Another foolish story was that I had been imprisoned and that my husband had shot me as a spy and then shot himself!

At the end of January I made, quite casually, a decision that turned out to be momentous and far-reaching. I made up my mind to go to Partenkirchen in the Bavarian mountains, take Lexel and Bolko and try to find a small villa which I could make my holiday headquarters during the War. Partenkirchen, which is about thirty-five miles from Munich, is a lovely spot surrounded by magnificent scenery and many lakes. It can be warm and sunny in the winter as at St. Moritz, and I thought I should be at peace with the children.

Throughout the War Bavaria was a place of peace for many a weary soul. The people embraced the War with reluctance, feeling that it was Prussia's fight and not theirs. Being a mountainous people and economically practically self-supporting, they attached little importance to sea power. They came into the German Confederation reluctantly in 1871, and always resented, and still do, the idea of being dragged about at the heels of Prussia.

A charming incident I know of will show what Munich was like during the War. The able and well-known Intendant of the Royal (now the State) Theatres was then as now Baron Franckenstein, brother of the present Austrian Minister in London. Baroness Franckenstein, a dear, kind friend of mine, had the good fortune to be born an Irishwoman. All during the War she remained in Munich doing her ordinary duties and living her ordinary life. Only once or twice during the four years was she subjected to any annoyance because of being technically "an alien enemy," and then only of a trivial kind. It was the custom of the late King Ludwig of Bavaria to take a daily walk through the principal streets of Munich accompanied by one of his daughters. He never once met Baroness Franckenstein without greeting her with marked attentions, frequently specially crossing the street to do so, and always made the same remark: "I hope you are well and that you have *good news from home*." A real King and a very great gentleman.

Then Princess Ludwig Ferdinand of Bavaria, the mother of my dear friend Princess Pilar, was just as gracious and kind. Born an Infanta of Spain, she was sister to the late King and is therefore an aunt of King Alfonso XIII. She sometimes got presents of food from the Spanish Royal Family, specially at Christmas, and she never failed to send Baroness Franckenstein a little plum pudding or a few mince-pies, accompanied by a sweet little note saying they were "just to remind you of home"

I know we British pride ourselves on our broad-mindedness, our tolerance and our chivalry to women. Nevertheless I am quite certain that the German wife of a high official living during the War in say Edinburgh would not have been treated as Baroness Franckenstein was in Munich; and I am quite certain that no member of the British Royal Family would have dared publicly to show courtesy to a German subject. Is it any wonder that I like and admire the Bavarians?

But even at Partenkirchen I was troubled by many things. I received very few letters and everything was opened, including letters from one of the Emperor's sons, written from Pless. My little secretary, Helene Wagner, decided to go to see the chief Postmaster. When she entered his office she saw two letters on his table addressed to me. She asked him to hand them over to her and he calmly announced: "You cannot have them, they have not been read yet." One was from the wife of my husband's General Director and the other from a doctor, or Lord Mayor, or someone, asking me to patronize and be present at a Charity Concert they were giving in Waldenburg, a factory town in Silesia, not far from Fürstenstein. I would have gone there, but the letter was handed to me only after the concert was over. The delay in delivering letters such as this prevented me from performing many little kind actions I would have been only too glad to do, and the people, very often strangers, sometimes neighbours and friends who asked me to do this, that and the other, never really believed that I had received their letters too late. They just thought I was "English" and did not want to help.

That I was not the only person in Germany torn in two by the War is proved by the following letter from the Grand Duke of Mecklenburg-Strelitz. By the way, it was not a shawl I sent him, but a muffler; men never seem to know the difference. Anything that goes round the neck they call a shawl!

NOYON, *January* 11, 1915.

DEAR PRINCESS,—

To-day again you made me a great pleasure by sending me a *Liebesgabe*,[1] some excellent cigarettes. You always find the most useful things and kind attentions. A thousand thanks again for all your kindness, I appreciate so much all you send me. I perfectly love the warm shawl, it is so nice and smooth and so becoming, I feel very proud wearing it! Smelling the good scent of it reminds me of everything else but war. Oh, this terrible war, no one knows how long it may last; the losses on both sides are quite terrific. All the fine English men-of-war that are lost, I only hope you had no friends on board. I have had no news from all my friends and I do not write by the way you kindly mentioned to me, as I do not like to write an open letter.

I am so grateful to you for having made enquiries about our imprisoned friends, such a pity you could not find out. I

---

[1] Charitable gift.

have now asked my Grandmother if I shall make official enquiries, but got no answer yet. Would you kindly send me my Grandmother's letter or a list of the names, I could not make out the spelling of all. In her last letter my Grandmother asks me to find out: Captain Aleck Vandeleur, 2nd Life Guards, and Captain Y. W. Lennox, 8th Black Watch, and writes how much sympathy she has with you. I hope you are quite well and comfortable at your new home. . . .
Yours very sincerely,

ADOLPHUS FREDERICK.

Early in February I got a letter from Prince Eitel Fritz saying that in the hundred days he had been at the front his Regiment, the 1st Prussian Guards, had lost one hundred officers and four thousand men. It was dreadful. He, the kindest of men, was terribly bitter about Germans having to fight " Indians " and " Senegalese." He had met Hans a day or two before at Mezières and the poor Prince got some comfort from recalling his last visit to Fürstenstein and my singing and playing after dinner. How the men in every army loved to envisage " home."

Many of the letters I received at this time were very sad, but the following gem gave us all a hearty laugh:

BLACK RIVER VALLEY CLUB, WATERTOWN, N.Y.

WATERTOWN, N.Y., *Feb.* 1.2.15.

HER MAJESTY THE PRINCESS OF PLESS,—

Reading about sad loss, and take notice at your Pikture of yourself and our German Heros. I would be very much pleased to send you some of our American Newspaper German and English Language to haf a good idea of the real War News from this awful and terrible War. The World would like to know whenever this terrible War gone to be ending hoping the End will come soon and let the World haf an everlasting Peace. I wish to hear thos German Heros haf a good time to read the real News from thos Newspapers and let Germany haf a fair Play, because the American people tont understand anything but Grape Jucie Politik.

WILLIAM GOETZ, Chef,
B.R. Valley Club, Watertown, N.Y., Amerika.

Colonel Gordon [1] of the Gordon Highlanders was taken prisoner early in the War and with Ivan Hay, Robin Grey and others was for a time in the Prisoners-of-War Camp near Magdeburg. I was fortunately able to do something to help and cheer them and would like here to quote a piece from one of Colonel Gordon's letters because it gives a glimpse of how British prisoners in Germany "carried on":

. . . I have asked my wife to write to you to further impress our mutual gratitude and to send you (hoping for your acceptance) photos of our only boy (aged two) with his Dad and also one of herself—I trust one day you will meet her. She is very pretty and one of the best. We two have always had a mutual admiration for you, exemplifying as you have always done, the ideal type of English beauty—Pardon me if I have said too much but my words are true. . . .

Ivan is bright and dull alternately but is always the smart good-looking English officer and gentleman. Delightful Robin Grey is always a host in himself—cheery and hopeful at all times. With a very small party I am being sent to Blankenburg Upstadt bei Berlin, and that will be my future address. I regret leaving behind my young brother-officers who did so well for me. Their names are Usher, Hunter-Blair, Houldsworth, Stewart of Appin, Pelham Burn, Robertson and Hamilton (Sir Ian's nephew). I daresay you have either met them or their friends. Splendid fellows they all are. Other senior officers often say to me, "What a nice lot." I am very proud of them. . . .

When they heard of the treatment I had received in Berlin many of my German friends wrote me dear letters (and took risks in doing so); others came to see me or expressed their sympathy in other ways. Even so, I longed to be for a bit with people who understood and loved England and the English, and before whom one could speak one's thoughts. I therefore wrote and asked the Grand Duke Adolphus if he thought his grandmother would welcome me at Neustrelitz. He was at home on leave and wrote as follows:

[1] Colonel W. E. Gordon, V.C., C.B.E., A.D.C. to the King (1913). Born 1866. Commanded No. 1 District Scottish Command, 1917–20.

NEUSTRELITZ, *February* 8, 1915.

MY DEAR PRINCESS,—

Your letter has reached me this morning. I am horrified they have dared to treat you like this. You have my fullest sympathy. Also my Grandmother, to whom I gave your kind message and told how they behaved to you, asked me to express to you how deeply she feels for you. I do not know why, but I had a kind of feeling something might happen to you and in my daily prayers I begged God Almighty to protect you from all disagreeable things. Alas! it has happened all the same! It is inconceivable; I cannot tell you how furious I am. I have seen what you did for our wounded and how they loved you at the hospital at Tempelhof. The authorities should be grateful to you! I have no words to describe what I feel, I am too furious. . . .

Please do not think I am a person who leaves his friends in a situation like this . . . my house will always be open to you and I will be glad to have the honour of receiving you. . . .

Patsy, at home in England, had never learned what it meant to be discreet and, as every one knows, was in consequence much criticized by narrow-minded neighbours and even by friends. Like most uncharitable people they never knew all the facts. There was I in Germany doing everything I could for British prisoners. From the Emperor downward I continuously bothered every one I knew. It was inevitable that at times one would be asked to make a return by trying to help some German prisoner in England (as Countess Brockdorff had begged me to help her poor nephew). Quite often I had to pass on these requests to Patsy and seldom hesitated to do so, because however one doubted her discretion, no one could doubt her courage or resource. How could anyone refuse to forward her this request from Ivan Hay: "Next time you write to your Mother please remember me to her and tell her there is a very nice young German named Theodor Bohrman, 7th Pioneers, in Netley which is quite near Newlands, and ask her to do what she can for him. He was wounded and taken prisoner by the British at La Bassée 25th January."

Patsy was indefatigable. She got a dreadful septic

thumb by neglecting it in order that she might go every day to the hospital and write letters for the wounded. Six weeks in a Liverpool nursing home was the result, but even that did not damp her ardent spirit. I used to love her letters. In one she wrote: " There are so many Joneses here amongst the convalescent soldiers on sick leave that they all get mixed up at the chemist's. So a tiny child called there and said: 'Look you, please sir, give me the medicine bottle the Doctor ordered for John Jones the Poacher'!" In another, speaking of the Censorship: " Oh, Dany, why can this letter get to you and I can't; God knows they might open me up, censor me and stamp me all over, if only they would let me come to you, my own little Dany." On another occasion, writing of Hansel having to be away from me at school, she said:

> It is too sad little darling H. can't be more with you; I can't see, even in the days of one's great-grandfather, what use Greek could have been. I know my brother's tutor was supposed to teach me Latin and Greek, also football; the two first I flatly refused to learn; the last I did learn till I got a kick on my behind from five brothers at the same time and was called a silly ass for getting in the way; so I gave that up too!

I must quote one or two serious bits which gave news of what was happening at home. Sometimes I got nothing for weeks and then a great bundle would come:

> *March* 13, 1915.
>
> MY PRECIOUS DARLING ONE,—
>
> I want you to know that the precious old Granny is ailing fast. But so happy, so peaceful; got her arms round my neck yesterday, and said I only want you, my darling, and *Peace*. She talks so much of her father. Well indeed, as Jessop[1] says, she has earned her long rest and happiness. Last night she said to me, " We must have our prayers to-night," so I knelt down; " Oh, I must kneel too"; but I made her sit still. I said the Lord's Prayer and " The Peace of God." But she said, " Oh, that's not enough." And she started

[1] Her maid.

saying such beautiful prayers quite on her own; and then she asked why her darling little grandchildren did not come down and see her. I said, "Which ones, darling." "My darling little Daisy and Shelagh and George." Little Dany one, don't be unhappy, or feel I am. Of course one dreads it, for there is no love like a Mother's. But I feel she is going to such perfect happiness. . . .

II

At the end of March, although forbidden actually to enter Berlin, I was "allowed" to visit Potsdam for the Confirmation of my eldest son if "escorted by my husband": in fact I was his prisoner. They tried to prevent my going at all, but I determined that nothing would keep me away from this important ceremony and I made myself so disagreeable that they at last gave way. At that moment it was supposed that Hansel, who was only just over fifteen, would join a Hussar Regiment at once. The boy of course wanted to go; had he not tried to join directly War broke out. I admired his spirit, but I did not want my son to go and kill Englishmen—or be killed by them. Fortunately the Emperor forbade him joining on the ground that he was too young and gave orders that he was to continue his studies.

During my few days at Potsdam I had the immense comfort of speaking English with the boy. It made me cry like a fool. I saw many old friends, including the Grand Duke Adolphus, who was present at the Confirmation ceremony.

Hans duly returned with me to Partenkirchen, where I found that Lexel had amused himself by cutting off his eyebrows and eyelashes. We had a comparatively happy Easter together, now that I was relieved from the dread of Hansel joining the Army at once. Another comfort was that one of the assistant butlers at Fürstenstein, *Unteroffizier* Seidel, was home indefinitely on sick leave, and was able to be with me and run my small house. He had often acted as my courier, spoke excellent English, knew all my friends, and was invaluable. Of course all men were in the Army and women servants almost unobtainable. I had Helene my Secretary, Elsa who was one of my lady's-maids, and with the help of local servants we managed quite well.

I tried to keep in touch with friends in other countries and find out how the War was really going. Towards the end of March Oscar Herren wrote from his place near Toledo: "This awful war makes me long to strike out the word Civilization from every dictionary, but I cannot believe it can last much longer. Here in Spain we are threatened with a famine and there are thousands out of work. . . ." And this from Marquess Pallavacini in Hungary: ". . . So it is really Hungary which bears the brunt of it and loses all her best sons, for in Austria only the German element is any good, the rest is pretty rotten. It is wonderful to see our people how they fight, and had we had better leaders in the beginning, we would be nearer to peace now. . . ."

So much was said in all countries about the treatment of prisoners-of-war, so many charges were made and denied that it is a duty to record any *facts* that came under one's personal notice. My own conviction is that, in the field, the fighting men of all nations were gallant and chivalrous. I think in the base Camps of every Army there were instances of petty persecution and cruelty, and this was liable to be the case especially in Prisoner-of-War Camps, where the Commandant was a civilian dressed up as a soldier, or where he had never seen active service. Every fighting man, whatever his nationality, had too much respect for other fighters to treat them with discourtesy, much less with cruelty. So much was said about the brutality of Prussian soldiers in Belgium and elsewhere that this extract from a letter of Colonel Gordon's comforted me immensely. The opinion of a senior officer and an experienced soldier such as he, was absolutely reliable. Writing from Garrison Lazarett No. 1, in Berlin, on March 23, where he was in hospital, he said:

. . . As from the very beginning I receive the most lavish kindness and consideration in the hospital. It is beyond all praise. My wife has told the King at my special request. I have been in poor health since April last. I had hoped to keep on my legs until the end of the war by taking care, but was recently defeated in my object when pain got the upper hand. The most kind commandant of Blankenburg, Captain Baron von Lochow, had me moved into Berlin, where everything possible has been done for me. . . .

Of course one way or another I heard a good deal of what my relations and friends were doing. Shelagh had her own hospital at Le Touquet, which had speedily won the reputation of being one of the best run in France. In March Ivan Hay wrote me from Magdeburg:

. . . I have very little news of home but am afraid my poor Mother worries too much about me and is very unhappy. Lady Helen Vincent is working in London at Guy's Hospital, Rachel Dudley is in France with the Australian Hospital and Edith Wolverton has a large convalescent home at Ditton.

Do let me know of any wounded officers who are in England as I always write to my father and he helps them if he can.

That was always the plea of the real fighting man. Let me help, even my enemies, if I can. I do not know if Lord Erroll was criticized by the Yellow Press at home for daring to be courteous and helpful to German prisoners, as Lady Oxford and Asquith, Patsy and many others were. But I am quite sure that even if he were it had no effect on him. Here is a letter I received from Lady Erroll. "Winnie" is the Duchess of Portland and "Elisalex" is Comtesse de Baillet Latour (sister of Alphy Clary), to whom the Portlands were so extraordinarily kind all through the War:

KILRONAN, BRIDGE OF ALLAN, N.B.,
September 1st.

DEAREST PRINCESS DAISY,—

How dear of you to write to me, and I am so thankful for news of Ivan, and to hear that he is well, and having a change, and it must be so healthy up there. He says so little when

MYSELF.

From a water-colour picture, painted at Mandelieu in 1914, by M. Edgerley.

he writes that I seem to know nothing of his daily life, but one can imagine what a blessing a change must be. I am going up to Langwell about the 27th of this month, and will give all your messages to Winnie and Elisalex. Yes, it is very lonely without poor Ivan, and one's heart is very heavy, and you too, poor dear, have many troubles and I do sympathize with you. I have come up here to be with my husband, as it is so lonely for him in the evenings, but I miss my garden dreadfully, though there is plenty of work to do here, and as you say, nothing like work to keep you from thinking. I had a line from Lady Desborough to-day, poor darling, it is heartbreaking for her, one can't bear to think of it. Lady Mar is close by here, which is nice. She is writing to Ivan. I am always routing up his friends to write, letters must be a godsend. I hope both your invalids are doing well and that you are not too anxious.

With much love, good-bye dear, and write again sometimes, it is such a comfort hearing. Yours ever,

MARY ERROLL.

Poor Lady Erroll, who could have foreseen then that when the War was over her eldest son, Lord Kilmarnock, Ivan's brother, would become British High Commissioner in the Occupied German Provinces and that, having meanwhile succeeded his father in the Peerage, he should die at his post ten years after the end of the War.[1]

Here are two entries from my diary:

April 5, 1915. Partenkirchen.

To-day, and since weeks, the attitude of Italy has been doubtful, and I feel myself perfectly convinced that unless Austria gives way to her and gives back to her what she once took,[2] namely Trento and Trieste, she will fight against Austria (which country she has always detested) and that will mean of course another enemy for Germany.

That Bismarck should have made a treaty with Italy knowing then the strength of England's Navy, I shall never understand, for since years I have looked on the map and smiled sadly thinking, "Oh, what blindness," for there is Italy with her

---

[1] The twentieth Earl of Erroll died suddenly at Coblenz, February 19, 1928.

[2] Historically this statement is not justifiable.

heel in the middle of the Mediterranean, a narrow land all coasts surrounded by sea. It is surely impossible to think for one minute that she would ever direct her Navy against that of England ; and can one blame her for thinking of herself first ? Is it not absolutely to be understood that she cannot risk everything by going against Great Britain ? For her own sake she must remain quiet and not stand firm to that old agreement she made with Austria and Germany.

Hans thinks there will be a peace in May ; little sweet Auntie Minnie, whose husband, Guy Wyndham, is in the War Office and of course continually with General Cowans and Lord Kitchener, even she writes to me and says : " Somebody told me there will be a peace on the 14th of May." Well, diary, I do not see this ; there may be a discussion which will last a month or two, questions asked, proposals made, but neither country will agree to them ; harder words will be used, more anger will be shown and then a more bitter war will begin. . . . Republics will spring up I believe, other changes will be made, and one or two Kings will disappear. . . .

Diary, the first week in July, 1914, I laughed and said to Baron Goldschmidt and others in London as I watched people after dinner : " Yes, but you are all dancing on a volcano ! "

He asked me the other day : " Did you *know* anything then ? "

How could I ; but I *felt* as I feel often and foresee. I have said it since months ; and I feel it now ; two or even three big men, whether Crowned or not, will have to fall, and it will not be on the field of battle ; one may get ill, one may be murdered—and one will not make any great difference—in fact the death of some of them will help peace. We'll see !

III

In all the excitements of the spring of 1915 I behaved very badly to my poor diary, quite forgetting it for weeks at a time. And yet it was really a great comfort ; I personified it in a way and talked to it as if it were a living friend, just as one talks to a dog, a horse, or even a cat when one is very much alone. It is a real relief, fulfilling some need deep-seated in the human heart. By April, the lovely Bavarian spring returning, I started to be good again. I had heard from Hans that the Empress might be going to Pless and, if so, I would have to be there to receive her. With this in prospect I just had to go to Munich to get some clothes. While there I wrote:

April 12, 1915. Munich.

Dear diary, I write in Munich. I came here to-day by motor with Duke Luitpold of Bavaria and his two cousins; one is the Princess Ludwig Ferdinand of Bavaria, and the other her daughter Princess Pilar. I had to get up at seven and be ready at eight and am now frightfully sleepy.

We went again (I have been often) to Duke Luitpold's new house in the mountains, which is not yet half-finished, but will be perfectly divine when it is; built in a sort of Tyrolean, yet Italian way, it has a touch of Byzantine in it. In the roof is a great, open terrace with pillars from which is the most lovely view. We had hoped to get up all the way in the motor-car, but they stopped in one little heap of snow as the wheels could not catch hold of anything and so we had to finish going up on foot which was very tiring.

It had been a long day through snow and puddles. . . . We had to go to a rotten little restaurant. I had taken my lunch with me in a little basket, just sandwiches as usual and some jam-sandwiches, such as I used to take to the Lazarett in Berlin. I ate a few in the Restaurant and they ate the rest and we shared the few biscuits which I had. . . .

I have just had a bath and am having some dinner. I took the two Princesses back to the Nymphenburg Palace in my motor-car, and then came here to the Hotel Continental and had some coffee and cake. I passed Clement and Rosario Schönborn on the way with their daughter[1]; and then, as I sat here quietly by myself drinking my coffee, who should be announced but Prince Ludwig Ferdinand. I was much too tired to welcome anyone, but thought it right to see him. I can't help laughing when I think that his daughter, Princess Pilar, said to me: "My father always judges women by the way they put on their hats." I suddenly remembered it and told him so. I had on a cap tied round with a white tie, a present from my maid Elsa which she found in Partenkirchen, and which she was awfully proud of; it is dark pink and white wool and really very nice. . . .

What a darling Lexel is; and please God he will stay as

[1] Marie Catherine (Cissy), now Princess Hansel of Pless.

near to me in thought and deed as he is now. He loves to give me flowers and make me garlands; he is such a pet, although he always has dirty hands, forgets his gloves and his hat and will wear the coat which does not match his trousers; but does anything matter in the world so long as one's heart is in the true place?

While I was in Munich I got a telegram from Hans saying he and Hansel would be at Fürstenstein for one or two nights, so I decided to rush off and see them. There was no time to wait for anything. As by now I was almost literally without a stitch of clothing, I borrowed some night-dresses from Rosario Schönborn and a frock to go to church in on Sunday, and away I went. During my stay I visited the hospitals at Kunzendorf (a village near by) and went twice to the one at Salzbrunn. I took with me Frau von Pohl. I must say everything seemed well done. I gave the wounded champagne in which to drink the Emperor's health and offered to provide wine twice weekly for those whom it suited.

While there I had a letter from Rosamund de Ramsey imploring me to do my best to help her dear old blind husband to get permission to go back to England. I was astonished that nothing had been done, and I decided to waste no further time with underlings but to write at once direct to the Emperor. Hans always tried to dissuade me from doing this, but what was the good of wasting time with underlings swathed from head to foot in red tape and with brains like a linseed poultice. This is what I said, taking the opportunity of discussing several other matters that were then troubling me:

YOUR MAJESTY, SIRE,—

I ask no forgiveness for this letter, as I too have things to forgive. Your Majesty's Empire is standing its ground, but all hearts are full of sadness and the world in tears. But God helps, I think, what is right for its own sake, and at such a time of victory Your Majesty can, at night, perhaps, before putting your head on the pillow, pause for one second and feel for individuals who are in misery, such as a real friend of mine, Lord de Ramsey, stone blind since fifteen years, who is now at Bad Liebenstein with Professor Graf Wieser. He has all his relations and four of his sons at the front; another of his sons whom I know so well, is at present at Schloss Celle—also a prisoner.

Lord de Ramsey has been in Germany since last June to try to be cured of his blindness, so has not been near his family for nearly a year; he begs to go home to his wife. I thought he was exchanged, indeed, that he had gone long ago. Oh, Sire, think of this old, real English gentleman of sixty-five, of the best family, and totally blind: and think of those, too, in solitary cells.

Sire, Germany has her enemies, as it seems, gradually falling. Then, in pity's sake, let there be no revenge. We are too proud to tease people with pain. Those captured from the *Untersee* boats in England are in prison, a vile thing —and wrong, I know: but for God's sake don't let Germany do worse by putting Englishmen into solitary confinement.

. . . but I shall be alone on a hill—or near a big tree and hold on to nature and truth. I will never again be in a crowd in Berlin. I shall never belong there any more; but for the sake of the prayers you once said (perhaps in English) to an English mother—then in pity let this dear old man go back to England, and let these others remain in prison, if it has to be, but not in solitary confinement!

God take care of Your Majesty and all that are yours; and do this for me. Your obedient subject and——!

DAISY OF PLESS.

P.S.—I have been dismissed without trial or judge to defend me--so I am a *servant* no longer!

When I told Hans at Fürstenstein what I had done he said that it was quite useless, that everything now went by rule in Germany, and not even the Emperor himself could personally do anything!

The following extract from my diary shows the spirit in which I wrote to the Emperor. I wanted to be firm and respectful, but not subservient and I wanted my request granted on grounds of justice and mercy, and not merely as a personal favour:

May 5, 1915. Partenkirchen.

The Court can give me no orders now. I remain a German subject, as they deserve all one's prayers and respect, and my children and husband are German. But I am no longer an " obedient servant " which is the way one signs oneself, and which I have signed so often to the Emperor. No—I am no longer that, I am nobody's servant; neither shall I play the rôle of the dressed-up housekeeper, which I have been for so many years, particularly since dear Vater died. Somehow I think, as I felt when Baby was ill, that Vater's spirit must be somewhere near, and that he knows that I wanted always to do what was best, and in the end he will help me. . . .

Winston Churchill's policy (I think it was his) of putting captured U-boat officers in jail in solitary confinement instead of treating them as ordinary prisoners-of-war, was, as I admitted to the Emperor, quite barbarous. It had naturally the most unfortunate results for British prisoners-of-war in Germany. On April 20, Ivan Hay wrote from Burg:

. . . Do write as often as you can as I am all by myself in a cell in the jail: as the British Government has put the German submarine people in jail, so the Prussian Government has put a corresponding number of us in prison. If you have got one or two English books you don't want I wish you would lend them to me. If you send anything to the *Gefangenen-Lager* they will send it on down here. Please remember me to Seidel and thank him for his message.

His nice reference was much appreciated by Seidel, who was really indefatigable in helping me in every way and in nothing was he more willing or untiring than in affairs that concerned British prisoners-of-war. I always found that the people who loudly expressed hysterical hatred were either writers in irresponsible newspapers, old maids who were safe, old men who knew the *only way* to win the War, or men in soft jobs behind the lines.

I used to get charming letters from prisoners-of-war, many of them people I knew only by name or perhaps had met once. As soon as I heard of English prisoners by name I always tried to write them a cheery letter and ask if they wanted anything; very often it had to be a dictated one, or else I would never have got them done at all. Here is a bit of a letter from one of Lord Albemarle's sons:

. . . I shall love getting the books and the parcel from the Army and Navy Stores, which you are so kindly sending, and for which I thank you many, many times. I have sent your message to my Mother and Father, who write me many letters. I am sure you do not remember me, as it is years since I came to see you in London, with them; so it was all the more kind of you to have written to me! If ever, in the future, you see someone with fair hair, a *very* large nose (rather like beak), and about six foot three high, you'll know it's me! In fact, I hope this apparition *will* appear to you, as I should like to thank you myself for all you have done for me. I am so sorry you have not been well, after your nursing in Berlin, but I hope you will be quite all right again soon. Of course we all agree with what you say about the treatment of the Submarine crews, and I think Winston Churchill is almost in a minority of one in England! After all, they only did their duty, so they ought not to be treated differently to others. Now I must send this. Thank you, again *so very* much. Yours sincerely,

RUPERT KEPPEL.[1]

P.S.—My name *is* Derek, but it is only my third name! I haven't heard of my uncle D.[2] for ages. I suppose he is still with the King.

Quite soon after writing to the Emperor I got a semi-official letter from Herr von Treutler from the Great Headquarters at Pless telling me that Lord de Ramsey was at last to be exchanged. So that was something done—but how little. A condition, characteristically German, was attached to Lord de Ramsey's release; it was that six interned Germans should be sent by England in exchange. My recollection is that this absurd stipulation was not accepted,

[1] The Honourable Rupert Oswald Derek Keppel, Coldstream Guards, son of the eighth Earl of Albemarle.

[2] The Honourable Sir Derek Keppel (brother of the eighth Earl), Master of the Household to His Britannic Majesty King George V.

in spite of the flattering inference that one Englishman was equal to six Germans. Herr von Treutler, who was the Prussian Minister in Bavaria, was the Foreign Office representative on the personal Staff of the Emperor with whom he was, at this time, a great favourite. It was therefore very satisfactory to hear from this high Foreign Office official so promptly: it again bears out what I have always said about the Emperor's prompt helpfulness whenever I appealed to him.

Towards the end of May or the beginning of June I heard that Julian,[1] wonderful Julian Grenfell, had perished, and that his brother Gerald was doubly bereft because these twain were as one soul. Julian left to his friends and to the British Army an imperishable example and the deathless message:

> Sing well, for you may not sing another;
> Brother, sing.

To me he stood as the ideal of a type to which belonged three splendid young soldier friends who perished in the early days of the War: George Wyndham's handsome son Percy, Robin Duff, and Lord Charles Fitzmaurice.

A short two months before his death Julian wrote immortal lines which will be a monument to himself and his comrades long after every war memorial now in existence has crumbled to dust:

> The fighting man shall from the sun
>   Take warmth, and life from the glowing earth;
> Speed with the light-foot winds to run,
>   And with the trees to newer birth;
> And find, when fighting shall be done,
>   Great rest, and fullness after dearth.
>
> The thundering line of battle stands,
>   And in the air death moans and sings;
> But Day shall clasp him with strong hands,
>   And Night shall fold him in soft wings.

[1] Captain the Honourable Julian Grenfell, Royal Dragoons, was killed on May 26, 1915; his brother Gerald perished on July 31 in the same year.

Julian's splendid death, far from fanning in my heart any hate for the combatants of other nations, gave me fresh courage and hope. His death, like his life, baptized his friends and the world anew with beauty, and, surely, could they have met, he would have shared the feelings expressed in the following letter by Alphy Clary, a brave young fighter belonging to an alien country:

> . . . It's horrible to think of war in Italy.[1] Every one who has seen a real modern battle, must shudder when he thinks that all that can happen in Milan or Ferrara, even in Venice perhaps. What *idiots* those people are there to let themselves be driven into such misery by quite few men. Sonnino,[2] Tittoni,[3] Salandra,[4] D'Annunzio and some little group of generals have decided on Italy's fate. People in England will, of course, be very glad that they have succeeded in buying Italy, but King George must feel a bit disgusted when he'll be obliged to kiss Vittorio Emmanuele!

I was sick of being idle and wondered if Prince Ludwig Ferdinand of Bavaria would care to have me in one of his hospitals in Munich. A cousin of the late King of Bavaria, he is a Doctor of Medicine by profession and, after he retired from the Cavalry, became Inspector of the Medical Services of the Bavarian Army. I wrote to his daughter Princess Pilar about it, and she replied:

> NYMPHENBURG PALACE, 25. IV. 1915.
>
> DEAR PRINCESS,—
>
> Your kind, nice letter gave us all such pleasure, that we all thank you for it. About the Lazarett question I cannot answer you yet, as the decision does not rest solely with my father. He asks me to say that he will be *very happy* to have you there. Also that he will do everything possible to get you in. The great difficulty consists in there being so many *Helferinnen vorgemerkt*. My father hopes he will be able to

[1] Italy declared war on Austria-Hungary on May 23, 1915.
[2] Then Italian Minister for Foreign Affairs.
[3] Italian Ambassador to France.
[4] As Italian Prime Minister, signed the declaration of war against Austria-Hungary.

make an exception and take you in before all those ladies are placed. In any case he has asked it: now we have to wait till it has gone its way round! As soon as I know the result I will write again and send you back your certificates.

I can understand that the wounded liked your smile and the nice ways you have!

Your Red Cross card is so nice! I would like to keep it, but suppose it is the only one you have—and don't dare.

I do hope all will be in order soon and that you will come. With best remembrances—also from my father and mother—very sincerely,

PILAR.

But the *Helferinnen vorgemerkt*, that is, ladies desiring and already promised employment, were numerous. I would have had to wait for centuries, nor could I expose Prince Ludwig Ferdinand to the odium of giving me, a Prussian, employment before Bavarian ladies. There was never any love lost between Bavaria and Prussia.

I know that, like Hans, lots of people thought I ought to have "gone to ground" at Partenkirchen throughout the War. But could I? To be there alone was to do nothing but think. I wanted work . . . work . . . work.

Nor was I going to stand being treated like a confessed criminal, what is, I think, called in England on "ticket of leave." Receiving a special permit to go to my son's Confirmation, or to go to my own home Fürstenstein, or wait humbly in the hope of being summoned to my own castle in Pless! Most of all did I resent my letters being systematically censored. When they censored my telegrams to Hans it was more than I could stand, and I telegraphed direct to the Chief of the General Staff and wrote to Count Schönborn begging him to make investigations on the spot. Here is a translation of his reply:

HOTEL ESPLANADE, BELLEVUESTRASSE, BERLIN, 19.4.15.

MY DEAR PRINCESS,—

I must in haste inform you that I have been to the General Staff where I enquired about the telegrams from you to Hans

Heinrich. I have learnt that through a mistake of a subordinate in the Telegraph Office, probably in Hamburg, these were laid before the Censor. The Chief of the Department concerned who has charge of all the messages, regrets this mistake of the official *very much*. He said to me that the Censor who was once always against you has since some weeks, retracted, and as only one or two of the officials have been informed of this restriction, the mistake has been made; he will take care that this does not occur again. I am glad to be able to give you this not unagreeable information and will report the same to Hans Heinrich. . . .

Had I succeeded in finding war work in Munich I probably would have remained in Bavaria throughout the War. However, that was not to be. My old friend of the Tempelhof Hospital, Professor Baron von Kuester, was by this time in charge of a military hospital train and I wrote asking him to give me nursing work under him, but only on the condition that he had found me efficient and useful and in every way a satisfactory subordinate. He replied as follows, and his letter, needless to say, gave me intense satisfaction. Here is the translation:

HALLE (SAALE), *June* 21, 1915.

YOUR SERENE HIGHNESS,—

I beg to thank Your Highness for your kind letter of May 31st, 1915. I am so happy to think that Your Highness is taking such a kind interest in me, and allowing me also to share in the sunny benevolence which is dwelling so fully in Your Highness's heart. As I was favoured to observe with what original, convinced and sacrificing love Your Highness without regard of person devoted yourself to our wounded, I will scarcely forget this beautiful picture for the rest of my life. This deep true conception of the Samaritan duty which equally values high and low, friend and foe, and only knows the one aim to help and make happy, one unfortunately rarely finds. I beg your pardon that I speak so openly, but I did not think at the moment of the Princess of Pless, but of the Sister Daisy who has been working with the old Professor von Kuester at the Tempelhof.

I heartily thank Your Highness for the kind invitation extended to me to come one day to Salzbrunn with my assistant Dr. Bode. We shall be very pleased to do so for a few days and will first inquire telegraphically whether you can conveniently receive us. When we meet we can discuss the details about Your Highness joining the Hospital Train. I also warmly thank you for your kind congratulations upon my receiving the Iron Cross. . . .

With many hand-kisses in true devotion, I remain, Your Serene Highness's obedient servant,

PROF. DR. FREIHERR VON KUESTER.

However unpopular I was locally, certain duties and responsibilities in Fürstenstein and the neighbourhood could not be neglected. I had heard, for example, that the Salzbrunn Hospital was not running quite smoothly and decided to go and see for myself. It was my husband's view at first that the War would only last a very short time and that the State should do everything for the wounded. Unfortunately, his initial orders about expenditure were not cancelled for some time and this caused a lot of trouble.

My diary will now take up the story for a bit:

June 22, 1915. Fürstenstein.

Back again in Fürstenstein; quite sorry to say good-bye to that little villa in Partenkirchen, where we had at least been very cosy; Duke Luitpold and all the Bavarian Royalties have been most kind to me. . . . Before I left Partenkirchen I bathed with little Lexel; it was the greatest fun in the world. Baby Bolko came with us too one day, but did not bathe.

Now I am back here since some days and have done all the usual things. Yesterday I gave coffee and supper to over a hundred soldiers, and the same thing happens to-day and all other days, and then I go every day to Salzbrunn and see what they are doing there. I had a few very serious words with the Head Sister, as nothing was being done in a methodical way. Sister Hanna from the Lazarett Tempelhof has arrived and will overtake a lot of the work for me, and other Sisters from there will be here in August . . . so before I go to Bansin the last days of this month or the first days of July, everything will go at last as I wish it to do. It is dreadful how one has always to wait for the permission of one's own General Director before one can do what one thinks is right.

Of course if Hans had given me permission at the beginning of this terrible war, everything would have been in order long ago, but the only thing he told me was that I should not spend a penny—and without money in this life it seems one can do nothing. This whole war was caused by money and every country has been paid to fight. But I am afraid England will find herself like a heavy money-box with a big hole in it, as she is now asked to pay all her Allies and Italy (whom she has bribed to fight against Germany—and break her old alliance), and England has now very little money to pay her own expenditures.[1]

I have just had a nice letter from Lord Albemarle. I copy it here:

LONDON, *June* 14, 1915.

DEAR PRINCESS DAISY,—

When we heard of it, we were very much touched by your kind solicitude for my boy R. K. in his unpleasant situation, and Gerty joins me in sending you her love and very many thanks. I have been working hard to get the U-boat prisoners in this country treated as ordinary prisoners of war, and I am glad to say that the new Coalition have thought fit to rescind Churchill's policy of reprisals upon officers who, after all, have only done their duty. They have now been sent to Donington Hall and other Detention Camps, where they have quite a good time. I think all countries will rejoice when this war comes to an end. . . . No one here has any interest in anything but the welfare of their relations who are fighting. No one goes to Cowes and thank goodness there is no Ascot. With again very many thanks to you and our united love, I am, Yours very sincerely, A.

June 26, 1915. Fürstenstein.

Dear diary, I have been all day at the Hospitals, I can scarcely stand any more. I wonder what on earth it is, and if I shall really ever be strong.

Just before leaving the house this morning I got a telegram from Hans telling me that a motor-car would arrive here to-day and would take me to Pless[2] for a few hours to-morrow, and bring me back here in the evening.

---

[1] This was the view then current in Germany.—D. OF P.

[2] The Emperor's Headquarters in the East were established at the Castle of Pless in the autumn of 1914.

To get from here to Pless and back would mean fourteen hours in the motor-car. No! diary, I have no intention of doing such a thing. I have always had the greatest admiration and respect for the Emperor and I have the greatest respect for all this nation—but I have far too much pride and self-respect to accept as a great honour the permission to go to Pless for a few hours and see the Emperor at the price of this awful motor journey. I shall simply answer to-morrow by telephone that I am not well enough to undertake such a long day, which is perfectly true, for I cannot stand such a terrible lot.

And I am glad to think that on the 30th I shall be at Bansin with Rosario Schönborn and her daughters; just with the ring round me of love and affection; and the little Grand Duke not far off with his motor-car, and he will take me probably wherever I want to go; and if people talk what the devil does it matter; they have talked enough already from morning to night. If I were to blow my nose at the present moment I believe half Germany would know it.

Even dear Clement Schönborn writes to me to-day and says that "he won't say anything more because I know the reason"! This means, of course, that he thinks even a letter addressed to me with the Reichstag stamp on it would be opened. . . .

I have not the slightest intention of going to Pless for a few hours—unless the letter which I expect to receive from Hans to-night when the motor arrives is a very nice and submissive one. I have already written the Emperor that I shall never again enter what we call "the social world of public life" in Germany, unless they apologize right through to the end. No telegrams will gain my forgiveness, and certainly not two hours in Pless, where I have my own rooms and where without seeing anybody in particular, I could perfectly well stay the night.

However, on thinking quietly and carefully over the matter, I decided that it would be best to go to Pless—but on conditions which in my own mind I had clearly fixed. There was much to be gained from a visit to the sacred Great Headquarters and, when it was over, I could easily spread the news by passing it on to others as *a great secret*—and I would make a point of doing so.

Hans sent a very nice letter with the motor-car, so

TEMPELHOF HOSPITAL, BERLIN.
Autumn, 1914.

I duly went to Pless, and from there direct to Bansin where I wrote in my diary a full account of what took place and cannot, I think, do better than quote it in full. On July 1st the British Army lost sixty thousand men—the worst day in its history. Fortunately for me I did not know it at the time or I might not have been so agreeable to them all:

July 8, 1915. Ostseebad Bansin.

. . . I see I arrived at Fürstenstein on the 22nd of June and I got the telegram from Hans on the 26th from Pless, telling me a motor-car would come for me on the 27th to take me there. One of the Emperor's cars came, so I got up at half-past seven in the morning and got to Pless about two in the afternoon.

The telegram said that I was expected there for *einige Stunden*, which means a few hours. So I wired to Hans to know where I was expected to sleep, purposing in my own mind to sleep nowhere but in my own house. When I got there Hans met me and asked me to have some lunch, but I had some tea instead. He told me I had to stay at Solza,[1] and that they expected me there with pleasure. I replied that I had no intention of going there, that I would even prefer to go back that night by motor to Fürstenstein; I did not want to go to Solza and begin recounting again the story of what had happened to me in Berlin, and all the miserable time since. They would have asked me question after question —and all about England and the War, and I was far too tired after a long motor drive to set off on two hours' further journeying to Solza, there to make charming conversation and break out in charming smiles.

As I washed my hands in my own dressing-room I was told that the Emperor was coming to see me at half-past four. Addressing my own reflection in the glass as I passed through my bedroom, I made this promise: "Daisy, you shall sleep in your own bed to-night, and nowhere else." And so of course I did.

The Emperor came at four-thirty and stayed till seven-fifteen. We talked of many things, but I am sorry to say, Hans was present all the time. The Emperor was distressed that the English Church and the English religion did not help

[1] The residence of my cousin Olivia Larisch, some thirty miles away.—D. of P.

towards ending this awful war. He wanted to know why all the Bishops were against him, and then I asked him if he had read the sermon of Dr. Lyttelton[1] at St. Margaret's, Westminster, which I had sent Treutler to read to him. He *had* read it; I then spoke to him of Patsy's letters, and said that he must not judge the whole English nation by the attitude of the English Press, as that was not the only feeling in England, and that mother could not be the only person in the country to feel all that she had written.

Oh! my dear diary, if I had been able to spend a few hours alone with him, I know I could have made him happier, as he is a very sad man, feeling terribly hurt by the one foreign country he loved—England. He never forgets it; he tried all these years to keep peace, and although I am English and they might hate me at home for saying this, I shall always proclaim it to every man and woman I know.

I next said to him that the whole thing had been done in such a terrible hurry; that the Germans had prematurely crossed the Belgian frontier. He said this was not true; that before the outbreak of war he had wired direct to Jules Cambon, the French Ambassador in Berlin, to tell him that if the French remained neutral, the Germans would do the same and not touch French territory. . . .[2]

He then spoke of the caricatures of himself in the English Press. I told him not to mind this as the German Press was the same about the King of England and the Czar of Russia, only he did not see those vulgar papers.

Upon the subject of the neutrality of Belgium I shall make Hans write to me more fully, if he can have the patience and the time, as it is difficult to remember all the Emperor told me.

When the Emperor left the room Hans remarked: "Now he has said good-bye to you." I murmured "Of course," knowing quite well that he had *not* said good-bye to me.

Hans then left me, and ten minutes later I got a message asking if I would come down to His Majesty. As I was just tidying myself and did not wish to show any special eagerness, I thought it a good excuse to say I was in my bath[3]; the

---

[1] Dr. Lyttelton, Headmaster of Eton, preached a highly controversial sermon at St. Margaret's, Westminster, March 28, 1915.

[2] The Emperor was yachting in the Baltic from July 5 to July 26, on which date he returned to Berlin.

[3] It was untrue. But, in a good cause, an *effective* lie is often worth while!—D. of P.

answer was that the Emperor would expect me at a quarter to eight.

So I got into my blue kimono, which was all I had with me, and I went down the little private staircase and into the Emperor's small sitting-room, but he was not there. I sat on the sofa quite calmly and did not of course look at or touch anything. Suddenly the door opened and in he walked. He looked rather shy to see me, and I felt rather shy to see him so suddenly; he then said he had got a little brooch for my birthday and he took it out of his pocket and gave it to me.

It is impossible to tell you, diary, or make you understand how extraordinarily secret everything in Germany is, especially in the Hauptquartier. I should not have dared to stay there with him longer, and I felt this, so I just looked at him nicely and took his hand and left the room and went upstairs again, never thinking I should see anyone else that evening.

I dined at eight, just some fish and soup in my room and some red wine. My room looked lovely, as it is all pink and blue with exquisite lacquer furniture and very pretty subdued light. After I had eaten my fish and pudding and drunk some wine, I sat on the low Japanese sofa and to my astonishment Hannussek[1] appeared and announced visitors; this he kept doing at intervals of about ten minutes whilst he ushered in groups of gentlemen of the Hauptquartier. So by degrees they were all there, arriving about five or six at a time, and there I lay on the sofa. Hans came in and saw me with my feet crossed, just like a Japanese, and said: "You have no shoes on!" "No, I did not bring any with me—only mules"; and I laughed with them all and said: "It seems that for once a lady in the Hauptquartier is quite popular," and they all agreed.

I must not forget to say that just before dinner Herr von Treutler came to me for a moment and said that if I got into any further difficulties in Berlin I was to go at once to the Imperial Chancellor, Herr von Bethmann-Hollweg.[2] The poor Chancellor has lost his son and his wife in one year, so I shall not bother him very much; but all the same when I get to Berlin later I will certainly see him, as I feel he might like to talk to me.

---

[1] A Groom of the Chambers, formerly my father-in-law's personal servant.—D. of P.

[2] I afterwards learnt that the Emperor had himself arranged this and given the necessary orders.—D. of P.

The last man to leave my sitting-room that night was Herr von Chelius, who lost his eldest son, and whose second son of eighteen is at the front. Poor dear, I felt so sorry for him, and his wife had written to tell him that I had written her such a nice letter. He told Hans when he went downstairs that I sat on the sofa looking like an Alma Tadema picture; and oh! diary, I know a woman in pale blue with the bright face I had that night, lying on a very low, golden and dark wood sofa, with big Japanese cushions and embroidery behind her in a room with lovely pink Japanese panels, and surrounded by a lot of men in *Feldgrau* uniforms, must have looked nice, though aloof and lonely: if I had been Hans I should have felt somehow very proud of my wife.

Next morning my husband expressed wonder as to how on earth I had managed to come to Pless, and I asked him:

"Did not the Emperor tell you to invite me to come?"

"Yes; but why?"

"The Emperor once gave me an undertaking to fulfil a promise which he had made to the Empress Frederick: it was, always to be nice to me and take care of me if people were not kind. I simply wrote reminding him and asked him to keep this promise, saying that I *wished* to come to Pless. You all in the Hauptquartier may be afraid of the man the Emperor is, but I know the human part of his character, and besides—I am afraid of no one!"

Accompanied by the Emperor's Doctor I started at ten o'clock to visit the hospital in Pless; I had to be back before eleven-thirty, as I had received orders to see the Emperor at that time. I drove there myself with a nice coachman I am specially fond of, and two roan horses; he always harnesses teams very light in the mouth for me to drive. As we went along I was busy asking him if he would have five nice horses for me to drive later on, and he said, yes, he would. It seems that we passed the Emperor quite close on the bridge and he saluted me, but as I did not see him I did not return the salute!

Herr von Bethmann-Hollweg had arrived from Vienna that morning, having been in Austria for an important interview with the Bulgarian and Rumanian Ministers. As I returned I saw Bethmann sitting outside with the Emperor, and was surprised that His Majesty expected me at eleven-thirty, as it meant that he would have to dismiss his Chancellor by that time. However, he did so, and we talked for half an hour under the dear tree in the corner, and as we parted he told me that the Imperial Chancellor wanted to see me.

I was much surprised, but did not show it, and at twelve o'clock Herr von Bethmann-Hollweg came into my sitting-room and was so nice and sat next to me; but alas, Hans was there and was in a hurry to get to Fürstenstein—that terrible building—as, the day being my birthday, he was allowed to spend it with me—and this was supposed to bring me a great joy!

Well, my luncheon came in at a quarter past twelve, and there dear Herr von Bethmann-Hollweg still sat, and Hans to my mind was almost rude—he kept on telling me to "hurry up and eat." I answered that I never hurry and wasn't hungry.

Bethmann-Hollweg spoke of the War with the Russians not being yet ended, and we agreed. There are too many millions there to suppress absolutely and because Germany has now arrived at Przemysl and Lemberg[1] those millions are not finished. He also spoke of the English. . . . It was impossible to talk seriously, as Hans was fussing, and food coming in which I did not wish to eat. Bethmann-Hollweg at last said: "But I am disturbing you, so I will go." And I wanted to hear more and have a *real* talk with him. He always was against the increase in the German Navy and he knew I was in sympathy with him in that. I was very sorry to miss that chance, as I feel he would have liked to talk privately with me.

I must tell you, that when I saw the Emperor in the morning, he looked at me and said:

"I suppose you are twenty-nine to-day; at least you look it!"

"Ah! Your Majesty, I will not tell how many years there are to add."

---

[1] The city of Przemysl in Galicia was retaken by the Austro-German forces on June 3, and Lemberg on June 22, 1915.

CHAPTER TEN

July-December, 1915

DEAR old Lord Chaplin had a great understanding heart. I thought—of course quite wrongly—he might not be very busy and wrote begging him to send me a long account of everything that was happening in England.

My letter, from my standpoint, reached him at a lucky moment, because he was full of affairs, and generously passed on all his news to me. I was particularly glad to hear about the Women's Legion which had just been born. Lord Chaplin was on the Committee which publicly initiated the idea in April, 1915, and his daughter Edie Londonderry was the Legion's inspiration and quite wonderful Chief from the beginning to the end. My dear old friend's falling in love with the pretty Commandant of the Guard of Honour at sight was so like him, filled as he was with delightful early-Victorian gallantry. But I feel sure he was mistaken in saying the Guard was armed—except perhaps with killing smiles. Here is Lord Chaplin's letter. Alas! I never saw him again, as he died in 1923:

BRIXWORTH, NORTHAMPTONSHIRE, *July* 11, 1915.

YOU DEAR OLD FRIEND,—

Your letter, which I received some little time ago, went to my heart. How can you? How can any of us? be otherwise than sad at a time like this. Our hopes have been cruel, as everybody's must be. Such a number of the Best, the Brightest and the Bravest: but many, thank God, recovering from wounds—and all with one idea, to get out again as soon as it is possible.

Alastair Gower [1] was shot through the knee of one leg and the thigh of the other, the bullet just missing the main artery. He had a narrow shave. He is now at Dunrobin, which narrowly escaped being completely *burnt* while they were all there: but it turns out to be not so bad as one expected, the injury being confined to the two top floors chiefly. I will give all your messages—and I read your letter to Horace and Lady Farquhar the other day when I was there. They are too kind to me, having placed a room on the ground floor at my disposal at White Lodge, whenever I like: and I go there constantly and get a little fresh air—away from the House of Commons. This Sunday they are at the Pembrokes at Wilton, so I have come down here, to be quiet for two days, where you two years ago, you dear kind thing, came over to see me, when I had been so desperately ill. And be sure of this: we all of us think of you often in your loneliness and trouble—and no one more than the man who writes this from his heart to-day. . . . I have had a hardish time myself, having been jumped into the position of Leader of the Opposition since the Coalition Government [2] was formed. It was necessary, of course, to have someone, and when I was asked by the Liberal Privy Councillors who came to sit on the Front Opposition Bench, and by many of our own friends, as the oldest Privy Councillor on the Conservative side of the House, I agreed at once; and have, I think, been able more than once to steady things at awkward moments; and to be of help to the Coalition Government in which there was at first, and still is, very considerable feeling on both sides—but chiefly perhaps, but not only, amongst the men who have had to give up their places and some of those who were disappointed in not getting them—and which I think is gradually disappearing. . . . As it is, there was a covert attack on Kitchener the other day, which I was instrumental in stifling altogether, and his reception in the City—and *en route*—on Thursday showed how right I was. He is the idol of the Country as I write to-day. On that there is no doubt and well he may be, for *he was able to say at the Guildhall* that the whole of the great armies he has raised in little over the ten months, are all of them now

---

[1] Lord Alastair St. Clair Sutherland Leveson-Gower, son of the fourth Duke of Sutherland and Millicent Duchess of Sutherland.

[2] The first Coalition Government under the Premiership of Mr. Asquith took office on May 26, 1915.

equipped, armed and provided for in every way. And though they don't say anything about it—I understand he has at least . . . divisions at Home fit and ready to go anywhere at any moment, besides the enormous numbers that we have altogether elsewhere. And yet on this man who has carried out this unexampled feat—and with more and more recruits coming in by thousands every day—some of the scum in the House of Commons moved, the end of the week before last, what was practically a vote of censure on him. But I don't believe, although we have got a hundred and fifty of our best men in the House of Commons at the Front themselves, or serving somewhere away from the House, that the lot who do this can muster more than thirty or thirty-five at most; and even they are getting frightened about losing their seats already.

My Edie is working hard at hospitals and all sorts of things about Women. She started a Women's Emergency Corps three months ago—making me go to a meeting at the Mansion House with the Lord Mayor in the Chair and make a speech to start it, the Chairman being profuse in his compliments to me afterwards. It was a difficult speech to make, for there is a prejudice against anything like a regiment of amazons. But I managed it somehow. They are now all drilled—in uniform—and able to do at any moment any number of things now done by men and so liberate men to go to the Front.

I went to a meeting three Sundays ago to inaugurate the opening of the First Hut provided for the Munition workers at some works within a motor journey from London—by the Young Men's Christian Association, which have done so much in the same way for all the soldiers' encampments all over the country. For the first time in my life I had to make a big speech on Sunday, preceded by a most impressive Religious Ceremony. The place, an immense thing a hundred and fifty or two hundred feet long, was crammed, and at the entrance was a Guard of Honour to receive us of Edie's Corps, all in khaki, armed, and as smart as they could be. The General commanding the District asked me whether he or I should inspect them, but I left it to him. But the officer in command looked so delightful in her Uniform and with a charming little touch of Side in her gait, that I fell in love with her at once. It was a most striking scene. This great place crammed with men and women in khaki—and hundreds of the workers from the Factories—the whole thing being dedicated to an officer who had fallen in the War. . . .

But how I wish all this dreadful time was over, passed away and done with like an evil dream—as it will be, please God, some day—and that I was asking you instead, if there was any chance of your being in Northamptonshire again next winter, not to pass this door without stopping to ask for your old and true friend—full of sympathy for you and your position which cannot be otherwise than a sad one.

HARRY CHAPLIN.

Of course it was reported all over Germany that I dared not put my foot in Pless ;. that I was in prison in Bavaria, was never seen in Fürstenstein, and so on. When it became known, not only that I had been there, but had remained some days at the sacred Great Headquarters, my enemies were chagrined and my friends delighted. The Crown Princess wrote :

SEEHAUS, 17 *July*, 1915.

DEAR PRINCESS DAISY,—

I am deeply touched and thank you most heartily for the lovely lilies ! It is sweet of you to send them to me ! I am so pleased to hear of your "august guests" being in Pless, with *you* at the head of your household. How very interesting to hear all the great news at first hand.

Everything seems to be going on beautifully. I had a long letter from poor Christa some time ago. She is well, and everybody is very kind to her, but she may only see her husband for two hours a day in Gibraltar. King Alfonso is very kind to her, happily.

It is lovely up here at the sea. My baby girl is a perfect darling, and she lies for hours at the sea-side and is getting quite sunburned. The boys are such big chaps now. If you have time, do write a line and tell me about Pless in its present form ! With so many thanks and best love, I am,

Yours very sincerely, CECILE.

Christa, to whom she refers, was, of course, the wife of Prince Salm-Salm. They were both big-game shooting in Africa when war was declared. He was interned in Gibraltar and she, poor dear, was living there in great seclusion. Although technically an "enemy subject" I am happy to say she never experienced, while on English territory, any of the indignities I suffered in my husband's country.

In spite of my rehabilitation I fully realized Silesia was no place for me just then. This was one reason why I went there to put everything in proper order at the hospitals. This done, I wrote to General von Perthes, the highest official concerned, stating that all the hospitals in Silesia that I had organized and placed at the disposal of the military authorities were now in smooth working order, and that I wanted to lay down my responsibility for them and have them officially placed under the supervision of the Territorial Delegate for Silesia. The General most courteously agreed, and I then felt free to make my personal plans.

As it gets very hot in Partenkirchen in the summer, I had decided some time before to take the children to Bansin for a holiday by the sea. Before I left I had a message from the Foreign Office in Berlin saying that a young diplomat, Herr von Bülow, who had just come back from Rumania, had a letter to me from the Queen which he wished to deliver in person. I telephoned that I thought it might well be sent by post but, as they would not agree, I said he might come to Partenkirchen. My diary will tell the rest:

July 21, 1915. Bansin (Baltic Sea).

I see the last words in my diary are "I will put in later what Herr von Bülow will have to tell me." A great deal has passed since then.

It has rained and been sunshiny; we have gone in the motor-car with the little Grand Duke. Fritz (my brother-in-law) came here and the two sisters of the Emperor are here and dined with me last night. Princess Mossy, the youngest, is accompanied by her husband, who is Prince Friedrich Carl of Hesse.[1] He was wounded and they have lost their eldest son. They are both so very, very dear and nice. The father and son lay together in the same room while they were

[1] He and his eldest son were severely wounded in France in September, 1914: the latter was later on killed in Rumania. In October, 1916, his second son, an airman, was killed.

out in the war and wounded. Princess Vicy is, of course, Princes Adolf of Schaumburg-Lippe.

The Herr von Bülow, who brought me the letter from the Queen of Rumania, was very nice . . . young, but quite intelligent. He was to have left in the evening, but he walked to the station and missed his train, so telephoned and dined with me, and we had a nice talk.

The dear Queen sent me a charming letter, which is now in the portfolio of papers which are to be preserved. Her letter, of course, contained little that was political, except the remark that she was not at all one-sided, and that they realized the extraordinary organization of the German army. She wrote though, that she was sorry that poisonous gases had been used : it wasn't fair in any war.

How strange it is, diary, the many friends I have and the extraordinary letters I get from people on all sides, including the Crown Princess of Sweden. It seems, that all neutral states are sorry for me, and this means, as the two sisters of the Emperor and I were saying the other day, that the name " England," whether buried deep, or whether some day lifting its head higher than ever, will always be remembered and loved. English people *are* loved and what is English is loved ; there is something fine in the people themselves, which can never be obliterated, and which works from one generation to another. It is like the perfume of a flower ; even if the mother-bloom drops from the tree, the little buds turn into blooms full of seed and therefore immortal ; and I do not say this because I am English ! I have seen so many nations and I can judge the feeling of people. . . .

Herr von Bülow, who is in the German Legation in Bukarest, was most intelligent and sees the mistakes that the Germans have made since years in their own politics ; but, of course, he lauds the pride and grandeur of his country. I wrote a reply to the Queen and sent it to him to have it transmitted to her. He is now going off to the front instead of to Bukarest, so I must write to him and wish him luck.

Last Sunday I received a telegram from the Empress, from Pless ; it was only to say that she was very happy and restful there, but that the weather was bad, and that she was sending me, through Hans when he came here, a photograph of herself and her little granddaughter. . . .

. . . all those enormous dinners to which society has been used for so many years, and now has to do without ! The privation is doing them all good. It is not that one could not have the dinners, but the cooks are all out at the front. Thank God, in the future people will, I think, be more satisfied with simplicity; in fact, it will be the fashion to live with less grandeur and pomp, which after all used always to make me miserable. I used sometimes to sit at dinners in Pless and look round the table and see about eighteen footmen, five *Leibjäger*,[1] six under-butlers, two head-butlers and others besides, and all that long, long menu, which I never bothered to eat; but I used to think of all the money that was thrown by every man-servant into the plates of all my guests, while so many poor people's plates were empty. We always had far too many servants and never less than forty footmen.

I do not say this because it is war and the world knows such misery. Anybody who bothers to read my diaries will see that I have said so years ago.

Hans is here and last night he told them all about the Hauptquartier, which interested the two Princesses and Prince Friedrich Carl very much.

I must write myself to the Empress and the Crown Princess as they both signed the photograph; the Crown Princess also put the name of her little daughter Alexandrine. Then I must write to Prince Eitel Fritz, to whom I sent some stuff to cure his mosquito bites; a bottle of Eau de Cologne and two chiffon veils to wear when sleeping, as he says the flies crawl over his face all night and he cannot get any rest, although he has a bed. Hans told me last night that the Prince is the finest man in the German army and doing the greatest things; but as Hans is not one to understand that a man can be thoroughly masculine and yet absolutely human, I did not tell him that I sent the fly-paper, Eau de Cologne and veils; never having had to suffer any discomfort himself, Hans would not be able to imagine what it is to receive at the front something that gives even for a minute a little sort of home-comfort feeling.

August 2, 1915. Fürstenstein.

I always hope to write my diary myself, but it is often impossible; something incredible turns up and I am prevented. I see the date of the last entry is July 21st, and now here I am again in Fürstenstein after a second visit to the sacred Hauptquartier in Pless.

I received a wire from General von Plessen, the Emperor's

[1] The Prince's personal huntsmen.

THE EMPEROR AND MY HUSBAND AT GREAT HEADQUARTERS IN THE EAST, PLESS, 1915

AN ANCIENT HEAD FORESTER OF PLESS.

Aide-de-camp General, telling me that Hans had had an operation for appendicitis, that I could come or not as I wished; silly old fool, what did he think? I had at least to go there and find out if it was an operation that mattered or not. Herr von Treutler was the only one who really did the right thing, as he wired me that Hans had no fever, so by this I knew, having seen so many operations myself, that there could be no poison. I rushed off at once to Pless with just a few kimonos, the same old things I brought with me from London and such clothes as Elsa could find and pack quickly. We got the telegram at twelve, and she and Seidel left at two-thirty. The little Grand Duke of Mecklenburg-Strelitz motored me to Ducherow; so I did not have to wait there an hour. I dined in Berlin that night with Fritz and Baron Nimptsch, and Fritz and I got to Pless the next morning in a through carriage arriving at half-past nine. The *Fürstenzimmer* or Prince's Waiting Room was opened for me at the station, and Fritz and I tried not to laugh—we did not feel inclined for etiquette. At the station there was a guard of soldiers and police to keep the crowd away. I had not the faintest idea what they were, but Seidel told me it was a great honour. So, dear diary, I have accepted it as that. General von Plessen, the senior General of the Hauptquartier, and Count Westphalen, the Master of the Horse, were at the station to receive me.

At the main entrance of the Castle the Emperor himself met me and walked round and round the terrace with me for some time, explaining to me all about Hans's illness, how sudden it all had been, and saying that if a doctor from Kattowitz, a young and fine operator, had not happened to be there at the time, it would have been too late. . . . We walked and talked of old days and my father-in-law, but nothing of the War; I noticed the Chancellor near by, so after some time I said: "Your Majesty, someone more important than me is waiting." I then said "How do you do" to the Chancellor, smiled at the Emperor, saluted like an officer, and went upstairs to my rooms—and my breakfast.

It seemed so funny to be there and yet feel that I was not the hostess. Baron von Reischach came to see me—he is Marshal of the Court and Master of the Household in Berlin—and said, that if there was anything I wanted I was simply to order it, cutlets, and so on, as they lived very simply. I only smiled and said, which is true, all I live on or care for is a little fish sometimes, bread and butter and jam, and this is mostly what I have had thesc last days. The cooking at Pless though seemed very good, but I did not eat a quarter of what was put before me.

Hans was very weak when first I saw him, but soon improved. One day I and some of the Emperor's gentlemen motored to Promnitz and had tea there. One poured out the tea, and I asked them laughing: "May I have some more bread and butter?" And they were all delighted and enquired if I did not feel uncomfortable in my own house, asking for things and feeling like a guest. I said: "No, indeed, it was the greatest rest I had ever had." Then we sat by the lake and picked some flowering bushes and some fir cones to take back to Hans. I gave them to him in the evening, but somehow he did not seem to be very pleased. It is so difficult to understand people! I just sat near him smilingly for a little while and told him of the afternoon.

Another thing we did was to drive and see the stags, as I had never before been to Promnitz so early in the year, I had therefore not seen a lot of male stags together; in September, when the males are fighting for the females, one never sees more than two stags at the same time, or at the most three. On our way there to the stags in the motor the Gentlemen gave directions about the route we were to follow; they knew all the roads as they ride every morning. So I simply sat there quietly. The forest tracks were awful for a car, but every time it bumped I only laughed: it was not *my* car. We passed a waggon full of straw; I felt that we we going into it, and said so; then bang—we did, and the whole glass on my side was broken to bits. I put up my arm, so none went in my face, only all over my dress and on the rug. I felt something tickling my neck and put my hand up and took a little weeny bit of glass off; there was a little blood; for a second the men were terrified. However, we went on just like naughty children. As we stood by the stags we suddenly heard a motor and saw two Generals sitting in it. It was clearly one of the Emperor's cars, a Hauptquartier car, so I said: "For goodness' sake hide *me*; a lady in a pink cotton dress does not belong to the Hauptquartier!" But they only laughed as I got behind them. The motor stopped and the two gentlemen got out. I nearly had a fit, and said: "Who on earth is coming?" And they said "General——"—I forget his name; but they told me he was of great importance, as he has the whole of the ammunition under his orders. He was introduced to me and also his Aide-de-camp. I had my camera with me and I photographed them, and then one of them photographed me with the others, and soon we all went home, quite sorry to leave the lovely woods and Promnitz.

The day I left Pless it rained, so at Tichau I sent them all a wire in German: "Of course it is raining now that I have left. All greetings. Princess of Pless." And the following day I got this telegram in German: "We quite understand that Pless wept over your departure. We hope, Serene Sunshine, that you will soon return so that the merry drive to Mr. and Mrs. Stag can be repeated. Best greetings."

August 4, 1915. Fürstenstein.

Before I left Bansin Princess Mossy had asked me why I did not tell the Emperor of all the trouble I have been through and the lies that have been circulated about me. So when at Pless I wrote to the Emperor one morning and said I wished to see him alone or with Herr von Treutler; so they both came one afternoon. I told the Emperor very distinctly all that had happened, and I gave Treutler copies of the different documents and letters. I also told the Emperor that General Löwenfeldt had been too frightened and too great a coward to come and see me in Berlin in October but, as I heard on all hands that he was only a very second-rate soldier, this did not surprise me. The Emperor was very nice and said that now that I had been twice in the Hauptquartier all trouble was at an end and that the people would see he was my friend.

He saw me alone, too, the day I left, as I wished to ask him about Switzerland, as the idea suddenly struck me the night before, that to go there as Hans proposed would only raise fresh suspicions. Why should I hide myself! I am too proud to do things on the sly, as if I did evil, and I had the feeling that, having been in the Hauptquartier, the mad cats and dogs that are against me might lift up their hands and say: "What does it mean, the Princess has been in the Hauptquartier where no women are allowed (the Empress has been there once), and now she goes off to Switzerland." They would have said that I went there with some secret about a Zeppelin, a flying machine, a new cannon, or some deadly gas, or something of the sort. Oh, diary, how people have tried to throw poison at me! How shall I ever be able to find in the future any true happiness in this country! Yet

I admire the nation most intensely and also the Emperor; but their smallness and suspicion and evil-mindedness are really too much to endure.

When the Emperor saw me alone he said it was better that I should not go to Switzerland; he even said that if I went he would cut off my head!

I saw all the Emperor's horses in Pless, and lots of the Gentlemen used to come and see me in my sitting-room after dinner and we used to talk till eleven o'clock. One morning Baron von Reischach brought in to introduce to me Captain von Müller,[1] a very charming man, and such a quiet, nice, kind, human face; and indeed he must be that sort of man, as one day I had the most dreadful headache and had to stay in bed all day, and as he passed my maid Elsa, he stopped her and asked how I was.

This sounds like nothing on paper, but at such a moment and in the Hauptquartier—which is like the whole machinery of a clock—it is difficult for anyone revolving with its wheels to think of anything except of what way to finish this terrible war, and how to stop the sounds of guns and the shedding of blood.

One day I showed the Emperor how I had written on a bit of paper and stuffed into the chair in my sitting-room on which he had sat the second or third day, the words "The Emperor's chair, July 27th, 1915." It was written on the point of the envelope which if one licks on it sticks. I had to go on my knees to take it out from where I had stuffed it, and he looked and laughed just like old times, and said how nice it would be if I left it on the chair and the next man who sat on it would walk off with it behind him. In these terrible days I am always so glad when anyone laughs.

At Bansin darling Lexel had for some time been complaining about pains in his little tummy. I had him examined and, while with Hans in Pless, received news that made me decide to have the boy at once removed to Berlin for an appendicitis operation. There was nothing to be done but rush off and collect him at Bansin and get him to Berlin with as little delay as possible.

Before I hurriedly left Pless nice General von

[1] The commander of the *Emden*. The passengers and crew of some of his captures spoke highly of the courteous treatment they had received at his hands. The *Emden* was driven ashore and burnt off Cocos Island on November 9, 1914, by the Australian cruiser *Sydney*.

Gontard[1] had promised to keep me informed about my husband's progress, which he did in this letter (he wrote in German):

MY DEAR PRINCESS,— PLESS, 8/8/15.

I have just sent off my telegraphic reply to your kind letter, for which I thank you very much; in which telegram I was able to report the best in regard to the Prince and his quick removal from the hospital to the Castle. Dr. von Niedner is satisfied with the healing of the wound. How happy and thankful will you be, dear Princess, to learn of the favourable result of the operation of your second son, and which caused serious worries about illness during the last weeks. These troubles are now, with God's help, overcome.

Your eldest son[2] made an excellent impression here with His Majesty and all the Gentlemen. He is a brave fellow with good inclinations and very well brought up. As he, nearly always all day long, was with his father in the hospital he has not been able to write letters. Now he is very happy that early to-morrow he will be able to speak to his mother, so that I must not venture into his narrative. I was very pleased that this evening the Imperial Chancellor on his return to Berlin has taken the young gentleman kindly under his care and in his saloon carriage.

I beg to enclose the address of Prince Eitel Fritz. According to his last report of the 26th July he was quite well, but since then I regret I have heard no more.

Trusting that your little patient will further progress, and kissing your Highness's hands, I am, Sincerely yours,

GONTARD.

Here is a letter from Princess Mossy (Princess Friedrich Carl of Hesse) whom I had left behind at Bansin with her husband. She was always a perfect darling, and, as always, wrote in English:

MY DEAR DAISY,— BANSIN, *August* 2, 1915.

Alas, we are off to-day and I am *very* sorry not to see you any more, but I do hope we may meet before long somewhere else, and that soon things will be looking better all round especially for you, and that time will help you to shake off

---

[1] Adjutant-General and Marshal of the Court.

[2] Hansel had of course been summoned to Pless on account of his father's illness.—D. OF P.

the misery thrown upon you without your fault, and that you will not continue to think of all the injuries inflicted upon you, by ill-meaning people, who misjudged you completely. I hope you were able to speak to the Emperor and if he, as well as we, all know the truth, never mind the rest. You have many true friends, like the kind Schönborns, and I am sure the darkness of this past year will turn into light again. May you be preserved from the heartrending grief of losing something very dear to you, which seems to change life entirely. Thank you ever so much for your letter and for your kind thoughts of sympathy. I am so glad to think your husband is improving. Also for the copies of those horrible letters many thanks, do you wish to have them back? I read them with great interest. We are very sorry to leave this nice place which really did us good. How pleased you will be to get back to those *dear* boys of yours. God bless and help you, dear Daisy. With much love, Yours affectionately,

MARGARET.

About this time Alphy Clary sent me the news that he was engaged and hoped to marry directly after the War. The spirit in which he wrote me was typical of the best men in every army and every country. Oh, how I sometimes envied those narrow-hearted people who only thought of their own country's point of view. I had relatives or dear friends in England, Germany, Austria, Hungary, France, Spain, Russia, Sweden—I heard at intervals from them all and knew how fine and unselfish they all were, and how the best elements in all the belligerent countries realized this, and yet had to go on killing and being killed. Alphy wrote:

. . . I am going to be married—of course after the war, so God only knows when that will be! Huge tasks are awaiting us men, when the great slaughtering will be finished, because we young people will have to build up everything again, that has been ruined, so as to secure eternal peace for our children and grandchildren; we'll have to work very hard for our country and home; I shall want a companion at my side then to help me continually—she is a delicious child and I'm sure you'll like her. . . . We have grown too serious and have seen too much sorrow ever to be children again, but the memory of the old days at Pless remains as something quite unspeakably sweet. . . .

At the end of August I paid my long contemplated visit to the Dowager Grand Duchess of Mecklenburg-Strelitz. She was of course the aunt of the Queen of England who, as a girl, had spent quite a considerable amount of her time at Strelitz. The Queen was always devoted to her Aunt, whose influence on her life has been ennobling and lasting. As the sister of the Duke of Cambridge and the Duchess of Teck, the Grand Duchess had many ties with England. Indeed she always spoke of it as *home*.

Event after event had kept coming along, forcing me to postpone my visit. At last, however, to my great pleasure it took place. My diary gives an account of my second hurried visit to Pless to receive the Empress, and then describes my visit to the Grand Duchess:

August 28, 1915. Neustrelitz.

Oh, diary! I have just read here in Neustrelitz the few pages I had time to write myself in Fürstenstein. I see they were written on August the 11th, to-day we have August the 28th. I went back to Berlin on August the 12th to be with little Lexel during his operation, and got a telegram that evening at six-thirty from Hans, saying: "Return to Pless as soon as possible. I am well." I thought it could only be that they wanted to say good-bye to me and to the house as a Hauptquartier, and that they were all suddenly leaving. I had said, while there, many times, "I suppose you will soon go West," as the Russian situation seemed to have changed. I told them I did not wish to be rude or impolite, or desire that they should think that I wished them to leave my house, but I imagined it would soon be their duty to go West. However one evening the Emperor said to me he would be in Pless till Christmas. At any rate, with Lexel ill I could not go to Pless at once.

Instead I sent Hans's telegram to the Imperial Chancellor to ask what he advised me to do, thinking that perhaps the Empress was going to Pless and that I had to be there. At half-past eleven at night Baron von Stumm, Under-Secretary at the Foreign Office, asked permission to come up and see me at the Hotel in Berlin. I was just getting into bed, but put on a dressing-gown and went into the sitting-room saying, as he was soon going to be married and that we had known each other for so long, he must forgive me for coming like that—my hair was not undone. He had come to say that I must go to Pless at once. I was very upset to think of leaving the next day, which was Friday the 13th, but he said it was imperative, as the Empress had left Berlin that (Thursday) night, so I must leave by the first train in the morning. I was furious—and have not got over it yet.

I arrived in Pless on Friday evening at half-past ten. They had sent the Emperor's car to meet me. Upon my arrival I spoke for a minute with Hans, who was playing Patience, and then I went to have my supper in my own room. . . .

I saw the Empress the next day at three o'clock. Her Gentlemen met me on the stairs—the son of one of them is prisoner in England, and I have written to him; his name is Herr von Trotha. Downstairs I was met by Countess Rantzau, the Empress's lady-in-waiting, a young "old-maid," who is not popular in the Hauptquartier. She certainly looks grumpy enough!

I had been out early in the morning for a walk, and they asked me if I had met the Emperor and the Empress, as they had gone to the garden and probably thought I had gone there too; but I had preferred to go alone on my island. I had on a short cotton country frock, and after luncheon—which I had by myself, as the Empress always has her meals alone with the Emperor—Hans said to me: "Are you not going to put on a long frock?" I told him that I had not got such a thing, as having been called away from Bansin suddenly, I had no smart clothes with me; besides I possess none now, and even if I did, I never wear long frocks in the country on any occasion. The three Gentlemen in the room smiled at me and one said, "Better take some gloves," so I sent to my dressing-room for the pair of long wash-leather gloves which I had carried in the morning. I felt inclined to express myself sarcastically at the idea that in the daytime, in the country, and while a war was on, one should fuss about clothes; and I was sorely tempted to pull my hair down and go in a plait and put a little sand on my shoes—in fact to look natural, as one would in England . . . just as one did in the old days of dear Queen Alexandra and King Edward, the days at Chatsworth and at Newlands and at Cowes—amongst the darlingest friends!

As I went downstairs I said rather frigidly to the lady-in-waiting:

"I am sorry I have not a long dress with me."

"Oh, it does not matter for a few minutes."

I felt like saying: "You stiff little German fool; who speaks of a few minutes!"

But I swallowed my laugh inside—as I had learnt to swallow my tears; and I went in to the Empress who looked extremely nice in a long mauve dress, long mauve ear-rings, and white lace. We sat on the sofa together and talked from three till five o'clock! At half-past four I said to her:

"Does not Your Majesty wish to go to tea; the Emperor will be waiting." So we got up, but she sat down again.

One little point was rather pretty. I said to her:

"I thought of Your Majesty last night when I went to bed, knowing how cosy you were" (as they both sleep in the same bed).

I dare say just to hold each other's hands is a comfort to them at such a miserable time in their lives, and she smiled back at me and said:

"How funny; I had thought of you, too."

But I had no hand to feel; as my rooms are just above hers, she would possibly know this.

In the evenings we made bandages with some old bits of linen she gave us. There were present General von Plessen, General von Scholl,[1] Count Moltke, General von Gontard, whom Prince Eitel Fritz loves and writes about; he was the Governor of all the Emperor's sons; then there was Major von Münchhausen, Herr von Chelius, who has lost his eldest son, poor dear—and several other Gentlemen who played cards with the Emperor.

I sat on the sofa next to the Empress, and at last when there was a silence I said:

"Now we *must* pretend and tell stories as the children do."

So I turned to General von Plessen: "Begin with your life-story, but it must begin very seriously and in a deep voice—and say 'It was once dark'—and 'I remember': talk just as children talk." The Empress laughed:

"We won't have the whole of his life-story; a few stories of the last twenty years would be enough."

I did not ask what she meant, but I guessed. I have heard there was always a fuss when Plessen went to England in the time of Queen Victoria, as he and the Gentlemen with him behaved none too quietly amongst the ladies at Court! He was a fearful old flirt, and Queen Victoria was shocked.

---

[1] A Hessian, sometime Adjutant-General.

Then I turned to Major von Münchhausen and said that his name matched with stories like *Don Quixote*, and that even if he did not fasten his horse by the bridle to a church steeple, his family must have done something of renown; he laughed and said they were much older than that of Don Quixote. Then I said:

"All the better, you must have more stories to tell us."

From that point they began to talk of family trees—in German *Stammbaum*. Of course I said the wrong word, and when I tried to repeat it I said *Standbaum* which made them laugh; I was thinking of a *standard-tree* into which most people in Germany think it right to turn their lives.

Then Count Moltke began about his tree. When he had done I said:

"None of you can match mine, as I have two Queens in my family tree, two sisters who married two Wests; one was the Queen of Provence and the other of Lorraine."

Then Moltke turned and said:

"But Lorraine is German now."

I said: "Now it may be, but then it was not. . . ."

At any rate, as usual I acted my part and *no one* knew what I was feeling! . . .

Nobody knows I have been to Great Headquarters in the East; nobody knows that the Empress has been there; nobody knows (or is supposed to know) where it really is; they only know that it is somewhere in Silesia! Not one man in the house seems to dare to do anything; they are all frightened of each other and all wait panting in the hope of some Order or title they may receive after the War.

One afternoon the Emperor and the Empress drove to Solza to see the Larisches. I asked the Empress if I could come and she sent a note saying that she was going alone with the Emperor. Then I heard that she was taking the lady-in-waiting and two Gentlemen with her, so I proposed to go with the lady-in-waiting, but was not allowed.

In the evening Baron von Reischach (the Marshal of the Court[1]) calmly said to me that the Larisches had been told to ask no strangers, using the German phrase, *fremde Leute*. (The Emperor and Empress had not yet come downstairs.) So I turned to him and several other men standing near and said:

"Is this what you call me in my own house, where you are

[1] The Baron, who was actually Lord High Chamberlain, and who had been Master of the Horse, carried out the duties of Court Marshal at the Emperor's Headquarters during the War.

all my guests? You are all afraid of the Emperor and of each other."

Then Reischach said to me:

"But it was the Emperor's desire, and no one could say a word."

I was angry and retorted:

"This is not the first Court I have stayed at and I know that the Master of the Household generally arranges things and proposes to Kings and Emperors and helps them, and what he proposes—if it is right—is nearly always accepted. Count Larisch married my first cousin. The tactless way in which you have spoken is highly characteristic, believe me, Baron von Reischach. I do not mind, but I am sorry that anything so extraordinarily rude should take place in this house. To say as you do 'It is war, dear Princess,' is no excuse for absolute discourtesy and lack of chivalry. I expect you are all afraid of each other," and I pointed my finger at them *smilingly*.

As I left the room I just bowed to them and I think I made them all feel very uncomfortable.

Of course the only excuse they can make is to say that in my position I could not drive with a lady-in-waiting; but this is the usual stiff German etiquette which does no good and has spoiled all her politics and prevented her from becoming a nation that could be—if not loved as she is respected—at least thought of with some degree of affection.

At any rate, that night the Emperor and the Empress were most impressively nice to me, so I expect they realized the mistake that had been made.

(Even on a Sunday when we went to church, the Emperor and the Empress being in our box and I on the other side of the Emperor, I noticed as we were about to sit down that Baron von Reischach pulled my chair back, not wishing me to sit at the same level as their Majesties, but of course I simply pulled my chair slightly forward and so sat beside the Emperor and Empress in my own *pew* in my *own church*: I just would and did.)

Oh! my dear diary, the more one lives in this country the more one realizes the feeling of cheap, jealous snobbery and mistrust which underlies everything. . . . They listen to all you say and repeat it in whichever way they like, either to make it better or worse; it depends on the mood they are in. They either wish you good or evil; some are very nice, some are not great gentlemen, because they have no great, old, family tradition, full of generosity and broadmindedness.

"Live and let live" is not their motto; it is rather "Live as I wish"; move as I say; sit or stand as I order; think as I think; speak as I do. . . .

How often have I thought of the absurdity of old Generals and people at Court here calling Princesses, *Durchlaucht*, which means Serene Highness. Can one imagine a well-born gentleman whom one has known for years in speaking to an English Duchess saying "Your Grace"? Servants do it, but that is all. To say "Sir" or "Madame" to a Royalty is different. I simply hate it that I am expected to kiss the Empress's hand! How dare a woman expect another woman to do such a thing—except voluntarily with love and respect such as one feels for the old Grand Duchess of Mecklenburg-Strelitz. One feels so young next to her, and to see her dear little proud face would make one do anything. It is like a home here, I love her. . . .

Well, diary, I will not write any more now; I must get up, as I promised the Grand Duke to be ready at twelve o'clock.

August 30, 1915. Neustrelitz.

Fritz arrived here last night and the children are both so, so happy! And the Grand Duke is a darling to them, really extraordinary, and I will help him all I can. It is a very pretty place, but alas, so many roads are public. He has built a little house for himself, as both the Grand Duchesses live here (his mother and grandmother). So when he marries he must have a cosy home of his own. I promised to help him since months, and now our architect Kimbel is here and we went yesterday to the house. I naturally thought the rooms would be bigger. I can only look upon it as absolutely hopeless, unless he does what I suggest, which is to build a high wall right in front so that from her bedroom window, his future wife, whoever she may be, will not see all the street and the public within about fifty yards of her balcony. He had talked of the possibility of making a garden, but his *Hofmarschall* lives close by and he has already put up a little wooden wall between the houses. Of course this must be replaced by a high stone wall, so that at least roses can grow all over it and a broad herbaceous border be made in front. There are fine woods in the vicinity, but even these are public. A high netting has been put round the garden to keep the rabbits and the game out, which cannot remain; it must be much lower down. It looks like a villa in a small watering-place. To the right there are flat fields and no view.

Poor dear Grand Duke, he is so nice; it seems to me absolutely sad I can't stay here long enough to change it all; and he longs for a little cosy home of his own and I long to help him, but I wish I had not, without seeing the place, advised a decorator for him, or bought anything. The stuffs I have ordered in Munich are much too fine for such weeny rooms, and here in this nice house—they call it a Palace—he could certainly find a cosy wing for himself. The rooms I am occupying and the rooms in front and at the side are all free; also the rooms where Fritz is sleeping now; as long as the two Grand Duchesses live, he could have had the Head Bailiff's little house where Queen Louise [1] died, which is absolutely private and has a lovely view on to the lake; and it could be made quiet and simple and homely. This Park House, which he is trying to arrange, he started before his father died, rather more as a bachelors' house. He did not expect he would become reigning Grand Duke so suddenly and had not at that time any schemes of his own. And I must say he thinks and reads and studies a lot, and is full of ideas and so clever and interested in the family museum.

Yesterday we went out shooting at ten in the most lovely woods, all undulating ground with fine trees. We saw lots of game and two stags. I was supposed to shoot one, but I am glad it got away, as I was only trying to please the Grand Duke and his *Jäger*, who would have been so terribly disappointed if I had not tried. But the night before I told the Grand Duke, almost in tears, that for me to shed blood now, at such a time, would only make me miserable. I like to see our own *Jägers* in Pless and the forests, that is all; Hansel can do the shooting in future. Five years ago I used to go shooting only to get to know the men and all about their families.

I made the *Jäger* go and put a white patch on a tree and I stood a long way off and said I would hit it, without any tree to lean against or high stick; I aimed at about seventy yards and hit the mark and the *Jäger* was perfectly delighted. I did this just to show them I shot easily. I don't know really, diary, how I did it; perhaps I should not have been able to do it for certain if I had tried a second time, so of course I did not try!

We then went to Hohenzieritz and met the children and

[1] Louise Augusta Wilhelmina, the famous Queen of Prussia (1776–1810), daughter of Charles, Duke of Mecklenburg-Strelitz.

the tutor and Fräulein Fenzl for lunch. The lunch was very late and instead of Baby's nurse asking for his at the usual time she kept him waiting, and I think, poor darling, all the excitement of these days and a motor-drive here, and always eating with us and the Grand Duke, was too much for such a little child. So suddenly in the middle of lunch he said he had a tummy-ache and I ran out to find where I could put him to sit on something. When I came back I found the Grand Duke holding Bolko's head; the darling had been sick in his plate. The little Grand Duke is really an angel. I never thought before a man would do this! He surely is someone who ought to make a woman very, very happy; and have dear little children, please God; he deserves all that is nice. I want all that is best for him as he wishes for me.

The day after Fritz came we went in the afternoon to Mirow, which is absolutely Louis Quinze, a perfectly divine little dream-house. I really forget who lived there, I think Queen Louise and her sister did so for a time. In one room there is a little door leading on to a road with no steps down, and from where the sister used just to jump on to her horses—she was not supposed to do so—and ride astride. So she did it privately, God bless her poor little heart!

I wonder if the people who die are happier than those who have to go on living!

No one else was with us except the Dowager Grand Duchess, but of *her* I must write at length and exclusively—whole pages in fact. There is one room in Mirow which is pale-blue and silver with a little niche for the bed. In there will go beautifully four silver-framed mirrors the Grand Duke bought in Innsbrück; and there is a charming sitting-room all painted, and a lovely dining-hall upstairs; in fact a little jewel of a house which makes me long that the Grand Duke should arrange to live in it instead of continuing building the Park House. This new villa is really not worthy of him and his name—which, after all, is supposed to be something. At Mirow there is, too, a most gorgeous lake and with a steam-launch one can get thence straight to Berlin by canal in about two hours.

Oh, diary! why does everything in life—whether sad or happy—bring back the remembrances of colour and of sound. I have left Neustrelitz with a greater love for England, since I met the darling Grand Duchess grandmother, grand-daughter of George III., most splendid of English ladies—a strong spirit in her, and dignity and charm and love. What tact

THE EMPEROR'S SISTER, VICTORIA, PRINCESS ADOLF OF SCHAUMBURG-LIPPE.
Now Frau Alexander von Zoubkoff.

and wonderful conversation ! How she must have influenced all those round her. She is irresistible even *now*, and yet she is in her ninety-fourth year and, as a little child of three, remembers George III. If she had gone to the last Coronation it would have been her fifth, as she saw four English Sovereigns being crowned.

One talks, diary, of a person of ninety-four, wondering if they can see, if their brain does not get dizzy, if they can walk ; one cannot believe that life at such an age can really be open to the influence of any great emotion ; one thinks of it as being more like a tired tune that is descending slowly to its last chord ; but I can assure you the company of the Grand Duchess does not in the least induce reflections like these. To have been with her every night for dinner, as we were, once for tea (with Lexel and Bolko), and then once in the morning on her balcony ; to have even barely seen her is to love her and absolutely respect an old age which is like a sort of lovely crystal cameo, etched with precious remembrance marks that can never be erased.

If I had one-tenth of the intellect that she has, I should be thankful. The power of remembrance with her is absolutely uncanny. Most people when they are old wander in their mind, but she can talk of the present and the past ; how diplomatically Peace could have been arranged before this, and could be arranged even now. . . .

She talked of Prince von Bülow, formerly Imperial Chancellor.[1] She talked of the Emperor as she has known him, and wonders how he is at this present moment. We spoke of the Empress Eugénie of France, of whom she so much reminds me ; although the Empress is younger she cannot do half as much or walk so quickly. The Grand Duchess also talked of Pietri,[2] who is always with the Empress, and even mimicked the way he looks and the way he rubs his hands when he is speaking. She really acts and changes the expression of her face, so that you can *see* about whom she is speaking. But to sit and speak with someone who can discuss and weigh Bethmann-Hollweg the present Chancellor, summarize the existing political situation in Europe, who knows every living Crowned head and knew all those

---

[1] Chancellor 1900–9.

[2] Franceschino Pietri, a Corsican, the devoted servant of Napoleon III., continued faithfully to serve the exiled Empress until his death at Farnborough Hill, Hampshire, in 1915, at the age of eighty-two.

as far back as seventy years ago; who can speak from personal knowledge of the Empress Eugénie leaving France; of the wars of 1864 and 1870!

One sometimes holds one's breath, gets quite confused; one would feel ashamed of oneself but for the reflection that she is *living* in it all again. Every word she says is like the present to her! As for us, we have merely read it in bad history-books in a hurry, or tried to talk about it with an uneducated governess. I feel quite home-sick and lonely in writing about her, the dear, great little lady, with her understanding eyes which are still quite clear. The large rooms in which she moves are an appropriate setting for *her* great personality, instead of what they might be to an ordinary woman—overwhelming.

She looked even better at ten in the morning than at ten at night! And I simply long to go back to Strelitz, and perhaps she will let me go before Christmas, just to rest there quietly downstairs with my feet up, as I ought not to walk too much. To think . . . And I could write and dictate and go to see the darling for twenty minutes a day, or perhaps not at all: I can always have a cold in my nose and the dear old servant there with long whiskers would quite simply tell me if he advised me to go to her or not. She has got to live, diary, to see realized the future plans for a peaceful Europe, which will be formed after this war. She *must* live for this, and I am going to pray for it, as it will be a most exciting moment, when all countries start arguing and scowling over the terms of peace; and that is why I think the war will last longer, for no one has even thought yet of a plan of peace or a map of peace.

She was such a fine woman and such an historic character that I shall copy here portions from one or two letters I received from the Grand Duchess Augusta directly after I had left Strelitz:

STRELITZ, *September* 5, 1915.

MY DEAR PRINCESS DAISY,—

It was indeed a real pleasure to hear from you so soon, such a dear letter too, and so like you in all its contents as if you were talking to me! I am so truly glad you felt a little bit at home, when here, resting your poor worried heart with me, the old lady of the *last* Century, and this is what makes you think so much of me, who am no more than others of the same date, or would be, were they alive ; and yet I am glad you like me as I am, and have given me your dear affection. We felt quite sad after you had left us, recalling though the charm of your presence, which had not left us, and will remain. . . .

The public like to invent sensations by making a fuss ; at present it is hammering nails into old Hindenburg as upon a cross. This is to be done here too, but I shall certainly not join in aping others. Need I tell you how glad I shall ever be to see you, only it would distress me, being unable to entertain you, as I would like to do.

Renewing my thanks for the dear letter, Ever your truly affectionate,

AUGUSTA.

When replying, I asked the Grand Duchess to forward letters to England to Queen Mary and Queen Alexandra for me. This she did. Here is her letter in which she conveys Queen Mary's kind message which, reaching me at such a miserable time, did much to cheer me up.

The letters dated October 7 and 11 reached me together at Salzbrunn, where I had gone to meet Hans and to inspect the surrounding hospitals and see the building operations at Fürstenstein.

STRELITZ, *October* 7, 1915.

DEAR PRINCESS DAISY,—

The Queen in her letter to me says, " Will you write and thank Princess P. for her letter and say that I forwarded her note to Queen *A*. Please tell her that G. and *I* think of her and are sorry for her in the difficult position in which she is placed."

She was pleased to receive so nice and cheering an account of her old Aunt, this being a comfort to her. I am sure you will be pleased to know this, therefore I write to you at once on receiving her letter. How are you getting on ? I so often think of you, looking forward to your visit after my dear grandson's return ; he told me he will not be away long. Just now he is motoring about, I hope, not *too* near the French, where bloodshed is raging. What do you hear of your brother-in-law ? Has he come back ; is he a support to you ? Did you receive the letter I sent you from Princess Margaret ?

I addressed it to Salzbrunn; should you not have got it, send for it there. I am keeping up as far as possible, though I suffer deeply from all this anxiety.

The Queen tells me of such fine weather at *Home*, which enables her to sit out in the garden; her second son [1] has come back, invalided, hoping to recover in Scotland from a nasty gastric attack. Princess Mary [2] has gone up to join him, keeping him company. Queen *A*. greatly fatigued, has gone to Sandringham. I hope you are keeping well and am as ever, Yours affectionately,

AUGUSTA CAROLINE.

STRELITZ, *October* 11, 1915.

DEAR PRINCESS DAISY,—

Thank you for your dear nice letter containing so much. Your news was very extraordinary; yet you have some friends, keep to them as your real support in difficult times. . . .

I had such a dear letter from my Swedish niece,[3] she had just heard from her brother [4] with good news *then*. My "Boy" [5] is now motoring about in dangerous regions; he works very hard so I feel rather nervous. . . . The "roll of honour" becomes longer each day, it cuts one to the heart. My niece [6] is doing wonders of kindness and thoughtfulness, much overworked I fear, could I but be of use and help her. In writing to my Rumanian niece,[7] do tell her how often I think of her and the happy time when we met in the dear old country. Your letter interests me in all it tells me, mine is empty but for the affection I feel for you. A.

My diary records one vividly painful incident during our few days' stay at Salzbrunn. We could not of course stay at Fürstenstein as it was upside down, and there were no servants. As usual we put up at our own hotel in Salzbrunn, most of which was being used as a convalescent home for wounded officers requiring Spa treatment:

---

[1] The Duke of York.
[2] Viscountess Lascelles.
[3] The Crown Princess of Sweden.
[4] Prince Arthur of Connaught.
[5] Her grandson, the reigning Grand Duke.
[6] The Queen of England.
[7] The Queen of Rumania.

October 11, 1915. Salzbrunn.

I sat on the balcony the last three nights in a comfortable chair to listen to a man who plays the piano beautifully. The Major came up and spoke to me last night about the fall of Belgrade and told me that the man who plays the piano is a professional music-teacher. And oh, diary, what do you think he played to-night? That old song of mine, *Two Eyes of Grey*, which, even when singing in England, has made me want to cry—and I thought that no one but Maudie Warrender and I have sung that song. It is never played in France or Germany or Vienna, and to my absolute misery and astonishment this man played it to-night on the piano. And there was I sitting quite near, knowing each word and not daring even to sing it; to sit alone and remember! Hans not far off playing Patience. . . .

Does the devil send little spirits round I wonder, just to tease one? And some of this pianist's favourite pieces are French waltzes, things that one used to hear at Ciro's Restaurant at Monte Carlo, or that Sophy Torby used to play, and which I and her girls used to dance to. And now here I sit with convalescent wounded men in this hotel in the year 1915, and queer little things like this happen. It is like a bird that sings in an awful, awful storm and then falls dead.

About the middle of October I had a letter from Prince Eitel Fritz from Noyon, which gave me great pleasure. It said that he and the Grand Duke Adolphus had met and dined together a few days before; but what really pleased me was to hear that the Germans had just unveiled in St. Quentin a monument which they had erected to the German and French soldiers killed there. The Emperor himself went to St. Quentin for the ceremony and afterwards took poor Prince Eitel Fritz with him to Charleville for a few hours. I also liked this because it proved (what I already knew well) that the Royal Princes fared just like any other officer of their military rank and that to them, as to every one else, even a few hours away from the trenches was a very rare treat. Above all, the erection of the monument told me that the old German chivalry was not really dead: Belgium, Nurse Cavell, the *Lusitania*,[1]

[1] The *Lusitania* was sunk by a German submarine on May 7, 1915.

the *Untersee* boats—many things—had conspired to make me at times fear that it was. I have often wondered since what happened to that monument or if it is still there! If so, surely it is a voiceless angel eloquently and continuously healing the wounds of war.

I had hated remaining inactive all these months. The plan of working in Bavaria having fallen through, and that of joining Professor von Kuester's Hospital Train not having materialized, I at last persuaded my husband that everything had blown over and that I might apply for and obtain work as a nurse. I wrote to the Crown Princess for her advice and help and this is what she replied:

MARMOR PALAIS, POTSDAM, 28 *October*, 1915.

DEAR PRINCESS DAISY,—

Many thanks for your kind letter. I am so pleased for you that your husband writes allowing you to do earnest work and not sit about in these bad times, and understand how much you would like to help.

Unhappily, I am afraid it will not be possible to have you on my Train, because, after the Train having had to give away its big *D wagon*, they have only one little room for the Office and personnel, and have sent away a nurse on that account. As it is very fatiguing, they have now decided to take only men for the nursing. My cousin Mariette [1] also wanted to go on a Train, but the family urgently disadvised her on account of it being *much too* tiring. But of course, dear Princess Daisy, if you feel up to travelling about *continuously* I will try and get another Train to take you; only I could always give you the advice *not* to go on a Train, but nurse in a hospital. I do hope you will not think me unkind for not being able to fulfil your wish, but on my Train everything has been settled since months and I cannot possibly change it.

I am so pleased you can come to Berlin again, and that all difficulties have been overcome, and feel so sorry for you, your heart must feel so sore.

My children are well, *unberufen*! My baby-girl is too sweet for words. With best love, dear Princess Daisy, I am, Yours affectionately, CECILE.

[1] Her Highness Duchess Marie Antoinette, of Mecklenburg-Schwerin, a daughter of Duke Paul Frederick of Mecklenburg-Schwerin.

From our own people who were prisoners-of-war I often got news of what was happening to my friends in England, as in this letter from Robin Grey at Blankenburg. Mrs. Astor is of course now Lady Ribblesdale; "Zoe" is Mrs. Farquharson of Invercauld; Alec was Lord Alexander Thynne, Lord Bath's brother. Poor Basil Blackwood (son of my dear old friend Lord Dufferin) went back to the front and soon after was reported "missing, believed killed." "Freddy Blackwood," Lord Basil's youngest brother, is the present Lord Dufferin. Fergus Bowes-Lyon was the brother of the fascinating little lady who is now Duchess of York. Robin's letter says:

October 28, 1915.

. . . I am deeply touched by all your kindness. Bless you. I have heard quite recently from Mrs. Astor and Mrs. Farquharson; the former is probably going to America next month for a short while. Zoe is back at 26 Bruton Street. Alec is at the front. You will have heard that poor Myles Ponsonby is killed, and Lord Petre and Fergus Bowes-Lyon and alas! many, many more. Freddy Blackwood has just gone back to the front, but Basil's hand is still quite useless and they did not let him go back yet. I am so sorry to hear that Betka Potocka has lost both her husband and mother. I am going to write to her as soon as ever I can. I only pray her two boys are well.

I think I must have made some sort of a fuss and got Robin Grey and one or two other officers transferred from Burg to Blankenburg, which was a much better camp. I wrote and told Colonel Gordon this and also that I was going to serve on a Hospital Train. He replied:

. . . Thanks to your kindly influence, we British here have been gladdened by the arrival not only of Robin Grey but also Major Gray and Captain Graham-Watson. I am in a position to say that they and those to whom they are very dear and precious thank you with full hearts. The officers themselves are overjoyed to be in this harbour of rest and peace and their happiness in their new surroundings is shared by their friends at home.

Since I last wrote, the Camp has been visited by Prince Max of Baden,[1] who by his sympathy and gracious courtesy rendered that Sunday a day long to be remembered—in fact, never to be forgotten. I think you are perfectly wonderful and can only hope that this new venture of yours in the call of charity will not overtax your strength. Needless to say your very presence will comfort many a gallant fellow maimed and weakened by honourable wounds. . . . The kindly thoughts and good wishes of your grateful and ardent admirers here will oft be with you in your good work; of that please be assured.

Well do I recall the song you mention, *Two Eyes of Grey*. Nothing so arrests the present and diverts one's thoughts into the past than does a song hallowed by sweet memories. I have still good news from home. Please come back soon safe and sound. Robin Grey sends you the best of good wishes, in which I join.

II

The good news to which Colonel Gordon referred was that at last I had succeeded in being accepted for service on the Military Lazarett Train commanded by Professor von Kuester. My diary will tell all about it:

November 3, 1915. Military Lazarett Train Y.

What an address, thank God I *can* give it. I left Berlin in a fearful hurry—lots of wires and so on; one saying that His Majesty wished that the Princess of Pless should go to the Serbian frontier; so here I am and really the meaning of the word kindness is difficult to express. I would wish to say so much. It was just luck, the *greatest luck* that somehow has come at last—since I brought dear Vater's picture and put it over my bed in Salzbrunn. To be on this very Train which is under Professor von Kuester, the dear nice doctor from dear old Tempelhof—and two other nice doctors from there. There is also a very nice doctor called Doctor Lemke who was with dear Vater in Dresden all the time before he died. And he spoke to me about it all, which somehow made me feel homely, and he even asked after Hannussek.[2] I

[1] The last Imperial Chancellor of the German Empire.
[2] My father-in-law's personal servant.—D. OF P.

felt inclined to kiss Hannussek and him, as it made me feel as if *Vater was near*. There are four Sisters, all seem nice; one has a pretty little face. . . . I only wish there was also the Head Sister from Tempelhof and then we would be homely. This Train is like a street, it is at least six hundred yards long, and will hold at a time two hundred and sixty wounded, whom we go now to fetch. . . .

I wrote to little Shelagh and Poppets and Patsy before I left, as to write to England from the Train is impossible.

I have always said give me people who are not in Society. It is in this class of men and women one finds a true feeling which is just happy doing good to others. Professor Graurt was so pleased at my starting that he sent me some flowers to take with me. And this Professor here! I would like to put the words "thank you" on a ring of pure gold and give it to him. . . .

The world must suffer to be kind; all happiness makes people selfish, and to suffer pain oneself—mental or physical—helps us to gain the sympathy and understanding to help others. The Professor has been so dear to me. I saw him for a minute in Berlin and he told me I could not come all alone; I must bring someone; he would try and get a carriage for me. I begged him not to say I wished for it. Just now I asked him what he did; he went to three chief people. I gave him my credentials, copies of telegrams received and sent by General von Gontard of the Hauptquartier which said, "Sein Majestät des Kaiser und König." So with these, and his goodwill, they somehow arranged things and I have three ordinary compartments and my own *cabinet*.

Oh, diary, from now I drop from me sad reflections. My real friends in Berlin are so glad that I have something serious to do—or to try to; and General von Gontard in Pless was so nice on the telephone, and Hans spoke for me too.

How old General von Perthes in Berlin must be grinding his teeth! When I got on the telephone to him to ask for a Pass he said it was out of the question, "I know nothing about such business." In fact, I closed the telephone up. It was strange, as other things I have wanted he *has* done for me; and when I told Princess Margaret of Hesse in Bansin that he had done all I asked him about my Lazarett, and so on, she said he had been most unpleasant to her. And Prince Miguel of Braganza and his wife are furious with him—something about a nurse I think. So I telephoned at once to Pless for a Pass—and here I sit conqueror—with a smile and very dirty hands. I sang a song to Lexel the other day called *Ten Dirty Little Fingers*, a child's song, and when I was going to sing downstairs at the Lazarett in Salzbrunn he said: "Mummie, I noticed lots of the soldiers have just as dirty hands as me; why don't you sing that song to them!"

Now I will go and tidy for supper. What a relief it is not to have to put on something *fashionable*; I was so happy and simple in perhaps a former life!

The blessed boys are at the little villa at Partenkirchen; I shall go there for Christmas I expect. Hansel is in Potsdam and came to fetch me the day I left. I write this as if it were days ago and it was only yesterday. I hope the days will go long. This period has not begun yet, but I shall be sorry when it is over I think. I only hope I shall get better at the carriage-crossings, but there are no metal hand-rails as in express trains, only ropes across; and one can see the railway lines underneath moving, and the doors of one coach are not always exactly opposite those of the other, therefore one has to open them after one has crossed and it is a twisty business. It will be part of my duty to hold these doors open to let the stretchers pass, so now I'll start practising it—and wash my hands and look at my dirty face first.

III

But my enemies were by no means defeated. After we brought our two hundred and sixty wounded back from Serbia, the Train was waiting at Magdeburg, when the Professor was peremptorily informed that I had only been given permission to make one journey in Lazarett Train Y. He demanded an explanation and said that if I were removed he would resign, as he had been travelling back and forwards for a year, was dead tired and could not stand any more worry. He wrote to Hans. I also wrote to Hans reminding him that I had joined the Train by order of the Emperor and saying that if I was removed I would never again put foot in the Prussian Court.

I had quite a good idea of who was at the bottom of most, if not indeed all, of the trouble. It was a woman. It was she who exaggerated and circulated the lies about my visit to the Prisoner-of-War Camp at

Döberitz. I had known her for years. She was so insignificant that I had hardly ever given her a second's thought. The War, however, proved that she possessed at least one quality in a remarkable degree, Malice. I never did her any harm, being always civil to her as one is to the crowds of nonentities whom one meets in life and who are about as significant as a chair on which one sits at dinner in a restaurant. As for her silly old husband, he was almost an imbecile and, had it not been for his Princely rank, would probably have been locked up. With his loose lips and pink wet eyes, his endless clumsy attempts at flirtation would have made any sane woman sea-sick, so his wife need not have bothered to be jealous ; nobody wanted him but herself and, as she was by instinct a snob, I suspect that his title was all she really cared for.

I had to wait in anxiety and annoyance for three days to know if I was going to be turned out of the Lazarett Train before I received a telegram from Hans telling me that it was His Majesty's desire that I should remain on the Train.

I made one more journey to Serbia and, on the way back, as the Train passed through Silesia, it was specially stopped for me at Salzbrunn. During the period of rest between journeys the Professor and one or two of the Doctors and Sisters came later from Magdeburg to Salzbrunn for a rest and change. My diary will tell what happened :

December 3, 1915. Salzbrünn.

I have seen all the wounded here and dined with the Doctors and Staff. Before going to bed I asked the Band to play *Heil Dir im Siegerkranz* which, in English, is the air of *God Save the King*. While they played and sang it I kept thinking of England, the Coronation, the darling days at Chatsworth, and all the happy meetings with King Edward—one of the greatest gentlemen I can ever hope to meet, and one with the kindest of hearts.

Yesterday I drove Professor von Kuester to see Fürstenstein, and on the way back told him of this characteristic example of German snobbery and small-mindedness. Herr Keindorff, our General Director, had said to me the night before, after we had talked business together: "Your Highness, I do not like to disturb you on such an impertinent matter, but I was asked if it was Your Highness's desire that Helene (secretary), the Swedish masseuse, the governess and tutor, and so on, shall eat downstairs in the same room with the convalescent lieutenants, as it seems that an objection was raised." I said to Keindorff: "Whoever is fit to write my letters for me and whoever is fit to dine with my children, is more than fit to dine with these men here, who if they were not in uniform, would probably be clerks in *your* office, or head men in the woods; some few might perhaps be doctors, but they would be the exception!"

By December 13 I was once again aboard Lazarett Train Y at Breslau, where we were awaiting orders. I wanted very much to be at Partenkirchen for Christmas and to spend it there with Hans and the boys. My idea was that I could go as far as Hungary in the Train, get somehow to Budapest, and from there to Vienna, where I could pick up Hans, and from which it is normally only nine or ten hours to Munich. Hans did not, however, manage to get to Vienna, but he and Lexel met me at Partenkirchen station where my maid Henriette and I arrived at eleven o'clock at night after a sixteen-hour journey. When we reached Partenkirchen—nothing but rain. Hans got bored, so he went to Fürstenstein to see his blessed building operations, and Hansel went to Munich to the Schönborns for Christmas.

Except for Lexel and Bolko my Christmas was therefore a lonely one, but I made the best of things. My greatest source of happiness was the knowledge that in the Lazarett Train I had been of some use and that the Staff and the poor wounded loved me. I have before me at the moment some of the dozens of letters and post-cards I received at Christmas and I cannot do better than close my account of 1915 by giving translations of a few that are typical of all the others; one from a soldier, one from a soldier's wife, and one from a Sister who served with me on the Train:

BRIEG, NEAR BRESLAU, *December* 4, 1915.

HER SERENE HIGHNESS THE PRINCESS OF PLESS,—

For the cordial and loving care that we enjoyed during the transport by the Hospital Train of the Johannite Order from the 27th to the 30th November I would like to offer my warmest thanks in the name of my comrades. It was admirable to see how the Noble Princess sacrificed herself by her love and care for the wounded and sick. Our warmest thanks also to the other noble ladies, as well as gentlemen. All this has inspired us with fresh courage and strength, and we shall, as soon as our health permits, hurry again to the front and join in the fight, until our good right for our dear German country has been gained. In deep devotion,

Reservist, I. DIRNER.
Field Artillery Regiment, Nr. 29, 2nd section.
At present in the Reserve Hospital,
Briegisdedorf-Brieg, near Breslau.

KLEIN-TSCHANSCH, BROCKANER WEG, *December* 9, 1915.

I beg Your Serene Highness to accept my humblest thanks for the greeting sent me through my husband. My husband had the high honour to be received by Your Highness in the Hospital Train from Weisskirchen in Hungary to Oppeln and Brieg on November 28th. May God give Your Highness further strength to comfort our wounded and sick soldiers.

Your humble servant, FRAU LUISE MILDE and Children.

The next one is from Sister Erna, whose English may be almost as shaky as my German, but whose warm heart was strong and sure:

BERLIN, 24.12.15.

DEAREST "SISTER DAISY,"—

My thoughts are often dwelling with you, full of gratitude for all your kind actions. It was through your kindness that I have spent many a charming hour which I shall never forget. The magnificent blouse gave me an immense joy, only it is *much* too beautiful for me. The wounded soldiers in the 6. showed great joy at the gifts from the Sister D. so beloved by all. Dr. Lemke and myself distributed them quite justly, and in every carriage there was great jubilation when Dr. Lemke announced with a voice of thunder: "Here are more gifts from the Princess of Pless." My night watch passed off very lonesome! Unfortunately one of the patients died on the transport at Dr. Bode's station. Now the Train lies again at Magdeburg and celebrates there the festival. I hope you arrived well at Partenkirchen, dearest Princess. May Christmas bring you only agreeable hours. On January 2nd we have to be at Ypsilon; it is also better so, to me only work may render life bearable. I would have preferred to remain at Basias! Fare you well! Once more my warmest thanks! Your always obedient and grateful,

ERNA VON GLASENAPP.

Even now, after all these years, it is good to look over such letters again and to remind oneself that in the midst of all the perplexities and annoyances of the War there were simple, homely, friendly men and women who accepted at its face value what one tried to do, instead of always seeing behind the simplest and most spontaneous act some hateful or even traitorous motive.

CHAPTER ELEVEN

1916

THE year 1916 opened very quietly at Partenkirchen with Lexel and Bolko, or " Baby Bolko " as we always called him. Even now, when he is more than two yards long, Lexel always speaks of him as " my baby brother." They are both such dears and such good pals. From his birth, as my readers know, Bolko's health had been a cause of constant anxiety. There was heart weakness, which, I am happy to say, was gradually overcome as he grew older. He was forbidden to run fast and I think it was at Partenkirchen during those holidays that Lexel was overheard admonishing him : " They say you will die soon anyway, so if I were you I would run as much as I wished and get in all the fun you can before it happens ! "

I wish I could describe the homely naturalness of Bavaria, and the naked-kneed but charming Bavarian Royal Dukes who used constantly to come to see me. We always dined in the nursery after the children had gone to bed. We never used to dress for dinner—all the men wore shorts with bare knees and stockings. These shorts for outdoor and sports wear are made of fine leather dyed brown or grey and ornamented with embroidery and fringes of leather or green silk. With them is worn a loose shirt, embroidered braces, a waistcoat which, for festive occasions, is of green velvet and is often richly and gaily decorated, and decked with silver buttons and fastenings ; a cloth, or sometimes for hunting even a leather jacket is customary, and the costume is completed by a soft green velour hat finished with the high feather aigrette or " brush " which is so characteristic. All over Bavaria this costume is worn by schoolboys just as the sailor-suit is in England and the kilt in Scotland. My boys frequently wore the Bavarian national dress, which is not only picturesque but extremely comfortable and hygienic; carried out in fine embroidered cloth and velvet it is very effective for evening or fancy dress wear.

In the evenings I would change into a fresh blouse and short skirt as everybody would have had a fit if I had worn even a tea-gown—silk would have frightened them. One day I remember asking, as we were all to dress up, what I should wear, and they said "dress as a flower." The only way I could think of to do this was to put some flowers in my hair—quite a mad idea but they liked it.

I will describe one typical evening. My little room was full of greenery and spring flowers, and after dinner we opened the balcony windows, turned out nearly all the lights, and each man produced a harmonica, flute or other instrument and we sang folk-songs and "yodelled." All Germans are of course, almost without exception, natural musicians and devoted to music. Herr Martner had given me a Tyrolean dress, a red silk bodice with a dark flowered silk skirt, and to please him I once put it on over my white silk blouse; I felt it was too awful, but they bravely pretended they didn't and Duke Luitpold even said I looked like a Rubens picture. Afterwards all the servants came in and danced, and my chauffeur sat and smoked as an equal with the Royalties and others. In Silesia, as I know it, this would be unimaginable; indeed no Prussian could have understood it, and it made even me feel rather shy. But Bavarians are extraordinary people. The next day the staff were all perfect servants again as if the music and dancing of the night before had been a dream. I loved those evenings, they were so restful, and I was so tired of what is called Society.

Duke Luitpold once arranged a party to go up in the mountains where there were chamois and caper-

ADOLPHUS FREDERICK VI, GRAND DUKE OF MECKLENBURG-STRELITZ.
His last portrait.

cailzie. It included Princess Othon of Schönburg-Waldenburg, Countess Montjelas,[1] Duke Ludwig Wilhelm[2] and myself. We all motored from Duke Ludwig Wilhelm's house at Kreuth in the mountains, near Tegernsee, until we were so high up that motors could go no further. There I got into a carriage and the others walked. It was the most glorious evening. We went up and up till we saw the chamois quite near us, and the ground was covered with strange little low-growing wild flowers. At last we got to the hut where we were to spend the night. I had suggested bringing some food from Partenkirchen, but Duke Luitpold said that it was unnecessary—simple provisions such as war-bread, biscuits, eggs, and butter, would be there. So I only took three oranges, which was unlucky, as all that we found in the hut was a very little butter, some bread, apples and that awful red sausage full of garlic. I had a spoon in my little basket and that had to do for everything. We stirred our tea (which luckily someone had brought) and spread our butter with the handle of it. But it was so remote and beautiful that I felt peaceful and at rest. We were all happy. We had two guitars and we played and sang and even danced.

We were to start about two o'clock the next morning, so we all went to bed early and I did not undress. I stupidly blew out my bit of candle, lay down on the straw mattress and then felt for a rug to pull over me. I had no matches—they were very precious then—so I didn't know what to do when I stupidly couldn't find the rug in the dark. I got up, fumbled about and at last found the door handle, opened the door and called out "please someone come here."

After a moment another door opened, and Duke Luitpold came out with bare legs and a coat. He is a very economical man, but nice, and I knew he would

[1] Wife of the Foreign Office official who was at that time in charge of American affairs.

[2] Son of the late Duke Karl Theodore and brother of the Queen of the Belgians. In March, 1917, he married Princess Othon of Schönburg-Waldenburg, her husband having been killed at Reims in September, 1914.

never give me a whole box, so I asked him for just one match. He struck one, gave it to me and shut the door, and I walked carefully towards the candle. Of course when I got there I had nothing but a thin red line in my fingers. So out I went again, this time with my candle, and shouted, and he came and lit it for me with a generous second match. I thought he would be furious, but he was very kind about it.

I could not sleep and about two o'clock, after a good deal of rumbling had been going on, someone called out that we must start in ten minutes. So up I got, still matchless, in the pitch dark.

Duke Ludwig Wilhelm walked in front with a lantern. Princess Schönburg and the little Countess Monjelas were angels to me. Even then I could not walk very well, particularly in the dark. I had a stick, and darling Lory Schönburg wanted me to lean on her. Of course, I couldn't lean on a woman, and every now and then we all three stopped to rest. After a short time Duke Luitpold saw I was in difficulties and told me to lean on him. I hated to do this, as I could not bear to be a bother to him when he had arranged all this so that I might shoot a capercailzie. In the end we compromised and I put my hand in his coat pocket. We got into bogs of half-melted snow; but, alas, there was no sunrise. It poured and poured with rain—we were drenched. I had on my mackintosh coat and skirt which let in more rain than any good tweed. Moreover, the skirt made such a noise as I walked that not only should we have been unable to hear the capercailzie, but the noise would have frightened them away. So I took it off and hung it on a bush. Underneath I had a pair of brown silk knickerbockers, brown stockings and high boots. So I pulled my jersey down as far as I could and we went on and on.

After two hours' walking we had to admit that it was no good. So we returned to the hut and had some more tea and hard bread. The others walked and I went in the carriage down to Duke Ludwig Wilhelm's house where at last we had a square meal—cold ham, bread and butter and sherry. When I got back to the funny little hotel I thought it must be at least two o'clock in the afternoon, instead of which it was only half-past nine in the morning. I had a bath in a borrowed india-rubber bath, but thank goodness I got some hot water. After that I went to sleep.

That evening I dined with Princess Schönburg and her mother, Princess Wittgenstein. Countess Montjelas and I danced, dressed up in dressing-gowns, odd bits of chiffon—anything we could find.

We did a lot of tobogganing and skating and there were many pleasant people at Partenkirchen at the time, including young Bismarck, a nice boy, grandson of the great Prince, and with plenty of the family intelligence. He recently married Mademoiselle Annie Tengbom, a Scandinavian lady I think, and is now a Secretary at the German Embassy in London.

II

It has already been hinted that in my opinion as early as 1915 the Emperor was no longer "all powerful" in Germany. This was, I think, proved by what happened about my going on Lazarett Train Y. In spite of the direct orders of His Majesty, Professor von Kuester was not only reprimanded for allowing me to continue on the Train, but was dismissed for doing so "without the permission of the Military Authorities in Berlin." Not only was he dismissed; he was placed under arrest for twenty-four hours. I was furious and wrote to the Empress, Prince Eitel Fritz, and every one else I could think of. The poor Professor was naturally in despair and I, who had brought all this trouble upon him, could do nothing.

To aggravate matters, scandal-mongers had circulated a story that a luxurious saloon coach had been put on the Y Train specially for my accommodation. It did not, of course, specify which high officials had been suborned in order to secure me this unobtainable privilege. I thought it well to write to Countess Brockdorff pointing out that the "saloon coach" consisted of an old third-class carriage with three compartments, each with wooden seats. I had one of these, my maid Elsa (who turned her hand to anything that wanted doing in the Train) the other, and the remaining compartment, part of one of the seats had been cut away to make room for a desk and a cupboard, the Sisters and I used as a rest room and store for all sorts of necessary odds and ends. In fact, I had similar accommodation to the doctors, accountants and the military escort.

I was relieved to learn that neither the Empress nor Countess Brockdorff believed a word of this nonsense—but many people did.

At the end of January I was in Munich for a few days and hearing that the Lichnowskys were there I telephoned asking the Prince to come and see me; I knew his wife could not do so as she had just lost her father, Count Maximilian von Arco-Zinneberg. My diary gives the following account of the interview:

January 30, 1916. Munich.

To talk to poor Prince Lichnowsky last night was really sad; and to see him again as I did at tea to-day. He is frightfully depressed, feeling that the Emperor and others blame him for the war between England and Germany. He seems to think still that because they were so nice to him and his wife Mechtilde in London that it meant that the political feeling against Germany had absolutely died. I cannot quite think this. The commercial jealousy was always there and in England they would *not* disbelieve in the idea of a German invasion and often talked of it; it was like a red rag to a bull.

Lichnowsky said to me, which I have maintained all along, that Austria ought to have accepted the submission of Serbia, as the Serbians had conceded everything, except the absurd stipulation that all her Ministers should be nominated by Austria[1]: they insisted upon appointing *some* of their own. All this could have been arranged and in time the Austrians

[1] If Austria made this "absurd stipulation," the fact has never become publicly known. Unfortunately Prince Lichnowsky cannot now be consulted about it.

and Hungarians would have taken up these posts quietly with tact and without fuss.

Lichnowsky also told me something which astonishes me, and which I must find out more about. He said that Germany could have forced Austria to have accepted Serbia's submission and that Berchtold, the Austrian Foreign Minister, would have done anything that the German Emperor and his Government dictated to him. Lichnowsky insists that the whole beginnings of this war was the fault of Germany; also that if the Germans had *not* crossed the frontier into Belgium, Belgium would have remained neutral.

What is a woman to think, or indeed the cleverest man, when a former German Ambassador in London tells her this: and the German Emperor tells her, as he told me in Pless, that the King of the Belgians refused to remain neutral; that he himself personally talked on the telephone to King Albert before the War broke out, saying that if Belgium would remain neutral the Germans would not cross the Belgian frontier; the King of the Belgians refused.[1]

January 31, 1916. In the train on my way to Fürstenstein.

Let me write here what I think, and we will see if one little bit of it comes true. Let me just state the facts which are borne out by my diaries and by copies of letters to Hans, written seven years ago when he proposed to enlarge and rebuild Fürstenstein. I begged him not to do so, saying there would be war, succession duty and many other things, and that it would bring him bad luck. Another thing. When *he* and others told me last Christmas that France would make a separate agreement, I laughed and said: "Do you ever read the papers; what do you all think in the Hauptquartier; you all seem blind. I see *no* possibility of a separate agreement in any single country: Serbia might be paid by Italy (that means by England), perhaps to lay down her arms. . . . France will certainly make no separate peace and England will go on for at least another two years until Germany wants peace and asks for it. The men here in Germany are getting more and more tired, and there will soon be no more left.

---

[1] On July 24, 1914, the Government publicly declared that Belgium would uphold her neutrality "whatever the consequences"; on the same day the German Government sent to the Entente Governments a note approving of the Austrian ultimatum to Serbia; and Sir Edward Grey, the British Foreign Minister, proposed an international conference in order to avert war.

In England itself there may be little money, but all her Colonies are rich and India will give her what she chooses to ask. . . .

India wants her freedom, and a little while ago hated the English Government—but now what has happened? They are to be given their full freedom, but as one of England's Colonies. They will have their own representatives and their House of Parliament. The high-caste men of India are exceedingly well educated, better than many Englishmen; they have been to Oxford or Cambridge or to Universities in America; they know France well and also other countries and speak many languages. They have seen now, as all Europe sees with astonishment, the absolute gathering together of all England's Colonies with open arms towards the mother-country. . . .

All these Colonies of England have come together like men answering to a mother's cry, and India has done the same for the simple reason that she sees herself free and acknowledged equal. Even South Africa has done the same, a country which only sixteen years ago was fighting England. England gave it a free government. This was a surprise at the time to every German—even to Dr. Solf the Colonial Minister. . . .

Before I got into this train I saw Prince F—— L——. He is not in the war and pretends to have a bad heart. He wears an orchid, far too much jewellery and smiles. . . . He is not really a man.

At Fürstenstein I visited all the hospitals and convalescent homes, entertained sick and wounded soldiers, had conferences with our General Director and did all the usual things.

I was, of course, still trying to get appointed to another Lazarett Train; meanwhile there was nothing to do but go on as usual. About the end of February poor Emmanuel Salm-Salm was exchanged for dear Colonel Gordon. I was delighted for both their sakes; Colonel Gordon got back to his wife and child in England, and Emmanuel and Christa were released from their captivity in Gibraltar. Emmanuel[1] rejoined his regiment a few days after he got back. I must not forget to say that before he left Colonel Gordon wrote me a delightful letter in which he spoke of

[1] Prince Emmanuel Salm-Salm was killed at the battle of Pinsk, August 19, 1916.

his Camp Commandant, " kind Baron von Lochow, who for me is the very ideal of a chivalrous knight."

On February 23, Hans wrote me: " People in Silesia are talking a lot about Conny being in Switzerland and meeting so many Englishmen. If you went too, it would be madness. The war is nearing its very end now so you can wait for a few months longer before you see Shelagh." Alas! it was not true. By March 5, he had changed his mind and wrote me from Great Headquarters: " Everything is going very well, but it will take some time. The resisting power and pluck of the French is beyond praise. They attack places we have taken, over and over again, and retake them with a tremendous loss of men. All this is very good, although it makes our progress a bit more slow. But it shows what importance the French attach to the place, so when it falls, the moral blow will be tremendous.[1] Now I must finish as I am awfully tired."

So much for what they knew about it all at Great Headquarters. That " resisting power and pluck " of both French and English was something no German could have measured beforehand, and Verdun never fell. One of their greatest national failings is an inability to judge others or put themselves in the other man's place. I think we English have that failing, also the French, but the Germans have it worst of all. On March 14, Hans was even more cautious and wrote: " But it will take several weeks before we get this place. The Emperor cannot go to the front, at least not where we go, so he has to sit the whole time at the H.Q., which bores him tremendously."

I was so touched by what Colonel Gordon had told me of the visit of Prince Max of Baden to Blankenburg and its effect on the prisoners that I wrote to the Prince to thank him and tell him how much his friendly action was appreciated; I, of course, seized

[1] The reference is to the battle of Verdun, which began on February 21 and lasted till August 31, 1916.

the opportunity of asking his help about one or two matters. I also told him the glad news that I had got another Lazarett Train. His reply, written in English, is that of a Christian gentleman:

KARLSRÜHE, 31.3.16.

DEAR PRINCESS OF PLESS,—

I just received your very kind letter, and have to thank you for it.

What you have heard from your English officers concerning my visits to them really interests me. Of course all prisoners are unhappy, and therefore ready to value any sign of sympathy more than in normal times. I feel this very distinctly, and am consequently happy if I can be of some help to them in any way.

I am glad to have made the acquaintance of Colonel Gordon, in whom I found a most rare and charming nature and character. Lieutenant Alastair Robertson I also remembered having seen.

I will see what I can do for your friends, but before I can do anything I beg you to be so kind and tell me in which camp Captain Keppel is to be found. . . .

I sympathize with all those who are not born in the country they live in and belong to one of the belligerent nations; it is a hard lot, more especially in a war like this, which has awakened the worst passions. My mother having been a Russian [1] I am able to understand this particularly well.

I am glad for you that you are nursing in a hospital train. Work is the only thing to make one forget, and in face of the wounded there is no difference between friend or foe. On this ground every right-thinking person will find full understanding all over the world.

I think the last time we met we were at Grosvenor House in London during the Coronation: it was then I saw the *Blue Boy*. Maybe we met again at the wedding of my brother-in-law and Princess Victoria? [2]

Once more I will do what I can to please you and your friends, only I too must spare my words of intercession for those cases which need them most. Please to believe me, dear Princess, Yours very sincerely,

MAX PRINCE OF BADEN.

---

[1] Princess Marie-Maximilianovna, Duchess of Leuchtenberg.

[2] Ernest Augustus, reigning Duke of Brunswick, married Princess Victoria Louisa of Prussia in 1913; Prince Max married Duke Ernest's sister, Princess Marie Louise of Brunswick.

III

Towards the end of March I had received the news that at last I had got another Lazarett Train and hurried back to Partenkirchen to see the boys and arrange things there. My diary says:

March 30, 1916. Partenkirchen.

This is my fourth day here and I leave on Saturday to get to Berlin on Sunday morning. Thank God all is arranged about the Lazarett Train and I have permission to go on it. It belongs to Herr von Friedländer; he is a rich Jew and pays everything. How well I remember about six or eight years ago saying to Hans, when he laughed at the way Jews were received in English society: "You will see it here some day, one wants their brains and one wants their money. Every Court has to accept the nicest of them—and there are very nice Jews."[1] Directly after that Friedländer was made "von" and another Jew, Schwabach, was also made "von," and both their wives go to Court. I dined with the Friedländers in Berlin the other night and their house is a perfectly magnificent one, full of the most lovely things, and in excellent taste.

On April 2, the Grand Duchess Augusta wrote to me:

To-day's account of those terrible Bombs thrown in London affects me deeply.[2] I can hardly keep up more, my poor heart, really brave hitherto, now trembles.

Am I really to leave you a Souvenir? I will do so, at your risk. When in May your visit really may come off, I hope you will see little Strelitz at its best, see the many changes, some improvements, my dear Fred is making; he is well and ever a comfort to the old "Granny" who often thinks affectionately of you!

And now I must let my diary tell something of what life was like on my new Lazarett Train D.3:

April 29, 1916. Lazarettzug D.3.

We are at Sainte Avold in Lorraine, waiting to go up somewhere to bring the wounded down; I am in all comfort, I have

---

[1] See pages 66 and 67.

[2] On March 31 there was a German airship raid on England. The German Airship "L.15" was brought down by gunfire near the mouth of the Thames.

quite a big bedroom, two compartments turned into one; two washing basins and my own private *cabinet*; next door where I now write I have another little room with two tables, two armchairs, my *chaise longue*, and nice little cretonne curtains. And in my bedroom I have all the little curtains of black cretonne with pink roses that I had in the other Lazarett Train; all the wood, and the beds for the wounded, is painted white, so everything is bright and clean. Yet somehow I miss terribly my dear old Professor von Kuester and Doctor Lemke, who was so intelligent and talks and writes beautiful English. I often think of the awful way they have treated Professor von Kuester and still nothing is done.

One morning I got up at half-past five and at half-past six went for a walk alone right in some woods—and oh! the birds sang in a way impossible to describe; every bird in a sort of rapture at the sunshine and the fully developed spring; and then in the distance one heard a sort of low thud-like thunder; and one knew the guns were at work. God, how sad I felt as the birds sang; and in a ditch near by were growing those yellow water kingcups which thrive in the lake at Newlands, and I could picture them all there. But now I must drop these thoughts and live, and think only of, the life which is before me till the War ends. . . .

Wine is drunk at lunch and beer at supper (which is just a homely cold affair); as I eat nothing they became quite anxious, and are touchingly sympathetic, so to please them I ate two eggs yesterday, and the day before, and they got some fresh butter and milk specially for me. I brought by mistake a gramophone (it ought to have been sent to Salzbrunn). And in Metz we just had time to snatch up some new records for it, and it is really a delight to them all: it is in the little sitting-room and they play it all the time. . . .

I was forgetting to say that at Gravelotte when we visited the museum an old woman was there selling post-cards; I guessed she was French and had seen the war of 1870 just on that spot. When I spoke French to her the poor dear old face changed; she had been looking so sadly out of the window; she said her German would never be perfect, though I could see how she was trying. Did she (or God perhaps) guess what I felt then when talking to her, and thinking of my hills in France, my land there by the sea, all those I so love in England, and my Granny. This old shop-woman had lost one son, one was still at the front (German of course), and the other a prisoner in Russia; I was careful to say very little as the doctor stood near me and I had a feeling he did not like it. . . .

The whole of the fields and all the " world " outside Metz seems a bare desert as the trees which used to stand there have been cut down now—for clearer sight and *Schützengraben*, cannons, supports for hidden mines, and so on. And of course Gravelotte and St. Privat are old great bare battle-fields with little white crosses—everywhere; and now and then a single tree; and then the many Memorials put up by the different countries, Baden, Saxony, Prussia, and so on in remembrance of their regiments in 1870. High on one little hill is a big stone where the Emperor William I., then only King of Prussia, once stood to watch the victory of Malmaison Hohe. . . .

The stone bears a lion, which somehow one had thought of only as a symbol of England's power! and oh! diary, as I stood in Pless in 1914 in a Sister's dress and was photographed by the doctor from the Lazarett, with my hand resting on the wall near a carved lion, I thought then: " That Lion is English; I am English; Europe is at war." And now on the old battle-field of Gravelotte I see again a lion; and the thought comes to me: " No Zeppelins over England will stop that Lion's roar." Dear England, suffering so. Germany is all pride and marvellous determination and courage worthy of the greatest respect. Does she go begging for men to join her colour and fight for their country? Oh, diary, and you English men and women, let me tell you with tears in my eyes that a wife here in Germany (at least in Prussia) is proud to send her husband out to fight and the children cheer him as he goes. I see in the papers that Asquith called a private meeting for the enlistment of married men and if by the 25th of May fifty thousand men, whether married or not, do not come forward they are to be fetched.[1] And Lord Crewe made a speech to the same effect, and it was to him in his own house, the month of May, 1914, on my way to Germany, that I said: " Make your men into soldiers; have compulsory service, it will do the men all the good in the world." I saw then no immediate danger of war but I thought how nice all my German footmen were, strong and straight and honest. And alone in his room Lord Crewe said to me: " No, we have neither the

[1] The Second Military Service Bill extending compulsion to married men passed the House of Commons on May 16, and became law on May 25, 1916.

money nor the necessity ; we have our Navy, which is all that England will ever want." And now two years has made all this change and I see no end. And I have a longing like a thirst to speak with those I love. As I crossed into France yesterday, and as we shall go to-morrow to Mars la Tour from Metz, I thought how easy it would be for me, with courage and money, to get into a cottage, cut my hair, dress up as a man, live hidden while I am searched for, and somehow get into the French lines and be sent to England. And as I write this a train passes loaded with *coal*; and I suddenly realize I am the wife of a German coal-owner. . . . And I should be treated here as a rebel, and not allowed to see my boys again. I have been through so much that somehow my courage seems to have left me ; such an attempt would require bodily courage as well as careful thinking. I had better wait.

IV

When the Train got back from France I was given leave. This happened very irregularly. If things were quiet at the front we would make one journey and perhaps have a long rest ; if the fighting was severe we went back and forward continuously as long as we were wanted.

I went to Fürstenstein and my diary says :

May 14, 1916. Fürstenstein.

I have been all over the building with Hans and just smiled and pretended I thought it all beautiful, or at least it would be so. I went into my old bedroom with the two architects. We talked of where the fireplace would be, where the door would be, and so on. But it all seemed to jeer at me, as much as to say : " Yes, you are right," for somehow I still feel and have always felt, as my diary will show since years, that this building will bring ill-luck to the family, that I shall never entertain in the new part of the house. Even if there was no war and one was to work as hard as one could, with a hundred men a day, it could not be finished for another six or seven years.

From Fürstenstein I again went to Strelitz to see my dear Grand Duchess. I wrote an account of the visit in my diary when I got back home. Here it is :

May 26, 1916. Fürstenstein.

The time in Strelitz was very pleasant. The Grand Duke was charming and nice, the same gentleman as always; but I got very tired, having to go from one house to the other, and one room to another, to help him to try and arrange things. He is going on with that little Park House villa which I think is awful. . . .

His mother must have been beautiful as a girl and has lovely eyes. One day we went into her drawing-room for tea, the Grand Duke wanted to put me next his Grandmother, but I at once said: "No, you sit there, I have been asked to tea by your mother and shall sit next to her and talk German, which is the most tactful thing to do." . . .

The poor lady had postponed her tea a whole hour, so of course it mixed up with her dinner, and she did this only to please the Dowager Grand Duchess, who will not adopt the new summer time. The lady-in-waiting to the Grand Duke's mother turned to me and said quite shyly: "Do you go by the old time or the new time?" I answered: "I go by the time of all Germany."

Really that time-question in Strelitz muddled us all fearfully, even Hélène and Elsa; I promised to go to one lady at ten and the other at nine, and tea with the other at five, and dinner at half-past seven. One never knew what time was what.

One day after having been on my legs and being polite all day long I lay on the sofa in my bedroom and rested. I said to Elsa: "I am dining with the Dowager Grand Duchess at her time, so how long have I got before dinner?" She said an hour and a half. "That is good; I'll lie down here for an hour and tidy myself in half an hour." Presently there was a knock at the door. I was too lazy to move and simply said rather irritably "Come in," and I kept on saying it each time the knock was repeated.

Suddenly the door opened and the Grand Duke's head appeared. He looked at me in absolute astonishment and I at him. He said: "It is dinner; it is on the table." And then I said: "I do not understand how it got there an hour sooner," and so on. We argued quite amicably for a second and laughed and I said: "Well, because of all this changing of the clocks on every side of the house one never knows where one is or what time it is: do not wait for me, I will be ready in half an hour; don't be cross," and he wasn't.

A few days after I wrote this account of my Strelitz visit I was again back in the Lazarett Train. I will quote from my diary just a few passages that give an idea of how one felt and wrote at the time:

June 1, 1916. Lazarettzug D.3. Valleroy, between Briey and Conflans.

Yesterday morning we walked in a meadow near a wood; Sister went further on with her doctor, and I stayed with mine and the *rechnung-führer* (financial manager) on a hill with a view and we sat on some damp hay. The nightingale sang; we stopped talking and listened: and the guns shook the air at the same time and scarcely an interval of peace. We found a bird's nest—the bird remained sitting; and the grass was a mass of spring colouring—every wild flower more beautiful than any of God's angels could have thought of in all Heaven. Contrasts, yes; they are the bricks of which our life is built, but oh! how the difference sometimes hurts. I passed a garden yesterday which is quite close to the train, and the air was delicious, full of the scent of the white Mrs. Sinkins picotee carnations; how I longed for a few to remind me of little Patsy's garden. I leaned over the gate and dared for once in a sort of hungry misery to talk French and ask the girl to give me one; but she did not wish to, saying they belonged to her mother. "She did not wish to," thinking I was German! And I longed to tell her the truth; but the others near would have understood. Oh! what these two years have taught me I never wish to think of again. I long to go back to Strelitz and see the darling old Grand Duchess. It comforts me to be near her and that dear, great gentleman her grandson.

Seven o'clock.

I am washed and tidied, having been out for a walk by myself. I jumped from the carriage and walked quickly in the wet grass, straight on, straight on, for fear that someone would see me and want to come too. I walked for one and a half hours near the river, passed over the railway lines, met two soldiers on horseback; they bowed, which is the "right thing" to do to a "Sister." Twice I fell in the slippery mud. . . .

Oh! diary, you cannot think what it is to be alone—with the distant thunder of guns—and then to reach down and pick a great bunch of some wild flowers. I never saw so many different sorts as the spring in France shows. And as you break the twigs, out of the grass fly the partridges; and oh! the larks! It was as if the air was laughing. The guns in the distance drive the birds away, so they come back down here where it is quieter. I was absolutely alone and thought of those I loved.

While I was near Metz, Prince Eitel Fritz was near Noyon, only about seventy miles from Paris, and from a hill near by could see the Eiffel Tower and the Sacré Cœur. I wrote to him asking for his help to have Professor von Kuester's wrongs investigated, but even he could do little, although his heart was full of goodwill. Like me, he loves Nature and, as thousands of soldiers have done, found his comfort in sunsets and flowers, having discovered that "every plant has its soul and its little will to be itself": he hated that by the War "the green meadow was wounded," and he knew that although people were often disappointing, Nature never was.

June 7, 1916.

Yesterday we drove in a shaky old carriage to Château Ficheroy, which they say was thought of for the Emperor as Headquarters. It is an ugly house with a nice old bridge and belongs to the owner of one of the iron mines. It was not chosen as a Headquarters being too near the river Orne (upon which I have tried for an hour to fish), and which being broad and very curved, is a distinct mark for the French flying machines. I cannot bring myself to write "Enemy flying machines"; they are not my enemies. I feel enmity towards no one; except the lying Press Agencies of all countries; and the Jew money grabbers and men of the Bourses of all countries; looking with jealous eyes on those eating out of the same dish as themselves, not hungry as a dog or other animal might be, but hungry for gold—which is now being paid for by blood.

Yesterday the news came of the loss of seven hundred lives off the Orkney Islands,[1] nine English boats being destroyed; *Queen Mary*, *Marlborough*, a cruiser and so on; one will see

[1] Battle of Jutland, May 31–June 1, 1916.

what the English Press say; two German boats destroyed[1]; at least this is the first Naval encounter of the two nations, and right up on the North of Scotland Germany with her mines and *Untersee* boats has done the best. Oh! I laughed at the dismissal of Tirpitz knowing it (as it will prove) to be a bluff just to make the Allied and Neutral nations believe that the German Navy intended to keep quiet.

Now to-day the news has come that thirteen thousand Austrians have been taken prisoners by the Russians.[2] . . . Oh! Austria, Austria, I love you; you are near me in feeling and I near you; and Prussia is like a cold hard unsympathetic mountain farther than the North Pole; I do not touch it and it is not near me, as I have always said; Silesia is to me different; and the only reason being that it once belonged to Austria before being snatched from a Queen's hand by Frederick the Great. The Austrians may not be great warriors but they are great gentlemen. . . .

Oh, diary, to-night the papers say that Kitchener and his Staff, on their way to Russia, have all been drowned.[3] I left London Saturday, the 1st of August, 1914, and I had sat next to him at lunch on Wednesday the 29th with Prince and Princess Lichnowsky at the German Embassy; at least I think these dates are right. I said to him, as there was an idea of his returning to Egypt: "Don't go; you are wanted in England, there is no one." I meant for home politics; the Irish Question and so on. I did not think of war then; I even begged him to stay in England and marry, and he looked at me through his dear bright but strange eyes, as one didn't match the other, and laughed. And now the German papers say he is drowned. I—close this book and pray that this is not true.

At this time Smith, friend to me and faithful nurse to my children, was at Kassel. I had sent her a little snapshot of the boys taken outside Promnitz and she wrote me such a warm, affectionate letter. It was queer where one found comfort during the War. Smith's chief solace was a maid in the household of Princess Frederick Sigismund of Württemberg

[1] The *Marlborough* was not amongst the six British ships sunk; the Germans also lost six ships.

[2] "Brusilov's Offensive" began on June 4, 1916.

[3] H.M.S. *Hampshire* sunk by a mine off the Orkneys, June 5, 1916.

who had been in France and England. She had often seen our Villa Liberia at Mandelieu, had lived for seventeen years with Miss Minnie Cochrane (who all her life has been Lady-in-Waiting to Princess Beatrice of Great Britain); the maid therefore also knew Milford-on-Sea and Lymington and the New Forest. I could so well understand Smith appreciating her.

Sometimes the ache to speak directly to an Englishman was unbearable. My diary describes an incident that bears this out. We were waiting at Caudry for our wounded and I was asked if I would care to visit a Hospital in the neighbourhood:

Now I am just back. A charming old *Oberleutnant* came with us, a middle-aged man, who gave me a book of the Hospital and who took me round to see everything. He let me speak to the Englishmen, although it was all in a hurry, as our Head Doctor who accompanied us thought only of his stomach and wanted to get back for luncheon! But I had just time to slip into the hand of an officer called Major Craig a piece of paper quite small, which I had pinned ready into my blouse and on which I had written how I would give all the world to be lying ill amongst them, that I was a sister of the Duchess of Westminster, and that my heart was with them all and I wished them a quick return to health. He was sensible enough to take the paper, doubled up like a pill, and not open it. I only pray God he will keep it a secret and not show it to a soul, otherwise they will say the most devilish things against me because I wrote a kind word to a wounded Englishman. I should be shut up in Germany.

The guns are booming; now they have announced that infernal lunch, so I must go and eat, but I do not wish to do so; and I must smile and say how marvellous the Hospital was; and no one knows what I felt—and wrote—and did—or of the little bit of paper I gave to Major Craig.

God help me! a miserable Lazarett Train stopped close to ours; we had time to go and look at it and found it was full of wounded English. I took Herr Rath with me (without the others seeing), and spoke to two of them. The window was opened; one was a Major Brown, he gave me his address asking me to write to his mother, close to Winchester. I told him it was quite near my mother; I spoke to another, but did not dare go in; it smelt dreadfully and the wounded told me it was full of lice! One soldier on board was dead and I longed to find his body and put a little flower on it! Now more English are coming; but I shall stay in my cabin, I cannot bear it; as I may do nothing for them, nor talk with them, except on the sly. I am a *German nurse* and in German uniform.

The work begins in half an hour and it is now four o'clock; I expect we shall load till eight; then travel all night, come back at once, and start again. Why did they send us suddenly to this Army, I wonder, right close to the front! Was it because I was on the Train, and they wished to torture me? God help me soon, but only death can set me free!

V

Most of our fine Silesians were excellent soldiers and such charming, grateful patients. As in every other country, it was those who stayed at home who were hard-hearted and malicious. When I got thoroughly hopeless and depressed, weighed down with the futility of my poor personal efforts in face of such a vast need, I would get a letter like this and take heart again. It was from a main hospital at Ingolstadt, was of course written in German; dated June 11:

MOST GRACIOUS PRINCESS OF PLESS,—

I like this very much, but it was much nicer in the Hospital Train as I was quite unexpectedly given the joy of seeing my most Gracious Princess. I shall not forget this day in all my life, when I was permitted to speak to my Princess in person; to few of our dear Silesians is given the privilege of meeting our dear Princess as Sister in the Hospital Train. By these lines I send, from my comrades and myself, our very best greetings and our deepest respect. . . .

Some time before this I had written to the Grand Duchess Augusta enclosing a letter for the Empress Eugénie, which I begged her to send on. In her reply she deplores the death of Lord Kitchener:

We have been and are passing through painful, sad and trying times; it is all I can do to keep up, yet my faith is the same, good must come after evil days. The death, the tragic end of our great man, struck me down so deeply! My faith (earthly one) was placed upon that firm rock! He was the "friend" the King proclaimed him to have been, well deserved; *they both*[1] deplore his death as he deserved; still their courage never fails.

You kindly are interested in my health; I was much upset for a time, now am better; letters from Home help me on. Your note to Emp. E. reached her safely; all my dear Nieces write such kind letters, always thinking of me when they meet, to hear my last news as to how I am going on. I am glad to have my dear "Regnant"[2] here for a time, am expecting his sisters' visit shortly; both are rays of sunshine to "old Granny," she, who thinks of you so often and wishes you so well. A. C.

I was as happy and content in my Hospital Train as anyone had any right to expect to be during the War. I was the Sister responsible for the Operation Carriage and eight other carriages, eighty patients in all. The constant occupation and trying to relieve the pain of others enabled me to forget my own.

Bolko at this time was at Heringsdorf on the Mecklenburg coast with his governess and fell and broke his arm. I was given ten days' leave to go and see him. Fortunately a child's broken bone heals easily; he slept well, was good and merry and had no fever and no pain. The change of surroundings did me lots of good.

Take what care I would, I was always getting into rows about something! Once when the Lazarett Train was at Magdeburg, I had an hour to spare before I need leave Berlin to join it. I decided to go to church, of course in my Sister's uniform, as I would not have had time to go at all had I stopped to change it. There was no end of a fuss about this. I always think that one reason why Germany lost the War was because everybody would stop anything, however important, to kick up a fuss about something that was nothing. I handed the whole incident over to Hans and, after a long time, he wrote:

---

[1] The King and Queen of England.
[2] The Grand Duke Adolphus.

GROSSES HAUPTQUARTIER, *July* 21, 1916.

Germany is, as you know, the country of regulations, therefore everything is *überlegt* (well-weighed) about several times, carefully looked after, if it is in conformity with the existing regulations, and then it goes through the official channel, which takes a lot of time. If somebody dares to do it differently, he gets at once into hot water. That was also the reason for the report, that you went to church in Berlin in nurse's dress. By the regulations this dress is only allowed to be worn out of doors by the professional *Schwestern*, just the same as only soldiers are allowed to wear uniform, and every civilian doing it would be prosecuted. When I explained it, that you wore it because you had to catch the train directly after church, it was all right.

I am glad little Bolko is better. . . .

The newspapers which announced that on your birthday the English flag was hoisted in Salzbrunn, had all to deny it. It was simply the West colours, red and blue, which some idiot mistook for the English colours

We are just in the midst of what is I think a decisive battle on the Somme [1]; decisive, as far as the French are concerned, because England will go on fighting even if France makes peace. But this will be easier work, as it is now. By the reports at hand to-day, the losses seem to be terrific on the English and French side. If you meet English wounded out where you are, be very careful with them, or there will be some new gossip. (By the way, I don't think that the Duchess of Connaught who was a German would bother very much about German wounded.) *Le jeu ne vaut pas la chandelle.*

I am glad you saw Hansel. He must look very nice as an Hussar. . . .

This new commercial submarine [2] is a marvellous thing. Can you imagine that she brings in one single trip the whole indiarubber which is necessary for the whole German army during one year. Three hundred tons. But it is the truth. . . .

The flag incident, to which Hans refers, was most annoying. Although I was not there, they followed the usual custom and flew flags with the West coat-

[1] The Battle of the Somme (1916) began with the battle of Albert (1916) on July 1.

[2] The *Deutschland* "commercial submarine" arrived at Norfolk (Va.) on July 10, and returned to Germany on August 23, 1916.

MY ELDEST SON, HANSEL.
In 1919.

of-arms and of the West colours at Fürstenstein on my birthday. Several stupid newspapers got hold of this and published statements saying that it was the Union Jack that was flown, and, of course, blamed me although I was hundreds of miles away and did not even know they were flying flags at all. In fact, I had forbidden them to take any notice of my birthday.

About this time dear Princess Vicy of Schaumburg-Lippe lost her husband.[1] We exchanged constant letters, but what can one really do on such occasions. She went to her sister, Princess Mossy, at Schloss Friedrichshof, the lovely home which the Empress Frederick had herself built near Cronberg, in Taunus, and where I first stayed with her as a shy, young bride. I was glad the sisters could be there together because Friedrichshof is a place of healing. Something of the gracious and sympathetic spirit of its creator remains, and always shall remain.

Very soon after her visit to Friedrichshof the Lazarett Train was going near Bonn and, on the off chance, I wired to Princess Vicy to see if she was there. My diary says:

> Yesterday we unloaded wounded, some of them at Bonn. I had wired to Princess Vicy and she sent her car and her Lady-in-Waiting to the Station and I rushed off to see her. I was dirty and untidy, having got up at half-past six; but I washed my hands in the Palace (I call it a villa) and we talked for just fifteen minutes, and I had to rush back to the Train. She is somehow a lonely woman, although an Emperor's sister. . . .

The following letter from my husband describes the Emperor and the Great Headquarters Staff hurrying off from France to attend an important conference at Pless:

> PLESS, *July* 28, 1916.
>
> On Saturday last after dinner—it was half-past ten at night—the Emperor asked me, at Charleville, if he could come to

[1] Prince Adolphus of Schaumburg-Lippe, uncle of the present Prince, died July 9, 1916.

Pless at once, and how long it would take to get the place in order. . . . I said twenty-four hours. So he said he would leave France on Monday the 24th and arrive at Pless on Tuesday night.

At nine p.m. the Emperor got here with all his people, and Jagow of the Foreign Office; at eleven at night Bethmann-Hollweg the Chancellor came; the next morning Hindenburg with Ludendorff and three Staff officers arrived. Lots of important conferences, which turned out well, were held.

Yesterday (27th), in the afternoon, the Crown Prince Boris of Bulgaria arrived with General Tchov, the Bulgarian Commander-in-Chief; and one hour later the Archduke Frederic arrived from Teschen.[1] General Conrad [2] and two other Austrians got here only at eight for dinner. Private conference between the Emperor and the Archduke from six to eight o'clock. At dinner, the most historical which ever took place at Pless, the absence of General von Falkenhayn was much commented on; he "had a bad toothache"!

All the Austrians left about midnight, but the others are all still here. The Emperor had intended to go back to the West to-day, the 28th, but is now staying till over Sunday, and perhaps a few days longer. The Crown Prince of Bulgaria, a charming boy, is occupying your rooms, as the whole house is chock full. Important decisions have been taken, which will probably do us good. Hindenburg and his Staff leave to-night or to-morrow; the Chancellor remains here, I don't know till when. That is all the news in brief. . . . About the result of the conference it is not difficult to guess.[3]

PLESS, *July* 30, 1916.

. . . Hindenburg and his Staff left on Friday night. I think that everything is arranged for the best. The Crown Prince of Bulgaria and his people left yesterday (Friday) afternoon. The Chancellor and Jagow are still here.

---

[1] The residence of Field-Marshal the Archduke Frederic (father of Princess Salm-Salm, and brother of the Queen Dowager of Spain).

[2] Field-Marshal Conrad von Hötzendorff, Commander-in-Chief of the Austro-Hungarian Armies, relieved of his command July 16, 1918.

[3] On August 29, 1916, Field-Marshal von Hindenburg succeeded General von Falkenhayn as Chief of Staff of the German Field Armies, and General Ludendorff was appointed Chief Quartermaster-General, German General Staff.

All this time I was in great anxiety about my father's health, as I had heard that he had been in a serious motor accident; it had even been rumoured that he was killed. I had a short leave and on September 4 I went to Friedrichshof to stay for a few days with Princess Mossy and her sister Princess Vicy, who was again staying with her. One evening we looked up my name in her mother's Visitors' Book on the occasion of my first stay eighteen years ago. Just for old remembrance I touched the piano and hummed through *Home, Sweet Home*. The visit was a lovely one and my diary reminds me that while there I received good news:

September 6, 1916. Schloss Friedrichshof, Cronberg.

Just now I had a telegram from dear Prince Hatzfeldt that all is well with darling Dads. How he has found out I do not know, but I realize how pleased he will be to be able to send me this great good news, and to have received it here in this home of friendship and gracious memories has been a great comfort to me. . . .

From Friedrichshof Princess Vicy and I went to Nauheim for a little change and while there had one or two very interesting letters from my husband, from which the following are extracts. The first one explains how Prince Hatzfeldt probably got the news about Poppets:

Pless, *September* 10, 1916.

I cannot tell you how pleased I am that the news about Poppets is good. . . . Hermann probably addressed himself through a neutral power to Benckendorff, his brother-in-law, and got the answer at once. What a dreadful time you must have passed.

We are so full up that all the younger Gentlemen live in the Train at the station. The Empress is here; also King Ferdinand and the Crown Prince of Bulgaria; to-night Enver Pasha[1] arrives. For lunch to-day the Archduke Frederick and all the Austrians come over from Teschen. It is more than I can stand, on my legs the whole day. To-day I had

[1] Turkish Minister for War.

to go to Mass with the Bulgarians at 8.30; at 10 to the Protestant Church with our Sovereigns, then walk with the King of Bulgaria in the Park, and then the lunch with lots of people to talk to. Bethmann is here too, naturally. To-morrow I go with King Ferdinand to Saybusch, the Archduke Karl Stephen's place in Galicia, for luncheon. . . . The work is terrific.

PLESS, *September* 14, 1916.

I enclose a letter from the Empress who has just left. She has been here since the 29th of August. The King and Crown Prince of Bulgaria left last night. So I too am off to-day. I go for a few days to Fürstenstein, Sunday the 17th to Berlin, and Monday to Königswart to go on with my cure. These last weeks were most interesting, as a very important bit of the world's history has been made here—but extremely tiring. We are all worn out. . . .

You need not be anxious any more about Poppets, after the explicit telegram of Hermann. Gerard [1] is an old idiot; and so is his colleague in London.[2] They have not answered yet.

While Princess Vicy and I were at Nauheim I had a long letter from Princess Mossy in which she said:

. . . Please tell Vicy dear, with my tender love, that I had a telegram from Sophie [3] yesterday in French, forwarded by the Greek Legation at Berlin, saying they were all well, no anxiety whatever about the King's health, that all communication was impossible for the moment, but she would telegraph officially if she had something special to say, and that all her thoughts were here. It was joy to hear from her at last. The last news I had of my darling boys, who are on the Rumanian frontier, was dated August 28, and they were then well, and full of expectation of what was going to happen, as they had just received the news that war was declared,[4] and shooting had begun on the Danube. May God protect them!

---

[1] Mr. James W. Gerard, United States Ambassador in Berlin.

[2] Dr. Walter Hines Page, United States Ambassador in London.

[3] The Queen of Greece.

[4] Rumania declared war on Austria-Hungary on July 27, and Germany on Rumania on July 28, 1916.

I trust you have had still more reassuring news about your father, and that you will spend nice and comforting days at Nauheim. Much love, dearest Daisy, from

Yours affly, MARGARET.

About the end of September I had a jolly letter from Jack Cowans from Cumberland Lodge assuring me that my friends had not forgotten me and that they often spoke of me. He got news of me from time to time through Violet Mar and others. Prince Christian sent his best love to myself and my husband. Jack added: "He is getting very old, dear old boy, and very deaf and blind" and was "wondering if he would live to see Peace." The poor Prince died about a year later.[1] The letter concluded characteristically: "Just remember we all love you and there is a silver lining to every cloud (not golden). Gold will be scarce in Europe for many a year."

I had some flowers sent from Fürstenstein to the Empress, and in a nice letter of thanks Countess Brockdorff said: "Her Majesty goes for a ride every morning, and is so faithful in visiting the wounded, the feeding establishments for the poor, and the like. Her Majesty was of course very much shaken by the deep sorrow that has befallen the poor Esmarchs.[2]

People who thought I was in a position to go about betraying the secret doings that went on at Pless would not have believed me had I told them the truth, which was that I was dependent entirely on my husband for the merest glimpses of what was happening. Apparently I had inquired if I could not go to Promnitz and live there quietly for a bit:

PLESS, *September* 14, 1916.

. . . You cannot come and live at Promnitz, as the whole place is in a dreadful state. . . . Then lots of the furniture has been taken to Nasse's house for Hindenburg. Nasse has

---

[1] October 28, 1917.

[2] Death of Prince Christian's sister, Henriette, at Kiel, October, 1916. Born a Princess of Schleswig-Holstein, she had morganatically married Professor Johannes von Esmarch.

gone to the Palais, the house next to the Castle. There is a list kept at the Secretary's Office of all the people who have been staying in the Castle since the War began, with dates and the names of the rooms. After the War a list will be made for each separate room. . . . Enver Pascha and his Staff stayed only one afternoon and night. He is a charming man, thirty-six years old and good-looking. Yesterday Count Roedern was here, the new Secretary of the Treasury and successor to Helfferich, who becomes Vice-Chancellor and Secretary of the Interior; he by the way is first cousin to Nasse, as Nasse's mother was a Countess Roeder.

Now I will finish as I must see Hindenburg and Ludendorff, and in half an hour I have to lunch and then catch the train.

VI

I was making desperate efforts at this time to get to Switzerland to meet Patsy or some member of my family and so receive first-hand news about my father. Dear Granny Olivia's death at Ruthin on September 4 had been a severe, though not unexpected, blow. The false report of my father's death, too, made me feel that another moment's delay was unbearable. Other people had received leave to go to Switzerland or Holland, so why should not I do so. Dutch neutrality at that time being very uncertain, I knew I was unlikely to be allowed to go there. But Switzerland seemed easy enough from Munich.

From the beginning to the end of the War the late Crown Princess of Sweden was more kind to me than I have any words to say. Such a friend. Time, trouble, risk; at need all these were as nothing. What a loss her death was to her family, to her friends, to Sweden. Here is a letter from her which shows what she was, and what she did for me, far better than I could tell it:

STOCKHOLM, *October 24th.*

MY DEAR D.,—

Thank you so much for your letter. I wired your message to Mr. Russell as soon as I got your letter, that was the one dated October 13th; then yesterday I got Mossy's note asking me to send Joynson Hicks [1] a wire from you, and that I have done.

I saw your nice little Swedish masseuse a few days ago and was so interested to have news of you in a more personal way, but I was sorry to hear she thought you so run down and in need of massage and quiet. Can't you try and come to some quiet place in Sweden and then she could perhaps continue to give you massage and help you in that way? I am sure it would do you a world of good.

I heard from England a short time ago that Lady Ripon is not dead but she is very ill and suffers terribly; it is too sad, isn't it? I have good news from home, my father [2] keeps well and is happily very busy but he feels dreadfully lonely at times and some friends write that it is like seeing half a person only! Patsy [3] is well and busy too in different ways; she has taken to singing and is very keen about it and takes a lot of lessons. Old Prince Christian has had a chill and is evidently not at all well; of course he is very old and his only sister died at Kiel last week and that was no doubt a great blow to him. His son, being in Germany, cannot go to him, and he feels that too of course. All due to this awful never ending war! With love, Yours, D.

In October Princess Mossy lost her second son, Maximilian, just before he became twenty-two. Another boy gone and inside a few months. I was terribly grieved for her and wrote and sent flowers. In my letter I told her that I proposed taking a little house at Berchtesgaden for the Christmas holidays, so that the boys and I could spend them together. I suggested that the Princess and her husband Prince Friedrich Carl should join us there.

FRIEDRICHSHOF, *October* 24, 1916.

MY DEAR DAISY,—

Your kind letter, full of sympathy and feeling touched me very much and I thank you with all my heart. What I feel like words cannot express. One struggles on and tries not to think, but at every step, wherever one turns to, the terrible pain sets in and seems to grow worse and worse. Your lovely lilies were on the Altar during the last sad ceremony, they

[1] The West family solicitors.—D. OF P.

[2] The Duke of Connaught. [3] Her sister, Lady Patricia Ramsay.

looked down upon that beloved child's coffin, the emblem of his innocence and pureness! He and his brother left this world untouched by all its wickedness and horribleness, they sacrificed their young lives for a sacred cause, doing a most noble duty. That must be my comfort some day, but at present it is the missing of those two bright lights in one's life, which makes one feel so miserable and heartbroken. They were my pride and joy and never gave any trouble or caused us one moment of sorrow.

I cling more than ever to those that are left, and they have been a great comfort in these dark days! What you propose about Berchtesgaden has been in my mind a great deal, and I think we all need a change very much. So if you will really let us live in your house, Daisy dear, we shall be most grateful. We can only get away in the Christmas holidays, so we would probably start from here on December 26th and arrive the 27th. It seems useless to make plans in these days, as they always get upset and all is so uncertain, but still I like to think of this one. May Fräulein von Nesselrode, my lady-in-waiting, make all necessary arrangements with your secretary, when the time comes? I think that will be the simplest way. My husband is *very* particular, and I am afraid would never agree to our plan, unless you let us look upon your house as a hotel, so *please*, Daisy dear, let all be done as he wishes, or else he will make us go somewhere else. If we may have the rooms for nothing, that is already a great advantage. I do hope Vicy will be able to go too. Should our other two boys, now eldest ones, who are at the front, be here for Christmas and accompany us, I suppose we could find rooms for them at another hotel, as you are sure to be full up. It is quite uncertain if they can get leave, but if they do, we should of course not like to separate from them. I hope you and yours have been well, dear Daisy, and that you have had good news from home. Once more *many* thanks for your warm-heartedness and much love from Yours affectionately,

MARGARET

The moment had now come which had hung over me like a sword from the outbreak of War. The moment so many women throughout Europe dreaded day and night. Hansel had to go. He was in the Royal Prussian Life Guard Hussars, and on October 25 was posted to his Regiment, which was in the

Second Army on the Western Front somewhere near St. Quentin.

At the end of October I paid a short visit to the Grand Duchess Augusta at Strelitz. As always, it comforted me to see her, and the only drawback was the infernal German etiquette:

November 3, 1916.

. . . I have had three very nice days, except that I felt rather lonely in the Palace without Fritz or the children or the Grand Duke or anybody; and the etiquette of big courts one understands; but when a little Court has a great deal of etiquette it bores me; like a woman who puts on a tiara with her tea gown; for instance, they come to call on me and I am supposed to return their call; and then this morning even at breakfast when the Grand Duke of Mecklenburg-Schwerin came to see me before the train left, I had to go and receive him formally in one of the drawing-rooms.

It seems so stupid. The Schwerin Grand Duke sent formally to ask when he could come and call on me, instead of just saying as we would have done in the old days in France or England, " Shall I come to-morrow at five or at luncheon ? "

The Grand Duchess Elisabeth, the mother, sent word that she wished to come and call on me but I did not understand it quite and said " No " that I was not ready, which was true. I thought she only wanted to see if my rooms were comfy—anyway I found her afterwards on the front terrace and then I asked her to come in with me, and she came in as if she was a guest, which made me feel idiotically stupid. I went and had tea with her at five and saw the Grand Duchess Granny again at six, and got down again from there at seven, just in time to dress for dinner.

I can never succeed in thinking of the Bavarians as Germans, although they speak the same tongue. They are dear, simple, homely people and as friendly and approachable as the Irish. Before the Revolution of November, 1918, Munich was one of the most delightful Courts in Europe. Bavaria is, of course, after Prussia, by far the most important State in Germany and the Bavarian Royal Family were, and are, delightful. As for my friend Princess Pilar, or to give her full name, Princess Maria del

Pilar, she is unique; she is more Spanish than German as both her mother and her grandmother were born Infantas of Spain. She has all the spirit of the South, and yet she hates etiquette and ceremony as much as I do. When I received the following letter from her I did not realize that her reference to a King for the new Kingdom of Poland could be any personal concern of mine:

DEAREST DAISY,— NYMPHENBURG PALACE, 5.XI.1916.

You must forgive me for not answering your dear letter before. I was always wanting to do it, but never found a moment. You don't know how happy you make me, when you are so nice to me or write so heartily. Thank you so very much!

I feel very sorry for you that your boy has to go to the front and can well understand your feelings knowing him in the West. My brother is coming one of these days for a fortnight's leave. I am so glad. This War is too terrible. It seems that it will never stop!

Yes, do telephone when you come to Munich. You know we are always glad to see you.

To-day the papers tell us that Poland is a Kingdom. I would like to know who is to be the King? Everything seems so funny! I suppose we will soon hear more about it—there can't be a Kingdom without a King. The people seem excited about it. Some say the War will stop at once, others that it will last a hundred years. I don't see why one thing or why the other—but still—I don't see a great many things.

Well! come to us or let us meet in town—whatever you prefer. Good-bye, and much love from your affectionate

PILAR.

Poland has always been, and I suppose always will be, a thorn in the side of Europe. Before the War, as my diary mentions more than once, Germany was responsible for much repressive legislation against her Polish subjects in Silesia. In August, 1914, the Czar hurriedly promised to make Poland an independent Kingdom with, I think, a member of his House on the Throne. But of course nothing definite was done. Then Austria-Hungary aimed at uniting Russian Poland with Galicia, but this Germany opposed.

In November, 1916, as Princess Pilar's letter says, Poland was proclaimed a Kingdom and the German Emperor set about looking for a King. He sounded my husband to see if he would like to wear a kingly crown but he was unfavourable as, at that time, he had quite other ideas about his own future. Hansel was then suggested but again Hans was unfavourable. Here is an extract from one of Hans's letters of that period :

PLESS, *November* 23, 1916.

The enclosures of your last letter interested me very much. The Empress is here, and this takes the whole evening. I am so glad that poor Poppets is not seriously hurt.

Prince Waldimar of Prussia (Prince Henry's son) was here a few days ago, and, as usual, had your rooms. In his attendance was Captain von Stegmann, the husband of the lady you spoke of as having been in Switzerland. He told me that, by the new regulations, it was quite out of the question that she could go there again. We must now wait for what will happen with the Duchess of Arenberg [1] if she wants to go again to Switzerland. Practically the thing is of no importance as the English authorities would not let your parents go out. But I want to see if you are treated in a different way to others.

You have no idea how much there is to do here. Politically this Polish question gives one heaps to do, I mean personally, as tons of business arrangements have to be made to meet the new state of things. And what this will really be, God only knows. The Poles here are very quiet, to judge by their Press, but in Posen they begin already to move with the object of joining the new Kingdom. The great difference between Posen and Upper Silesia is, that there they have a Polish nobility, which luckily does not exist here.

I am writing to Treutler by the same post. This letter goes under your secretary's address. I am sending a short note to you by the same post. Wire when both have arrived.

As is generally known, the Polish question trailed on for years and is not settled even now. I do not know how Marshal Pilsudski styles himself, but he maintains the state and dignity of a King. The Emperor, of course, wanted to give her a German

[1] Hedwige, wife of the 9th Duke of Arenberg, was a Princess of the noble Belgian House of de Ligne.

King and because the Hochbergs were descended on the distaff side from one of the old Polish Kings this would have answered very well. I know that when my husband and sons went to Poland soon after, they were welcomed with great enthusiasm, towns were decorated and great celebrations held. When Hans refused to accept the Polish Crown for himself or Hansel, a suggestion was made that it should be given to Lexel. As a preliminary measure they even went the length of "converting" him to the Roman Catholic Church! But of course the downfall of the German Empire cancelled all these plans. I had in my possession a great many highly confidential and secret documents connected with this and other important matters, together with certain letters which, if published, would compromise many European Statesmen. The dispatch-box containing these was stolen from my maid at a Railway Station in Berlin. I may say that I know quite well where the box went, although, unfortunately, I could not organize a counter-theft after the manner of a detective novel. But here my lifelong habit of having copies made of all important letters I receive or send stood me in good stead. The thieves may like to know that exact and authenticated copies of every document are in existence and are safely deposited in the strong-room of my bank in London. One day they may come in useful in clearing up dark patches of contemporary history.

VII

When I was at Strelitz the Grand Duchess Augusta seemed to be in her usual health. At any rate she did not complain. But she would never do that, having always the feeling that she must suffer in silence with the wounded. Directly I left she became ill and for nearly four weeks was without food, taking only a little wine and water. On Tuesday, November 28, she spoke for the last time to those she loved and told her grandson that she knew the end was near and only hoped that God would take her without her having to suffer too long. There was a good deal of pain and she was given narcotic injections.

In December the darling old Grand Duchess Augusta died. It affected me quite as much as did the death of Granny Olivia. How glad I was that I paid that last visit to her in November. Here is what her grandson wrote. The ties of affection that bound those two were extraordinary—unique I should say. I never saw such close intimacy, love and communion between youth and age:

NEUSTRELITZ, *Monday night.*

I have no peace and no time to write, but the first line I do write you shall get. You know what I have lost and that my heart is broken, nothing can ever replace what the darling was to me. Your kind and most hearty sympathy helped me a great deal; thanks so much for all you wrote. I did what you asked me and put one of your lilies from your flower-heart into the darling Granny's coffin. As long as the coffin was open I could go and look into her dear face and kiss her most darling hand. I had long talks with her; one night I went and I had the kind of feeling she was calling me. It was about midnight, I was sitting in the Park House and I at once went to the Schloss to see her and there she lay so peacefully on her bed in her bedroom. It was the last night, next morning she was taken to be put into the coffin. I sat there for a long time and had the true feeling that her spirit was with me and peace came over me. And now I know, that she will be with me all my life. The darling was and will be for all my life my best and most dear friend. If I have to settle serious things, I'll think of her, she gave such good advice. Yesterday was the day of her funeral, I can't tell you what I suffered; only God knows how my heart is looking! Oh! do please pray for me. I know you'll do it. I can't stay here for Christmas; I am going to France next Saturday, first to Brussels, where I am getting presents for the soldiers and then to Douai or thereabouts. I'll send you my address as soon as I know. Christmas I'll spend with the wounded at the Hospitals and try to help them and forget my own grief. I have the so sad duty to return to you the letter my darling Granny did open no more. . . .

On December 8 we celebrated our silver wedding. How could we be glad about anything! Private sorrows and public griefs jostling one another so quickly that you had scarcely time to realize one before another overcame you. For our wedding anniversary Hans wrote:

I have bought a little brooch for you the other day in Berlin and told them to send it so that it arrives on the 8th in your hands. This is not a proper silver wedding present, but only a little trifle to show you that I have not forgotten the day. The rest we can talk later. I was half a day in Berlin to attend a meeting, and travelled there from here with the Crown Prince, who had just arrived from the funeral in Vienna,[1] and I spent Sunday in Fürstenstein. Lexel is very well. Much taller and thinner. . . .

Yesterday the Emperor Karl and the Archduke Frederic came over for luncheon (forty-eight persons). To-day our Emperor is returning the visit to lunch with the new Emperor in his Train, as the Schloss in Teschen is the Imperial Headquarters. I did not go, because there is very little room in the Train. So our Emperor took only two A.D.C.'s and a doctor.

Now I must finish, as it is time for post. I will see you (nearly for certain) in Fürstenstein before Christmas. But for Christmas I have to be here. A big kiss to Bolko and a very big one for you.

The next letter from Hans contains a good deal that is of public interest. Throughout this book I have tried to present things as they seemed to be at the time; not as we now know them to have been. This, I always think, is the truly interesting—and sometimes valuable—thing: how did the events look at the moment to those immediately concerned. What I always long to know and never can is how Helen of Troy or Cleopatra felt and thought about things in their secret hearts *before* they *knew*.

PLESS, *December* 6, 1916.

I hope this letter will just reach you on the morning of the 8th, as your letters don't seem to be any more delayed. Well, it is twenty-five years that we are married, and I can only say, that I feel very proud, that I had such a brilliant idea twenty-

[1] That of the old Emperor Francis Joseph of Austria, who died November 21, 1916. Although the German Emperor went to Vienna to kneel at the coffin of his Ally, he did not actually attend the funeral, as he wished to avoid taking precedence of the new Emperor.

five years ago. You have decidedly succeeded in making me extremely happy during this long time, and I trust to God, you will find your happiness again too, when this beastly war is over and Hansel is safely home. I am sure that in a year's time we will have peace and, surrounded by our three dear boys, we can have proper silver wedding festivities (which would also please the people) either here or in Fürstenstein, which will be ready by then, or in both places, one after the other.

The idea of the coming peace makes one of course talk again of the War, for the simple reason, that if the War is not finished, there will be no peace. I just hear that Bukarest[1] is to fall to-day. The Greeks are at last moving in our favour. It does not require much perspicacity to guess, that after the Rumanians, it will be Sarrail's turn. If Briand, who started the Salonika expedition against the advice of Joffre, will overlive Sarrail's defeat, is more than doubtful.

This morning the news came of the resignation of Asquith.[2] It will probably be a new Cabinet with Carson, Bonar Law and Lloyd George. All very active men who want to go ahead. We can only welcome their intention as the War will be sooner over. The amount of stuff of all sorts, especially food-stuffs, we have found intact in Rumania, is tremendous, and will help in a great way.

Nothing could have exceeded the kindness of the Emperor and Prince Eitel Fritz in keeping me informed of the well-being of my "so big little boy."

On December 15 the Prince wrote: "We have always warm weather, rain and fog, like the winter climate in England. But we are quite happy about it as the enemy does not shoot so much as by sunshine, and there are no aeroplanes by night when it is cloudy. I see Hansel nearly every day; he is going on very well and is taking his signal course, which will soon finish. He is getting broader and stronger and more manly, although he is only seventeen. On Christmas Day I will have him and Mirbach[3] here in our quarters and we will spend the evening together; I hope to make it a little nice for him."

[1] Bukarest was occupied by the Germans on December 6.

[2] December 5.

[3] General von Mirbach, commanding the 1st Guards Division in which Hansel was then serving.

Like the good soldier he is, the Prince was arranging presents and Christmas cheer for his soldiers and the wounded who were near.

I decided that I must spend Christmas at Fürstenstein, and do what I could to make it a little gay. One always hoped and believed it would be the last one to be spent in such utter misery.

I sent a carrying bed for the wounded as a present to Hospital Train D.3, and little gifts to Dr. Andress, the Doctors, Sisters and Staff. To the Emperor, Empress and Countess Brockdorff I sent flowers: flowers frail as hope and as eternal.

After supervising feasts and presents for the sick and wounded at Fürstenstein I went to Berchtesgaden to the children and dear Princess Mossy and her husband and family. Her sisters, Princess Vicy and Princess Charlotte (of Meiningen) were also there, so we had a real, homely, family party. Princess Mossy was so tender and nice, so unselfish in putting aside her grief, and her husband was such a great gentleman, that it was a joy to have them. The Emperor sent me a coloured reproduction of his portrait by Adams; the Empress telegraphed on Christmas morning and every one was kind. We went for walks, tobogganed, played with the children and pretended we had forgotten the War. We were buoyed up by the fact that in the Reichstag in December Bethmann-Hollweg, speaking in the name of the Emperor, said that His Majesty had decided to suggest the initiation of peace proposals to the Allied Powers.

Even the dear old Berchtesgaden Stationmaster, who always insisted on opening the Royal waiting room for my arrivals and departures, sent me a present of a pound of home-made sausages. God alone knows what was in them! Bless his dear old Bavarian heart! He had written on a not very clean piece of paper the beautiful Bavarian invocation which is in daily use, especially in the mountain districts, *Grüss Gott!* It is the popular abbreviation of *Gott grüsse Sie*—May God greet you.

CHAPTER TWELVE

January-December, 1917

NEW YEAR, 1917, found us all still at Berchtesgaden. Princess Vicy, Prince Friedrich Carl and Princess Mossy and their four children—the two sets of twins—myself, Lexel and Bolko! The ladies-in-waiting to the two Princesses and some of the others slept out, as they say, but how the remainder of us squeezed into the little house called Gmundschloss I have now no idea. On such occasions affectionate goodwill makes everything easy.

Already, as we know, Prince Friedrich Carl and Princess Mossy had lost in the War their two eldest boys, Prince Friedrich and Prince Maximilian, both under twenty-four. Their next four boys were twins—I don't quite know how one says it. The two eldest twins were Prince Philip and Prince Wolfgang, aged twenty-one. Wolfgang arrived before Christmas, but Philip did not do so till later. Dear Princess Mossy. Always gay and courageous. Two sons gone; two to be continually anxious about; and her two "baby twins," Richard and Christopher, growing daily older and more anxious to join their brothers at the front. They were, of course, nephews of the Emperor, and yet vile gossip said that all the members of the Imperial family were kept in safe places. It was not true. My diary gives an attractive glimpse of our little party:

January 3, 1917. Berchtesgaden.

I am not quite well and am writing this in bed. Last night Prince Friedrich Carl, his sister-in-law Princess Vicy and her lady-in-waiting, Hannah Lohe, dined downstairs. Princess Mossy and I had a cosy dinner alone in my own private sitting-room; the sudden arrival here yesterday of her other twin, Philip, was a great surprise and delight. Alas! he is the eldest now. We had to get him a room out as this little house is more than full. As it is, the younger Hesse twins sleep together, and so do Lexel and Bolko.

Yesterday every one but I went to Königsee; some walked home. Prince Friedrich Carl, who is so kind and nice and full of a great charm, drove Baby Bolko back alone and they talked of stars and beasties and other lovely things. . . .

I am most happy to be able to record that all four of Princess Mossy's boys survived the War. The two elder ones are happily married, Prince Philip to Princess Mafalda of Savoy, the lovely daughter of the King and Queen of Italy. If they read this book I send them greetings and warm, good wishes.

Owing to the kind thought of Prince Eitel Fritz, we had Hansel also with us for New Year, that dear Prince writing to say it would do the boy good to have a few days' rest and be a pleasure to me. When Hansel went back I sent champagne and cigars with him—as a thankoffering!

For some time fantastic and disquieting rumours had been reaching me about what came to be known in England as the Cornwallis-West case. It had been going on for some six months, but I knew nothing except what could be learned from gossip and conjecture.

Poor dear Patsy had been indiscreet and, like myself, had her small kindnesses and indiscretions swelled to the dimensions of a public scandal by envy and malice. I need not write about the affair here, as the Editor of this volume and Major Rutter gave a full and impartial account of the matter in their *Life* [1] of General Cowans.

I must, however, give a letter from my father, showing how he viewed the whole matter. This letter and an incident in Ruthin town which I will describe are quite enough for me:

[1] *General Sir John Cowans, G.C.B.*, by Major D. Chapman-Huston and Major O. Rutter. Two volumes. Hutchinson. 1924

NEWLANDS MANOR, LYMINGTON, HANTS, *January* 14, 1917.
MY DARLING DAISY,—

If you have lately received the English papers you must have read about a certain lady being accused of all sorts of things. *Don't believe a word of it*, and rest assured from me that the charges are wicked and vile fabrications and the accusers are vile and vindictive, but they managed to give an entirely wrong impression of what passed on certain occasions, as well as misconstructing what the poor soul meant to the miserable creature who was the cause of all the trouble. The public realize all this now and write *innumerable* letters to her all deprecating strongly the judgment as in every way based on false testimony uttered by persons of corrupt minds. *Don't think any more about it.* I will send you a newspaper about it and hope it may reach you. How are you, dear soul? I trust enjoying the snow and sunshine. Happily we have no snow here, but it is cold. Mary Hughes and Ella Willett are here, which I am glad of as they are both cheerful and pleasant. Every one wants cheering in these days! Good-bye, darling,
Your ever devoted POPPETS.

What my father says about the "innumerable" letters had proof in rather a remarkable way. A short time after I received his letter he and Patsy attended some public function in Ruthin. As I write I have before me a photograph showing their welcome outside the Old Town Hall. The Market Place is simply black with cheering people; flags are everywhere and spectators crowd the windows and even the lamp-posts. Patsy received an ovation Royalty might have envied. That was concrete evidence of what the inhabitants of North Wales, who watched every action of her life from the time when she was seventeen till she was seventy, thought of the whole wretched affair.

When Princess Mossy got back to Friedrichshof she wrote me such a long and splendid letter in which she said:

. . . And when cruel disappointments and trials come, think of the many friends you have, and above all of your sweet children; they are treasures and you can be proud of each. Let Hansel become your friend and adviser more and more, treat him as a grown-up man, and trust him; he seems so steady and quiet and everybody likes him. We got home safely Sunday afternoon and found deep snow, there has not been so much here for years. If only we had you all here for tobogganing. The boys took to it at once, but since yesterday school has begun, and they only come home late in the afternoon. Philip left yesterday, and so it is lonely and quiet once more.

I often go up to the little Chapel on the hill where my beloved eldest boy rests; it is so peaceful there, and does me good, but oh, the pain and sadness that comes over one. Vicy writes that she misses the comforts and cosiness of the Gmundschloss, at Bayrischzell, and no wonder too. I often think of my pretty room. Please remember us to Ina,[1] your dear boys, and Herr Brinlock[2]; and let me thank you again for everything, dear Daisy, also in my husband's name, who sends you every sort of message.

I am longing for the picture to come, and cannot say how grateful I am for that, it was too dear of you. With much love,

Ever yours affectionately, MARGARET.

About the middle of February I received the following telegram from the Emperor: one could not at the time tell exactly all that it implied[3]:

PLESS CASTLE, *February* 11, 1917.

On my departure from Upper Silesia I would like to tell you how well I have been looked after here and to let you know how thankful I was to feel how carefully everything had been thought out to make my careworn life as agreeable as possible. With best greetings.

WILHELM I.R.

Patsy's letters were always a joy. She was one of those rare people—their price is above rubies—who would insist on seeing the gleams of fun that glint through the saddest things. Some long time after the War broke out all the men servants had, of course, gone, including the butler. Somewhere or another

[1] My cousin, Ina FitzPatrick.—D. OF P. [2] The tutor.

[3] The departure was due to the collapse of Russia; on March 12 the Russian Revolution began, and on March 15 the Czar abdicated.

Patsy got hold of a man and his wife as butler and housekeeper. His chief recommendations were that he was not too old to stand up and that he had once been with the Archbishop of Canterbury. What he must have thought of the difference between the atmosphere of Lambeth Palace and that of Ruthin or Newlands history does not say.

His name was Maycock and his wife wore the trousers. She always addressed him as "Maycock," while he not only addressed her but always referred to her as "Mrs. Maycock." Patsy, who, like me, never could remember anyone's name, would ring the changes on Maycock, Junecock, Blackcock or anything else that came into her head.

Shelagh was at home for a few days' leave from her hospital in France, and Patsy decided to make a fuss of her by giving a luncheon party. Poor old Maycock with no footmen did his best and stayed himself by taking a little more than was good for him so early in the day. "Mrs. Maycock" in the kitchen cooked the small joint the War Food Regulations allowed and which Patsy by accumulating the family meat tickets had saved for the great occasion. We never had table-cloths at Newlands, but that day, as an evil fate would have it, one was used. Every one was seated. Enter Maycock, bearing the precious minute joint. The floor was polished, Maycock a bit dazed. He slipped, caught at the table-cloth to save himself and lay on the floor covered by gravy, silver, table-cloth and all the rest of it. Every one, of course, laughed. Maycock never moved. His poor false teeth had flown out and broken. Little Dolly Crowther, who took such care of Patsy in her last years, and who now takes equal care of me, was helping behind the scenes and rushed to Maycock's help, asking what was the matter. But the poor old man could only splutter and gurgle. Patsy kept poking him with the stick she always carried, shouting all the time: "Get up, get up, Maycock, Junecock, Blackcock, get up! Woodcock, get up!"

It was little Dolly and some of the guests who eventually got the poor darling out of the room; collected the dishevelled joint from a corner and in due course lunched at a table—without a table-cloth.

In nearly every one of Patsy's letters there was something to laugh at. Here are bits from one written early in March, 1917:

Dads and I have just been reading your darling letter together, snatching it from each other.

"Do let me read it!"

"No, I will read it myself. Who on earth is Eupatoria?"

"Ah, darling, do let me explain."

"No, no. You don't know who it is any more than I do."

—And both of us nearly in tears.

Oh, my Dany, I can never tell you how wonderful Poppets is—or how wonderful we think your darling letter, and how he grasps the truth of everything. My Pet, how you must have suffered. Oh, my Dany, yes; how I long for you and I to have our little "New Moon" home, and darling Baby with us—and Hansel and precious Lexel coming to see the old Granny, and doing just exactly what they please with her.

Well, to tell you about darling old Poppets. We just make him lead the life of an ordinary county gentleman since his accident—that is, not letting him be constantly going to Meetings and taking the Chair in stuffy hot rooms. Well, last Friday there was a large Meeting at Milford about growing War Food. He had a bit of a cold, so I sent down a message to say we were coming, but that I did not want him to take the Chair and speak.

Up we marched through a mass of people, when I found placed by the platform *an arm-chair* with a cushion! Poppets made one dash at the cushion, threw it back over his shoulder, where it hit a poor old lady's bonnet making her look drunk to the world, exclaiming, "Good Heavens, who put that cushion there?" Then he sat down.

Mr. A., a very little man quite crooked because he had been trying to cut down a tree and put himself under it when it did fall, and fat B. who looks a cross between an old actor and a eunuch, began dancing and bowing to each other like two mad goats, arguing as to which should take the Chair. Finally the fat man *stomached* the little thin man into it with a flop. When the thin man recovered his breath he began a long-

MY SISTER SHELAGH WESTMINSTER AND HER DAUGHTERS, URSULA AND MARY.
In the water-garden at Newlands, 1918.

winded speech by saying: "Ladies and Gentlemen, I know very little about the subject. I never fed a pig in my life."

At last the fat man's turn came and he got up, his arms full of papers which he kept quoting from and then dropping; I saw Poppets drumming with his fingers—as he does when he is thinking—and humming to himself! Then he attacked one side of his head—the bad side—and scratched it violently. Before I could say one, he was up on his legs, knocking all their silly arguments flat, giving them *facts* on every subject. He spoke for twenty minutes, without one single stop or stammer—and sat down amid loud applause. Then at the top of his voice: "Now, my dear little Patsy, I think we will go; the rest will bore us." And out he marched—people still clapping: he ate a huge dinner, slept like a top, and insisted on going to a concert next day. But now I must tell you another of his strange freaks. His hair all over is turning *quite black*. I swear he is putting nothing on it.

God bless you, darling precious one. Oh God, how I long to see you. I have written to the little Duchess of Marlborough. Geoffrey Brooke was lunching with Miss Paget[1] the other day who was so nice and said she had heard from you. I will find out about Alec Thynne. I heard from Jack Cowans yesterday, he said he was writing to "that dear child Daisy."

II

I have always felt that when I die I want to be cremated and about this time—I'm sure I don't know why—I decided to have a suitable casket made. Most likely when I do die it will be a case of the Empress Eugénie over again. She had her tomb made in France thirty years before her death, and when it was wanted no one could find out where it was, and she had to remain unburied for a year while another was being made. So it is really often quite useless taking too much thought for the morrow.

The casket for my ashes (I call it my "ash-tray") was made of nice bright shiny steel with a gold daisy in relief and four little gold legs. When my maid

[1] Sister of Lord Queenborough. She has a house near me now at La Napoule and is a dear friend.

unpacked it she was terribly disappointed as she had hoped it was a box of chocolates, then very scarce. What was so astonishing was that the whole of me could go into such a small space.

This casket incident happened in Munich in March, where I had gone to do some shopping. While there dear old Count Wolff-Metternich came to see me. How it recalled the happy days in London before the world got upside down. Duke Ernst Günther and his wife Dora also came and were enchanted because I was able to provide honey for tea. It came from Fürstenstein, as did all sorts of delicacies throughout the War. Hardouin, our French Head Chef, knew I didn't like "ordinary" food and was always afraid I would starve to death. He used to be quite wonderful at sending me and the children regularly wherever we were, cakes, sardines, jam, and even home-made chocolates and potted meats. Where he got sugar goodness alone knows; but of course he would have plenty of poultry, game. butter, cream and eggs under his own control.

On March 20, Aunt Minnie (Mrs. Guy Wyndham) wrote me a long newsy letter in the course of which she said:

> The Duchess of Connaught's death did not come as a surprise to us, for all through her illness we feared the worst—too many complications: she will be very greatly missed. So many of our old friends have gone, dear Daisy. Wasn't it sad Harry Cust dying? I feel to have lost one of my greatest friends, he was always so brilliantly amusing and his place will be impossible to fill.

When I heard of the death of the Duchess, I of course wrote at once to Sweden to Princess Daisy. I did so from the Nymphenburg Palace outside Munich, where I had been spending a few days with Prince and Princess Ludwig Ferdinand and their girl Princess Pilar.

The following letter from Princess Mossy (Princess Friedrich Carl of Hesse) refers to the beginnings of the

Russian Revolution,[1] said at the time, I know not with what truth, to have been engineered by communists in Berlin with the connivance, if not indeed with the encouragement of the German Court and Government! If that dastardly charge be true then Germany indeed deserved to pay, and has paid, for such infamy[2]:

FRIEDRICHSHOF, *March* 24, 1917.

MY DEAR DAISY,—

Thank you so much for your kind letter. I hope you had a nice time at Nymphenburg, and that Vienna will also make an agreeable change for you. If you are still with Princess Ludwig Ferdinand please remember me to her. She sent me such kind messages through Professor Hass, whom I hear you also saw, and promised to help in his beneficial work for East Prussia. It would be very dear of you if you could make him to hold his *Vortrag* in several towns in Silesia. . . .

The state of affairs in Russia is bewildering. May good come of it for us, and bring on peace soon. I feel so sorry for the Emperor and Empress; it is too horrible to see that nobody is ready to help them, and all leave them to their fate. May their lives be spared; they are such good, dear people, although he is too weak and unfit for such a position. Our Emperor was looking very well and in the best of spirits the other day.

Oh dear, if there could but be an end to all this misery soon. Of course I felt deeply for the other Daisy.[3] Hoping you are pretty well, and with much love also to your dear children, ever, Daisy dear, Yours affectionately, MARGARET.

The Russian news had bad results for the Grand Duke Michael and Sophy. They, who had never known what it was to be poor, found the greater

[1] In March, 1917, a Constitutional Government, so-called, was set up with Prince Lvoff at its head; on August 15 the Czar was sent to Siberia.

[2] "(*a*) On July 27, 1915, I reported that I had learned that the Germans were picking out the revolutionists and Liberals from the many Russian prisoners of war, furnishing them with money and false passports and papers, and sending them back to Russia to stir up a Revolution."—Gerard, James W., *My Four Years in Germany*, p. 293. (*b*) On February 17, 1917, Lenin, a refugee in Zurich, was sent for by Ludendorff, who offered to convey him and his friends back to Russia to organize pacifist propaganda. Lenin laughed—and went."

[3] The Crown Princess of Sweden.—D. OF P.

part of their income gone. They had to give up Kenwood and economize in every possible way. Their huge magnificent villa Kasbek at Cannes was a white elephant as long as the War lasted. When things got more settled Sophy leased it to Major and Mrs. Thomas Moss and she and the Grand Duke went to live in a smaller adjoining villa which they also own. Speaking of elephants reminds me that they were Sophy's pet adoration. Kasbek was full of them, great and small, in china, wood, bronze and every conceivable material.

I have often said that the Emperor never failed in the little attentions which endear a man to women. What mother in all the circumstances could fail to be highly gratified by, and grateful for, the following telegram:

ON THE FIELD, *March* 28, 1917.

Yesterday when on an opportune visit to the First Garde Division I saw to my delight your little big boy. Heartiest greetings. WILHELM.

The very moment I was receiving this telegram Patsy was hearing in England rumours to the effect that the Emperor had not only turned against me, but locked me up. She and I used a sort of code in our letters. I was "the little girl with golden hair," Patsy herself "Eupatoria" (one of her names), the Emperor was "the governess" and so on. Patsy wrote on April 10:

Do you remember a darling little girl with big blue eyes and quite golden hair, that I tied up in pigtails to make it fluffy. Well, I hear she is being persecuted by her governess and shut up like a prisoner. I can't believe it, for she is such a bright little thing, always so good. I don't and won't believe it. The papers are absolutely impossible and write and say anything they like, not the sort of papers we read, but the common papers Sanders or Mrs. Ennet would get. Poppets is wonderfully well. I often send little Biddy about six slices of bacon for her breakfast and she gets it and it is such a treat to her. And I put on the outside: "If anyone opens this and won't let my poor little girl have it, I hope it will make them very, very sick." So she always gets it. Please my precious one let me know if you are with dear friends—and well. I hope the kind people who open this letter will send it on for a Mother who loves and longs to hear of her child.

In Germany in the set in which I moved nearly all marriages are, or at any rate were, "arranged." I had felt strongly for some time that the Grand Duke of Mecklenburg-Strelitz would be happier if he were married. His grandmother was old and he used to try and save both her and his mother anxiety by keeping all his troubles to himself. He was terribly alone, and had no one to confide in. It was in these circumstances that he and I became real friends. We often discussed his marriage. During the War it was difficult to make plans or bring about meetings in an unostentatious way. However, I had some time before thought of a young and charming Princess, a relative of our own. The suggestion was acceptable to both sides. I was pleased about it all and so was Hans, who knew everything, and fully approved.

In the spring of 1917 the feeling against me in Silesia as an Englishwoman took another and much more ominous form. Silesia was always inclined to be socialistic in a moderate way; now the ultra-Democratic element was becoming aggressive and was raising its voice against the government and the nobility.

I proposed to visit Fürstenstein in May and Hans advised me, if I did so, to live in the utmost retirement and not see anyone. Uncle Bolko wrote me (in German) from Rohnstock:

ROHNSTOCK, *May* 13, 1917.

DEAR DAISY,—

That you will shortly come to Fürstenstein I have learnt elsewhere and we trust then also to be able to see you. Like Hans Heinrich, I also would like to ask you to be very careful and *not* to show yourself *at other places*. As I have often told you there are the most adventuresome and silly rumours abroad about you, which have even led to enquiries being made of us, which we naturally have rejected as being silly and without taste. It is said that you are an English spy and as such, have been arrested or even already shot.

In any case among the people there exists a bitter feeling against you and you must not be surprised if you possibly get insulted.

One of the greatest comforts, indeed luxuries, I enjoyed throughout the whole War was receiving all the time the English papers. I think I had *The Times*, *Daily Telegraph*, *Morning Post*, and *Daily Mail*, and *The Sketch*, *Tatler* and *Punch*. They all came with extraordinary regularity. These I used to lend to special friends with the strictest conditions about their return as eventually they all went to British prisoners-of-war, who, in turn, passed them on to other prisoners. It shows how precious they were that Muriel Münster[1] wrote and asked me if, before returning it, she might cut out and send to her cousin, Lord James Murray, who was a prisoner, a picture which appeared in the *Tatler* of his father the Duke of Atholl who had died a short time before. Of course, in such exceptional circumstances, I at once agreed.

Another very interesting thing is that throughout the War we were able to send money to England quite regularly. In the summer of 1914 I had signed a lease of Arnwood, a charming old house in a small Park in the New Forest and which belonged to the Newlands Estate. The rent for this and other payments were regularly made. I am sure I do not know how. It was all done by the Administrative Staff at Fürstenstein.

In April Hans was in Vienna and wrote an account of his impressions to Hansel who passed it on to me in the following boyish letter, which gives also a glimpse of what the writer thought about the duration of the War. It may safely be assumed that his view was the one then current in the Officers' Messes of the 1st Guards Division:

[1] Princess Münster von Derneburg was before her marriage Lady Muriel Hay, the daughter of Lord Kinnoull; she died in 1927.

FROM THE WEST, *April* 30, 1917.

Daddy wrote and told me that it was nearly like peace in Vienna. For *money* you could get everything you wanted, but the poor people who have not got any money, were starving. Everybody there seemed to be terrified of a revolution. It would serve them jolly well right if there was one. Germany I think will never be able to make anything out of Austria because they hate us and will not let us interfere in their business—which from their point of view I can very well understand.

I don't think there will be Peace either before two years, or a year and a half. I don't see any reason for the others to stop. I don't even quite believe that we can starve England by our Submarines. . . .

I hope your legs are all right again! Perhaps you walk too much.

Hansel's remark about submarines was very interesting because towards the end of April Mr. James W. Gerard, the American Ambassador, paid a visit to the Emperor at Great Headquarters in the town of Charleville-Mezières for the purpose of making it plain that should unrestricted submarine warfare and frightfulness be revived, it would not only be ineffectual against Great Britain, but would mean the entry of the United States into the War on the side of the Allies. During this visit Hans saw quite a lot of Mr. Gerard.[1] It is remarkable that a mere boy like Hansel should have foreseen the uselessness of the weapon which Tirpitz, Hindenburg, Michaelis, Ludendorff, Kühlmann and the Conservatives believed would bring England to her knees in three months. Needless to say I shared Hansel's view, knowing quite well that nothing would bring England to her knees.

A letter from Princess Mossy written at this time expresses so well how Germans saw their own situation

[1] "One day we had tea in the garden of the Villa formerly occupied by the Emperor, with the Prince of Pless (who is always with the Kaiser and who seems to be a prime favourite with him), von Treutler, and others, and motored with the Prince of Pless to see some marvellous Himalayan pheasants, reared . . . in captivity. . . . At lunch I sat between the Emperor and the Prince of Pless. . . ."—Gerard, James W., *My Four Years in Germany*, page 231.

during the War that I will quote a bit of it. I do not understand why Germany felt she was being hemmed in, treated unjustly, and that the civilized world (assisted by the uncivilized) was in a conspiracy to obliterate her from amongst the nations. But she did, and, as a matter of fact, still does. It is a psychological factor of immense importance that was not, and still is not, sufficiently taken into account. Until this primary factor in German mentality is fully understood and, somehow or another, resolved, there will never be a real feeling of peace in Europe. Princess Mossy, although the youngest sister of the Emperor, is a woman with great experience of affairs, tact and judgment. She could never be accused of an unduly emotional, much less an hysterical point of view. She wrote:

FRIEDRICHSHOF, *May* 19, 1917.

. . . I quite see how cruel and unjust it seems that all your kindest and best intentions are misunderstood, misconstrued, even turned against you; but never mind, keep up your courage, and wait for better times. As long as your conscience is clear, what does all the rest matter; of course it hurts, I know it but too well, but then it is what unfortunate Germany is going through during these three years, and what we Germans all feel, that injustice is heaped upon us by the whole world, and that every lie is believed, and all our most sacred and ideal motives are trampled upon and disbelieved. You are going through the same personally and in small as our poor nation is suffering at large. . . .

In a casual little letter Hansel sends me the news that he has got the Iron Cross, but, of course, does not bother to tell me why. I used to get very tired writing letters and, to save myself, asked the boy to show one I had written to him to Prince Eitel Fritz. At this he was rightly very indignant:

FROM THE WEST, *May* 30, 1917.

Just a few lines to tell you that I got the E.K.I. Rittmeister von Radowitz got it at the same time. He told me to send you his best love. I will answer your long letter soon. Just now I have not time. I did not give Prince Eitel Friedrich your letter to read because to begin with if you write *me* a letter it is for *me* and not for Prince Eitel Friedrich; also I do not know P. E. F. well enough to show him my letters. I am now *Brigade-Beobachter* (observer) and have got rather much to do. Perhaps somebody can explain to you what that is. The weather is lovely and I live and sleep underneath a birch and am extremely dirty! If there were not such an awful lot of flies, mosquitoes, etc., it would be very much nicer; I can so well understand a horse getting absolutely mad with rage. If you send me something please send me a little wooden cigarette-case. *Please* don't believe everything that people tell you—especially now in war-time, because ninety-nine per cent. is bosh!

During the first days of June I had a letter from my father telling me that Patsy had been very ill and suffered from hæmorrhage. Specialists were summoned from Liverpool and decided that an operation was unnecessary. Even so, the meagreness of the news that reached me kept me very anxious.

III

In November, 1916, the young Archduke Karl, whom I had treated like a boy at Fürstenstein in June, 1910, had succeeded his great-uncle the old Emperor Francis Joseph. I honestly believe that from the moment he ascended the Throne the young Emperor and his wife the Empress Zita did their best to bring about an honourable Peace. We know now that the Empress's brother, Prince Sixte of Bourbon-Parma, who was serving as an officer in the French Army, made on behalf of his brother-in-law, secret Peace proposals both in France and in England.[1] The Emperor Karl saw that the continuance of the War meant disaster for both Austria and Hungary and did his utmost to save his two countries. This fact must never be forgotten. His Peace intentions were disapproved of in Germany and it is ironic to speculate that, had they been successful, the German Revolution might never have taken place

[1] On March 31, 1917.

and the Emperor William II. might still be at the head of the nation. A letter from Alphy Clary, written in June, gives a glimpse of how Austrians regarded their new Sovereign. The "Elisalex" to whom he refers is his sister Countess Baillet-Latour, who was in England throughout the War. She was all the time with the Portlands and their kindness to her was extraordinary:

> . . . I've had a letter from Elisalex dated May 7th, *such* joy; poor dear, she was ill again, but thank God is well and always with the P.'s, who are perfect angels to her, such staunch loyal friends.
>
> I wonder if you realize what a glorious man our beloved young Emperor is and if you heard his speech, when he talks about "peace without hatred." He does everything he can to do away with that ghastly hatred between the countries. . . .

About this time I had a long letter from the Grand Duke Adolphus Frederick telling me all about his grandmother's affairs. Going into and putting everything in order and as she wished it, he naturally found most trying. At the moment, too, he was suffering from one of his terribly trying periodical attacks of hay fever. Until I knew him I had never realized how severe and almost indeed incurable this disease can be. Since then I have met an American man who, because of it, has to spend two or three months at sea every summer; it is the only thing that relieves him. The Grand Duke still missed his grandmother terribly and it gave me a melancholy pleasure to be told that he found comfort in recalling the "beloved country" where he had "the best time he ever had, the best friends," and "delicious Ruthin" and my "most kind parents."

In June a great many British prisoners were moved from Crefeld, which was a popular camp, to Schwarmstedt in Hanover, which was very unpopular. It was two hours' walk from a station and miles from anywhere. The accommodation was wooden huts, possible in summer, but cold and dreary in winter. In

July I had a letter from Mrs. Leicester, whom I did not know, begging me to get her son, Second-Lieutenant G. W. Y. Leicester of the Cheshire Regiment, moved from this camp and, if at all possible, exchanged and sent to Switzerland. The boy had a badly injured face which required very careful and prolonged treatment.

Now Hans, Uncle Bolko, Princess Mossy—all my friends and admirers—might say what they thought best about being discreet, keeping quiet, avoiding bothering the authorities and so on. But how could I refuse Mrs. Leicester's appeal. That I did not know either her or her son made no difference. She was a fellow-Englishwoman begging for help, and mine, for what it was worth, I could not deny her. Many people, total strangers, wrote to me in this way, but that was merely because I was the only Englishwoman married in Germany whose name they happened to know.

Without seeming to exaggerate it is difficult to explain how hopelessly tactless Germans often are. The very day I heard from Mrs. Leicester I had a letter from a lady in Silesia, the wife of a minor official, asking me to gain a great favour for her husband. She was of a position which, before the War, might have entitled her to be presented to me at a Bazaar or public function. That is to say, she was entitled to be addressed as Mrs. Really Truly Secret Court Sanitary Counsellor Schmidt—or some such nonsense. She ended her plea for assistance by saying: "The starving of England is, I still believe, the best way to end the War"! I may as well add that the request was an indiscretion—she wanted her husband to be made an Excellency. Needless to say Mrs. Sanitary Counsellor received no aid from me on her ever upward social climb.

In July my dear father died. I had been uneasy for some time, but not anxious, as Patsy had said how well he was in the beginning of June. It was the greatest blow I experienced during the War. To be away from him when he needed me most.

When my father brought my mother home to Ruthin as a bride in 1872 they were overwhelmed with the warmth of the greetings that welcomed them. Addresses and presentations were made, and, in a collective reply, my father speaking of Patsy said: "The sunshine of her face will often gladden the cottage door, and I will undertake to say that the social duties she owes to other classes of society will not be omitted." Speaking for himself he added: "I desire to show my friends by a close attention to the duties of the position in which Providence has placed me how grateful I am for all that has been given to me. . . . I have ever held the opinion that the possession of property, or rank or station in this life is attended with grave responsibilities. . . . A man should hold his possessions as a sacred trust, and, as far as landed property is concerned, he should so manage it that as many as possible should benefit by it and enjoy it."

He faithfully kept his word and served as Lord-Lieutenant for fifty-four years. For each moment of that time he was at the disposal of every honest individual and useful cause that claimed his help. After his death they found on his desk the notes for a speech which he was about to make on the continuance of every effort to bring the War to a successful end. As for little Patsy, all she could write was: "Great Heart is dead."

One of my greatest comforts at this time was the beautiful letters that reached me from every direction. Most of them, necessarily, from Germany. Prince Eitel Fritz, the Grand Duke Adolphus, the Hatzfeldts, Princess Mossy—the most touching letter although, poor darling, she was consumed with anxiety at the time about her sister, the Queen of Greece, and her brother-in-law, the King, whose position was very precarious just then.[1] Countess Clary Kinsky, too,

[1] King Constantine of Greece, under pressure from the Allies, abdicated on June 12, 1917, in favour of his second son, Prince Alexander.

was angelic—but I cannot mention, though I thank them, all. The Larisches (Hansie and Olivia and Fritz and May) and Fanny Sternberg were my greatest consolers. Thus, one of the bitterest moments in my whole life brought its own sweetness.

When the news of my father's death reached me I was at Nauheim, in Hesse, doing a cure. But how could one settle down to "do a cure" in such circumstances. I longed for occupation; work; necessary and relentless work. Hermann Hatzfeldt was not only Head of the Red Cross, but Imperial Commissioner and Military Inspector of all Voluntary Sick Nursing and, at the beginning of August, he wrote from Great Headquarters and asked me if I would care to go to Uskub in Serbia to nurse at the War Hospital there.

One day soon after my father's death Princess Pilar came to see me. She was so sympathetic and understanding that I wanted to pour out everything —and found I could not say a word. It is often like that at moments of great tension in our lives. Sometimes this involuntary silence is even the cause of lifelong tragedies. I felt so guilty that I afterwards wrote to the Princess and tried to explain. This is her reply:

PRIEN A CHIENSEE, VILLA ROSEN-ECK, 18.VIII.1917.

MY DEAR DAISY,—

Yes, I did understand you in your silence! I wanted to say so much, but could not either. Sometimes I thought you must think me stiff and cold and yet I was afraid to speak.

The letter of Hansel you copied for me is awfully nice. I sent it to my mother, so that she may be quiet too. We have good news from my brother [1] thank God. He is very satisfied with the kind of war they are having now down there. He says it is much better, although more exertion for the horses, than in the trenches. It seems they all like it better.

I am so sorry you feel so lonely and that you have nobody with you at Nauheim who understands you. Of course I don't think there are very many people in the world who

[1] Major Prince Adalbert of Bavaria.

understand one truly—especially you—as you are different from the everyday people. That was the first thing that made me care for you at once, before I knew you really. Now that I know you I care for you with all my heart—I love you—and will always do so, as I will always understand you: you may be sure of that.

I remain here till the 24th. Then I return to Nymphenburg. I had a nice pleasant time here at my aunt's; I am sorry to leave and yet I am glad to go back to my mother, who feels lonely—and back to my work. I can't think of myself as passing my life without doing anything, as so many people do, leading the life of a Princess such as existed some centuries ago: I cannot.

I hope to see you when you go back to Munich. Meanwhile don't forget me. Thanks for your dear letter. A heart full of love! Your affectionate, PILAR.

Bethmann-Hollweg, who became German Imperial Chancellor in 1909, was by the middle of 1917 in high disfavour throughout Germany because of his lukewarm support of the ruthless submarine warfare. I do not speak of his political career because I do not know enough about it to do so. He was an honest, rather too impulsive man; when in August, 1914, he described the Belgian Neutrality Treaty to the British Ambassador, Sir Edward Goschen, as a "scrap of paper," he was saying exactly what he thought —one of those thoughts best kept to oneself! He really believed that "necessity knows no law," but in the circumstances it was very unwise to crow it from the housetop.

He never agreed with von Tirpitz about the submarine blockade and eventually forced the so-called Grand Admiral to resign. Later the German public got to think Bethmann was truckling too much to America and, generally speaking, neutralizing the aggressiveness of the War. The Emperor had by this time been converted to the doctrine of frightfulness, and von Tirpitz (as I had prophesied he would be) was recalled to power. At the behest of the extremists the Emperor, who had been Bethmann's personal friend from the days they were young men at Bonn University, dismissed him. This happened in July. I was terribly sorry, because Bethmann was right to dislike submarine warfare, fear and wish to conciliate the United States, and distrust the extreme militaristic party. I, of course, hated them and for every reason was angry at their triumph. Had the Emperor stood by his Chancellor, defied the military party, encouraged the Emperor Karl to press forward his Peace overtures, decided to restore Alsace and Lorraine (Lorraine alone would by then not have been enough), a negotiated and perhaps not unduly humiliating Peace would have been then quite possible.

The Emperor sacrificed Bethmann.[1] From that moment his own doom was sealed, because, win or lose, he could never again be anything but a puppet in the hands of the military and naval dictatorship.

Oh! the blindness to the inevitable result of American participation in the War! It is unbelievable. The military machine—the most stupid of all machines—ruined the Emperor and the Dynasty and . . . lost the War. I repeat, the *German Militarists lost the War*. That the Emperor was too weak to withstand them was his misfortune rather than his fault. I doubt if, by that time, Napoleon the Great could have withstood them. All his life, and all through the War, in his secret heart of hearts, the Emperor desired Peace. To my mind in modern times it is the people who make their Kings; not Kings who make their people. In 1917 the whole German people demanded "frightfulness."

Before the War the Emperor was loud, swaggering, aggressive, showy, because there is an element in the German character that is all these things, and admires them. He was narrow in his outlook, bigoted in his sympathies, intolerant in his attitude to foreign nations, because the Prussian spirit in Germany is all these things. The Prussian loves to ride rough-

[1] The Cabinet Council at which it was decided, on the advice of Admiral von Holtzendorff and others, to prosecute anew the U-boat warfare, was held at the Castle of Pless on January 9, 1917.

shod over others and thinks he has a right to do so. It suits them all now to blame the Emperor for these things and to call it Hohenzollernism. Hohenzollernism is only Prussianism in the open. They say its spirit has (with the Emperor) completely disappeared. It may be so, but I for one think that sudden national conversions are as rare and unsatisfactory as sudden individual conversions.

To me personally Theobald von Bethmann-Hollweg was always considerate and charming and was very amiable and attractive in private life.

One day I motored over from Nauheim to Friedrichshof to see Princess Mossy. My diary's account of the visit throws some light on current events. It was a long and tiring journey, but well worth while:

August 19, 1917. Nauheim.

. . . Princess Mossy has seen a lot of the Emperor lately and says he is very well but " Oh, how even *he* is misunderstood in this country," and this is very true, diary. She also wondered how they would call the new German Chancellor in England whose name is Michaelis.[1] I said they will probably call him " Michelangelo " or "Michael's angel."

It was very nice walking in her garden full of roses, and in the house such lovely pictures put there by her mother, the Empress Frederick. We spoke about the Peace Propositions of the Pope and both agreed it might be a very slight beginning, as all countries are tired of this slaughter. I think that next April will see an Armistice, with the frontiers still guarded. This will continue until Peace is agreed upon, which will take four to six months. Each country will want to gain something; and what makes me smile through tears is to know that each country is losing *all* and *can* gain nothing. England will keep her old name and prestige among her Dominions and retain what she has already got in Africa, as the German colonies there will prefer to remain under the English Sovereign, and will not want to go back to Germany. . . . German rule never appealed to them, and they and the Germans never understood each other.

I told Princess Mossy that it is years ago now since I begged

[1] Dr. George Michaelis was Imperial Chancellor from July 14 to October, 1917.

the Emperor to give back Lorraine to the French; I also said I did not realize then when I said this to the Emperor, that Bismarck had always been against the annexation of Lorraine in the 1870 War. To regain Alsace was quite different, as it had once been German. Princess Mossy answered: "My dear, it was *not* Bismarck; it was *my mother and my father* who were always against it, saying the French ought to have paid more money, but that Germany need not have taken Lorraine in 1870, though she might have kept Alsace."

By the end of June or beginning of July masses of German troops were being moved from the Western front to force an end to the Russians in the East. Hansel's division was amongst those transferred, and he used to give me in his letters vivid little accounts of what was happening to him. He has an inquiring and accurate mind and thinks and writes with the greatest exactitude. My vague and generalizing imagination and dislike of meticulous detail often bores him. Mentioning the exact number of foreign words spoken by the Austrian is typical of dear Hansel—who is always an angel to me, bless him. All the boys learned to speak Polish, and of course German, English and French are as their native tongues:

FROM THE EAST, *August* 2, 1917.

I am attached to another Battalion as Liaison officer. . . . The War here is so funny after the West, because the Russians are absolutely harmless and have got hardly any ammunition for their artillery. Yesterday I interviewed an Austrian prisoner who had escaped from Siberia and had sneaked himself through the Russian lines. He had been in America as a workman eight years ago and could talk a few words of English (about twenty-seven) and a few words of German (about twenty-two) and understood everything in Polish. You ought to have heard me examining him about the Russians in these languages. You would have died of laughing!

You ask me if the political movements at present interest me. Of course they do! Everybody is very glad Bethmann has gone because he was not strong enough to guide Germany in a war like this and would have absolutely ruined the country. He has done enough damage as it is.

A few weeks later he again touches on the military situation in Russia as he saw it. I cannot think why my restoration to health was to bring about the danger of his being " sat upon " when he came home. As a matter of fact, Hansel has such poise and integrity of will that, even as a small boy, he was a very difficult person to squash effectively:

FROM THE EAST, *September* 18, 1917.

I am so glad the cure is doing you such a lot of good. But all the same I do not mean to be sat upon when I come home!

The Russians have destroyed everything. In fact, one cannot understand—if one has not seen it—how human beings can turn into animals. For instance, when retreating they kill, murder, destroy and burn everything they see and can get hold of. The other day I was in Riga [1] which is a very nice town and absolutely German. The inhabitants are all delighted Germany has taken it.

Bolko must be very funny praying in all languages. Daddy wrote to me that you were going to Uskub to nurse. I hope I will still see you as I am coming on leave about the 23rd or 24th of this month. I go straight from here to Berlin where I must see the dentist for three days and get some things. Then I can go anywhere. I am sure to get leave for about a fortnight.

I do not know how it was in England, but in Germany during the War sending boys to suitable schools was very difficult, almost impossible. Lexel was growing very rapidly and was being educated by tutors who succeeded one another with embarrassing rapidity. Something was always happening to bring about changes. At this time he was at Fürstenstein, with Herr Reder as his tutor and Herr von Selle keeping a supervising eye on him from Waldenburg. There was an idea of sending him to school in Görlitz, a noted educational centre. This meant finding a family there to board him, as, of course, in Germany there are very few boarding-schools as we know them in England. This in turn raised all sorts of difficulties about food. Ordinarily Herr von Selle would have

[1] Riga was occupied by the German Army on September 3, 1917.

accompanied him to Görlitz and remained with him as his Governor, but this was impossible as he had war work to do in Waldenburg which necessitated his presence daily. Eventually we decided that as the boy was growing so fast he must remain for the present at Fürstenstein, where he could at least have plenty of plain country food. Baby Bolko was, of course, with me.

In October Princess Mossy wrote:

> . . . So sorry to think of the many worries you have had ever since your poor father's death. It is indeed difficult for you to do anything for those at home, being so far off, and in these times too. Our little Wolfgang is here on a short leave; he was in hospital at Bukarest for some time with dysentery and jaundice, but is well again now, thank God. Philip is in Russia. Our stay in Switzerland passed very quickly. My poor sister is recovering, and the King will I hope be well, after an operation which will have to take place soon. What they have been through and the way they have been treated surpasses everything. Oh dear, how much suffering everywhere! In haste, much love, from yours affectionately,
>
> MARGARET.

In October Hansel got his leave. The Division was being moved back to the West, and in between he got about three weeks. We all met at Fürstenstein and spent a happy time there in perfect weather. We saw Hansel off in Berlin and then Bolko, Fräulein Staehle and I went to my rooms in the little house in Romanstrasse in Nymphenburg. I had to prepare for Belgrade and make arrangements for Bolko and Fräulein Staehle to go off to my little villa at Berchtesgaden and remain there.

In the first letter he wrote me after he got back to his Regiment, Hansel mentioned plans for a great German offensive in the spring:

FROM THE WEST, *November* 21, 1917.

Lexel, the rascal, never wrote and told me what you talked about me the evening after I had left. What was it? I am writing you this letter to Belgrade, as I do not think it will reach you any more in Munich. I wonder what you will feel like in a town like that because I am sure it will be awfully dirty and smelly. I hope you will have a decent room to live in and will be able to have a bath at least *once* a week. I would like a brown leather coat for Christmas. We are living in what one calls a *Waldlager*. Quite nice little houses made of wood, with moss and green fir-tree on the top so they cannot be seen from the French flying-machines. In the afternoons we play football sometimes, and Prince Eitel Fritz runs like the devil.

About the War; I do not think it will end till next autumn or winter. There will be a tremendous offensive of the Allies in the West next spring with American help. (I think particularly in flying-machines.) If they don't succeed then they will stop. And they will not succeed, because we will have time to prepare ourselves during the whole winter.

During 1917, in spite of the so-called success in Russia, official Germany was becoming daily more and more nervous about the likelihood of success. One of the results was that war regulations of every sort were tightened up. In April, for example, it was forbidden to write letters to or receive letters from prisoners-of-war or interned civilians. My kind friend Major von Gosler in Berlin was in despair when he had to write and tell me of this. From August, 1914, this humane man did all he could to make corresponding with prisoners as easy as possible. He was an important official of the department handling all letters from abroad, and I would not like this book to appear without some acknowledgment of his unfailing help and kindness. Another dear friend who helped me all the War to get letters through via Holland was Daisy van Brienan.

Perhaps here I had better say something about what Serbia was like during the War, or rather that part of it controlled by the Austrians.

Belgrade was of course full of Austrian soldiers, and the hospital I was to serve in was an Austrian official one with the very grand name of the Imperial and Royal Hospital Brcko.

On my arrival in Belgrade I was met by a very nice fat Hungarian Professor who conducted me to

MY DAUGHTER-IN-LAW, MYSELF, AND MY ELDEST SON, HANSEL.

At La Napoule, 1927.

a little three-roomed house formerly belonging to a Serbian officer and his family of seven! When we got to the house Mr. the Professor insisted on standing with his heels clicked and pressing a large soft felt hat to a very large soft fat tummy in the ridiculous way people did because one was a Princess.

I said, pointing to a hideous sofa: "Will not Mr. the Professor sit down." He did. The legs came off the sofa, and Mr. the Professor remained on the floor for quite a time.

That night I slept well, which was a great comfort, as for weeks I had suffered from insomnia and used to lie awake swallowing my thoughts and trying quite ineffectively—I who could never count anything—to count sheep. However, the bed of the Serbian officer, his wife and an instalment of the seven children was quite comfortable and I was in a beautiful dreamless oblivion when suddenly, in the middle of the night, up went my feet and down my head. The back of the bed had come off and all my pillows and most of me was on the floor. I had been told to "keep my feet up," but this was carrying things too far.

Next day I begged the official whose duty it was to provide equipment for the quarters occupied by the Sisters to try and get me a small iron bed and a wooden chair. Elsa and I had heard revolting and terrifying tales of the vermin, smells and sanitation of Belgrade and we thought the less upholstery the better. Greatly daring, I also asked for a bath. Men so annoy me on occasions like these. They always say: "It's no good asking because you won't get." I say, "It's quite hopeless getting if you don't ask." So I always ask and, nearly always, I receive. When I got back from the Hospital there was a nice big broad bath in the corner. Privately I felt quite certain it was stolen from an hotel or somewhere, but that was no affair of mine. The Serbian servant got some hot water, and Elsa made me a delicious bath with lots of perfume and bath salts. It was like Paradise. After wallowing a long time I got out and was sitting down doing my hair when I suddenly noticed that the room was full of water. I had pulled out the plug, but, as no escape pipe had been fixed, the water merely spread all over the room. After that each time I had a bath the water had first to be bailed and then sponged out.

The food we got was awful. Anchovy paste smeared on war bread was considered a great delicacy. Onions and garlic were in constant use. I think one associates a special smell with each city one knows. London (best smell of all), Paris, Berlin, Madrid, Vienna, Moscow, Calcutta, Dublin, Buenos Ayres, Oslo, Budapest, Breslau have all their own individual and peculiar odour, but I can never think of Belgrade except as a mixture of anchovies, garlic and drains.

The Brcko Hospital not only received soldiers, but civilians, including women and children. Soon after my arrival I disgraced myself (in my own mind) very much. I was on duty during an operation by which a man was having a piece of diseased bone cut away. I was holding open the incision with two pairs of instruments like pincers and as soon as the piece of bone was removed matter gushed up and all over me. I became faint, but dared not let the wound close, so I asked the observation Doctor to take the instruments from me. He did. I was led out in a fainting state and soused with cold water. I was both annoyed and angry and full of contrition. The operating Doctor said it did not matter, as something of the sort happened to every Doctor and nurse at least once in their lives. The amount of matter that streamed out of the poor patient was almost unbelievable; it ran all over the floor, nearly covering one of the Doctor's boots. He did not seem to mind and only said: "Well, at any rate I have had my foot-bath!"

I was feeling very depressed and wrote to Hansel saying I would soon be catching crawfish—an amusement we both loved and often shared—in Heaven with Poppets. Hansel would have none of that and replied:

FROM THE WEST, *December* 21, 1917.

. . . There will be no nonsense about your going on catching crawfish in Heaven. You will first catch a few thousands in the *Schwarzen Graben* and *Daisysee* with the family and then eat them, before you are allowed to sneak away and catch them all alone! I never knew you were so greedy! *Haben Ihrer Durchlaucht verstanden?*—Has Your Serene Highness understood?

I think now we will have Peace in a year. Russia is absolutely finished and will not "come down"—as you call it—any more. When we get our troops from the East to the West—which I suppose is going on all the time—England and France will have to give in before America can help them one little bit.

I thought you would not like Belgrade and the garlic.

I could not get leave for Christmas as I had been back on duty such a short time, and many others had a better right. I did, however, manage to do so for the New Year. I went to Berchtesgaden to Bolko, where Hans and Lexel joined us.

We all had the feeling that somehow, in one way or another, 1918 was going to be a decisive year.

CHAPTER THIRTEEN

January-December, 1918

EVEN now, looking back across ten years, one cannot review the events of 1918 without emotion. I suppose that, for good or ill, it was one of the most fate-filled years in history. In retrospect how trivial our own personal and domestic chronicle appears in comparison with events that must remain memorable as long as time itself shall last. In January I was still at Berchtesgaden, in Bavaria, glad of the change and quiet, and yet restless to get back to war-work; and while I was thus fussing about matters that seemed to me important the great Russian Empire was in collapse; Kerensky had disappeared, and his successor Lenin and those who were associated with him had embarked upon a course the end of which no one can even now foresee.

In Germany the immediate result of the Russian collapse was greatly to enhearten the nation and Army, and strengthen the hands of the Military Chiefs, who now thought all they had to do was to concentrate their entire efforts on a sweeping victory in the West under Hindenburg—that god with the feet of clay. On January 27 the Emperor's birthday was celebrated at Great Headquarters in the West with marked enthusiasm. Was not the Ukraine going to make immediately a separate Peace and, as Hans wrote, was it not "chock full of every foodstuff for man and animal." As a result of the Russian peace negotiations the price of goose flesh in Silesia had already fallen at this date from six to four marks per pound. It was extraordinary how the delusion about Ukrainian plenty grew and flourished; why even in realistic England in 1920, Mr. Lloyd George not only waxed lyrical about "bursting Russian corn bins," but quite a number of people even believed him.

Early in January I heard from Shelagh that Patsy was dreadfully ill. I consulted Hans about the possibility of getting to England to see her, but he said it was absolutely out of the question. In these circumstances both he and I thought it much better to distract my mind by returning to Belgrade to nurse. My sister-in-law Lulu Solms, the Crown Princess Cecile and all the friends whom I consulted, approved; Prince Gottfried Hohenlohe, who in the autumn of 1914 had become Austro-Hungarian Ambassador to Germany, was most kind in facilitating all the necessary arrangements, providing me with a *laisser-passer* and so on.

I have just been re-reading a letter which Fanny Sternberg wrote me from Vienna just then. It is so dear and comforting that even now it brings tears to the eyes. And yet her son Leopold was terribly ill at the time, all his wounds having broken open again and his shrapnel-smashed leg still in plaster, and yet Fanny, who naturally was in despair, could find time and energy to write and comfort me. In a letter of sympathy about Patsy from Prince Eitel Fritz, he enclosed a snapshot of the grave of his dog, a companion for eleven years, who had just died in France. The Prince spoke of him as "the faithfullest friend I ever possessed." It seemed a comparatively trivial thing and yet how well I understood his feelings and his grief, and it helped to still my own.

Both Princess Mossy (of Hesse) and the other Daisy (of Sweden) were indefatigable in getting through to me news of Patsy; and the dear Swedish Princess could understand my mood so well because had not she herself been unable to go to her own mother, the Duchess of Connaught, during the illness that preceded her death in March, 1917.

At the end of January I started for Belgrade, leaving Bolko behind at Partenkirchen with his faithful and reliable governess, Fräulein Staehle. Lexel went to

Fürstenstein where Hans saw him at intervals when he went there to inspect the building operations; the stage of putting in ceilings and fireplaces, and deciding on panelling and coverings for the walls, had at last been reached. I suppose all this helped Hans to forget the War: he aimed at having the private Chapel the finest and most striking thing in the house and, I think, succeeded.

At the end of February in Belgrade I received terrible news.

The Grand Duke Adolphus had drowned himself in a canal in the Park at Strelitz. I could not believe it. I had written to him at Christmas and received in reply a nice chatty letter from Strelitz where he was on leave. He spoke of it being the first Christmas without "his darling Granny," and was so grateful because I did not fail to "mention her in every letter; she was a darling." He also spoke of the progress being made at the Park House, where he had just hung in the passages some old coloured English prints. There was, too, a reference to the young Princess whom I hoped he would marry, and also to her mother. It was a dear letter, quite hopeful, and dated January 10. Yet in less than seven weeks he had gone . . . voluntarily. One says that; but was it voluntary? Such events are mysterious and baffling. All one can know is that to face them a human soul must feel utterly defenceless and alone. Then the consuming grief and regret that one was not there in time of greatest need to help, perhaps even to prevent.

So much nonsense was written about the death of the Grand Duke both at the time and since, that I must, in fairness to his memory, set down what I know. A stupid story, constantly repeated, is that it was discovered by the German Secret Service that he had been spying in the interests of England, and that he was given the alternative of being shot as a traitor or taking his own life. The Yellow Press took the opportunity of insinuating that, like me, the Grand

Duke was more English than German, and that I was, somehow, the cause of his death. A great friend of his and of mine wrote to me as follows.[1] I was far away in Belgrade at the time, and personally knew nothing of the details, but her letter may be accepted as the full and authentic account of what took place, as far as the exterior aspect of the tragedy was concerned : the heart's secret is mercifully folded with my dead friend in the great heart of God :

Your telegram I received here yesterday evening and had waited for it. Terribly quick and unexpected this tragedy comes, and I look upon it as an insoluble puzzle. At the end of January we were some days in Berlin together, where he was pleased and contented and so full of future plans. One cannot understand or conceive what has made this horrible issue possible. So far as I can judge, his character was not at all disposed to melancholy. Lonely he certainly was, but I had not the impression that this troubled him, and understood that he felt himself well and was continually busy with things he ordered or directed. The death of his beloved Granny had, to be sure, taken from him his truest adviser and her loss he had grievously felt. Even so, there was the near prospect that he would not need to live any longer so solitary. . . .

He was the truest friend of my son and had given him much good advice, especially as he knew life. What must the poor thing have suffered those last days and no one to help him. I know how heavily you will feel this misfortune. This naturally loving nature, loved by all who knew him. . . .

Can you imagine that the charming *Parkhaus* has for ever lost its creator. What joy he had with it. All that can make life desirous was his ; he had all means at his command. He was so good for the Poor and Needy, and if he could make a pleasure for anyone he did it. We have suffered a great loss which cannot be replaced. You will also feel this and I heartily sympathize with you and embrace you in mutual grief.

The facts which are known to me are as follows : He went out with his dog at four o'clock on the 23rd inst. As he did not come back to dinner his people began to be disturbed. They made a search at once but found nothing. Military

[1] The original is in German.

Police with dogs then searched further and at mid-day the next day the Bodyguard first found his dog sitting near his cap at the Canal. After dragging the Canal they found the body with a shot wound in the temple. So far the weapon has not been found. This is all I know.

My diary tells how deeply I felt this blow, but the passages are too intimate to be transcribed here. His Granny loved and admired "Fred" more than anything in the world, and I have never seen, between old and young, anything to equal their mutual understanding and devotion. He loved flowers so much and was so tender, gay, gallant and considerate that together we had christened him *Rosenkavalier*, while my two youngest boys always called him "Uncle Freddie" or "Uncle Strelitz." I think the loss of his Grandmother, the apparent endlessness of the War, his heart in England and his home in Germany, and the two countries fighting with each other, just tore him in pieces and he could stand it no longer. Then there was that terrible exhausting chronic hay fever, which, so I am told, leads to the utmost depression.

Never mind. He went alone (as we all must) to join that great band of compassionate hearts, each one of whom died because of our sorrows and the sorrow of the world.

II

On March 3, 1918, Germany signed the Treaty of Brest-Litovsk with the infamous Lenin and Trotsky. At the time this was officially looked upon as both a military and a diplomatic victory. All the same it gave many people in Germany a shiver of horror down the back, and I was one of them.

For some time Princess Mossy had been arranging with Princess Daisy that I should go to Sweden and have a real rest and change. In a dear letter promising, if I came, to do everything possible for me, the Crown Princess remarked: "What do you say to Molly Crichton going to marry Algy Stanley? She is still such an invalid that it seems strange. I see Birdie

Ilchester has got a little girl, and Marjorie Anglesey has just had a daughter which makes three, and no son." "Molly" was, of course, Lady Mary Grosvenor, whose first husband was Lord Crichton. He was killed early in the War, and she afterwards married Lieutenant-Colonel the Honourable Algernon Stanley. As I write these lines I see in the papers a description of the wedding of her girl Kathleen to Lord Hamilton, the eldest son of the Duke of Abercorn.

In March, I think it was, Prince Lichnowsky's account of his Mission to London, written and printed for his family alone, was, owing to a deliberate and well-meaning indiscretion, published without the author's knowledge. In consequence the Prince was deprived of his rank *à la suite* in the German Army, and, later, expelled from the Prussian House of Peers. There was a tremendous outcry throughout Germany. Even kind Fanny Sternberg wrote: "He has really made a fool of himself, and cannot show himself anywhere"; and Hansel, from the Western front, vividly expressed his young astonishment on a post card. I longed to write to the Prince, but did not dare to put my name to a letter addressed to him, as I knew all his correspondence was being opened.

In France something had happened that might well have seemed to Germany ominous. On March 26, Allied unity of command was at last achieved at Doullens. Two days later Hans wrote to me as follows: The quotation displays an almost unbelievable ignorance of the national psychology of France and England and a childish notion of what was happening in Ireland: [1]

FROM THE WESTERN FRONT, *March* 29, 1918.

Everything is going on extremely well, much better than was expected. We must have made by now fifty thousand English prisoners. They were taken quite by surprise with

[1] The Princess is here a little unfair. The Prince was fully justified in claiming a great German victory when he wrote on March 28. On March 22, Byng's Third and Gough's Fifth Army, numbering six hundred thousand, faced one and a quarter million German

our offensive. This accounts too for the tremendous amount of war material of every sort which fell into our hands. They had not even the time to blow up their ammunition depots. But what now ? I think, that the French will try to help with a flank attack, and when this will have been repulsed and the English driven still more back they will take to the boats, putting the blame on the French, who came too late, and pretend that the state of Ireland makes it necessary to retire from the Continent. Which of the two will make Peace first, is impossible to know to-day, but there is no doubt, that this battle brings us a great deal nearer Peace. . . .

What do you say to Lichnowsky's book ? Can you imagine a man making such an ass of himself. Tactlessness and vanity are the two main features in his character. He can thank God, if he is not put into prison and kicked out of the army. . . .

We will have Peace soon and then you can go to England. It is only a question of weeks. Lloyd George cannot last over this defeat, by far the biggest in English history.[1] And Clemenceau has already declared that he would only stay in office as long as Lloyd George did.

Even as these lines were being written by Hans the issue of the Battle for Amiens was being decided against Germany, and that, whether they realized it at the time or not, was, for the Central Powers, the beginning of the end. I have never known whether Hans wrote with his tongue in his cheek or not. I cannot think that, having been at Great Headquarters throughout the War, it would have been easy to

troops ; the Fifth Army retired, and the Germans captured sixteen thousand prisoners and two hundred guns ; on the 23rd the Germans crossed the Somme, threatening Noyon and thus Paris ; on the 24th they were within twenty-five miles of Amiens and, had they only been able to bring up their supplies of ammunition and food, must have captured it and thus opened their way direct to Paris. Ludendorff had planned to be in Amiens by the 24th and was only prevented by the fact that, in previous battles, the Germans themselves had by their artillery fire made the country through which they had to pass a crater of death. This, and the matchless gallantry and stubbornness of the British troops, saved the day. The Allies had (at last) learned their lesson ; on the 26th, as the Princess reminds us, the Agreement of Doullens was signed. From that moment the German offensive began steadily to fail.

[1] This was quite correct. At the moment it was written Haig had no reserves in France, and very few in England.

deceive him as to the actual situation, nor throughout the War did I ever notice that he deliberately sent me misleading information. I can, therefore, only conclude that the Germans really did think that all was going well for them, and that the Battle for Amiens was a victory and not a defeat. That is perhaps not so impossible as it sounds. Did not England in May, 1916, win a Naval victory at Jutland and in the official announcement hail it as a defeat! On April 7, Hans wrote from the West:

I saw Hansel yesterday, after I had missed him twice. He is very well. They have plenty to eat, as they took tremendous storages from the retiring army. He gave me some chocolate, which they took from the French, and which I am sending to Lexel and Bolko. I sat with Hansel for an hour in his room, which he has to share with another officer. The beds are good, but not a single window pane is left, as the place was some days ago under artillery fire. We had tea with his General. Prince Eitel Friedrich, who lives in the same village, was there too. We have been living in our train since the 20th of March. Everything is going on well. If our enemies would only shake off Lloyd George and Clemenceau, peace would come soon. By the time you will get this letter, you will have heard of more interesting news from the front than I could tell you.[1] Now I must finish. The Crown Prince has just arrived for luncheon and the courier is leaving.

Towards the end of April I received from Princess Daisy a letter which set my mind at ease a little about Patsy, but dashed my hopes of a visit to Sweden. Somehow one seldom thought of the Neutral Countries as having serious food difficulties or being short of housing:

SOFIERO, HELSINGBORG, *April* 20.

DEAR DAISY,—

Many thanks for your last letter. I'm afraid it looks as if it won't be possible to get any rooms for you to live in here, there's been such a rush on them, I'm so sorry but perhaps

[1] The reference is to the beginning of the great German offensive in Flanders on April 9, 1918; it caused Haig to issue his famous "Backs to the Wall" Order on the 12th.

we could manage it later. Fröken Holmberg hasn't come back from Germany as far as I know, at least she hasn't given any sign of life as she promised to do. Will you be able to arrange to go to the watering-place in Germany that she frequents during summer, and get her to give you massage again? We are here in the country for a week's change and rest and to see to the garden. The sea is so beautiful and calm and blue; it helps one to forget all the awfulness in the world around one. The question of when it will end seems as far off as ever.

I'm thankful to have heard that my father [1] has returned safely from the East and is well again, I only heard a little while ago that he was quite ill in January. The children too are all well and happy and that is much to be thankful for. How are you getting on with your nursing? Isn't it very tiring? I don't think I could nurse, it's not at all my line. So many at home though seem to have developed a taste and ability for it. Much love from Yours affectionately, D.

On the same day Fanny Sternberg wrote me from Vienna that: "We have passed through great excitements and all regret so much that the Emperor let Carl Czernin [2] go—just at such a moment."

We were all devoted to dear Czernin and his wife Marichi. Of course he could not remain on as Foreign Minister when his young Emperor, behind his back, was sending his wife's brother, Prince Sixte of Bourbon-Parma,[3] who was an officer in the French Army, to the French President Monsieur Poincaré, and all over the place with secret offers of Peace. I must admit that, from the moment of his Accession in November, 1916, the Emperor Karl had longingly turned his eyes towards an Armistice, but a Sovereign cannot do one thing and his Foreign Minister another.

Oh! what a warm and sustaining thing the true

[1] The Duke of Connaught had spent the winter in Egypt.

[2] Count Ottokar Czernin was appointed Austro-Hungarian Foreign Minister in December, 1916.

[3] On April 11, 1918, the French Government published the text of the Emperor of Austria's letter to Prince Sixte of Bourbon-Parma proposing peace negotiations; on April 15, Count Czernin resigned.

friendship of woman for woman can be. I like and appreciate the friendship of men, but, inevitably, there must be many deep feelings, needs, emotions—mostly quite illogical and inarticulate—which they can never understand. Here is a letter from Princess Pilar of Bavaria such as only she can write. I remember as if it were yesterday how its arrival comforted and strengthened me:

NYMPHENBURG PALACE, MUNICH, 21.IV.1918.

DAISY DEAREST, No I have not changed, nor *will* I change, concerning you. I care for you very much and I understand your ways. I do not care what other people say; I am sorry if they do not understand you, but it won't change *me* or my feelings, be sure of that. A letter of mine must have got lost by the way. Your other letter, before this one, was so very dear and so dreadfully sad. And this one too. You have learned to smile to hide your tears; I think we must all learn to do so; and we all do, but yet I am sorry, that you have come to that.

This war has shown us *how* people really are—many we found nice before, have turned out to be the contrary, while others we never had cared for, showed a heart. I found your letter on my table when I returned home yesterday evening from a lecture about Spain given by a young Spaniard of only seventeen; it was very good. I had rather a lonely feeling about me and wished for sun and a blue sky. Then I found your letter; it gave me so much pleasure; it comforted me. Only I would like you to be happy.

I did get an Order, or a kind of one, like all, at the Golden Wedding.[1] I take it as remembrance; that is all. When do you come back? It is spring already. The Park is in bloom all over. Won't you come soon?

All my love. I won't change. Love from my parents.

PILAR.

At the beginning of May I was officially asked if I would undertake the post of Director of a new Soldiers' Home about to be opened at Constanza[2]

[1] The Golden Wedding of King Ludwig III. of Bavaria and his Consort was celebrated in Munich with considerable pomp in the spring of 1918. Ten months later His Majesty abdicated.

[2] Constanza (Rumania) had been captured by Austrian and Bulgarian forces in October, 1916.

for Austro-Hungarian soldiers returned from the Russian campaign. I gladly consented, partly because all my friends were constantly urging me to give up the work in Belgrade which was much too hard, and partly because I much preferred Austrians and Hungarians to Serbians. The authorities in Belgrade were all as kind and considerate as circumstances would allow, but the city in war-time was a dismal spot. Constanza was healthy and on the sea. Above all, Sisters Edith and Clara, my two nice faithful friends from the Tempelhof days, were there and anxiously desired me to join them.

From the end of 1917 onwards in Germany there was a great deal of pandering to the Socialistic element which was daily becoming more openly aggressive. Many people considered this a great mistake, rightly holding that it was indefensible to pass new and extremely radical laws when so many men were serving in the Army and could not therefore make their wishes known. I suppose the truth is that you cannot make a whole nation submit for four years to what is in effect a military dictatorship without breeding a strong reaction towards revolution. It is unwise not to foresee and consider that the nation most amenable to the iron discipline essential to success in modern war, is the very nation most likely in the end to perish by internal revolution, whether the war be lost or won. This consideration might cause rulers and politicians to hesitate who are otherwise undismayed by the prospect of War. Both the Russian and German people accepted war discipline and restrictions far more readily than England or France, and yet both succumbed to the heady wine of unexpected and unfamiliar freedom.

I do not know where Hansel got his information, but, on May 24, he wrote to me: "It is quite possible that the war will be finished and Peace signed in November. You will not perhaps believe this?" A day or two after receiving Hansel's note I heard from Prince Eitel Fritz, who said: "I will take care of your big boy so far as one can do so in this war. Soap and cigarettes would be beautiful, thank you." Peace was likely in November; but soap and cigarettes were an immediate and daily necessity!

During April and May the German Armies were making their desperate and final effort to seize Amiens. I do not quite remember, but rather think that by the end of May that effort was finally spent. Here is an inside picture of those momentous days as painted by Hans:

FROM THE WEST, *May* 29, 1918.

I saw Hansel yesterday. He is extremely well and in excellent spirits. We left the G.H.Q. the 27th at night and on the 28th at 2 a.m. the artillery began.[1] Two thousand batteries began firing at the very same second. The enemy was taken quite by surprise, from what French prisoners told me. I interviewed some already at midday on the 28th. I went out early in the morning, directly our train arrived, with Count Dohna (the commander of the *Moewe*). He had never seen a good land fight, and we had great fun. We motored directly towards the famous Chemin des Dames which our troops took at 11 a.m. I could not get to Hansel that day, as it was too far to walk to where his Brigade was fighting, and motoring was impossible.

Yesterday, however, I motored over to Hansel, crossing the Chemin des Dames at two different places. It was very difficult for the motor, as the road was full of shell holes. There were only three English Divisions north-west of Rheims, nothing but recruits, who offered no resistance. Opposite Hansel's lot were Frenchmen, who ran, too, like hares. Our losses are extremely small. The enemy must have lost about forty thousand men, as we took about twenty-five thousand prisoners.

While I made my trip to Hansel, the Emperor went to another place (one cannot send him very much forward) and met an English General, called R——, whom they took the day before. The Emperor described him to me as a man of thirty-eight years of age, a Welshman, looking like a sergeant-major. This General's opinion was that the resisting power of England

[1] The Battles of the Lys continued from April 15 until May 27; the (third) Battle of the Aisne began on May 31, 1918.

was over, because she has no more men. The fact is that the English were a dangerous enemy, so long as they could stick to their trenches, but now, as we have passed the trench country, the fighting goes on in the open field for which they are not trained, and their leadership is naturally very bad.

Those fights, which I talk of, are only the *beginning* of the second act of our offensive ; you will have heard already more about the development of it, by the time this letter reaches you. But I hope that this second act will be the last one.

About these insulting newspaper cuttings : the Emperor was not furious about *you*, but about the papers. It was I who showed him the cuttings, and he agreed with me that proceedings should be taken at once.

The "insulting newspaper cuttings" to which Hans referred were some which he had sent me concerning the death of the Grand Duke of Mecklenburg-Strelitz, and which I had returned. Here is one of them. It shows the infamous depths to which certain German newspapers can descend. That, during war, was perhaps understandable and excusable; but many of them are just as bad or even worse now in time of peace. The British public, used to the British Press, with its extremely high standards of honour, probity and decency, has no idea of the malicious vulgarity of many German newspapers considered quite reputable in that country:

The mystery of the suicide of the Grand Duke of Mecklenburg-Strelitz has not been cleared up yet in spite of great publicity. Some papers, especially Austrian, announced that the young Prince had been married morganatically to a Hungarian, Frau von H., who would not set him free when he thought of marrying a Princess of Anhalt. Likewise a well-known opera singer, Frau S., was mentioned in connection with the death of the Grand Duke. Although it will hardly be possible to lift the veil from the Strelitz drama during the War, it must be said in the interests of truth, that neither the singer nor that Baroness (who by the way possessed no legitimate rights) had anything whatever to do with the tragic end of the Grand Duke. Every one who is acquainted with Strelitz and its surroundings knows the real motive and to play hide-and-seek in this case is of no avail whatever. The evil influence of the deceased (as a big Berlin paper has already mentioned) is the wife of a German Prince and magnate who is an Englishwoman by birth and—as many symptoms in her surroundings have indicated—has remained English in her thoughts and in her mind. (The lady in question can only be the Princess of Pless.—The Editor of the Paper.) This lady, a greatly celebrated beauty, had won a fatal influence over her Grand Ducal friend. The mutual relations finally ended in a public scandal. The consequence of it was that the Grand Duke was obliged to stay far from his capital, having been given to understand that his rôle as the head of his country, and as a soldier, was no longer acceptable to his subjects. Shortly before his death he is said to have received the visit of his sweetheart. It came to a tragic issue and those who have followed the course of the conflict were not surprised at the end.

The Grand Duke had never considered marrying a Princess of Anhalt. As this book shows, he was repeatedly in his capital in the months immediately preceding his death. He was there in November, 1917, settling things after his grandmother's illness and death. He was there again at Christmas for the purpose of visiting the wounded and the hospitals and he was there on sick leave at the time of his death. I had not been there, nor had I seen him since the spring of 1916. The article from beginning to end was a tissue of lies.

On June 1, the Princess Margaret (Daisy) of Sweden wrote me another letter from Sofiero, their lovely country home on the Baltic, where they were revelling in a rest after nine months in town. The children were running wild. Her brother to whom she refers is, of course, Prince Arthur of Connaught, the "friend" the Grand Duke Adolphus, and his "cousin" Queen Mary of England:

I've not had any news from home lately but when last I heard all were well, and my brother in America on a special Mission. I know whom you mean by the friend who had such a dear old Granny; poor thing, how sad it was; have you ever heard the real story? His cousin at home really liked him and she was so unhappy about it, but glad her aunt the old Granny had gone before. I hope you are getting the best out of the nursing you can, it may of course be a help in spite of the hard work. With best love, Yours,

D.

III

In June we kept the anniversary of our Silver Wedding in beautiful Munich, which had now become dear to me. Pilar was there and her parents, and many kind friends; and I could have Bolko and his really nice, kind governess, Fräulein Staehle, in from Partenkirchen. I went back to my little furnished house on the outskirts of the city close to the Palace of Nymphenburg. Lexel was at Fürstenstein, and Pless was of course now empty.

But it was very difficult to settle down to anything when constantly receiving from my husband letters containing passages like the following. The idea of Paris being blown to pieces by huge guns gave me constant nightmare. That beautiful city where I had spent the earliest days of my honeymoon and which I had loved since years, had been under long-range shell fire since the end of March from the one or two German guns christened by the British "Big Berthas"; but this was not taken very seriously in informed circles in Germany, being merely an advertisement to cheer up the troops and the civilians. Hans's letter described something far more menacing:

FROM THE WEST, *June* 4, 1918.

Here are the two last photos of Hansel and me. On the one of them you can see his E.K.I.[1] He was not in the least astonished to see me, but greeted me by saying that he was sure I would come that day, because I had always managed to arrive when something important had been going on. . . . That we got in such a short time to the Marne, is beyond every

[1] Prince Hansel had been awarded the Iron Cross, first class, for his gallantry in the German advance of March 1917, when he repeatedly crossed and re-crossed the Somme bridges carrying dispatches. The Emperor deputed Prince Eitel Fritz to hand the boy the coveted Decoration.

expectation. Yesterday I met Engelbert Arenberg, who was of course even more unwashed than in peace time. We went with the Emperor on to the top of a hill, from where we could see with the naked eye a great part of the fighting. Everything is going on so marvellously well, that it can only be now a question of a few weeks, till, at least, the French will give in. Our line is at present seventy kilometres (forty-four English miles) from the centre of Paris. A few kilometres further, and we can place our *ordinary* big guns, of which we have scores. This means that in a few days Paris will be shelled so that not one stone will be left on the other, simply wiped off the face of the earth, like so many other French towns which I have seen. Would not the French prefer to make peace, to avoid this disaster.[1]

I got a letter from Patsy from Geneva. I am answering it to-day.

Having, with the approval of Hans, put the matter of the scandalous newspaper reports concerning the Grand Duke Adolphus into the hands of our Berlin lawyers, I also wrote to the Emperor. I did so through my ever faithful and indulgent friend, Princess Mossy. Here is what she said:

FRIEDRICHSHOF, *June* 10, 1918.

DEAR DAISY,—

Just a line to say, that the Person I am very fond of, and to whom you wrote through me, let me know that he had received the letter, and would do what he could to help you, and put your mind at ease. So I hope this will comfort you and cheer you up. You can be sure that you will never be forsaken by your friends so there is no reason to worry, nor to believe that they distrust you. Just do as they advise, and put up with all the complications and difficulties of these terrible times. I can assure you it is not easy for anyone, and all have their share of trouble. Hoping you are pretty well, and with much love, Yours affectionately,

MARGARET.

The Emperor himself replied at once, doing so through the Chief of his Personal Staff, General von

[1] Paris was bombarded at intervals by long-range guns between March and August, 1918; the "ordinary" range German guns never got near enough for this purpose.

Plessen. I realized that he adopted this method in order that his attitude in the matter should become publicly known and that his condemnation of the outrage should have all the weight carried by his own official action.

This was the last personal kindness the Emperor did for me. It was done at a time when his country, his throne and even his person were in grave danger. In such circumstances not many men or women would have stepped aside from stupendously important affairs to interfere on behalf of a perhaps silly woman who had been libelled by a scurrilous rag. Yet the Emperor did so, and the loyalty and fineness of this action would of itself place his name, in my humble opinion, on the starry roll of the noble friendships of history. In that letter written just after his mother's death in 1901 he said he would never allow me to be "maliced"; and as far as he could prevent it he never did.

Here is a translation of General von Plessen's letter:

GREAT HEADQUARTERS, 10.VI.18.

YOUR SERENE HIGHNESS, MOST GRACIOUS PRINCESS,—

His Majesty sends you his best greetings and thanks for your letter of May 19th, which has arrived here on June 8th, and directs me to reply as follows:

You may be sure that His Majesty did not believe one word of the gossip concerning the late Grand Duke of Mecklenburg-Strelitz.

The newspaper article which treats of this matter in such a brutal way had been forbidden by the Chief Censor. The author of the article nevertheless published it and—at the request of the Prince of Pless—will be prosecuted by the State-Attorney. The investigation is still proceeding.

The authorities have been instructed not to in any way inconvenience, Your Highness. However, in order to prevent any misconceptions, it would be well for Your Highness to avoid in public life everything that might appear in the least unusual.

His Majesty would be glad if Your Highness would lend your time and valuable strength more to the narrower home country in place of the unquiet activity in Hospital Trains and foreign Hospitals.

With the expression of my most complete esteem, I have the honour to be, Your Highness's devoted servant,

VON PLESSEN, Aide-de-camp General.

Von Plessen's reference to Foreign Hospitals was also very characteristic. The Prussians and Austrians hated, and still hate, each other. The Emperor Francis Joseph, the most egotistical man who ever lived, looked upon the German Empire as upstart and shoddy, and the German Emperor, and indeed every German, simply squirmed when one spoke of the Holy Roman Emperor. The Austrian Kaiser was the last of the Cæsars; whereas the German Kaiser was only the third of what?

Although I had in principle accepted the offer to go and work in Constanza, when it came to the point, I was reluctant to leave the Imperial and Royal Hospital Brcko in Belgrade where every one was so kind, particularly Dr. Theodor Hüttl, the Chairman of the Surgical Department of the Hospital and a most skilful surgeon, and Dr. Bohm, the Head Staff Surgeon and Commandant.

I had been there from the end of November, 1917, and, at the end of June was, as I have said, given two months' leave. After a short stay at Nymphenburg with Bolko and his governess, I sent them back to the mountains and myself went to Klitschdorff to spend a few days with Lulu and Fritz Solms. They were devotedly kind to me and Lulu looked so pretty and sweet with her white hair, girlish complexion and very young face and figure. From there I went to Fritz for a day or so at Halbau on my way to Fürstenstein. When I got home I wrote to Hermann Hatzfeldt to ask whether he advised me to go to Constanza or return to Belgrade.

On July 18,[1] the French launched their counterstroke after the attack on Amiens. It marked definitely the beginning of Victory for the Allied Armies. While

[1] The fourth Battle of Champagne, July 15–18, 1918.

at Halbau I received the following interesting letter from Hansel, who writes an excellent description of the beginnings of a modern battle:

FROM THE WEST, *July* 27, 1918.

As soon as I have time I will write to Uncle Fritz too, but just now we are in an awful mess.

On the 15th in the morning at 1 a.m. our Artillery fire began, and continued till five o'clock. In the meantime Engineers were to build bridges over the Marne which flowed between the French and German trenches. At five o'clock our Infantry was going to attack. Everything would have gone all right if the whole offensive had not been betrayed. When the Engineers started to work searchlights suddenly flashed up from the enemy side and revealed the whole place in their cones of light. Immediately French Artillery, which was only waiting for that moment, shelled the place so that nearly all the boats and a lot of the poor devils working on the bridges were blown to bits. Somehow or other we managed to get one bridge so far ready that our first Battery was able to get over at seven in the morning.

The Infantry got over all right and took the chain of hills above the valley of the Marne in a swift attack. Instead of going on then and keeping the enemy running, and so preventing him from bringing up his reserves, the Infantry had to stop because our Artillery could not cross the Marne and support them.

It would take too long to explain everything to you, but you can perhaps imagine what it means to cart artillery, ammunition, and everything else that troops need over bridges which are badly shelled during day and night. Besides that, enemy bomb-squadrons threw many bombs on every bridge and every little group of trees—where they perhaps thought somebody could hide—from early in the morning till late at night. They also tried to block the valley by gas, but did not succeed because the wind was too strong.

I was afraid I had lost one of my horses (*Mougu* out of *Marabout*—you must know the mother). I think I wrote you about it.

When we saw that the offensive could not continue, we tried to send all our horses back over the Marne, because they certainly would have been killed otherwise. As I needed one with me I could only send one back. . . .

On the night of the 19th–20th we went back on the north side of the river, as it was not possible to maintain such a position: the French luckily noticed nothing till the next morning.

Halbau must be lovely now. I think I am the only one who has never been there.

Hans had to visit Berlin on some Parliamentary affairs and from there he dashed to Fürstenstein to see either me or the building operations—I was not in the least sure which. Anyhow men never grow up and must always have some ploy or another on to keep them a little out of mischief: nothing could do that completely. When he got back to Great Headquarters he wrote me:

FROM G.H.Q., *August* 1, 1918.

The day after I arrived (Saturday) I had breakfast with the Emperor alone and with one A.D.C. I had Count Freytag's letter in my pocket, and when the A.D.C. went out with some order, I told the Emperor about you and read the letter to him. He was very angry about this behaviour towards you and told me to give the letter to Plessen and to tell him to write at once to the *Generalstab*. This was done, of course, the same day. The Emperor asked me, why you wanted to stick to Belgrade, instead of nursing in Germany. This was just my chance and I said: In the beginning of the War, my wife tried to occupy herself with the Silesian Hospitals and Breslau, but they kicked her out. So she went to Berlin, where the same thing happened. Then she travelled in Hospital Trains, but this was too tiring in the long run, and so she went to Belgrade. He said it was disgraceful the way you had been treated. I answered, especially after all she has done for Silesia and Germany, even having her clothes made in Breslau, and her lace schools, cripple-homes and Hospitals. He is full of sympathy for you, and I am sure, he will always be a true friend to you, and you will see it after the War is over.

When the Emperor asked why you did not occupy yourself in Germany, he said too, that I should talk this over with Ernie Hohenlohe. But I will not do it unless you want it, as I don't know how far you are booked for Belgrade or Constanza. If you want me to arrange something with Hohenlohe for Germany or the West, then tell me so. I think that the

West front with the English wounded would not be advisable, as it would only be a cause of new gossip.

That bit of poetry you sent me is very nice. I pray for our dead every night, and am sure they pray for us, and especially for Hanse. He has been in a hell of a fire on the south of the Marne. . . .

A week later Hans wrote me again. His letter is very interesting, because, on the 8th, the beginning of the final British attack on the Germans had begun, and the King of England was at the front to see it launched:

FROM G.H.Q., *August* 10, 1918.

The Americans publish the names of sixty-four thousand officers and men killed, wounded, made prisoners and missing of their seven Divisions which took part in that engagement. This means a loss of ninety per cent., or practically the annihilation of those seven Divisions. A propos of Americans, I read in some paper some time ago that Mrs. Leeds, an immensely rich American widow, who paid some fabulous sum for a famous necklace (so it must be Mrs. Nancy Leeds) is engaged to Prince something of Greece,[1] brother of the real King. As they have no Family Regulations in the Greek family, she will become a Royal Highness. But the future of the American fortunes seems to me rather doubtful.

I like very much your long letter with all what just comes in your head, what you call "jabbering." I am only sorry that I cannot answer in the same way, because here there is a lot to do, and very little time to write letters.

IV

From that moment events just hurled themselves along.

From Fürstenstein I went to the Villa Silva at Carlsbad to join Hansie and Olivia Larisch for a bit, as my two months' leave from Belgrade was not yet over. While there I had a letter from the Swedish Princess Daisy. They were still at Sofiero. She said:

---

[1] Prince Christopher of Greece married the late Mrs. William Leeds in February, 1920.

I sent the wire to your mother which Mossy let me know about; I hope she understood.

Have you heard—it's very sad—Bertie Paget, 10th Hussars, has died, and Mary Greer's eldest son has been killed and now she's got none left; and he was only married this year too! The Albemarles too have lost a son[1] and one is a prisoner. Such sadness everywhere! When will it all end? An officer from home wrote me the other day: "Thank God this war can't go on for ever!" No, thank God, it can't; but it can last for a long time yet.

Some day you must come and see this place; we have to leave here on the 5th of September and are so sorry. It is less peaceful in town. Love from Yours affectionately,

D.

During the last days of August and the first part of September Hans was on leave; it was a great pity because far-reaching events of the utmost significance were taking place at the front, and I did want to know about them. I do not think that, even then, Germany was seriously uneasy; at all events Hans was not, because on September 4, before his return to Great Headquarters, he wrote to me:

The situation is good. The continual attacks of the enemy are only the proofs, that *they* must finish the War before the winter, or they would wait till they had more Americans at their disposal. But it is also possible that England at last comes back to her senses; i.e., that she realizes that she becomes more and more a vassal of America. I don't know, if an arrangement with us would not be preferable and give England a greater independence.

Best love to Olivia and Hansie.

Even the most highly-placed Germans were unbelievably badly informed about the Allies, their plans, objective and resources. On September 5, darling Princess Mossy wrote me: ". . . They seem desperate on the other side to come to some sort of a decision soon. Is it that they fear America becoming too powerful? Perhaps; otherwise they would wait till next year when they could have still greater quan-

[1] The Honourable Albert Keppel, Lord Albemarle's youngest son, was killed August 1, 1917.

tities of coloured people to fight for them, as America manages to bring over any amount."

I have not quoted anything from my diary for a long time. Here is a bit that gives a glimpse of my life at Carlsbad and at Fürstenstein during the last agonizing days of the Great War:

September 9, 1918. Carlsbad.

I went to a shop and bought a small piece of ham for which I paid forty kronen; this would be in English money about sixteen shillings. How funny it seems to talk of food and buying it. If one thinks of it, during the whole of this war, it has really not been necessary to starve except, I fear, amongst the very, very poor people, and that is why in a sense I almost would prefer to eat nothing.

One learns a lot though, diary, and in strange ways that make one see things very differently. Elsa, my maid, is the dearest girl with the dearest heart and loves God and believes in things in the most charming manner; in fact she talks sometimes about everything in a most extraordinary, peaceful, sure way which does one good, and helps one.

The other day when I was at Fürstenstein there were three old women working on the *Schlossplatz* in the pouring rain. I simply could not bear it—as just in front of me they were putting down a new elaborate marble floor for me to walk on. So I went with tears in my eyes—I felt I should sob—and said: " No, I don't allow this; go back to the garden, take shelter, do not work any more, you will be paid all the same."

One old woman I had known for many years; I pointed out that their coats were dripping wet, which was true. They did not seem to mind, but smiled and off they went. Elsa said to me afterwards: " Oh, Your Highness, they are used to it since so many years, they don't mind. They go back to their little home afterwards. Those sort of people are often happier than those that are placed in life quite differently." I dare say she was right.

While at Carlsbad I read, on the 9th September, the *Daily Mail* of August 21, which was, I think, quite wonderful, considering the War and the muddled state of Europe.

By September 16 Hans was back at Great Headquarters and wrote: " What do you say to Lansdowne's new party and his programme?[1] I think it might lead to peace. He seems to share my opinions that America will be a greater danger for England in the future than Germany." Even while Hans was writing this the great German Retreat had begun and Allied victories had taken place in Palestine and Macedonia. Concerning these tremendous events I feel that I really ought to use my letters and diary as much as possible, as they give what one then knew, without any of the vagueness and inaccuracy brought about by things that have happened since. By September 22 I was back in Belgrade, having passed a day or two in Vienna on the way. I wrote:

September 22, 1918. Belgrade.

Hansie Larisch said to us all the other day in Vienna (we were discussing Ottokar Czernin's marvellous and rightful letter which he wrote to the papers, as he was not allowed to speak it). Well, Hansie said: "Germany will have to give back Alsace-Lorraine to the French."

I merely thought of the words I had said to the Emperor seven years ago in Pless: "Give back Alsace-Lorraine to the French, Your Majesty, and they will be on their knees before you and there will never, never be a European or any other war."[2] At that moment he did not quite know what to say (and I think he was also not certain of his own thoughts) for he turned and said to the guests at the table: "What do you think she wants me to do now? She wants me to give back Alsace-Lorraine to the French." No answer was given him. Well, we will see what the future brings!

In two days Prince Lonyay is coming here from Constanza as he has been transferred somewhere else. I do not know who will be his successor there or what he will be like, but all this the Prince will be able to tell me when I see him. I must know what exactly my responsibilities are to be and if I will have a proper Staff of doctors and nurses.

Prince Lonyay, I should explain, was the man who had married the widowed Crown Princess Stephanie

[1] In November, 1917, the late Lord Lansdowne addressed a letter to the Press which advocated the opening of peace negotiations with Germany; it was refused publicity by *The Times* and other prominent newspapers, but was issued by *The Daily Telegraph*.

[2] See pages 270 and 449.

of Austria. He was therefore a brother-in-law of Prince Philippe of Coburg and Prince Napoleon, both of whom had married sisters of Stephanie. They were all, of course, the daughters of old King Leopold II. of Belgium; a great man in the true sense of the word, the King was in a way too big a personality for the small somewhat provincially-minded people whom he ruled.

On September 29 Hansel wrote me from the front that:

> One hears from men who come back from leave that the frame of mind is not very good at home. The people have forgotten the war and only think of gaining money and feeding themselves. Even the educated classes hardly realize that their country is fighting for its existence.[1] They cannot understand what this little word " existence " means, because they have not seen how France is ruined, thousands of villages burnt and plundered, and how their women and children are killed by shells and bombs. . . .

A letter full of intelligent foresight from a lad not yet nineteen. On the very day it was written Bulgaria capitulated. Five days later King Ferdinand abdicated and his son Boris succeeded him. From that moment Crowns—Imperial, Royal, Grand Ducal and Princely—rattled down one on top of the other in a great heap. Bulgaria and Turkey were finished and Austria, at last, had summed up the moral courage to desert her Ally. Poor Austria, she was on the verge of collapse and revolution, and one supposes that with nations, as with individuals, it is conceded that self-preservation is the first law of being. On October 7, Hans wrote: " We seem really to get nearer Peace, only God knows what sort of Peace it will be. Max of Baden,[2] the new Chancellor, is the one who

[1] Acute political and economic conditions already prevailed throughout Germany; on October 3 all the German Secretaries of State resigned.

[2] Prince Max of Baden, heir presumptive to the Grand Duke of Baden, became German Imperial Chancellor and succeeded Admiral von Hint as Foreign Minister on October 4. Count Georg Hertling had resigned the Chancellorship on September 30.

was once engaged to the Grand Duke Vladimir's daughter—at the time we were in St. Petersburg."

By now the civil and military situation in Germany was involved in mystery and uncertainty. Even Hindenburg, as I afterwards learned, was completely at sea! One day advising an immediate Armistice, the next insisting upon continued resistance, right up to the end declaring his "hopefulness" and then, when he had failed ignominiously, retiring. Is it any wonder the poor Emperor did not know what to do.

Had the civil population stood firm even then much, if not everything, might have been saved. But, on the collapse of Russia, a wave of communism had insidiously spread like poison gas over the whole of Germany. Germany indeed beat the Russians, but in their stead a much more elusive and deadly enemy invaded her. The German Empire fell at Brest-Litovsk—not in France.

V

It seemed almost an absurdity to try to arrange one's personal life while Empires were breaking into pieces before one's very eyes.

I was on my way from Belgrade to Constanza with Helene when we were stopped at Herkulesbad, in South Hungary. I decided to return to Belgrade, collect Elsa, Seidel and the luggage, and make for Vienna or Munich. We travelled from Herkulesbad to Orsova on the Danube by carriage and from there up the river to Belgrade by steamer. It was small, overcrowded and filthy and took about sixteen hours to do the journey instead of ten. At Semendria at midnight in the dark a lot of Germans got on board and Helene and I talked with them. They took her for a nurse as she had on a blue cap with red crosses on it. She and I huddled together on a sort of black box—God knows what was inside—but we sat there for hours. At last a German Major spoke to us. He sent his servant to fetch us some wine—which I thought was awfully nice of him, as by then he knew who I was, but very rightly and bravely said to me: "Well, my wife could hardly speak a word of German; we have been married now since years; but she talks it much better than you do." He had asked me what nationality I was and at first I said I was a Swede; I had been this so often during the War. Then, when he proved friendly, I was too proud to continue to sail under false colours and told him I was English. Anyway we became quite friends, and he told me he was related to Countess Brockdorff in Berlin. He sent through official channels a *dienstliche Depesche* for me (which otherwise Seidel would never have got), directing him to join me at Budapest.

When at length I got safely back to Belgrade I learned that Seidel, having sent my luggage to Uskub, had fled with Elsa to Vienna. This sounds improper because I have quite forgotten to mention that they were married some months before. Belgrade was by this time in a turmoil, so I continued my journey to Budapest, there to await my fugitive servants and wandering baggage. I was much upset by reading in the *Daily Mail* of August that the Entente Powers insisted on the Abdication of the Emperor. My diary will give some idea of what took place in Budapest during the last hectic days of the ancient and once great and powerful Austrian Empire:

October 26, 1918. Budapest, Hotel Ritz.

It is terrible that they now propose the German Emperor should give up his Crown for the sake of peace.[1] He is one of the dearest, truest friends I have. Weaknesses he most certainly has, like all men and women, but a true heart! If Germany is left without an Emperor I do not know what will happen; but I only pray as I think of it that he will accept this demission for the sake of peace; as Christ died for mankind on the Cross, so the Emperor must die for the present,

[1] On November 9, 1918, Revolution broke out in Berlin, the Emperor decided to abdicate, and Prince Max of Baden became Regent, with Herr Ebert as Imperial Chancellor.

and later with all my heart I wish that the people will recall him again as Sovereign.

Our journey here was not very pleasant. We travelled by boat in weeny little cabins with refugees of all countries, so it seemed to me, one end dirtier than the other, as Helene got a louse on her coat. There were Hungarians, Serbians, Rumanians, and so on.

When we got to Belgrade at three o'clock in the morning only poor Dr. Bender was there, sent by the General von Rhemen to meet me. Thank God for this, as we saw no one in civil clothes and could not find Seidel. Dr. Bender told me Seidel and Elsa had gone, also Baroness Rhemen, Frau von Spetzler and her daughter; but that the General had found rooms for me. He asked: "What do you care to do, Princess? There is a boat leaving for Budapest in ten minutes; will you go by it or will you stay here?" I scarcely knew what to answer but I thought as Elsa and Seidel had gone and Helene and I were very tired, I would decide to come here direct: the journey took two days.

The King-Emperor[1] came here yesterday and had a big meeting to-day. Well, as Count Esterhazy said, there is little use in all these meetings as there is no Chancellor and they all spend their time in giving new advice to the unfortunate, stupid, weak little Emperor.

Esterhazy, to my astonishment, is quite against Czernin. When I asked him why he himself had not remained Prime Minister[2] he simply said: "Well, they would not do as I wished." I answered: "You are young, you could not expect this all at once." He told me later that his one wish was to get to England. Strangely enough I have never met him there and did not know he cared for it so. He too has wished for some time past to make a separate peace and end all this murder. . . .

Yesterday Count Schönborn-Buchheim, the head of the Schönborn family, came to see me; he is the brother of Ninie Hohenlohe-Langenburg and Irma Fürstenberg. His wife was in a Sanatorium on the other side of the Danube; he said her nerves and health were absolutely ruined through the War. We talked politics and he promised to return to-day, but

[1] On October 16, 1918, the Austrian Emperor issued a Manifesto proclaiming a Federal State on the principle of Nationality, but excluding Hungary.

[2] Count Esterhazy was appointed Hungarian Premier on June 15, and resigned office August 9, 1918.

to my astonishment this morning I heard he had gone. I suppose he decided suddenly to take away his wife, as during the night there was a throwing of bombs and a row just across the Danube opposite here. I laughed and said: "Well, to-morrow night they will probably come here, as all the banks and hotels are this side of the river." A lot happens now in a short time. Schönborn advised me to leave, but I had to wait for Seidel and my luggage from Uskub. . . .

All Austria is now in bits and every part wishes to become an independent state, the Croats, Bohemians, Hungarians, and Poles.

This afternoon the Head Surgeon from Belgrade in the Brcko Spital came to see me (he left soon after I got there nearly a year ago). And then Dr. Hüttl came; I hope they will all come and dine with me to-morrow. We had worked happily in Belgrade. I eat and sleep and live in this one room, a bedroom, and I see every one here who cares to come. Many hotels are shut and all rooms are now turned into bedrooms. Yesterday Georg Pallavacini's wife came, a nice little thing. We talked of her step-father, Count Andrassy [1] who, I see in the papers to-night, has gone to Vienna to undertake a new position. What he will do there I do not yet know. Esterhazy comes again to-morrow. I hope if he has time he will try and take me out for a walk, as I have been here three days and have not moved, but somehow there is such an unrest all round one that it is more peaceful to stay in sitting on a chair.

In the very middle of all this beloved Princess Mossy wrote to me: "Oh! Daisy, what a mess the world is in and how dark everything seems! But good will come of it, I am sure. We must keep our courage and think of building up in the future." What a great, unselfish heart that woman has. Every inch the granddaughter of Queen Victoria and the daughter of the Empress Frederick. Her brother's Crown all but lost and her country on the verge of ruin, and she talks quietly of *rebuilding*.

Budapest and Vienna were now very uncomfortable and quite dangerous, so I decided to make my way to Munich as soon as possible. I rather liked the

[1] Appointed Austro-Hungarian Foreign Minister on October 25, resigned November 1, 1918.

idea of being in the midst of turmoil and revolution as I am not in the least afraid of crowds and find danger of any kind exhilarating. But I had to think of Lexel alone in Fürstenstein, and Baby Bolko with only his governess to look after him at Berchtesgaden.

VI

At last I got away from Budapest and back to my little lodgings at Nymphenburg during the first week in November. There I hoped to be joined by the boys when we would all go together to the quiet and peace of Partenkirchen. In a day or two the wandering Elsa and Seidel turned up with the wretched luggage. Hans, it appeared, was at Fürstenstein and wrote that, owing to the threatening attitude of the people, neither Fürstenstein nor Pless were safe.

On November 6, I heard a noise of aeroplanes overhead and my two maids and I rushed to the windows to see what they were. There were five of them, coming from the direction of the Austrian frontier, which is only about forty miles away. We thought they were going to drop bombs. Instead they showered over Munich thousands of poisonous pamphlets inciting the people to revolution, having been sent for this purpose by the Communists of Vienna. That day there was a great popular stop-the-war meeting in the big field opposite the Exhibition Ground. It was really quite quiet, and only demanded the end of a war, which Bavaria had never liked and of which it had long been tired. But the imported poison gas from Russia via Vienna did its work.

Eisner led the crowd through the city. A few determined police with batons could easily have dispersed them. But no one did anything. The King was seventy-three, the Crown Prince Rupprecht and all the Royal Princes under sixty were at the front. The small garrison, which like nearly all garrison, home, and base troops, suffered from chronic "grouse-itis," left their barracks and joined the crowd. A Workmen's and Soldiers' Council was formed, sat in the Diet buildings all night, and early the next morning, November 7, proclaimed the ancient Wittelsbach Dynasty deposed and a Republic set up. That evening the aged King Ludwig III. left for the Castle of Anif, near Salzburg, in Austria.

The next day, November 6, a Government with Eisner, an alien half-mad Jew and a communist, at its head was set up in Conservative Catholic Bavaria. I left turbulent Munich for the peace, quiet and stability of the mountains.

A day or two after I arrived in my little villa in Partenkirchen a Workmen's and Soldiers' Council was formed in the town, and five of its members were billeted on me. My diary says:

November 15, 1918. Partenkirchen.

They are all very, very nice to me and I have given parties for them and their friends twice in my little house; and then in the village hall two big parties of two hundred men; this means simply providing cigarettes and beer, otherwise it is all done at the expense of the community. The little I do is simply done most truly from all my heart, as one must not forget those men have all been at the front since four years and in my eyes, as I see things clearly coming, they are our only defence against Bolshevism.

They simply want, as far as I can learn by talking to them, a certain right to what God made the world for, and that is that the poor shall not hunger and want, and that fields and green grass shall be free for men and women to walk over. Of course this does not mean that some paths cannot be marked private, but since Vater died I have hated to see at Fürstenstein and Pless new roads built to hide every single soul that could pass near us, chains hung everywhere with the words upon them *Verbotener Weg*. God's heavens are not *verboten* and there all, thank God, will some day be on the same level and only the soul and heart may speak. Work we shall have to do, but it will be a work of kindness to all.

After a fortnight at Partenkirchen I felt that I must return to Munich and find out all that had happened to the Royal Family, particularly my dear friend Pilar and her parents, Prince and Princess Ludwig Ferdinand. Every one at Partenkirchen was *most kind* to me, but I felt isolated and lonely and longed to talk intelligently with people who shared my outlook. Also, I wanted authentic news of the great outside world. At Partenkirchen one was completely isolated.

When I arrived at Nymphenburg I found that Pilar's brother, Prince Adalbert, had returned from the front; Prince Ludwig Ferdinand was no longer in uniform; they did not then know where Duke Luitpold was; and the upstart Government had ordered them to leave the Palace of Nymphenburg.

I think it was the day after my arrival; we were standing by the piano talking about politics and I suddenly said to Pilar: "One day Bavaria and Prussia will separate; I feel it coming." It has not happened yet, but I know I shall live to see this prophecy come true.

While I was at Nymphenburg I received from a Hungarian friend the following tragic little account of how things were in Vienna. It was written about the middle of November:

I truly did not imagine that a Peace would be like this. Since yesterday I am in command as a Guard-officer over the men guarding the King's Treasury at the Hofburg Imperial Palace. If you could only see me! One's whole pride rears itself up. The Guard-officers at the Schönbrunn Palace *themselves* broke in and stole private property of the Emperor. Consequently this incapable new State Council allows the Court Jewels and valuables to be guarded by *real* officers. Here I stand as a simple Guardsman, here, where my father for many years was Royal Treasurer and Keeper of the Seal; I remember so well as a little chap when I visited him how I admired the Guardsman on duty.

If the papers continue to insult and slander us officers then I shall leave at once, as for that I am too proud still.

The German-Austrian is showing himself really as quite an unprincipled individual. Old Generals have in public made speeches soiling the honour of the old faithful Army of the Emperor. I will not talk about the proletariat!

A few days ago some English officers arrived in Vienna and are staying at the Hotel Bristol. When they walked through the Ringstrasse even better-class people cheered them. A fortnight ago they were still our enemies.

How well one understands the chagrin and bitterness of this aristocratic son of a long line of Hungarian Princes and courtiers.

On November 27 I wrote in my diary:

I see so distinctly a future when England and Germany will be (and have to be) friends—not alone, but with many others; that means without signed treaties, which are no use, but with just a good understanding, and what the Soldiers' Council call *Kameradschaft*.

Thank God my boy Hansel was safe and sound: here is his description of what happened when he marched into Berlin on December 11, 1918, with what had once been the Imperial Guards:

Many thanks for all your long letters which I only received yesterday, as we have had no post for at least five weeks.

This morning I managed to telephone to Daddy, but could not tell him much, as one dare not talk or write openly of the things that are going on here. I still hope to be able to come to Partenkirchen for Christmas.

Yesterday we marched in to Potsdam. Most of the old men (*Kriegsverein*) howled at seeing the coming back of the men who for four years have defended a proud country, and now find, instead of a home, a manure heap which one formerly called Germany.

In spite of this the joy of the people was very great. We were bombarded with flowers as in a Carnival at Nice. . . .

INDEX

www.ingramcontent.com/pod-product-compliance
Ingram Content Group UK Ltd.
Pitfield, Milton Keynes, MK11 3LW, UK
UKHW022350071025
8280UKWH00003B/34